ESSAYS ON JAINA ART

Ananda K. Coomaraswamy

Essays on Jaina Art

Edited, with an Introduction by

RICHARD. J. COHEN

INDIRA GANDHI NATIONAL CENTRE FOR THE ARTS
NEW DELHI

MANOHAR
2003

First published 2003

ISBN 81-7304-534-8

Published by
Indira Gandhi National Centre for the Arts
Janpath, New Delhi 110001
in association with
Ajay Kumar Jain for
Manohar Publishers & Distributors
4753/23 Ansari Road, Daryaganj
New Delhi 110002

Typeset by
Ajay Art, Delhi 110085

Printed at
Lordson Publishers Pvt. Ltd., Delhi 110007

Contents

Preface

It is with great pleasure that I present Ananda K. Coomaraswamy's studies of Jaina art. This has been not only an opportunity for me to discover his seminal and profound contributions to the study of Indian painting, but also a chance to appreciate the breadth and depth of his intellect and personality. Jaina art and its symbolic inventory hold a special place in Coomaraswamy's formulation of the history of Indian painting, indeed Indian civilization itself. He was the first to recognize its chronological place in the succession of style.

Coomaraswamy's interests and expertise cover practically all the facets of South and South-East Asian artistic traditions.While some of his publications have been reprinted over the years, his corpus has never beern rationalized in print, in such a way as to promote a better appreciation of his methods of work and thought. In 1987, under the inspired leadership of Dr Kapila Vatsyayan, the then Member Secretary of the Indira Gandhi National Centre for the Arts, it was decided that the work of Coomaraswamy will be systematically organized according to thematic criteria. Nothing less than a new appreciation of Coomaraswamy's role will emerge as a result of Dr Vatsyayan's energetic plans. I would like to thank Dr Lalit M. Gujral for inviting me to undertake the project, and for his careful and wise guidance.

Philadelphia
August 2003

RICHARD J. COHEN

Introduction

Richard J. Cohen

FOUNDER OF THE FIELD

Ananda Kentish Coomaraswamy's writings on Jaina art practically span the entire period of his active working life as an art historian (see the bibliography). He wrote his first words on the subject in 1914, and ended with a book review in 1943, four years before his death. As many have noticed, one can identify two distinct varieties of intellectual style within this period: technically oriented expository writing, roughly from 1908 to 1930, when he opened up and defined many areas and categories of South Asian art for study and consideration; and the last sixteen years or so of his life, during which he developed his theoretical ideas, often speculative and controversial, on art, metaphysics, religion and culture.[1] While the study of Jaina art never dominated the core of his research interests, Coomaraswamy took to its investigation, especially Jaina painting, with characteristic energy and dedication. As in so many other areas of cultural study, he led the way in recognizing its value and recovering its identity. Of the many personal qualities that Coomaraswamy possessed, one in particular contributed mightily to his success in achieving his goals: namely his ability to bridge the gap between western cultures and the cultures of South Asia. With gentle, yet firm persistence, he forged ahead, confronting the critics. Notable are the friendships he struck with the British intellectual and historian of painting, Sir William Rothenstein (1872-1945),[2] and the American philanthropist and teacher of painting, Denman Waldo Ross (1853-1935). The former joined Coomaraswamy and others in founding the India Society (London, 1910) to promote public interest and awareness in Indian culture, and generally facilitated Coomaraswamy's access to quality publishers, such as in the case of his *Rajput Painting*,[3] while the latter facilitated Coomaraswamy's settlement at the Boston Museum of Fine Arts, and the purchase of South Asian art for the museum.[4]

Roughly between 1907 and 1912, Coomaraswamy engaged himself in a campaign to awaken Indians to the importance of their cultural heritage and the power and potentiality it held for them in their struggle against foreign domination. In doing so, he played a founder's role in establishing the study of Indian art (pre-modern and modern) through his lectures and writings, such as 'The Present State of Indian Art',[5] 'The Relation of Art and Religion in India',[6] 'The Aims and Methods of Indian Art',[7] 'On the Study of Indian Art',[8] and 'The Modern School of Indian Painting'.[9] He was writing also to counter the egregious and biased statements of such scholars as Sir George Birdwood, curator of the Indian collection at the South Kensington Museum, and chairman of the Royal Society of Arts, who had publicly argued against the existence of fine art in Indian culture.[10] It was during this period that

[1] Lipsey, Roger William, 'Signature and Significance: A Study of the Life and Writings of Ananda K. Coomaraswamy', New York University, Ph.D. Dissertation, 1974, p. 7.

[2] *Men and Memories,* 3 volumes, London, 1931-39; see Vol. II, Chapter 28, 'An Indian Pilgrimage', p. 249, in which he describes a visit with Coomaraswamy in Allahabad in 1911.

[3] London: Oxford University Press, 1916, 2 volumes; reprinted, New York: Hacker Art Books, 1974.

[4] Ross was an instructor of painting at Harvard University, and wrote *On Drawing and Painting*, AMS Press edition, 1971.

[5] *Modern Review*, Calcutta, Part I, July 1907, pp. 1-5; Part II, August 1907, pp. 1-9.

[6] *Transactions of the Third International Congress for the History of Religions*, Oxford: Clarendon Press, 1908, II, pp. 70-4.

[7] *Essays in National Idealism*, Colombo (1909), pp. 17-50.

[8] *Art and Swadeshi*, New Delhi: Munshiram Manoharlal, 1994, 2nd edition, pp. 46-55; 1st edition published by Ganesh Press, Madras, 1911.

[9] Ibid., pp. 116-27

[10] See 'Fine Arts in India and the East: Part I', *Hindustan Review* (Calcutta), December 1912, pp. 494-501; 'Fine Art in India and the East: Part II', *Hindustan Review* (Calcutta), January 1913, pp. 79-

Coomaraswamy became intellectually engaged in equating nationalism with the study of cultural history, and utilized his proficient and prescient eye to identify and collect cultural and art artefacts with which he could exemplify and define the Indian nation. We find him writing in 1909, in the preface of *Essays in National Idealism,*

> To a few it may appear strange that in a book devoted to the ends of Indian nationalism, so much space should be given to art, so little said of politics. It is because nations are made by artists and by poets, not by traders and politicians. Art contains in itself the deepest principles of life, the truest guide to the greatest art, the Art of Living. The true life, the ideal of Indian culture, is itself a unity and an art, because of its inspiration by one ruling passion, the desire to realise a spiritual inheritance. ... Thus, once more by the inspiration of a ruling passion—the religious and national ideal in one—the Art of Life will be realised again; only by thus becoming artists and poets, can we again understand our own art and poetry, and thereby attain the highest ideal of nationality, the will and power to give. ... It is possible to find in true art not merely the spiritual, but, or rather therefore, the material regeneration of India. ... The causes which have led to the degeneration of Indian art, and prevent its revival, are identical with those that prevent the recovery of her political efficiency. ... I do not believe in any regeneration of the Indian people which cannot find expression in art; any reawakening worth the name *must* so express itself. ... There can be no true realisation of political unity until Indian life is again inspired by the unity of the national culture.[11]

Coomaraswamy traveled to India three times between 1909 and 1913.[12] During the second trip, which seems to have lasted from the summer of 1910 through the summer of 1912, he moved about extensively, lecturing and collecting art. He became well acquainted with the Tagore family and spent much time in Calcutta. His commitment to the Indian nationalist campaign, and own personal understanding of how the re-discovery of traditional Indian arts could participate in a national political awakening came to full maturity at this time. In *Art and Swadeshi,* which was published in 1911 while he was traveling in India, is displayed the tremendous breadth and depth of his knowledge, interests, intellect, and political commitment. There are articles on 'Swadeshi, True and False', 'The International Congress of Applied Chemistry 1901: and Aniline Dyes', 'Facial Expression in Indian Sculpture', 'Song-words of a Panjabi Singer', 'Education in Ceylon', to name a few. In the lead article 'Art and Swadeshi', we find him linking the rediscovery of India's artistic capacities with its political and economic future.

> Indian design is an inexhaustible treasure-house of fine invention. But have you ever reflected that all this invention belongs to the past—that modern India, Anglicised India, has produced no beauty and romance, but has gone far to destroy the beauty and romance which are our heritage from the past? Go into a Swadeshi shop—you will not find the evidence of Indian invention, the wealth of beauty which the Indian craftsman used to lavish on the simplest articles of daily use, the filmy muslins or the flower-woven silks with which we used to worship the beauty of Indian women, the brazen vessels from which we ate and drank, the carpets on which we trod with bare feet or the pictures that revealed to us the love of Radha, or the soul of the eternal snows. ... India, above all nations, was beautiful once, and that was not long ago. It is the weakness of our national movement that we do not love India; we love suburban England, we love the comfortable bourgeois prosperity that is to be some day established when we have learned enough science and forgotten enough art to successfully compete with Europe in a commercial war conducted on its present lines. It is not thus that nations are made.[13]

He was invited to deliver a lecture before the Indian Society of Oriental Art (founded in 1907), Calcutta, entitled 'On Mughal and Rajput Painting'.[14] This lecture took place at the home of Sir John George Woodruffe, the famous scholar of *tantra.*[15] At the request of the Society, Coomaraswamy organized an exhibition of Indian art at the United Provinces Exhibition at

86; 'Indian Images with Many Arms', *Burlington Magazine* (London), XXII, 1913, pp. 189-96, an abbreviated version is found in *The Dance of Śiva*, 1918 (see footnote below).

[11] *Essays in National Idealism* (Colombo: Apothecaries Co. Ltd., 1909), pp. ii-iii. Reprinted by Munshiram Manoharlal, New Delhi, 1981.

[12] Lipsey, op. cit., p. 132.

[13] *Art and Swadeshi*, pp. 1-3.

[14] Published in *Art and Swadeshi,* Madras: Ganesh Press, 1911. This same article with slightly less and modified text, with fewer plates was published in *The Modern Review* (Calcutta), January 1911, pp. 71-5.

[15] Lipsey, op. cit., p. 152.

Allahabad.[16] It was through this effort, and his personal research program, that Coomaraswamy toured North India, collecting examples of medieval miniature painting, while greatly enriching his understanding of the artefacts. It seems that the art dealer, Radhakrishna Bharany of Amritsar, helped Coomaraswamy purchase many of the paintings he later used in his studies and publications.[17] He returned to India a third time in 1913, once again enhancing his already impressive collection.

Coomaraswamy experienced a disappointment at this time, which prevented him from settling in India. He proposed that a National Museum of Art should be established, preferably in Benares, and that he should be appointed its director. He offered his large personal collection to the venture. Government support was not forthcoming, as it was felt that such a museum would only facilitate the agenda of nationalists lobbying for *svarāj* (self-rule). The result was that he returned to the west, where he made a home and accommodated himself to its pleasures, pressures and politics. The settling down of Coomaraswamy in the west undeniably tempered his nationalism and influenced the discourse he used to contextualize and define Indian art. In particular, I am thinking of Coomaraswamy's selection of 'Rajput' art to label the folio painting not associated with the Mughals. At the time, he was struggling with the handicap of having not enough examples to decide confidently the answers to questions concerning geographical location and diffusion of style. Through, his own collecting efforts, he became aware of folio paintings produced in the Pahari region and Jaipur. Thus, he naturally settled on a term, the basis of which was identification of the 'ruling class' under whom the art had been produced. This had been the sum and substance of the label 'Mughal painting'. As Pramod Chandra has noted, we have lost awareness of Coomaraswamy's original reason for selecting the label 'Rajput painting'.[18] This has resulted in a tendency to generalize all non-Mughal folio painting produced in North India with the Rajput class, rather than specifically identifying the associations of painters and patrons. Coomaraswamy lived and worked in a westernized intellectual world, and created categories which responded to and were created for *observers* of Indian culture.

Through the articles 'Mediaeval Indian Painting',[19] and 'On Mughal and Rajput Painting',[20] Coomaraswamy can be credited with bringing to the attention of the world the existence of Mughal and Rajput painting, and the need to research their histories. In the former article, he describes Indian painting as having three main divisions: early, medieval and modern. Defining the early period, he says, 'The paintings of the early period range from the second century BC to about the seventh century AD, the latest examples thus belonging to the time of greatest attainment in Hindu and Buddhist sculpture (the seventh and eighth centuries). The best known examples are those of the Buddhist caves at Ajanta; but even these have been only imperfectly described and reproduced.'[21] He offers no specific evidence or examples of painting representative of the second century BC, up to the earliest paintings of Ajanta. Moving on to the medieval period, he begins with a statement which suggests he was *unaware* of the existence of Jaina manuscript illustration altogether: After the seventh century we know nothing of painting in India, except for occasional literary references, until the time of the Great Mughal.[22] The remainder of the article, and the greater part of it, is a description of Mughal and Hindu painting, beginning with the reign of Akbar. Others had already published examples of Mughal painting, as Coomaraswamy notes. He promotes the idea that, in spite of an apparent hiatus, the 'Hindu tradition in painting however survived in certain districts. ...'[23] Characterizing Hindu painting as chiefly religious in subject matter, and situating it within the Mughal school and the Kangra Valley school, he provides one example of each. Here, I believe, we witness for the first time

[16] *Catalogue of Ancient and Modern Pictures and Sculptures Exhibited at the United Provinces Exhibition,* 1910-11, Calcutta: Indian Society of Oriental Art; edited with N. Blount, 42 pages.

[17] Pramod Chandra, *On the Study of Indian Art,* Cambridge: Harvard University Press, 1983, p. 98.

[18] Ibid., pp. 94-7.

[19] *The Modern Review* (Calcutta), April, 1910, pp. 314-32. This article is not in Rama P. Coomaraswamy, ed., *Ananda Kentish Coomaraswamy, A Working Bibliography* (New Delhi: Lalit Kala Akademi, no date).

[20] *The Modern Review* (Calcutta), January 1911, pp. 71-5.

[21] *The Modern Review* (Calcutta), April 1910, pp. 314-15.

[22] Ibid., p. 315.

[23] Ibid., p. 315.

Coomaraswamy's selection of the artistic rendering of Śiva as symbolic of the very basis of the Indian (Hindu) world view. The subject of both of the Hindu paintings is Śiva: in one his worship (in form of a *liṅga*) by Umā (in Mughal style), in the other his cosmic dance (in Kangra style).[24] Coomaraswamy seizes the opportunity to explain the esoteric nature of Indian art, as well as to suggest to his audience that Indian culture has something to offer the West.

> The race imagination saw in the form of Śiva's dance, what men of science now express in mathematical discussion of the ether; and what they saw they expressed in their own language of poetry and form; and we of modern times, prove only the littleness of our imagination if we think that we are greater because we express in mathematic formulae, what others saw in form and colour or heard in music. 'Into deep darkness do they go that bow the knee to ignorance; into yet deeper darkness, as it were, they go, who bow the knee to knowledge.' Are we not in danger of this deeper darkness now; and is there not a more profound superstition of facts, than any possible superstition of the imagination? Perhaps the greatest value in any art for us may lie in its power of helping us to grow out of this new superstition of today; if this be so, how far has modern art departed from its real self, in seeking merely to reflect the appearances of things with photographic vision!
>
> In India, the religious, philosophical, and artistic consciousness is unified in a way incomprehensible to the western mind; and however great the effort, it is necessary to realize this before Indian, or any Oriental art can be really studied or fairly judged.[25]

Coomaraswamy closes this article with a description of the stylistics of the Kangra example, and notes that,

> we are at first impressed with the rather unaccountable fact of the survival of such a purely Hindu tradition in a remote Himalayan valley, until some fifty years ago. Until we know more of Indian art history than we do now, we cannot fully account for this. As regards the work itself, it is always easily recognizable by certain peculiarities in drawing, especially of the eyes, and secondly by the marvellous purity and brilliancy of colouring, and absence of atmospheric modification; the general effect of a picture like that just referred to is rather that of mediaeval European stained glass or enamel, than of painting as now generally understood. There is no doubt that the whole, both in subject and treatment is more remote from modern European thought and feeling than the work of the Persian and Mughal schools; and this makes its acceptance slower and more difficult.[26]

Coomaraswamy's recognition of the 'peculiarities in drawing', which mark the Hindu school, such as the eyes, brilliance in colouring and absence of atmospheric modification is profound. He grasps the 'essence' of an indigenous Indian style, elaborated earlier in the Jaina (and in a few cases Buddhist) manuscript illustrations dating from the eleventh to fifteenth centuries; a style which later some scholars called 'Apabhraṃśa', 'Gujarati', 'western Indian', or 'Jaina'. He does not reference this earlier material, as it does not figure in the article, and apparently was unknown to him at the time. Since the 1960s, with the discovery of many new examples of painting from the early fifteenth and sixteenth centuries, painted in various centers in northern India, from Gujarat, through the heartland of Madhya Pradesh, up to Delhi and over to Jaunpur (Awadh) it has become increasingly clear that such terms as 'Jaina', 'western Indian', and 'Gujarati' do not capture the geographically diffuse articulation of the continuance of the indigenous Indian style that Coomaraswamy identified. Of the many terms coined, I prefer, for the time being, 'Apabhraṃśa' as I believe that it is an appropriate characterization of a continuous artistic tradition that existed in literate society, which in turn promulgated literary illustration. This tradition, while it is mostly apparent only in its 'Jaina' form, through the thousands of Jaina texts produced in Apabhraṃśa languages between the ninth and fifteenth centuries, actually enjoyed wide appeal in many cultural circles. Proof of the persistence of an Apabhraṃśa style in literature (and consequently in art) is provided by the early texts in Awadhi and Dakkani, composed by Sufi authors, which display many of the formal characteristics of earlier Jaina narrative works.

[24] Two years hence, Coomaraswamy published an article carrying the title 'The Dance of Śiva', *Siddhānta Dīpika* (Madras), XIII (1912). It was republished as the feature chapter in the now famous, *The Dance of Śiva: Fourteen Indian Essays* (New York: Sunwise Turn, 1918), which bears the photograph of a Chola Bronze of Śiva performing the cosmic dance. Coomaraswamy succeeded in establishing the symbol which would become the twentieth century's cultural icon for India.

[25] Ibid., p. 321.

[26] Ibid., pp. 321-2.

In the article entitled 'On Mughal and Rajput Painting',[27] he has qualified the label 'Hindu painting' by enhancing it with 'Rajput', formulating a distinction which I shall allude to momentarily. He continues to be unaware of the continuity in medieval painting attested by Jaina manuscript illustration:

After the first great period of Indian painting, of which the painted chaityas at Ajanta are witness still, we have to face an almost entire absence of actual remains, until we reach the middle of the sixteenth century. We know, of course, from literary references and other indications, that the art was continuous. But no mediaeval wall paintings are preserved, although a few Buddhist painted book covers are found.[28]

Coomaraswamy draws several interesting and important distinctions in this article. He organizes *all* painting into three categories, wall painting, painting on cloth, and portfolio painting. Whether he intends to or not, he exposes some of his personal biases, such as when he submits wall painting is the 'noblest', giving as examples the work of 'the Italians and the Ajanta artists'. Curiously, he favors the Japanese use of cloth painting, hanging one piece, alone, in a room sparsely furnished, in opposition to 'the modern inartistic fashion of hanging many pictures, more or less incongruous, and none of them designed for the place they occupy, upon the walls of rooms already overcrowded with furniture and knick-nacks'.[29] Apparently he knew of no Indian paintings on cloth, and the various purposes to which they were put. Coomaraswamy associates all 'Indian' painting with the category of portfolio painting, 'with a few exceptions of paintings on the walls of palaces of the sixteenth, seventeenth and eighteenth centuries'. He appears to suggest that the earlier wall painting, such as that of Ajanta, belongs to something other than 'Indian'. Coomaraswamy makes a distinction between 'book illustration', which he says is 'more characteristic of Persian than of Indian art', and 'picture painting' which he associates with Indian art, having 'immense variety and depth of content, humanistic and religious. The pictures fall into two groups, Rajput and Mughal.'[30] With respect to Persian painting, he is polite, but somewhat dismissive, claiming that, 'It tells us of magnificent adventures and of scented gardens, not of the love of God or the infinite joy and sorrow of the lives of women or men, nor does it reveal to us the character of men or the souls of animals and trees and mountains. Its types are conventional rather than ideal, and one wearies of the languid mannerism, notwithstanding its marvellous charm.'

At this point, Coomaraswamy attempts to describe the two groups of Indian picture painting, the Rajput and Mughal. He typifies Rajput painting as 'specially serious, epic and romantic, [expressing] a profound sense of sympathy for all natural life and a sense of the fundamental unity of all created things. The Rajput painting represents the remains of mediaeval Hindu painting, almost entirely free from foreign influences.'[31] In describing Mughal painting, Coomaraswamy says it is an art characterized by a 'profound interest in individual character. Its types are neither ideal nor conventional but rather, realistic, or to use a more expressive term, actual'. He notes Mughal painting is more concerned with kings and courtiers, 'than with the visions of saints or the lyric symbolism of an agricultural race'.

Since Coomaraswamy is breaking new ground here, we need to forgive him his partiality and remember the limitations imposed by the available data. Going one step further, Coomaraswamy suggests that by the close of the seventeenth century, Rajput and Mughal painting fuse into a new painting form he elects to call 'Indian'. More problematic is his statement that Rajput painting 'is an art in its old age, beyond its time of most supreme achievement (which may have been in the eighth or seventh century, not far from the latest painting at Ajanta)', whereas Mughal painting 'is an art in the full vigour of its youth, with infinite courage for experiment, and the conditions for almost over-rapid evolution.' While I tend to agree with the latter statement, the former is simply wrong, but pardonable, as Coomaraswamy did not have enough information.

It must have been at this time (1912) that Coomaraswamy discovered miniature painting at

[27] *The Modern Review* (Calcutta), January 1911, pp. 71-5. The article is an abstract of a lecture he presented to the Indian Society of Oriental Art in Calcutta in 1910. It is erroneously noted in Dr. Rama P. Coomaraswamy, op. cit., item # 111, as published in the April issue of *The Modern Review* (Calcutta) of 1910, which is actually the publication date of 'Mediaeval Indian Painting'. See fn. 19 above.

[28] Ibid., p. 71.

[29] Ibid., p. 71.

[30] Ibid., p. 72.

[31] Ibid., p. 72.

Jaipur, which prompted his qualification of 'Hindu' with the addition of 'Rajput'. However, he retains the category 'Hindu' for such non-Rajput painting as that found in South India which he says is of a 'different character ... [and can] fairly be called decadent and ... almost exclusively mythological'.[32] From an aesthetic point of view, he is most impressed with what he calls the Kangra Valley paintings, 'with their burden of love and their lyric humanistic symbolism'.

By 1910, it appears that Coomaraswamy had begun to move beyond his peers' knowledge and understanding of the 'history' of Indian painting; an understanding which had been based on and limited to the encounter between the British and the inheritors of medieval Mughal society; an encounter made problematic by British notions of cultural development. He was moving to a fuller, sophisticated appreciation of the differences and subtleties existing within the subject; an appreciation acquired through the expending of his own energy and funds. He was engaged in creating the basis for his later survey writing, and preparing himself to understand the unknown as it presented itself.

INTRODUCING JAINA ART

Georg Bühler's interest in epigraphy and the archaeological excavations conducted at Mathura by Führer in the 1890s led him to become the first scholar to write about art objects belonging to Jainism.[33] There is some confusion, however, concerning who was the first scholar to publish an investigative article on Jaina painting. In his article in the *Journal of Indian Art and Industry* in 1914, entitled 'Notes on Jaina Art', Coomaraswamy begins by referring to an article by Wilhelm Hüttemann, entitled 'Miniaturen zum Jinacarita',[34] which he states was published in the *Baesseler Archiv*, Band II, heft 2, in 1913. Hüttemann's article actually appeared in the *Baesseler Archiv*, Band IV, heft 2 for 14, thus raising the question which article appeared first. Since Coomaraswamy's article contains images reproduced from Hüttemann's piece,[35] one is led to conclude that he had them in hand. He must have had page proofs of Hüttemann's article. Coomaraswamy had collected specimens of Jaina art during his trips to India between 1909-13, viz., illustrated manuscripts, cloth paintings, embroidered pieces, and manuscript covers, and was reserving them for later study and publication, as he was more engaged in work on 'Rajput' painting. However, at this time, scholars such as Herman Jacobi, Ernst Leumann, Maurice Bloomfield and Wilhelm Hüttemann were publishing new material relative to Jainism. Coomaraswamy must have felt compelled to document his own efforts in recovering Jaina art, in addition to establishing the study of Jaina painting on a firm footing; thus the article with the somewhat breezy title 'Notes on Jaina Art'. I do not mean to suggest that Coomaraswamy's article is a less scholarly piece of work than Hüttemann's. Hüttemann presents selected examples, in line drawing form, of only one manuscript, a *Kalpasūtra,* held by the Museum für Völkerkunde, Berlin. His approach is philological, presenting pictorial information and analysis from an internal point of reference, often with direct quotation and translation of text. He describes selected miniatures from the manuscript, attempting to interpret their symbolic significance or heritage within the Indian religious context. I believe that Coomaraswamy was too busy studying the Rajasthani *qua* Jaipuri and Pahari miniatures he had collected in India, as well as checking collections in British institutions for Indian folio paintings, for him to focus on the Jaina material at this time. He was busily publishing research on Hindu and Buddhist art, photographed samples of Indian art in *Visvakarma*,[36] and a book on *The Arts and Crafts of India and Ceylon*.[37] In addition, he was involved in intellectual circles and debates around the London scene, many of which centered on the arts and crafts movement, post-industrialism (a term Coomaraswamy seems to have coined), socialism, the potential for hostilites breaking out in Europe, and Indian involvement in the event of war. As Lipsey has noted, it was during this period that Coomaraswamy developed two distinct sides to his public posture:

[32] Ibid., p. 73.

[33] 'Specimens of Jaina Sculptures from Mathura', in *Epigraphia Indica* 2 (1894), pp. 23.

[34] Miniatures on the Lives of the Jinas.

[35] The 'images' are actually line drawings, credited by Hüttemann to a Marg. Hüttemann, p. 49.

[36] *Visvakarma: Examples of Indian Architecture, Sculpture, Paintings, Handicraft, First Series; One Hundred Examples of Indian Sculpture.* Introduction by Eric Gill. London: Luzac, 12-14, 30 pages, 73 plates.

[37] Edinburgh: Foulis, 1913.

His writings in this brief period in England can be divided into two groups: calm and restless. The historical writings—*The Arts and Crafts of India and Ceylon, Rajput Painting, Buddha and the Gospel of Buddhism,* etc.,—based on research and an exchange with the past, are calm and lucid, while the writings directed towards contemporary problems are restless, unrealistically demanding, impulsive. The division can be made in another way; there is an Eastern Coomaraswamy, occupied with traditional art, philosophy, and social order, and a Western Coomaraswamy, deeply in sympathy with the most rebellious Western thinkers and seeking to impose his own orientalized version of their thought.[38]

We know from his articles in *The Modern Review* of 1910 and 1911 that Coomaraswamy had already posited the notion that medieval Indian painting reflected the continuation of a much older tradition of painting, in part represented by the remains at Ajanta. With the publication of 'Notes on Jaina Art', he was able to begin to fill in part of the gap in the record. We find him predicting the existence of still older materials.

The paintings are not only very important for the student of Jaina iconography and archaeology, and as illustrating costume, manners and customs, but are of equal or greater interest as being the oldest known Indian paintings on paper, and representing an almost hitherto unknown school of Indian art, based like Rajput painting on the old traditions, but carrying us back at least a century and a half further than the oldest available examples of Rajput pictures. It is, indeed, probably that when the Jaina libraries of western India are made more accessible, they will be found to contain illustrated manuscripts still older than the beginning of the fifteenth century.[39]

He was, of course, correct. Jaina libraries in western India have provided some of the earliest examples of palm-leaf manuscripts, reaching back to the twelfth century.

In an earlier article on Mughal painting, Coomaraswamy had suggested that 'book illustration' is more characteristic of Persian painting, while 'portfolio painting' is characteristic of Indian painting. He seems to qualify his characterization by comprehending his collection of Jaina paintings to be 'chiefly documents of Indian art', and to be 'the chief exception to the general rule that Indian manuscripts are not illuminated'. He adds that in the illustrated Jaina texts, 'there is no attempt at an organic relationship between text and illustration, such as always appears in Persian manuscripts'. Thus, the illustrated Jaina and Persian manuscript traditions are likened to one another and compared, with the Persian tradition cast in a more favorable light. His reason is that 'the Jaina miniature is simply a square or oblong picture that looks as if it had been pasted onto the page, rather than designed as a part of it. This may not arise so much from the fact that the painter and writer must have been separate persons, as from the fact that Indian painting was highly developed long before the sacred books were habitually preserved in written form.' If we may take exception, it is here, where Coomaraswamy measures the combined effect of the illustrations. He occupies himself too much with providing an explanation for why 'on the whole, the archaeological interest of Jaina painting exceeds its aesthetic significance'. He makes additional, similar statements, such as 'In most of the manuscripts, the drawing is indeed very highly accomplished, but rather of a workshop character than deeply felt. Many of the miniatures are overcrowded with detail, the statement of fact rather than the expression of emotion.' Since Coomaraswamy was practically the first scholar to publish a scholarly article on Jaina painting, he was not in a position to say much about the antecedents of his examples, which were chiefly illustrated manuscripts of only two texts, the *Kalpasūtra* and the *Kālakācāryakathā*. He does attempt to draw parallels with Nepalese Buddhist illustrated palm-leaf manuscripts, such as the *Prajñāpāramitā,* wherein he compares the placement and involvement of illustrations vis-a-vis text. But he does not seem to be aware of the *raison d'être* of the illustrated *Kalpasūtra* or *Kālakācāryakathā* and their relationship with an aesthetic which is functionary and necessarily hieratic. Jaina architecture and sculpture displays a similar self-aware aesthetic. Practically all illustrated Jaina manuscripts, or single folios such as *yantras* (meditation pieces) or *vijñaptipatras* (an invitation to a monk to remain settled for the monsoon), perform a specific role and function within Jaina socio-religious discourse. They are used for personal study (usually by monks), or for teaching in groups. They belong to a textually focused cultural world in which existed a need for particular formalisms, and which in effect shares aspects of the printed text.

[38] Lipsey, op. cit., p. 190.

[39] 'Notes on Jaina Art', *The Journal of Indian Art and Industry,* Vol. 16, 1914, p. 81.

In lieu of a narrative treating the historical development of Jaina painting, Coomaraswamy offers other kinds of information which, practically speaking, is needed as background for the reader to understand the content and flow of the manuscript illustrations. The article is divided into nine sections, the majority of which discuss the history of Jainism, the life of Mahavir and other Jinas, a summary of the story of Kālaka, an explanation of technical terms, Jaina cosmology, a physical description of the plates. Much of the information is derived from publications by Georg Bühler, James Burgess, Herman Jacobi and Ramakrishna G. Bhandarkar. Coomaraswamy, in response to his subject, ironically reproduces Jainism's own strategy which requires the text itself to be contextualized by detail.

In brief comments on style, Coomaraswamy does allude to the unusually elongated eye, protruding into space, even in the profile view. Attempting to find a source for this stylistic feature, he offers a literary reference, *Rāja-taraṅgiṇī* 1, 210: 'The corners of their eyes were captivating and illuminated by a very thin line of antimony, which appeared to play a part of the stem to the ruby-lotuses of their ear-ornaments.' But this reference is more germane for the eye in profile on the side of the head facing the viewer, and does not explain the treatment of the other eye which projects into space. Karl Khandalavala takes up the question of the further eye in Jaina painting, and mentions a suggestion of the learned and beloved Shwetambar cleric, Muni Shri Jinavijayaji, who thought that 'the guild masters of the later period felt that the face of a deity or heavenly being in profile, with only the nearer eye shown, might give the impression to the worshipper that the god-head was one-eyed, which was not desirable'.[40] Khandalavala remained skeptical, although he does not offer another solution. It is important to note that Khandalavala's treatment of style in Jaina manuscript painting, which he incorporates into a chapter called 'Aftermath of Ajanta', and which he links to ninth century paintings found at the Kailasa cave, Ellora, agrees in substance with Coomaraswamy's belief that Jaina painting, as well as other Indian styles, such as Rajput and Orissan, represent continuities of older Indian traditions.[41]

[40] Karl Khandalava, *The Development of Style in Indian Painting,* Delhi: Macmillan India, 1974, p. 50.

[41] Ibid., pp. 53-67.

Discussing the apparent lack of aesthetic value of the hieratic style of the Jaina manuscript illustrations, as compared to the achievements in expression displayed through Buddhist painting at Ajanta, Coomaraswamy resorts to his comrade-in-intellectual-arms, the eighteenth century savant, William Blake, whom he believed was the 'most Indian of modern Western minds'.[42] Here, Coomaraswamy selects the tonsure ceremony of Mahavir, as he prepares to renounce the world and live the life of an ascetic, as an example of Jaina art capable of evoking a passionate response. 'Like Blake, the poet thought that "there were listeners in other worlds than this". Such examples go far to prove that there must once have existed an Indian school of Jaina painting comparable with the classic Buddhist art of Ajanta.'[43]

FURTHER WRITINGS ON JAINA ART

In early 1916, Coomaraswamy traveled to the United States with his dancer wife, Ratan Devi, who had arranged the tour. Due to his anti-war position, there were legal difficulties leaving England, as well as protecting his property from confiscation and dealing with his *persona non grata* status in some circles in England. In the United States, he met Denman W. Ross, a teacher of drawing and painting at Harvard, and a donor of art to the Museum of Fine Arts, Boston. This fateful meeting resulted in Coomaraswamy deciding to leave his home in England, to sell a portion of his art collection to Mr. Ross, who purchased it for the Boston Museum, and to accept a newly formed post of 'Keeper of Indian and Muhammadan Art' at the Museum. In 1917, Coomaraswamy left England, never to return.

Coomaraswamy immediately published an article in the Museum's *Bulletin* for 1917, concerning several of the Jaina manuscripts purchased from his personal collection by Ross. 'Illustrated Jaina Manuscripts'[44] is, in fact, a distillation of comments he made in his 'Notes on Jaina Art' of 1914, and contains no new material or further discussions. In 1922 he published a short description[45] of a sculpture of a seated Mahavir

[42] See Lipsey, op. cit., Chapter IX, 'England, 1912-1916: Blakean Protest', pp. 187-209.

[43] 'Notes on Jaina Art', p. 90.

[44] *Museum of Fine Arts (Boston)*, XV, 1917, No. 90, pp. 40-1, 4 figs.

[45] 'Jaina Sculpture', *Museum of Fine Arts (Boston)*, XX, 1922, No. 120, p. 53, 1 fig.

(Ninth Century AD, Bundelkhand, North India), donated by Denman W. Ross.

In 1923 Coomaraswamy began publishing the volumes of the *Catalogue of the Indian Collections in the Museum of Fine Arts, Boston. Part IV: Jaina Paintings and Manuscripts* appeared in 1924. Coomaraswamy had added to the museum's Jaina collection during a visit he made to India in 1921. Some of the information descriptive of Jainism, the life of Mahavir, other Jinas, as well as the *Kālakācāryakathā*, given in the introductory sections of the *Catalogue* is repeated from his 'Notes on Jaina Art' published in 1914. I have not repeated this material, but have annotated the *Catalogue* chapter. The rest of the prefatory information suggests that Coomaraswamy was following closely scholarship in the field of Jaina history and art historical studies, as he provides the reader with the most current under-standing of the position of Jaina painting within the Indian tradition. He appears to temper his assessment of the overall quality of the Jaina manuscript paintings from his earlier statement which suggested 'the archaeological interest of Jaina painting exceeds its aesthetic significance.'[46] We find him more qualitative and aware of the existing diversity of types within Jaina art. His sensitive and expert references to the exact nature of the drawing, and his analogy of the illustrated Jaina manuscript to a musical score, reveal the depth of his own experience and knowledge. He surely benefited in this regard from his marriages to Ratan Devi who was an accomplished musicologist and dancer, and to Stella Bloch who was a painter, also a student of dance and music.

> In discussing the qualities of Jaina painting, accordingly, it must be understood that the reference is to the illustrations in the fifteenth-century manuscript in the Museum collections and to those of similar manuscripts elsewhere. The art is one of pure draughtsmanship; the pictures are brilliant statements of the facts of the epic (the life of Mahāvīra), like the *Buddha carita,* is essentially an epic, where every event is seen in the light of eternity. To call this pure drawing, implies that it is an art of symbols and indifferent to representation. On the other hand, it is not calligraphic, that is to say that elegance or an elegant combination of lines is not deliberately sought, and in this sense the draw ing is more like script (such as that of the accompanying text) made to be clearly and easily read. There is no preoccupation with pattern, color, or texture for their own sake; but these are achieved with inevitable assurance in a way that could not have been the case had they been directly sought. The drawing has in fact the perfect equilibrium of a mathematical equation, or a page of a composer's score. Theme and formula compose an inseparable unity, text and pictures form a continuous relation of the same dogma in the same key.[47]

Coomaraswamy created a firm foundation for the further study of Jaina art, especially Jaina painting. He was decades ahead of his time. The descriptive part of the *Catalogue* is meticulous and rich in detail, including a figure for each manuscript illustration. I had at my disposal, in the Van Pelt Library of the University of Pennsylvania, W. Norman Brown's personal copy of the *Catalogue,* autographed by Coomaraswamy, and annotated in Brown's own hand. I have incorporated Brown's suggestions and corrections where appropriate. We find confirmation of Coomaraswamy's prophetic role in the study of Jaina art with the publication by W. Norman Brown of the *Kālakācāryakathā*[48] in 1933 and the *Kalpasūtra*[49] in 1934. Ernest Bender, who was Brown's student, published editions of the *Nalarayadavadaṃtīcarita*[50] and *Sālibhadradhannacaritra*,[51] which also find a place in Coomaraswamy's *Catalogue.*

We are now in Coomaraswamy's most productive period, during which he further enhanced his language and philological skills, and produced much good analytical and survey work, resulting

[46] 'Notes on Jaina Art', p. 90.

[47] *Catalogue of the Indian Collections in the Museum of Fine Arts, Boston, Part* IV: *Jaina Paintings and Manuscripts*, Boston: Museum of Fine Arts, 1924, p. 33.

[48] *The Story of Kalaka; texts, history, legends, and miniature paintings of the Swetambara Jaina Hagiographical work, the Kalakacaryakatha*, Washington, DC: The Lord Baltimore Press, 1933.

[49] *A Descriptive and Illustrated Catalogue of Miniature Paintings of the Jaina Kalpasutra as executed in the Early Western Indian Style*, Washington, DC: The Lord Baltimore Press, 1934.

[50] *The Nalarayadavadaṃtīcarita (Adventures of King Nala and Davadanti) a work in Old Gujarati, edited and translated with a grammatical analysis and glossary by Ernest Bender.* Philadelphia: American Philosophical Society, 1951.

[51] *The Sālibhadra-Dhanna-Carita: the tale of the quest for ultimate release by Salibhadra and Dhanna: a work in Old Gujarati, critically edited and translated, with a grammatical analysis and glossary, by Ernest Bender.* New Haven: The American Oriental Society, 1992.

in his highly respected *History of Indian and Indonesian Art* (1927). The *History* represents an extraordinary effort by Coomaraswamy to summarize vast quantities of secondary information, together with his own ideas, formulated from his collecting and surveying research in India. Since the idea for the book is based on presenting the information through a scheme of historic periodization, the Jaina material is embedded within larger fields which focus on regionalisms, most often emphasizing Hindu or Buddhist reflexes. I have selected two short extracts which directly address Jaina architecture and painting. In contrast to the *History's* substantive contribution to the study of Indian art and its influence on South-East Asia, it does not represent an especial addition to the study of Jaina art.

In 1930, Coomaraswamy published a short article in *Eastern Art*,[52] noting the gift by Denman W. Ross of a Jaina manuscript on palm-leaf dated AD 1260. The codex (originally 285 folios, 56 missing) is a copy of the *Sāvaga-paḍikkamaṇa-sutta-cuṇṇi,* a commentary on a text which instructs Jaina laity in the need for and methods of repentance. The acquisition was noteworthy, as the manuscript contains six illustrations and was the fifth oldest extant Jaina manuscript, the oldest outside of India, known at the time. A year later, Coomaraswamy published another short article, this time in the Museum *Bulletin,* concerning yet another gift by Denman Ross of two important manuscripts.[53] The older dates from the middle of the fifteenth century, a codex of the *Bālagopālastuti*, a Sanskrit composition by Bilvamaṅgala in praise of the youthful Krishna. It is a non-Jaina text executed in the 'western India' style, as Coomaraswamy and others, such as W. Norman Brown and Stella Kramrisch, had begun to call the style which had formally been called 'Gujarati-Jaina'. The later manuscript, a codex dating around AD 1600, is of the *Kumārasambhava* of Kalidasa, and clearly of a Jaina source as it is dedicated to the twenty-third *tīrthaṅkara,* Pārśvanāth. These two codices are important for the study of the western Jaina hieratic style as one of the sources for later styles which develop in response to the patronage of Vaishnava and Rajput interests.

[52] 'An Illustrated Śvetāmbara Jaina Manuscript of AD 1260', *Eastern Art* (Philadelphia), II, 1930, pp. 236-40.

[53] 'Two Western Indian Manuscripts', *Bulletin of the Museum of Fine Arts* (Boston), XXIX, 1931, pp. 4-11.

ART AND LITERATURE AS METAPHYSICS

By 1935, Coomaraswamy had entered a bold new phase in his intellectual work. One senses that his *History of Indian and Indonesian Art,* published in 1927, represents his last and best effort at descriptive art history. He had decided to move towards a methodology which was essentially comparative and interdisciplinary, a method which sought to commence with the object and lead to the subject. He was never convinced that a purely 'historical method' could adequately explain cultural contact and changes. What he did believe in was the study of symbols, their circulation and cycles within and between cultures. Beginning with his first article on Jaina art, Coomaraswamy displayed his confidence and credulity in symbols. Much of the substantive value of 'Notes on Jaina Art' lies in its meticulous presentation of background information on Jainism, especially with respect to Jaina symbology as it relates to the paintings published in the article.

In this regard, his last and most interesting think-piece on Jaina painting, the article entitled 'The Conqueror's Life in Jaina Painting: Explicitur Reductio Haec Artis Ad Theologiam',[54] is typical. Roger Lipsey said 'that Coomaraswamy restored certain kinds of knowledge; this will be perhaps nowhere more evident, and was nowhere more desirable, than in the field of symbols'.[55] Through this article on the meaning of the 'biography' of the Jina, 'The Conqueror', Coomaraswamy attempts to bring us closer to the symbol, in fact to transcend the symbol by going beyond the objectivity of the traditional approach, through grasping the transparency of diachronic symbolism. He begins by explaining his point of departure and certain assumptions regarding the intersubjectivity of Indian traditions.

> Professor Brown and Mr. Ramachandran have provided us with authoritative and almost exhaustive denominative accounts of the iconography of Jaina painting, in western and southern India. It has long been recognized that as compositions and in symbolism the illustrations of the lives of the Jainas or 'Conquerors' are by no means contemporary inventions, but rather slightly varying recensions of archetypal formulae of which the date of fixation can hardly be determined for want of documents. In this respect the Jaina

[54] *Journal of the Indian Society of Oriental Art* (Calcutta), III, pp. 127-44, 14 figs.

[55] Lipsey, op. cit., p. 692.

compositions corresponds to those of folk art, which are evidently the lineal descendants of types of an unknown and in this case certainly a very remote antiquity. In this connection, it is the purpose of the present article to call attention to certain characteristics of the Jaina formulation, as to which there can be said what is also true of Indian iconography generally, viz., (1) that the forumulation is in hardly any detail a private property of the sect that makes use of it, and (2) that ultimate explanations can only be found in the Vedic metaphysical tradition, and/or cognate traditions. In other words, the miniatures are not merely illustrations of the life of this or that one of the twenty-four Tīrthaṁkaras (virtually, 'pontifices') but in the last analysis are illustrations of a universal 'Book of Genesis' (*bhāva vṛtta, jātavidyā*) or cosmogony. In this respect, of course, what can be said of the pictures is equally true of the texts which they 'illuminate' in more than one sense.[56]

Now, this is a subtle opening gambit. Coomaraswamy, while pointedly praising as 'authoritative' the scholarship of W. Norman Brown, one of the most important American Indologists of the twentieth century, and T.N. Ramachandran, an important early archaeologist/ art historian, further comments that their work is 'denominative'; that is, to suggest a kind of boundedness, limited by methodological stricture. More weighty is his statement that 'ultimate explanations can only be found in the Vedic metaphysical tradition, and/or cognate traditions'. In a footnote to the title of the article, Coomaraswamy adds additional clarification to his point of reference by referring to the twelfth century Jaina savant, Hemacandra:

[In Hemacandra's] description of those who are considering a painting, the first place is given to those 'versed in Holy Writ' (*āgama-vit*), whose judgement is based on the picture's 'agreement with the meaning of Writ' (*āgamārthāvisaṁvādi*), the second place to the 'very pious' persons who delight in the representations (*bimbāni*) of the holy personages as such, third place to the 'technical experts' who criticise the draughtsmanship, and fourth to those 'others' who are charmed by the colours. These points of view correspond approximately to the well known classification of references as respectively anagogic (*paramārthika*), moral, allegorical, and literal. In the present article, the reader is invited to consider Jaina painting from the first of these points of view, that of the *āgama-vit,* the *vidu, ya evam vidvān.*[57]

In other words, Coomaraswamy places Brown and Ramachandran in the third category, that of 'technical expert', and invites his reader to join him in Hemacandra's 'first position', that of the *āgamavit,* the one versed in the Holy Writ. Certainly, what follows the article's introduction requires generous leaps of faith, some would say the faith of the already converted. As an Indologist, in fact my teacher was Brown's student, I admit to having trouble accepting, even following Coomaraswamy's convoluted attempts at cultural fission and fusion. His use of Vedic sources, especially given the state of Indology's understanding at that time, is simply uncautious in the extreme. And yet, I am intrigued by his premise that 'the formulation is in hardly any detail a private property of the sect that makes use of it'. As a student of Jainism and Prakrit languages, I am aware of the probability, nay the existence of boundaries beween the hardened categories we glibly call Hinduism, Buddhism, and Jainism. In this case, the over cautious owe a debt of gratitude to one of the few historians of Indian art who ventured to balance (I feel successfully) on the beam of epistemology. Though he tried his hand at drawing, Coomaraswamy never became an artist. He married women artists, and we need to look more closely at the relationships for influences. Yet, having the opportunity to examine his career, I see an 'artist', in development: a creative mind susceptible to continuous growth, a mind dedicated to the proposition that we need to move from naming to the numinous.

[56] 'The Conqueror's Life ...', pp. 127-8.

[57] Ibid., footnote 1.

Catalogue of the Indian Collections in the Museum of Fine Arts, Boston

Part I
General Introduction

[In 1923, Coomaraswamy began publication of the *Catalogue of the Indian Collections in the Museum of Fine Arts, Boston*, Part I (1923), entitled, *Part I: General Introduction*, provides a short two-page introduction to Jainism, to prepare the reader for the subsequent volume containing the museum's holdings of Jaina art.]

[PREFATORY COMMENTS]

The catalogue of the Indian works of art in the possession of the Museum of Fine Arts will be issued in parts, of which the present Introduction is the first. In this introduction emphasis is laid only on those aspects of Indian thought which are most significant from the standpoint of the student of works of art actually represented or likely to be represented in the Museum collections. All of the objects comprised in the collections will be described, and almost all of them illustrated.

The Collections as now existing are mainly the gift of Dr. Denman W. Ross, including a large number from the 'Ross Collection', and also the greater part of the 'Coomaraswamy Collection' of paintings and bronzes, presented to the Museum by Dr. Ross in 1917. Other important gifts include a series of sculptures from the Amarāvatī stūpa, and other objects presented by the Government Museum, Madras; Miss Louise M. Nathurst's collection of Indian jewelry; the jewelry from the Gardner-Brewer collection bequeathed by Mrs. Arthur Croft; the Mughal hunting carpet given by Mr. Winthrop Ames; several fragments of Gandhāra sculpture and Mughal and Nepalese paintings given by Mr. Edward W. Forbes; a Siamese Buddhist figure and a number of pieces of jewelry bequeathed by Mr. Hervey E. Wetzel; a South Indian bronze presented by Sir William Beardsell; and some pieces of sculpture and other objects given by Dr. Commaraswamy. The remainder of the collection consists of purchases, other gifts, and loans, the former including the Indian portion of the Goloubew collection of Persian and Indian miniatures purchased by special subscription in 14, and the numerous sculptures and other objects purchased in India in 1921 from the Marianne Brimmer fund.

In connection with certain of the inscriptions quoted in various sections of the Catalogue, I am glad to take this opportunity of acknowledging kind assistance received from Sir J.H. Marshall, Director of the Archaeological Survey of India, from Dr. L.D. Barnett, of the British Museum and from my colleague Mr. John Ellerton Lodge.

I have considered it proper to suggest a date for each piece: in many cases this dating is made without hesitation, in others it must be regarded only as an approximate estimate.

Boston, 1923 ANANDA K. COOMARASWAMY

Introduction

JAINISM[1]

From the correspondences in Jaina and Buddhist tradition it is practically certain that Mahāvīra, otherwise called Vardhamāna (Jñātiputra) is identical with the Nigaṇṭha Nātaputta who is referred to in Buddhist texts as the leader of a rival sect in the time of the Buddha himself. Thus the founder of Jainism, like the Buddha, taught in the sixth century BC.[2]

What he taught, and the manner of his teaching, also closely paralleled the doctrine and ministry of Buddha. Jainism is essentially an ethical philosophy intended for ascetics, the Nigaṇṭhas, 'Freed from all bonds', who leave the world to dedicate their whole lives to the search for truth, and its proclamation. They practiced a more severely ascetic rule than that of the Buddhists. As in Buddhism, however, there was also recognized a laity, who without renouncing the world, still adhered to the Jaina doctrines, and supported the Jaina mendicants. The members of the lay community, if they could not reach the highest goal, could still walk on the path towards it.

Though retaining one and the same body of doctrine, the Jaina community as a whole was early divided into two parts, the Digambaras, 'Clothed with the sky', whose ascetics wear no clothing whatever, and the Śvetāmbaras, who are 'Clothed in white', and who alone possess an order of nuns. The Jaina teaching, like the Buddhist, takes for granted the Brāhmaṇ doctrines of *Karma* (Deeds, causality) and *Saṁsāra* (The Ocean of Life and Death). Its highest goal is *Nirvāṇa* or *Mokṣa*, the setting free of the individual from the *Saṁsāra*. The means to this end are the three Jewels of Right Knowledge, Right Faith, and Right Walk. Just what the Buddha is to the Buddhists—originally a man like other men, who nevertheless by his own power has attained omniscience and freedom, and out of pity for suffering mankind teaches to them the way of salvation which he has found—that is the Jina to the Jains. The Jina, the Conqueror, is variously known as Kevalin (Omniscient), Buddha (Enlightened), Mukta (Delivered), Siddha (Perfected), Arahat [*sic*] (Adept), and Tīrthakara, 'the Finder of the Ford'; by which to cross the Ocean of Rebirth. The last title alone is peculiar to Jains, all the others belonging to the common usage of Brāhmaṇs and Buddhists as well as Jains.

The cardinal doctrines of Jainism may be enunciated as follows: Human personality is dual, spiritual and physical; man has free will, and is himself alone responsible for all that is good or bad in his life; the human soul may control and be freed from its physical entanglement, becoming an Arahat in the world, and a Siddha in *Nirvāṇa*, enjoying then its true form of being and possessed of the four infinite powers; and those Siddhas 'who have revealed the broad fording-place of virtue' are called Tīrthakaras (Finders of the Ford). But just as in Buddhism, the Jina, who is at first a mere man, is subsequently deified and becomes the object of a devotional cult.[3]

It will be seen that this system differs from that of Upaniṣads in its dualism, and from Buddhism in its acceptance of the idea of the soul. It resembles the Sāṁkhya in its dualism, and Buddhism, both in its establishment of a monastic order, and in its attitude towards the lesser gods, with a rejection of the idea of a Supreme Creator. Like all other Indian religions, it has for its end the spiritual freedom and perfection of every individual.

While the Buddhist community no longer exists in India, except in Nepal and Ceylon, but is represented throughout Eastern Asia, the Jains have survived in India to the present day, but have not established adherents abroad. The Jains are to be met with in nearly every large Indian town, chiefly amongst the merchants. They have been politically, and are still economically powerful. To them the architectural splendor of many of the cities of Western India is largely due, as likewise, that of the great temple cities of Śatruñjaya and Girnār, and the beautiful temples at Mount Ābu. They now occupy an important position chiefly in Gūjarāt, Rājputāna and the Pañjāb, and also in Kanara.

[1] See especially, P.C. Nahar and K. Ghosh, *Epitome of Jainism*, Calcutta, 1917.

[2] For the details of the legend of the title of Mahāvīra, see section of the Catalogue dealing with Jaina Painting.

[3] It was, I think, first pointed out by Jacobi (*Gaina Sutras*, S.B.E., Vol. XXII, p. XXI) that the impulse to image worship equally amongst Buddhists and Jainas must have originated in the lay community and results from the experience and doctrine of Bhakti, or devotion.

Catalogue of the Indian Collections in the Museum of Fine Arts, Boston

Part IV
Jaina Paintings and Manuscripts

[In 1924, *Part IV: Jaina Paintings and Manuscripts*, appeared, with the same short introduction. The content of the first part of the Introduction, pp. 3-11, 'Jainism' and 'Life of Mahāvīra and Other Jinas' is taken, almost *verbatim*, from 'Notes on Jaina Art'. In discussing the contents of the *Kalpasūtra*, especially the biographies of Pārśva, Neminātha, and Ṛṣabha, the following text was added, beginning on p. 12.]

Much briefer lifes of the Jinas Pārśva (who is very possibly a real personage), Nemi and Ṛṣabha follow. They are similar in most respects to the life of Mahāvīra with only a difference in the names of persons and places. We give here certain episodes peculiar to Pārśva. The name Pārśva is in some way connected with a black serpent seen by his mother before his birth. His cognizance is a serpent. Later in life he is guarded by the serpent king Dharaṇendra who enters into the story in connection with Kaṭha. The *Pārśvanātha Caritra* relates the story of nine prebirths of Pārśvanātha and Kaṭha (originally brothers, Marubhūti and Kamaṭha), in each of which the former is slain by the latter, but dies forgivingly. When Marubhūti is reborn as Pārśva, Kamaṭha is reborn (1) as Kaṭha or Kamaṭha, who becomes an ascetic and (2) as the Asura Meghamālin. The rest of the story follows:

'One day Pārśva sees Kaṭha surrounded by a great concourse of people, performing the severe five-fire-penance (*pañcāgnitapas*). And he sees that Kaṭha has thrown a great serpent into a fire-pan which stands upon the fagots of the fire. He asks the reason for this pitiless practice, inconsistent with Kaṭha's own austerities. Kaṭha replies that kings might understand elephants and horses, but that sages alone understood religion. Pārśva has the fire put out; the agonized serpent is reborn as Dharaṇa, the wealthy king of the Nāgas in Pātāla, the subterranean home of the serpents. Kaṭha, as the result of his false practice, is reborn as an Asura by name of Meghamālin.

'Pārśva, happening to see on the wall of his palace a picture of the Arhat, Nemi, who had taken the vow early in life, decides to do the same, and to undertake the enlightenment of the world. Preparatory to his consecration he distributes vast alms. To the songs and music of the people he goes to a hermitage where the very trees and plants rejoice over his presence. At the foot of an Aśoka tree he renounces power and wealth, plucks out his hair, and, at the age of thirty, obtains the knowledge due to mental perfection. He wanders from place to place, instructing, and acclaimed as a Saint. While standing in the forest of Kāuśāmbī in the *kāyotsarga*[4] posture, the serpent-king Dharaṇa comes in great state to do him honor, performs a mimic representation, and during three days holds an umbrella over his head to protect him from the sun. He wanders again, to many places, to find out where dwells the enemy Illusion. The Asura Meghamālin (the soul of Kamaṭha) attacks the Lord Pārśva with tigers, elephants and scorpions, but, when he shows no fear, they slink off, as tho ashamed. Meghamālin then tries to submerge him in the waters produced by a

[4] *Kāyotsarga:* 'The posture of one who stands upright, or sits, with his two arms hanging down, and without any regard for his body, is called Kāyotsarga (abandonment of the body).' Hemacandra, Yogaśāstra IV, 132. 'The ascetic stands unmoveable, his arms held stiffly downward, his knees pressed together, his feet four fingers' length apart, his toes stretched forward.' R.G. Bhandarkar, *Search for Sanskrit Manuscripts*, 1887-91, p. 98, note. By this penance are cleared away past and present sins that require expiation. The *Kalpasūtra* mentions this penance only in connection with Pārśva: but our pictures represent Mahāvīra also in this posture.

fearful thunderstorm; even then the Lord does not budge from his place and his pious meditations. Dharaṇa, finding out by superior insight that Kamaṭha is attacking the Lord, fashions by means of his serpent hoods an umbrella over his head: the Lord stands there like a royal hansa [swan] bird, submerged in a deep trance, retaining his equanimity in the face of both Kamaṭha's attacks and Dharaṇa's devotion. Dharaṇa then excoriates Meghamālin's hatred of the Lord, pointing out that he had done him no injury, but on the contrary, had saved him from the sin of burning up Dharaṇa on the occasion of his uncanny practice. Meghamālin then repents, resorts to the Lord, and goes home, determined to devote himself to piety. Thus ends the drama of the persecution of the soul of Marubhūti by the soul of Kamaṭha, carried on through ten existences.'[5]

The following account of the birth of Neminātha, the son of King Samudravijaya and Queen Śivā, is given in Ch. X of the *Satruñjaya Māhātmayam* (Weber, A., trans. by Burgess, J. in *Indian Antiquary*, XXX, 298, 1901: 'At Sauripura, Śivā the wife of Samudravijaya, dreamt at dawn the fourteen great dreams, and at the very time, the 12th of Kārtika-vadya, Chitrānakṣatra, she gave birth to a child of dark color with the mark of a conch; then on the top of Meru the fifty-six Dikkumāris and sixty-four Indras celebrated the birth of the Jina, Samudravijaya also celebrated the event and gave his child the name of Arishtanemi (the 22nd Jina). He was nursed by a crowd of Apsarās and waited on by gods who had assumed his age at Indra's command. After this Samudravijaya went into the garden to amuse himself, when Indra seeing the Svāmi in the lap of his mother joyfully saluted him and said to the gods that Samudravijaya, in whose house the Svāmi Nemi Tīrthaṅkara had appeared as a son, was indeed meritorious and happy, praising the lord exceedingly for his bravery. Some of the gods present answered Indra that his praise of the boy before them was unseemly for they had once dried up the whole ocean and had pulverized great mountains with ease; and desiring to see the strength of the Jina, they had come to the garden consecrated by him. There they saw the boy caressed by people, some saying 'live long', some kissing him, some holding his fingers, some making him laugh by nodding their heads, etc. When, afterwards, they found the Jina in his cradle resting alone, they carried him off by stealth up into the sky. When they had gone some thousand *kos* up, the lord in meditation, knew what they were about, and to convince them of his powers, sunk them several thousand *kos* below the ground. Seeing their plight Indra pitied them, and coming to Nemi requested him to deliver them, as they had committed this fault through ignorance; and, after liberating them and putting the lord in his cradle, Indra returned to Svarga. Samudravijaya and others witnessing the power of Nemi, were highly pleased and returned home, celebrating a festival befitting the occasion in the Arhant temple. Henceforward the lord grew up protected by the gods under orders of Indra.' At Dvārakā the lord Ariṣṭanemi gradually grew into a young man.

Indra now describes the peculiar virtues of Nemi to the gods. The latter unbelieving, assumed human form and waged war upon Dvārakā; Balarāma and Krishṇa were defeated and made prisoner. 'Then Krishṇa's wives went to their brother-in-law, Nemi, and said humbly that he, being a Jina, a Tīrthaṅkara, was of unlimited power, and that though his brothers had been carried off he was unmoved and his valour would be of no account unless it were shown now. Nemi considered for a while and then came out to the assembly, when Samudravijaya who was about to proceed against his enemies was brought back by Krauṭṭku, who told him his efforts would be fruitless as these enemies could be defeated only by a Tīrthaṅkara. In the meantime Mātulle the charioteer of Indra had brought a chariot by his master's orders and told Nemi to mount. He did so with the weapons of war and completely defeated the gods. Indra came down and praised him greatly, requesting that he would pardon the gods for their folly. The gods bowed when they saw Indra and prostrated themselves to the Tīrthaṅkara, who pardoning them, went to Surdārāpura and released Anādhṛshṇi, Balarāma and Krishṇa. Indra requested the lord to take them to holy places—Śatruñjaya and others for their benefit. The lord, sitting in the *vimāna* of Indra, went with them to Śatruñjaya, told them its history, and thence came to Girnāra and then to Dvārakā. Leaving Nemi and his brothers there, Indra and the others went to their respective abodes.'

The following account of the episode of Kṛishṇa conch was obtained by J. Burgess from a

[5] M. Bloomfield, *Life and stories of the Jaina Savior Pārśvanātha,* Introduction, Baltimore, 1919.

Jaina priest (*Indian Antiquary*, III, 1874, p. 138): 'His cousin Krishṇa was also of superhuman strength, and was able to blow a large conch from which it was believed no other person could produce a blast. One day Neminātha saw it lying on the ground, and asking why that toy was lying there, he took it up and blew such a blast upon it as quite alarmed Krishṇa who began to inquire who it was that could blow upon his *śaṅkha*. On finding it was his cousin, he became jealous of him as a rival, and accordingly directed his hundred *gopīs* to excite amorous thoughts in Nemināthа and shame him into marriage, thinking intercourse with women the only way to put down his strength. The *gopīs* began to tease him and tell him as he was grown up to manhood he ought to marry. At first he refused, but after a great deal of reviling and reproaching he consented, and Krishṇa selected for him Rājīmatī the daughter of Ugrasena of Girnār—whose palace is still shown, being a ruin near the Junāgaḍh fort beside the Bhumriyo kuo. When the wedding day came and Nemināthа approached Junāgaḍh, he saw a flock of sheep and herds of cattle collected to be sacrificed for the people that had assembled to celebrate the wedding: the sheep were bleating piteously, and, struck with pity for them and the vanity of human happiness, and to save the lives of so many animals, he resolved to become an ascetic, gave up the world, and retired into the Girnār hills, followed by his intended bride, and there they both led a platonic life.' A similar account is given in the *Śatruñjaya Māhātmayam* Ch. XIII, where it is stated that the conch Pañcajanya had been bestowed upon Krishṇa by the god of the sea.

[Pages 17-22, 'Summary of the Story of Kālakācārya', are identical to 'Notes on Jaina Art', pp. 85-7, except for the following, which was inserted on p. 21.]

III. *Kālaka in Bharoch with Balamitra.*
IV. *Kālaka in Pratiṣṭhāna with Sātvāhana.*

Balamitra and Bhānumitra, nephews of Kālakācārya were king and crown prince of Bhṛgukaccha. Their sister Bhānuśrī had a son Balathānu. The two brothers hearing of their uncle's residence in Ujjayinī sent an ambassador, with whom Kālakācārya returned. In Bhṛgukaccha he preached to his nephews, their sister and her son. The latter was converted, and so too were many nobles and townspeople. The household priest or Balamitra making objections, begging was forbidden. Kālakācārya departed to Pratiṣṭhāna in the Marāṭha country, to the pious king Sātavāhana.

V. *Kālaka's Disobedient Pupils: and His visit to Sāgaracandra*

The pupils are disobedient: Kālaka leaves them and visits his pupil's pupil Sāgaracandra, arrives after dark, and unrecognized owing to the darkness of the night, engages in disputation with him. The repentant pupils came in search of him.

[A few similarities to 'Notes on Jaina Art' withstanding, the remainder of the introduction to the catalogue contains substantially new material.]

SUMMARY OF THE STORY OF ŚĀLIBHADRA

The story of Śālibhadra is told in a number of versions. The following is a summary of the original Sanskrit text of Dharma Kumāra from a manuscript in the British Museum, kindly communicated by Dr. L.D. Barnett:

'A poor village boy named Saṅgama, son of a widow, when half starved gave to a hungry ascetic mild-rice (pāyasa) that his mother had with much difficulty obtained for him. The boy promptly died, and as a reward of his precocious piety and intelligence was reborn as the son of the merchant Gobhadra and his wife Bhadrā in Rājagṛha, and was named Śālibhadra. He married thirty-two wives of his own caste, and lived in worldly happiness.'

The following summary of the story of Śālibhadra is based upon Professor Maurice Bloomfield's digest of Pradyumnasūri's *mahākāvya*,[6] p. 167, and our manuscript:

The saintly youth Saṅgama, son of the poor window Dhanyā, grows up in the village of Śāligrāma, in Magadha. He becomes a herdsman. One day he asks his mother for a dish of sweet rice-milk. She cannot afford to buy the materials, but her neighbors make her a present of them,

[6] *The Śālibhadra Carita, a story of conversion to Jaina monkhood:* by M. Bloomfield, *JAOS*, XLIII, 4, 1923, pp. 167ff. I am greatly indebted to Professor Bloomfield for an advance proof of this valuable article.

and Dhanyā gives the dish of rice-milk to her son. Just then a great ascetic, about to break a month's fast, arrives. Saṅgama, with profound devotion, hands him his dish of rice-milk; and receives the blessing of the ascetic. Ultimately Saṅgama abandons life by fasting.

He is reborn as Śālibhadra, the son of the merchant prince Gobhadra and his wife Bhadrā, in the city of Rājagṛha: his conception is announced in Bhadrā's dream of a field of ripe rice, which suggests Śāligrāma (rice-village). The ruler of Rājagṛha marries his son to thirty-two beautiful women, and proposes to retire from the world. Meanwhile Mahāvīra arrives, and Gobhadra, in spite of the protests of his wife, and son, takes his vows at the Lord's hands. Subsequently he dies by fasting and is reborn in the Saudharma heaven. Thence he descends as a god to visit his son and bestows upon him rare treasures and divine grace and beauty and great prosperity.

Merchants now come from abroad with rare and magnificent shawls whch they offer to King Śreṇika, who, however, thinks that he cannot afford to buy them. Śālibhadra's mother then buys the eight shawls, cuts each into four parts and presents them to Śālibhadra's wives, who in turn place them at his feet. Cellaṇā, King Śreṇika's queen, hearing of the shawls, begs him to take the shawls from the merchants by force. He finds that Śālibhadra's mother has secured them, and repenting of his former parsimony, offers to buy them from her. She, however, can do nothing as she has already given away the shawls. The king's messenger reports these matters to the king, who wonders what sort of man this wealthy Śālibhadra must be. The king sends his messenger to invite Śālibhadra to visit him. His mother Bhadrā goes instead and invites the king to visit Śālibhadra; he agrees, and is received in state, and seats himself upon a jeweled throne. The occasion of the king's visit is the means of Śālibhadra's enlightenment (*pratyekabodhi*); for he reflects that even the highest ruler is a mere living creature with hands and feet like himself. The only real king is the man of great virtue. Śālibhadra, with his wives, nevertheless pays his respects to the king, who is delighted.

Bhadrā now prepares a great shampoo for the king. As he is being rinsed, his signet ring falls into the water, and is lost, but when the water is poured away, it is discovered in the jeweled bath, where, however, its glory is dimmed by the splendor of its surroundings. The king is somewhat cast down by this; but recognizes Śālibhadra's superior spiritual powers. He returns to his palace. Śālibhadra's *vairāgya* (disgust of the world) now ripens. He purposes to abandon the household life and to become an ascetic (*sādhu*). Bhadrā endeavors to dissuade him, but the only compromise he will make is to abandon his wives one by one on successive days, thus postponing his final renunciation of the world for thirty-two days.

In the same city lives Śālibhadra's sister, Subhadrā, whose husband is called Dhanya. She tells him in tears that Śālibhadra is daily abandoning his wives. Dhanya remarks that such a gradual process of renunciation is far from admirable. Dhanya's seven other wives protest against this criticism on Dhanya's part, as he is making no renunciation whatever himself. He exclaims in reply that his wives have become his spiritual guides, for what they have said has suggested to him to wait upon the Lord and to become a homeless ascetic himself.

In the meantime Mahāvīra has taken up his residence on the Vaibhara mountain. Dhanya with his wives resorts to the Lord. Śālibhadra hears of this and reproaches his mother for her resistance. She now realizes that Śālibhadra cannot be dissuaded; accordingly she visits the king in order to borrow the royal insignia for the ordination ceremony (*dīkṣā*). The king himself promises to make the necessary arrangements.

Śālibhadra with his mother and wives, and accompanied by the king, now resorts to Mahāvīra's *samavasaraṇa* palace and receives ordination at his hands. Dhanya and his wife Subhadrā follow him into the homeless life. The king and the sorrowful women return to Rājagṛha.

Śālibhadra and Dhanya enter upon a life of severe asceticism. At the end of twelve years they return to Rājagṛha in the following of Mahāvīra. They are about to break a month's fast; and visit Bhadrā's palace as mendicants, 'emaciated, silent, unmoved'. But Bhadrā, eager to do honor to the returned spiritual heroes, is so deeply moved that she does not recognize them in their changed guise, and so misses the honor of offering to them the food with which they shall break their fast. With perfect equanimity they move on, and receive food from a woman named Mathatahārika, who had in the former birth been Śālibhadra's mother in Śāligrāma.

Śālibhadra and Dhanya now determine to pursue their path to the end; they practice more severe asceticism, and attain to death by starvation. Meanwhile Bhadrā and her daughter-in-law, accompanied by King Śreṇika go out to do honor to the great ascetics. On finding them at the point of death, they are profoundly affected. The king, however, so comforts Bhadrā that she is able to encourage her son in his efforts toward final victory. Śālibhadra and Dhanya are reborn in the Sarvārthasiddha heaven, where they enjoy the highest bliss.

JAINA COSMOLOGY[7]

The Universe is eternal, and has the form of a spindle resting upon an inverted cone. The spindle and cone together are sometimes represented diagrammatically in the form of a woman with arms akimbo.[8] Above the summit of the spindle is the paradise of the Siddhas, who have attained release and passed beyond rebirth. This paradise is all of white gold. It is known as the Īṣātprāgbhārā and by other names. In the middle is a white rock Siddha Śilā, Śilātala or Sīlā, having the form of an inverted umbrella, thick at the middle and diminishing outward to an infinitely small dimension. Above this rock is the abode of the Siddhas (Mahāvīra and other Tīrthaṅkaras).

A description of this place to which perfected souls pass, leaving their bodies here below, is given in the *Uttaradhyāna Sūtra*:

'Twelve *yojanas* above the Sarvārtha (heaven) is the place Īṣātprāgbhārā, which has the form of an umbrella. It is forty-five hundred thousand *yojanas* long, and as many broad, and it is somewhat more than three times as many in circumference. Its thickness is eight *yojanas*; it is greatest in the middle, and decreases towards the margin till it is thinner than the wing of a fly. This place, by nature pure, consisting of white gold, resembles in form an (inverted) open umbrella, as has been said by the best of Jinas. [Above it] is a pure blessed place, which is white like a conch. ... There at the top of the world reside the blessed perfected souls, rid of all transmigration, and arrived at the excellent state of perfection.[9]

The Īṣātprāgbhārā is inhabited by fifteen varieties of Siddhas, of whom the Tīrthaṅkara-siddhas are first.

It should be noted that the miniatures, as well as Jaina tradition, appear to identify the place described as Īṣātprāgbhārā with the actual Siddha Śilā. In the miniatures, the place resembling in form an (inverted) white umbrella, is represented in section as a crescent, very thin at the margins and relatively thick in the centre. This crescent has been pointed out to me by a Jaina priest, in the actual miniatures, as the Siddha Śilā; and some of the miniatures, moreover, are thus labeled in a contemporary hand. Hüttemann is certainly mistaken in describing the crescent as that of the moon.[10]

Below the Īṣātprāgbhārā are the five heavens (Vimānas) of the Anuttara gods, that of the Sarvārthasiddhas being central, and those of the Vijayas, Vaijayantas, Jayantas and Aparājitas being disposed in a horizontal plane around it. All things below the Īṣātprāgbhārā are included in the Saṅsāra or sphere of change, mortality and rebirth: nevertheless the gods of the highest heavens reside in these heavens for periods almost inconceivably long.

Below the five heavens of the Anuttara gods are the nine heavens of the Graiveyakas, arranged one above the other; the Graiveyaka and Anuttara heavens together form the upper half of the spindle.

Below them are the twelve heavens of the Kalpabhavas (sixteen according to the Digambaras), arranged one above the other, completing the lower half of the spindle. All the gods inhabiting the various heavens (*vimānas*) above the 'waist' are called Vaimānikas.

The 'waist' is formed by Mount Meru, the axis of the universe, and the lands and seas disposed about it horizontally. Here belong the Bhavanādhipati (Asuras, Nāgas, etc.), Vyantara (Rākṣasas, Kiṅnaras, Gandharvas, etc.), and Jyotiṣka gods (Suns, Moons, Planets, etc.), and finally, also men.

The geography of the worlds about Mount Meru is as follows: There is a central continent around Meru, called Jambūdvīpa Bharata. Around this is the Salt Sea, separating it from the continent called Dhātukī-dvīpa. Around this again is the Black Sea, separating it from the continent called Puṣkara-dvīpa. The four parts

[7] This subject is treated in great detail by W. Kirfel, in *Die Consmographie der Inder*, Leipzig, 1920.

[8] E.g. in a diagram reproduced by Kirfel, loc. cit., tafel 4.

[9] Jacobi, *Gaina Sutras*, II, Sacred Books of the East, Vol. XLV, pp. 2-13.

[10] Hüttemann, *Miniaturen zum Jinacarita*, Baessler Archiv, 1913, p. 74.

of the two outer continents, and the two parts (Bharata and Airāvata) of Jambūdvīpa, constitute the 'Ten Regions' or 'world'. The inner half of Puṣkara-dvīpa is separated from the outer half by a range of impassable mountains, the Manuṣottara Parvata. Each continent has an elaborate system of rivers and mountains.

The southern segment of Jambūdvīpa, called Bharata-varṣa, is the land of India, where the twenty-four Tīrthaṇkaras, of our age (*avasarpiṇī*) have made their appearance. It will be seen that the Bharata-varṣa of the map, with its mountain ranges to the north, its two great rivers, and the sea round it except on the north corresponds to the actual geography of India, with the Himālayas, Indus, and Ganges, and the Indian Ocean.

The cone below the 'waist' contains the seven hells or underworlds (Nārakas).

FURTHER EXPLANATION OF VARIOUS TERMS

I. It should be observed that every Jina has his own particular complexion, cognizance, and *dīkṣā*-tree. These are as follows in the case of the four chief Jinas whose lives are illustrated in the miniatures:

Jina	*Complexion*	*Cognizance*	*Dikṣā-tree*
Mahāvīra	Yellow	Lion (*keśari-siṃha*)	Aśoka
Pārśva	Blue	Serpent (*sarpa*)	Dhātakī
Neminātha	Black	Conch (*śaṅkha*)	Veṭasa
Ṛṣabha	Golden	Bull (*vṛṣa*)	Vaṭa (banyan)

II. A more particular account must be given of a *Samavasaraṇa*. This is, briefly, a walled enclosure prepared by Indra, or the minor gods, intended for the delivery of a religious discourse by a Jina immediately after he becomes a Kevalin. The following description of a *Samavasaraṇa* is extracted from the *Samavasaraṇa Sthavana*:[11]

Whenever the Jinas exhibit the condition of Kevalin, in which all substances manifest themselves, there the Princes of the Air (Vayu-kumāras) cleanse the earth for one yojana all around. The Cloud-princes (Megha-kumāras) rain down fragrant water, the gods of the Seasons spread heaps of flowers, and the Vāṇa-Vyantaras make the surface of the earth variegated with rubies, gold, and gems. There are three ramparts: the innermost, intermediate, and outermost. [The first] is constructed of gems, with the battlements of rubies, by the Vaimānakas; [the second] of gold, with the battlements of gems, by the Jyotiṣkas; [and the third] of silver, with the battlements of gold, by the Bhavanapatis. In a round Samavasaraṇa the ramparts are 33 *dhanus* and 33 *angulas* wide, 500 *dhanus* high, and 1 *krosa* 600 *dhanus* (counting both sides) distant from each other. Each rampat has four gates made of gems. In the centre is a gem-studded pedestal, with four doors, three steps, and as high as the figure of the Jina, 200 *dhanus* broad and long, two and a half *krosas* high from the ground level. [In the centre of the dais stands] the Aśoka tree, twelve times as high as the body of the Jina, and exceeding a *yojana* in breadth. Then [underneath] is [a pedestal called] a *devacchaṅda* [and on it are] four lion-thrones accompanied by [four] footstools. (The four lion-thrones are occupied by the Jina himself on the East, and on the other sides by three reflections of the Jina produced by the Vāṇa-Vyantaras.) At every gate the Vāṇa-Vyantaras put up flags, parasols, makaras, ... garlands, pitchers; a triple arch (*toraṇa*), and incense vases. Having entered from the East and from left and right, having sat on a seat facing the East, having placed his feet on a footstool, and having saluted the congregation (*tīrtha*), the Lord discourses on the Law. (The congregation consists of gods, men, and animals.) There are two step-wells in each corner when it is square and one [at each gateway] when the Samavasaraṇa is round.

The *Kalpa Sūtra* and the *Ācārāṅga Sūtra* do not expressly mention either the Samavasaraṇa or the Siddha Śilā. But the constant representation of these places in the miniatures shows that the mention of Mahāvīra's preaching (*samosarai*) the Law to gods and men, after attaining the state of a Kevalin, was understood to imply also the place of preaching, the Samavasaraṇa; and in the same way the statement that he became a Siddha implied that he went to the Siddha Śilā.

III. The Eight Auspicious Objects (*Aṣṭ-amaṅgala*)—Representations of the Eight Auspicious Symbols constantly recur in Jaina art.

[11] Bhandarkar, 'Jaina Iconography', *Indian Antiquary*, Vol. XL, pp. 125-30 and 153-61.

The names of the auspicious objects are given as follows in the *Aupapātika Sūtra*; Sanskrit or English equivalents are added in parentheses: (1) Sotthiya (*svastika*); (2) Sirivaccha (*śrīvatsa*); (3) Nandiyāvatta; (4) Vaddhamaṇaga (powder-box); (5) Bhaddāsaṇa (throne of fortune); (6) Kalasa (water-jar); (7) Maccha (fishes); (8) Dappaṇā (mirror).

JAINA LITERATURE[12]

In course of time the Jaina community achieved (or condescended to) a systematic organization. There came into existence monuments, monasteries and schools. To this development of a cult corresponded a literary, scientific, and artistic activity, of which the earliest results brought the doctrine into fixed forms. Probably most of the original canonical Jaina literature (the 'old books' now lost) thus took shape early in the third century BC. Bhadrabāhu, the author of the *Kalpa Sūtra*, is stated according to Jaina tradition to have died 170 or 162 years after Mahāvīra himself (528 BC according to Jaina tradition); that is to say, Bhadrabāhu died 358 BC. The *Ācārāṅga Sūtra*, which confirms the traditions of the *Kalpa Sūtra* regarding the life of Mahāvīra, is the first of the eleven *aṅgas* or sections of the canon of the third century AD.[13] The whole Śvetambara canonical literature, known as Siddhānta or āgama consists of (1) the Twelve Aṅgas, (2) the Twelve Upāngas, (3) the Ten Paiṇṇas, (4) the Six Cheda Sūtras, (5) the Four Mūla Sūtras, and some other separate texts.

The *Kalpa Sūtra* contains three separate sections (1) the *Jinacarita* (lives of Mahāvīra, Pārśvanātha, Nemināthа and Ṛṣabha), (2) the *Sthavīrāvalī* (lists of Elders) and (3) the *Samācārī* (rules for monks).

This Prākṛt literature was probably in the main handed down orally until the time of the Council of Valabhi (AD 454 or 467), when new redactions were prepared and the method of teaching novices from books was substituted for purely oral instruction. The canonical literature as it stands dates from this period, though at that time, and even subsequently, additions may have been made. In any case, it is certain that the *Kalpa Sūtra*, including the main account of the life of Mahāvīra, 'has been held in high esteem by the Jainas for more than a thousand years'. The oldest available MS. of the *Kalpa Sūtra* appears to be the illustrated Pāṭan MS. on palm leaf, dated equivalent to AD 1237 illustrated by Nahar and Ghosh in their *Epitome of Jainism*. A MS. commentary dated equivalent to AD 1307 is also known. But no doubt the *Kalpa Sūtra* has been handed down substantially in its present form from at least the fifth century AD.

The non-canonical literature consists of commentaries on the canon, and of original works on Dogmatics, Ethics, Discipline, etc., and hymns addressed to the Jinas; it also includes a vast literature of stories. The language of this literature is partly Prākṛt, or Jaina-Mahārāṣṭrī, partly Sanskrit. The most important text of the uncanonical literature, from the present point of view, is the edifying *Kālakācārya Kathānakam* so often appended to the texts of the *Kalpa Sūtra*. The *Kathā-kośa, Prabandhacintāmani*, and other collections of stories, compilations in the main of the fourteenth century, depict a court life similar to that which is represented in the illustrations to the *Kalpa Sūtra*.

JAINA PAINTING

The tradition of Jaina art is as old as that of Buddhist art, and developed under similar conditions, and partly in dependence on Buddhist art. Remains of a pre-Kuṣāṇa Jaina stūpa have been excavated at Mathurā.[14] There are very extensive rock-hewn caves with relief sculptures not earlier than the second century and mainly of the first century BC at Udayagiri and Khaṇḍagiri in Orissa.[15] In one of these caves there are remains of paintings. Jaina sculptures of later periods are well known and need not be referred to here. It is worthwhile to remark, however, the remains of frescoes, apparently Jaina, of the seventh century, have been described by Professor Jouveau-Dubreuil, from Sittanavasal near Pudukottai in southern India.[16] It would appear from his account that these are comparable in merit with those of Ajaṇṭā, though far less

[12] The best account of the Jaina literature will be found in Winternitz, *Geschichte der indischen Literature*, Vol. II.

[13] H. Jacobi, Sacred Books of the East, Vols. XXII, LII, and Abh. für die Kunde des Morgenlandes, Bd. VII, Leipzig, 1879.

[14] V.A. Smith, *The Jaina Stūpa and other Antiquities of Mathurā.*

[15] Cambridge History of India, Vol. I, pp. 639ff.

[16] Jouveau-Dubreuil, *The Pallava Painting,* Pudukottai, 1920.

extensive. The only other evidence bearing on the history of Jaina painting before the thirteenth century is a reference in the *Pārśva Carita,* Sarga VI, to a picture of the Jina Nemi painted on a wall.[17]

The earliest illustrated manuscript known is one of the *Kalpa Sūtra*, on palm leaf, dated equivalent to AD 1237 preserved in the Pāṭan *bhaṇḍār* (monastic library).[18] Here, as in Nepalese MSS. and in the later Jaina MSS. on paper, the illustrations take the form of square panels applied to the page without organic relation to the text, though as will appear later, the intrinsic quality of the painting and the script are in perfect accord. Indian art has never developed book illustrations as such (illustrated MSS. of any kind are very rare), and the square panels we have referred to must be regarded, as it were, as excerpts from the surfaces of painted walls (of the type of the Degaldoruwa Vihāra in Ceylon)[19] reduced in size and added to the written page. It is very evident from the practical identity of the composition of the pictures in all the manuscripts that the art as we meet it represents the survival of an old hieratic tradition in which the stories of the lives of the Jinas had long been presented in accordance with familiar formulae.

After the thirteenth century the next dated illustrated manuscript is the *Kalpa Sūtra* of the Indian Office Library, dated equivalent to AD 1427.[20] There is another illustrated *Kalpa Sūtra* in the British Museum (MS. Or. 5, 149) dated equivalent to AD 1464 (see previous footnote); and a number of other fifteenth-century MSS. of the *Kalpa Sūtra* in the Museum of Fine Arts, described below: not all of these are dated, and it is possible that some are earlier than the fifteenth century, particularly the *Kālakācārya Kathā*, M.F.A. 17.2279.

There are other illustrated *Kalpa Sūtras* probably or actually of fifteenth-century date, in the Freer Gallery, Washington, in the Museum Für Volkerkunde, Berlin (MS. 1, C. 2,367) and in the Royal Library, Berlin,[21] and in the Nahar Collection in Calcutta, and others in the various Jaina libraries in Pāṭan and Jaisalmer.

In discussing the qualities of Jaina painting, accordingly, it must be understood that the reference is to the illustrations in the fifteenth-century manuscripts in the Museum collections and to those of similar manuscripts elsewhere. The art is one of pure draughtsmanship; the pictures are brilliant statements of the facts of the epic (the life of Mahāvīra, like the *Buddha-carita,* is essentially an epic), where every event is seen in the light of eternity. To call this pure drawing, implies that it is an art of symbols and indifferent to representation. On the other hand, it is not calligraphic, that is to say that elegance or an elegant combination of lines is not deliberately sought, and in this sense the drawing is more like script (such as that of the accompanying text) made to be clearly and easily read. There is no preoccupation with pattern, color, or texture for their own sake; but these are achieved with inevitable assurance in a way that could not have been the case had they been directly sought. The drawing has in fact the perfect equilibrium of a mathematical equation, or a page of a composer's score. Theme and formula compose an inseparable unity, text and pictures form a continuous relation of the same dogma in the same key.

The physical peculiarity in the delineation of human forms, particularly the angularity of the features and the projection of the further eye, are incidents of local color independent of the quality of the art, the inevitable stigmata of time and place. In a wider sense the same applies to physical peculiarities such as the broad chest (often so much exaggerated that a distinction of the male from the female form is almost lost) and lion waist, and the large eyes with their corners extended to the ear,[22] which are the common taste of India and not peculiar to Jaina works.

That the handling is light and casual does not imply a poverty of craftsmanship (the quality of roughness in 'primitives' of all ages seems to unsophisticated observers a defect), but rather

[17] M. Bloomfield, *The life and stories of the Jaina Savior Pārśvanātha*, 1919.

[18] Nahar and Ghosh, *Epitome of Jainism*, Calcutta, 1917, pp. 696, 706.

[19] A.K. Coomaraswamy, *Mediaeval Sinhalese Art*, frontispiece.

[20] H. Jacobi, S.B.E., Vol. XXII and in Abh. für die Kunde des Morgenlandes, VII, 1, 1879, and Ziet. der deutsch. morgenlandischen Gesellschaft, XXXIV, 1880. A.K. Coomaraswamy, 'Notes on Jaina Art', *Journal of Indian Art*, 1914.

[21] W. Hüttemann, *Miniaturen zum Jinacarita*, Baessler Archiv, 1913.

[22] Which might be illustrations to the *Rājatāraṅginī*, 1, 216, 'the very thin line of antimony which appeared to play the part of the stem to the ruby lotuses of their ear-ornaments'.

perfect adequacy—it is the direct expression of a flashing religious conviction and of freedom from any specific material interest. This is the most spiritual form known to us in Indian painting, and perhaps the most accomplished in technique, but not the most emotional nor the most intriguing. Human interest, and charm, on the other hand, are represented in Ajaṇṭā painting and in late Rājput art.

The colors employed in the illustrations of Jaina manuscripts are gold (either as gold leaf forming the foundation of the painting, or gold paint), yellow (which takes the place of gold as representing flesh, in MSS. where gold is not employed), black, white (pure white and a pearly white), red, blue, green, and pink. In a majority of MSS. not only is there a marginal legend (sometimes written however upon the picture itself) describing the scene, but also a thumb-nail outline sketch of the subject; it may be inferred from the presence of these sketches that the scribe having left the picture space blank, the painter, in going over the work to be done made these diagrammatic notes for his own guidance. It is to be presumed, accordingly, that the scribe and the painter were not identical persons.

A word may be said on the form of the Jaina MSS. They consist of oblong leaves, averaging some 11.5 x 26 cm. A central string hole is indicated by rubrication, but never used; the indication of the string hole thus survives as a vestigial ornament. Almost all MSS. were rubricated; more elaborate decoration is rare. The MS. leaves are guarded by cardboard covers (*paṭarī*) which may be painted or covered with printed cotton or embroidery. Hinged cards, i.e. folders with one broad and one narrow leaf, called *puṭhā,* are sometimes used for convenience of reading. The MSS. are not as a rule tied by a cord (though elaborate book braids (*kora*) are sometimes employed), but wrapped and tied in handkerchiefs, which may be elaborately embroidered.

It is hardly necessary to lay stress upon the value of the Jaina paintings as illustrations of the manners and customs, costume, textile designs, architecture, and furniture of mediaeval India. We see for example, the routine of the king's daily life—his athletic exercises, toilet (with female attendants), darbar ('adorned' as Indian authors would say, by the presence of military officers, courtiers, brāhmaṇs and dancers), consultation of brāhmaṇs, the receiving of instruction from holy men, worship of the symbols of the Jinas, riding forth in state on richly caparisoned horses or elephants, or in a horse-drawn two-wheeled *ekka.*

Women observe pardah: they naturally play a somewhat restricted part in these lives of the saints, where they are of importance mainly as the mothers of the Jinas (we must not forget that in India, motherhood is at once a glory and a source of great power). They appear also as dancers and as nuns. Armies are represented on the march, and as investing walled cities. Monks are constantly represented, sometimes giving instruction, sometimes with pages of sacred texts which they expound, and often with a table before them supporting a book. Animals incidentally represented include the elephant, horse, ass, lion, monkey, bull, deer, dog, cobra, parrot, goose (*haṅsa*) and scorpion, and in some of the cosmological diagrams a further variety including tigers, hares, peacocks, cranes, ducks, crows, and other birds, fish, and the mythical *bheruṇḍa*[23] (here a flying elephant carrying other elephants).

Kings wear a *dhotī*, tiara, and jewellery, with the upper half of the body and the feet bare: kings and male attendants and soldiers have long hair knotted in a chignon and black beards and mustachios; beardless figures other than Jinas and monks are in almost all cases those of women. The Śaka king Gardhabilla and his men wear coats of the *aṅgarkhā* or *jāmā* type, as in the Rajput and Mughal paintings. The fastening is sometimes on the right, sometimes on the left side. The Śakas are also represented in what appears to be chain armor, covering the thighs, with a short coat above. Male figures other than kings are bareheaded: no turban is anywhere represented. Queens wear the *dhotī*, and a tight-fitting bodice (*kañcukī colī*); with or without the tiara. Their long hair hangs in a single braid, ending in a tassel. Saints in glory are dressed like kings, elsewhere in monastic robes, which are white, voluminous, and semi-transparent (the books appear to belong entirely to the Śvetāmbara sect).

[23] *Bheruṇḍa* or *bhāraṇḍa:* see Weber, *Śatruñjaya Mahātmayam*, trans. J. Burgess, *Indian Antiquary*, XXX, 1901, p. 289, footnote; and Coomaraswamy, *Mediaeval Sinhalese Art*, pp. 84, 85; also W. Kirfel, *Die Cosmographie der Inder*, tafel 5, lower right hand corner (the same form is also found on the Mughal hunting carpet, gift of Mr. Winthrop Ames, in the Museum of Fine Arts).

The formulae of Jaina painting naturally exhibit numerous resemblances and parallels to those of Rajput and other Indian paintings. Thus, the viewpoint is much elevated, so that in landscape subjects the horizon reaches nearly to the top of the page, leaving only a narrow strip of sky in which are depicted heavy storm clouds. The manner in which these clouds are represented is totally distinct from that of Persian and Chinese art, but like that of Rajput painting, and of older sculpture, and like that of eighteenth-century Sinhalese painting, where, however, the formula is reduced to more arid terms. A lotus rosette is occasionally employed to fill space (cf. Pl. 1, folio 49 with *Mediaeval Sinhalese Art*, frontispiece). Water is represented by an accumulation of jagged peaks not exactly like anything else in Indian art, but in a manner related to that of the South Indian palampore designs.

The nearest relatives of Jaina paintings are the Nepalese book illustrations, typically of the eleventh and twelfth century on the one hand, and the earliest of the Rajput *Rāgmālās* on the other. Nepalese painting has incidentally a physically similar quality of outline, but with far more aesthetic intention and great reliance upon subtleties; it is refined, and exhibits a taste and preciosity quite alien to the brilliant notation of Jaina art. Rajput painting, on the other hand, though likewise founded upon older traditions, is a new development reflecting the inspiration of the mediaeval Vaiṣṇava devotional revival, and is far more emotional than either Nepalese or Jaina art. Moreover, the early, Rajput *Rāgmālās* are essentially paintings rather than drawings; their concern is with human experience spirit ually interpreted, using genre as a medium, and relatively realistic. In all these respects the *Rāgmālās* are nearer to Ajaṇṭā than to Jaina painting. But as in Jaina painting the physical surfaces of the Rajput 'primitives'—the texture of the color and the quality of the line—are rough, and justifiably so because of the spiritual impulse and profound conviction underlying them.

Unlike Rajput painting, but like Nepalese Buddhist art, Jaina painting is a formal art of hieratic tradition. Hence at a later period (seventeenth and eighteenth centuries) it preserves its character unchanged, only exhibiting a more perfunctory treatment and a change of local color partly under Mughal influence. In its uncanonical phases (illustrations to the *Śālibhadra carita*) when the artist is left to his own resources it approximates to the contemporary painting of Rajputana (Jaipur), and shows Mughal influence in costume.

Bibliography of Jainism

Barodia, U.D., *History and Literature of Jainism.* Bombay, 1909.

Bhandarkar, 'Jaina Iconography'. *Indian Antiquary,* Vol. XC.

Bloomfield, M., *The life and stories of the Jaina Savior Pārśvanātha.* Baltimore, 1919.

——, *The Śālibhadra Carita,* a story of conversion to Jaina monkhood. *JAOS* XLIII, 4, 1923, pp. 167ff.

Bühler, J.G., *Jaina Sculptures from Mathura. Transactions of the Ninth International Congress of Orientalists,* Vol. I, pp. 219-21. London, 1893.

——, 'Note on Jaina Mythology'. *Indian Antiquary,* Vol. XXX, pp. 27-8. Bombay, 1901.

——, 'Digambara Jaina Iconography'. *Indian Antiquary,* Vol. XXXII, pp. 459-64. Bombay, 1903.

——, *The Iconography of the Digambara Jainas.* Verhandlungen des XIII internationalen Orientalisten-Kongresses, p. 74. Leiden, 1904.

Coomaraswamy, A.K., 'Notes on Jaina Art'. *Journal of Indian Art,* no. 127. London, 1914.

Daji, Bhau, *The Inroads of the Scythians into India and the Story of Kālakācārya. JRAS,* Bombay Branch. Bombay, 1872.

Forbes, A.K., *Rās Mālā.* 2 volumes. London, 1856.

Guerinot, A., *Essai de bibliographie Jaina.* Ann. du Musee Guimet, Bib. d'Etudes, Vol. XXII. Paris, 1906.

Hüttemann, W., *Miniaturen zum Jinacarita.* Baessler Archiv., Bd. 11, Heft 11, 1913.

Jacobi, H., *Das Kālakācārya Kathānakam* (edition and translation). Zeit. der deutschen morgenlandischen Gesellschaft, Vol. XXXIV, 1880.

——, *Gaina Sūtras.* Sacred Books of the East, Vols. XXII, XLV.

——, *The Kalpa Sūtra of Bhadrabāhu* (text). Abh. für die Kunde des Morgenlandes, Vol. VII, 1. Leipzig, 1879.

——, Articles in the 'Encyclopedia of Religion and Ethics'.

——, *Das Kālakācārya-Kathānakam.* Zeit. der deutschen morgenlandischen Gesellschaft, Vol. XXXIV, pp. 247-318. Leipzig, 1880.

—— *Über die Entstehung der Śvetāmbara and Digambara Sekten.* Zeit. der deutschen morgenlandischen Gesellschaft, Vol. XXXVIII, pp. 1-42, Leipzig, 1884.

—— *Jaina Sūtras, translated from Prākrit,* 2 volumes. (Sacred Books of the East, Vols. XXII and XLV.) Oxford, 1884-95.

—— *Eine Jaina Dogmatik, Umāsvāti's Tattvārthādhigama Sūtra.* Zeit. der deutsch. morgenlandischen Gesellschaft, Vol. LX, pp. 287, 512ff.

Jaini, J., *Outlines of Jainism.* Cambridge, Eng., 1916.

Jaini, Jagmander Lal, 'Some Notes on Digambara Jaina Iconography'. *Indian Antiquary,* Vol. XXXIII, pp. 330-2. Bombay, 1904.

Kielhorn, F., *On a Jaina Statue in the Horniman Museum. JRAS,* London, 1898.

Kirfel, W., *Die Cosmographie der Inder.* Bonn, 1920.

Kudalkar, J.S., *The Jaina manuscript-bhandars at Patan.* Annals of the Bhandarkar Institute, III, 1. Poona, 1921. (Mentions illustrated MSS. on p. 51.)

Lalubhai, Lalcand, *Dhanā Sālibhadra.* Ahmadabad, 1887.

Nahar, P.C. and K. Ghosh, *An epitome of Jainism.* Calcutta, 1917.

Smith, V.A., *The Jaina Stūpa and other Antiquities of Mathurā.* Archaeological Survey of India, New Imperial Series, Vol. XX. Allahabad, 1901.

Stevenson, J., *The Kalpa Sūtra and Nava Tatva,* two works illustrative of the Jaina, Religion and Philosophy. Translated from the Magadhi. London, 1848.

Stevenson, S., *The Heart of Jainism.* Oxford, 1915.

Vinson, J., *Legendes bouddhistes et djainas traduites du tamoul.* 2 volumes. Paris, 1900.

Winternitz, M., *Nejamesha, Naigamesha, Nemeso. JRAS,* London, 1895.

A complete Bibliography up to 1905 will be found in the work by Guerinot cited above.

List of Donors

Marianne Brimmer Fund. 21.1673, 64,65.
Ananda K. Coomaraswamy. 22.706.
Denman W. Ross. 17.2276-2300; 19.142; 22.364.

LIST OF MANUSCRIPTS AND PAINTINGS MANUSCRIPTS

1

17.2276. Manuscript of the *Kalpa Sūtra* and *Kālakācārya Kathānakam*, 108 leaves, 6 lines to a page. Prākṛt language, with *tīkā*, Nandināgarī characters,[24] with 17 miniatures. Thick paper. Contemporary covers (*paṭarī*) of coarse red printed cotton. Fifteenth century, or possibly earlier. Leaves. 280 x .095 m. Ross-Coomaraswamy collection.

This is the MS. C.A. referred to on Pl. 91 of 'Notes on Jaina Art' (Coomaraswamy, *Journal of Indian Art*, Vol. 16, 1914), where 14 of the miniatures are reproduced, including two in colour. See also Museum of Fine Arts, Bulletin no. 90, August, 1917, *Illustrated Jaina MSS.*, Figs. 1 and 2.

The *Kalpa Sūtra*, with 15 miniatures, occupies 89 leaves of the MS.; the *Kālakācārya Kathānakam,* with 2 miniatures, 8 leaves. The text is written in black ink, and is decorated with plain red borders, the central string holes rubricated, but never used. The miniatures are painted with yellow (in lieu of gold), crimson, black, green, two shades of blue, and occasional touches of bronzy gold, against a scarlet background. Occasionally a pearly white pigment is also used. The title of each picture is written on the margin of the MS. or on the picture itself. A minute sketch of the subject of each picture is also given in the margin (the painter's memorandum of the subject to be represented in the allotted space).

A short benedictory colophon concludes the text of the Samācārī section of the *Kalpa Sūtra*. The Kālakācārya text in Prākṛt differs entirely from that edited by Jacobi, loc. cit. Dr. L.D. Barnett tells me that this version is unknown to him. It consists of only eighty-five verses beginning:

Devimdavimda namiyaṁ sivanihisampatti parama sāsaṇa yaṁ, Nijjiya paramaya samayaṁ naṁda usiri vīra sāsaṇayaṁ. 1,

continuing in v. 3,

Atthi Dharāvāsapure naranāho vayarasiṁha nāmo tti Surasuṁdarī piyāse putto Kālayakumaroya. 3.

and concluding

Sūri ravi eha surīṇaṁ sesehiḥ viyaṇacaṁda sūrihiḥ ejjo savaṇassa kahā saṁkaliyāsuya samuddaū. 85.

The final colophon in Sanskrit immediately following reads:

Samāpto'yam laghuparyuṣaṇākalpaḥ paraṁkāthāyā digmātraṁ. Śrīḥ. B(emi). Maṁgalam mahāśrīḥ.

Udāra gambhīra kṛtajña puṇya manuṣya ratnāvali. Rohaṇādriḥ: nityotsavo vatsalatā nidhānam aekeś-vaṁśo vijayī jagatyāṁ 1.b.

Śrī Jñānakīya gacche maunī Śrī Śāṁti Sūri saṁtāne, bhaṭṭāraka Śrī Siddhasena Sūri paṭṭe Śrī Dhaneśvara Sūri śīṣya Śrī Mahendra Sūri paṁḍita Guṇacaṁdra nimittaṁ Kalpa Pustika svayameva lilekhe

Jaitīsīha putra Saṁgha-vībuṁcā bhāryā Ratnāde Bhramāde putrī Lalatū Madī sānyadhyena pustika lekhitā.

'This Laghuparyuṣaṇākalpaḥ is completed. The rest is a mere outline of the story. Prosperity! Utmost Prosperity! May it be well with the blessed community.'

'A mount Rohaṇa for the series of jewels of greatful and holy men, ever happy, a treasury of charity, the Ukeśa lineage is a conqueror in the world.'

'The *Kalpa Sūtra* book itself was written on account of Mahendra Sūri and Paṇḍit Guṇacandra, disciples of Dhaneśvara Sūri, on the pontifical throne of the Lord Siddhasena Sūri, in the lineage (succession) of the Silent Śrī Śānti Sūri of the Jñānakīya sect.'

'The book was written on behalf of Lalatū and Madī (?) daughters of Ratnā and Bhramā, wives of Saṁgha son of Jaitīsīha' (or 'for the use of Saṁgha, his wives and daughters').

The Ūkeśa (Oswāl) family is well known. Rohaṇa is perhaps Ruhaṇa in Ceylon.

[24] WNB corrects this to 'Devanāgarī characters'.

LIST OF MINIATURES

Folio 1. Mahāvīra enthroned: elaborate architecture settings, lion cognizance on base of throne. Legend, Mahāvīra.
Plate I.

Folio 2. The Jina as Guru, or spiritual teacher: the hand raised, holding a rosary. Legend, *Guru*.
Plate I.

Folio 6. Indra, seated on a throne, four-armed, holding elephant goad (*aṅkuśa*), noose (*pāśa*) and a golden fruit: umbrella of dominion in upper left-hand corner, the elephant Airāvata, vehicle of Indra, very small in lower right-hand corner. Legend, *Indra rūpa*, 'Picture of Indra'.
Plate I.

Folio 9. Indra and Mahāvīra, the former standing with two hands raised in respectful greeting (*añjali hasta*), with elephant goad and golden fruit in other hands; the latter seated on a lion throne. Legend, *Indra sya Mahāvīra,* 'Indra and Mahāvīra'.
Plate I.

Folio 15. Hariṇegameṣī bringing the foetus to the Rāṇī Trīśalā. Cloudy sky. Legend, *Rājñī* (or *rājī*) *rūpam Hariṇegameṣī.*
Plate I.

Folio 34. The Fourteen Dreams of the Rāṇī Triśalā, viz., elephant, bull, lion, Śrī Devī, banners [*sic.*], garland, moon, sun, banner, gold vase, lake, milky sea, palace, jewel heap, and fire. Legend, 14 *saunā.*
Plate I.

Folio 36. In two compartments, filling the whole page: to left, the Rāṇī Triśalā reclining (she is understood to be present at the interpretation of the dreams, but behind the pardah). Legend, *Rājā rūpam.* To right, Rājā Siddhārtha enthroned, a Brāhmaṇa seated before him, expounding from a book. Legend, *Svapna lakṣaṇa pāṭhakaḥ,* 'Interpreters of the significance of dreams'.
Plate II.

Folio 41. Tonsure of Mahāvīra: he is seated in a rocky landscape beneath the Aśoka tree, plucking out his hair, and is attended by Indra (two hands holding the elephant goad and golden fruit, the two others receiving the discarded royal robes of Mahāvīra); Indra's elephant Airāvaṇa (Airāvata) below, high horizon and stormy sky above. Legend, *Mahāvīra loñca,* 'Tonsure of Mahāvīra'.
Plate II.

Folio 53. Samavasaraṇa of Mahāvīra; the Jina seated in the triple walled, four-gated enclosure. Legend, *Mahāvīra samosaraṇa.*
Plate II.

Folio 55. Mahāvīra as a Perfected Being, enthroned in the Īṣātpragbhārā above the Siddha Śilā; clouds above and below. Legend, *Siddhi.*
Plate III.

Folio 59. Pārśvanātha enthroned: the Jina is green, and above his head appear the hoods of the seven-headed cobra by whom he was protected when practising the *kāyotsarga* austerity. Elaborate architectural setting; cobra cognizance on pedestal of throne. Legend, *Pārśva pratimā*, 'Image of Pārśva'.
Plate III.

Folio 66. Neminātha enthroned, in elaborate architectural setting. The Jina is blue; conch cognizance on pedestal of throne. Legend, *Neminātha.*
Plate III.

Folio 72. Ādinātha enthroned, in elaborate architectural setting; bull cognizance on pedestal of throne. Legend, *Śrī Ādinātha.*
Plate III.

(*Folio 98.* Conclusion of *Kalpa Sūtra.*)
(*Folio 99.* Commencement of *Kālakācārya Kathānakam.*)

Folio 100. Court of Gardabhilla; the king enthroned, a general and soldiers in attendance before him. Legend, *Gardabhilla.*

Reverse, Kālakācārya instructing the Śaka king: he holds a book [sic] [mouth cloth] in his right hand while the index finger of the left is raised (*tarjani hasta*) in exposition. Legend, *Śakaraya.*
Plate III.

Folio 106. Conclusion of the *Kālakācārya Kathānakam,* with colophon.

2

17.2277. Manuscript of the *Kalpa Sūtra* and *Kāthānakam*, 78 leaves, 9 lines to a page, Prākṛt and Sanskrit language, no *ṭīkā*. Nandināgarī [*sic*] [Devanāgarī characters, with 34 miniatures. Thin paper. No covers. Dated Saṁvat, 1554=AD 1497.

Leaves. 30 x .11 m. Ross-Coomaraswamy Collection.

This is the MS. C.B. referred to on p. 91 of *Notes on Jaina Art* (Coomaraswamy, Journal of Indian Art [*sic*] [and Industry], Vol. 16, 1914), where 21 of the miniatures are reproduced including one in colour. See also Museum of Fine Arts, Bulletin no. 90, August, 1917, *Illustrated Jaina MSS.,* Fig. 4.

The *Kalpa Sūtra* with 28 miniatures, occupies 72½ leaves of the MS.; the *Kālakasūri Kathānakam* (in Sanskrit), with 6 miniatures, 5½ leaves. The text is written in black ink, with red borders and central circles not perforated; the first page with a blue pattern border. The colours employed are crimson, black, blue, white, and scarlet on a gold-leaf ground; the gold being left uncoloured to represent flesh, etc., but covered with scarlet to form the background. The miniatures are not labelled: there are marginal sketches, but much faded.

The Kālakācārya text in Sanskrit naturally differs from the Prākṛt text edited by Jacobi, loc. cit., and from that of the previous MS. no. 1 (M.F.A. 17.2276) and that of MS. no. V (M.F.A. 17.227a). It has been printed as a supplement to an edition of the *Kalpa Sūtra* published by Shah Naginbhai Ghelabhai Javheri as no. 18 of the Sheth Devchand Lalbhai Jaina Pustakoddhar Series, Bombay, 1914. It consists of sixty-five verses, beginning:

> *Oṁ. Śrī Vīra vākyānumataṁ suparva kṛtaṁ yathā paryuṣaṇā ravyam etat Śrī Kālakācārya-vāraṇa saṁghe tathā caturdhyām śṛṇu paṁcamītaḥ 1,* etc., mentioned Dharāvāsa in v. 2 and Surasundarī in v. 3 and concludes
> *Śrīmat Kālakasūrayaścirataraṁ cāritram-atyujvalaṁ saṁpālpa pratipadya-cāṁtā samāya bhakti pratijñāṁmudā*
> *Śuddha dhyānam nidhāna līnamanasaḥ svargālayaṁ ye gatā, stẹ kalpāṇa paraṁparāṁśkṛtadharāyacchaṁtu saṁghe' naghe 65.*

The final colophon following this reads:
Colophon:

Iti Śrī Kālakasūri Kathānakaṁ. B(emi?). Śrī Saṁvat 1554 varṣe Bhādravā śudi 8, somavāsare. Davāḍā vāstavya Śrī Śrīmālajñātīya Śre(ṣṭhi) Sāraṁga Śre(ṣṭhi) ... bhārya Mānūṁ suta Karaṇā, bhāryā Māīṁ laghu bhrātṛ Mūlā bhāryā Pūtali Śre(ṣṭhi) sadhāraṇa pramukha suśrāvakaiḥ Śrī ... (portion erased) *m upakāritaṁ Śrī Kalpa pustakaṁ.*

Acandrārkka vācyamānaṁ cira jīyāt. B. Śrī B. 1.

'Thus the blessed Kālakasūri Kathānakam. It was presented by worthy lay-disciples, namely the merchant Sāraṅga of the Śrīmāla clan residing in Davāḍā, his wife Mānū, his son Karaṇā's (the latter's) wife, mother and younger brother Mūlā, his wife Putalī, and other contributors of the mercantile community, on Monday the 8th lunar day in the light fortnight of Bhādrapada in the year Saṁvat 1554.'

LIST OF MINIATURES

Folio 1. Mahāvīra enthroned; elaborate architectural seeting; lion cognizance on pedestal of throne. No legend.

Plate IV.

Transliteration of the text shown in the figure, being the commencement of the *Kalpa Sūtra:*

Namo arahaṁtāṇaṁ namo siddhāṇaṁ namo āyariyāṇaṁ namo uvajjhāyāṇaṁ namo loe savva sāhūṇaṁ.

Eso paṁca namokkāro, savva-pāva-ppaṇāsaṇo maṁgalāṇaṁ ca savvesiṁ paḍhamaṁ havai maṁgalaṁ

Teṇaṁ kāleṇaṁ teṇaṁ samaeṇaṁ samaṇe bhagavaṁ mahāvīre paṁcahatt' uttare hotthā;2[25] *taṁ jahā: hatth' uttarāhiṁ cue caitta gabbhaṁ vakkaṁte, hatt' uttarāhiṁ gabbhāo gabbaṁ sāharie hatth' uttarāhiṁ jāe, hatth' uttarāhiṁ muṁḍe bhavi*

Folio 2. The Eight auspicous objects; with the Jina as Guru, the right hand holding a rosary, and raised in exposition, and attended by two worshippers. Legend, *Aṣṭamaṁgalāka.*

Plate IV.

Folio 5. Court of Indra; Indra enthroned, four-armed, holding spear (*śakti*), elephant goad (*aṅkuśa*), and fruit, the right hand raised with forefinger extended; with three ministers, each four-armed and with weapons. Legend, *Indra.*

Plate IV.

Folio 6. Indra descended from his throne and kneeling with two hands raised in adoration of Mahāvīra whom he perceives on earth. Legend, *Indra namokṣanam,* 'Indra's salutation'.

Plate IV.

[25] The Figure 2 signifies the repetition of the preceding words.

Folio 10. Hariṇegameṣī removing the foetus from the Brāhmaṇī Devānandā, who reclines on a couch. Legend, *Garbhāpahāra Hariṇegameṣī,* 'Hariṇegameṣī (the foetus) from the womb'.
Plate V.

Folio 11. Hariṇegameṣī bringing the foetus to the Rāṇī Triśalā, who reclines on a couch. Legend, *Hariṇegameṣī garbha prakeṣepa,* 'Hariṇegameṣī placing (the foetus) in the womb'.
Plate V.

Folio 12. The Rāṇī Triśalā reclining on a couch attended by a maid. Legend, *Rāṇī Triśalā.*
Plate V.

Folio 13. The Fourteen Dreams of the Rāṇī Triśalā. Legend, *Caüda* (sa)*sauṇā.*
Plate V.

Folio 19. The Rāṇī Triśalā relating her dreams to King Siddhārtha. Legend, *Rājā sa rāṇī che,* 'This is the king and queen'.
Plate V.

Folio 21. Toilet of King Siddhārtha: the king seated, a wife or female attendant dressing his hair. Legend, *Majjana*, 'Bath-house'.
Plate V.

Folio 22. King Siddhārtha's court: the king enthroned, giving orders to three of his officers. Legend, *Rājā sabhā,* 'The king's darbar'.
Plate VI.

Folio 23. Above, the Rāṇī Triśalā relating her dreams to King Siddhārtha; below Brāhmaṇas with manuscript rolls discussing the interpretation of dreams. Legend, *Sabba lakkhaṇa pāṭhaga rājā*, 'The king's interpreters of all prognostics'.
Plate VI.

Folio 24. Above, the Rāṇī Triśalā discussing her dreams with King Siddhārtha; below, two Brāhmaṇas with manuscript rolls (horoscopes) discussing the interpretation. Legend, *Savva lakkhaṇa vicāra*, 'Discussion of all the prognostics'.
Plate VI.

Folio 28. Nativity of Mahāvīra: the Rāṇī Triśalā with the child, reclining on a couch, attended by a maid with a fly-whisk. Legend, *Janma*, 'Birth'.
Plate VI.

Folio 29. Festival of the anointment: Mahāvīra seated on the lap of a larger figure, two attendants holding vases, rocky landscape below. Legend, *Janmābhiśeka*, 'Birth festival.'
Plate VI.

Folio 32. Almsgiving on the first birthday: the king enthroned, before him a table, and three ministers. Legend, *Saṁvat sarīdāna* [*sic, Saṁvatsarī dāna* 'Birthday gifts'].
Plate VI.

Folio 33. Mahāvīra in the golden palanquin borne by the gods on the occasion of his going forth to adopt the monastic life. Legend, *Sivikā,* 'Palanquin'.
Plate VII.

Folio 34. Tonsure of Mahāvīra: he is seated in a rocky landscape under the Aśoka tree, attended by Indra, who carries the elephant goad in one hand, and receives the discarded royal robes with two others. Legend, *Dīkṣā,* 'Tonsure'.
Plate VII.

Folio 37. Samavasaraṇa of Mahāvīra; the Jina seated in the triple-walled, four-gated enclosure. Legend, *Jñāna samosaraṇa*, 'Preaching of wisdom'.
Plate VII.

Folio 38. Mahāvīra as a Perfected Being, seated in the Īṣātprāgbhārā above the *Siddha śilā*; trees at each side, clouds above, rocky landscape below. Legend, *Mukti śilā,* 'Rock of release', that is, *Siddha śilā.*
Plate VII.

Folio 41. Above, Pārśvanātha enthroned, the hoods of a seven-hooded cobra rising above his head; below, his nativity. Legend, *Śrī Pārśvanātha.*
Plate VII.

Folio 44. Above, Pārśvanātha as a Perfected Being, seated above the *Siddha śilā*; below, standing in water, practising the *kāyotsarga* austerity.
Plate VII.

Folio 47. Four scenes from the life of Ādinātha (Ṛṣabha): nativity, tonsure, as a Siddha, and in *samavasaraṇa.*
Plate VIII.

Folio 48. Twenty seated Jinas, representing the Tīrthaṅkaras between Ṛṣabha and Nemīnātha, whose lives are not related at length in the *Kalpa Sūtra.*
Plate VIII.

Folio 50. Four scenes from the life of Nemīnātha: nativity, tonsure, as a Siddha, and in *samavasaraṇa.*
Plate VIII.

Folio 54. The Eleven apostles of Mahāvīra; with an *oṁkāra* ideograph. Legend, *Gaṇadhara 11.*
Plate VIII.

Folio 61. The Jina [sic, monk (Devardhi?)] enthroned in a *mandir*, with a lotus below and two peacocks above.
Plate VIII.

Folio 72. Obverse: the Jina (Mahāvīra) enthroned in a *mandir*, with high *sikhara* worshipped by two kings, four monks, and two women. Conclusion of *Kalpa Sūtra* on this page: the text (end of the *Samācārī* section) reads:

> *hūṇaṁ samaṇīṇáṁ bahūṇaṁ sāvagāṇaṁ; 2; bahūṇaṁ devāṇam bahūṇaṁ devīṇaṁ majjha-gae c'evam āikkhai, evaṁ bhāsai, evaṁ pannavei, evaṁ parūvei, pajjosavaṇā-kappaṁ, nāma ajjhayaṇaṁ, sa-aṭṭhaṁ, sa-heuyaṁ, sa-kāraṇaṁ, sasuttaṁ, sa-atthaṁ, sa-ubhayaṁ, sa-vāgaraṇaṁ, bhujjo; 2; uvadamsei tti bemi. Pajjosavaṇā-kappo sammatto. Aṭṭham ajjahayaṇaṁ sammattaṁ b. graṁthāgraṁ 1716, b. śrī. śrī. śrī.*

Reverse: above, Conversion of Kālakakumāra, the prince receiving instruction from a Jaina monk; below, Kālaka returning home (?) [*sic*, trying out horse].
Plate IX.

Folio 73. Above, Kālakakumāra returning home (?); below, in a golden palanquin borne by the gods [*sic*, Kālaka is borne in a palanquin by men when going to enter religious life. His father had ordered a festival].
Plate IX.

Folio 74. Above, Kālakācārya instructs the Śaka king [who has received a command from his overlord to kill himself, to leave for India]; below, Kālakācārya at the kiln, changing the potter's clay [*sic*, bricks] to gold, with one of the *Shāhis* on horseback.
Plate IX.

Folio 75. The Siege of Ujjayinī; slaying of the magic ass.
Plate X.

Folio 76. Above, Kālakācārya seated, addressing Gardabhilla, who is a manacled prisoner in [the] charge of a soldier; (below) Kālakācārya at the door of a monastery, two monks sleeping within (perhaps representing Kālakācārya's visit to Sāgaracandra) [*sic*, Kālakācārya leaving his disobedient disciples].
Plate X.

Folio 78. Obverse: Kālakācārya seated in converse with Indra in the form of Brāhmaṇa. Reverse: *End of Kālakasūri Kathānakam,* and colophon with date (quoted above).
Plate X.

3

17.2278. Manuscript of the *Kalpa Sūtra* (*Jinacarita* and *Therāvali Sūtraṁ* only), 107 leaves of 7 lines to a page, Prākṛt language, Nandīnāgarī [*sic*, Devanāgarī] characters, with 27 miniatures. No covers. Probably seventeenth century. Leaves .255 x .105 m. Ross-Coomaraswamy Collection.

This is the MS C.C. referred to on p. 91 of 'Notes on Jaina Art' (Coomaraswamy, *Journal of Indian Art*, Vol. 16, 1914) where seven of the miniatures are reproduced. The colouring as in M.F.A. 17.2277, except that the background is bright blue in place of scarlet. Most of the pictures have legends, often repeated with slight variations in a later hand. No marginal sketches.

LIST OF MINIATURES

Folio 4. Fourteen Dreams of the Brāhmaṇī Devānandā; the lady reclining below, the dreams represented above. No. Legend.
Plate XI.

Folio 8. Court of Indra, the god, four-armed, holding elephant goad, noose, and fruit, enthroned beneath umbrella of dominion, and entertained by a dancing girl and two musicians. Legend, *Indra sabhā*, 'Darbar of Indra'.
Plate XI.

Folio 10. Indra kneeling with two hands raised in respectful adoration of Mahāvīra. Legend, *Indra nāmokṣaṇaṁ bhaṇai,* 'Indra offers salutation'.
Plate XI.

Folio 17. Above, Hariṇegameṣī taking away the foetus from the Brāhmaṇī Devānandā; below, bringing it to the Rāṇī Triśalā. Legend, *Garbhāpahāra garbha saṁgharaṇa,* 'Removing and transferring the foetus'.
Plate XI.

Folio 21. The Fourteen Dreams of the Rāṇī Triśalā: the queen reclining, the dreams represented above. Legend, *Triśalā svapna 14*.
Plate XI.

Folio 35. Above, King Siddhārtha at wrestling exercise; below, his toilet. Legend, *Malla juddha sājai*, 'Wrestling practice'.
Plate XI.

Folio 39. Interpreters of dreams; four bearded Brāhmaṇas, one with a horoscope, discussing the dreams [*sic*, above, king tells dreams to interpreters; below, interpreters interpret dreams]. Legend, *Rājā svapna pāṭhaka,* 'The king's interpreters of dreams'.
Plate XII.

Folio 46. Above, the Rāṇī Triśala, with a confidante, with gestures of grief expressing her fear that the unborn child may not be living, as it makes no movement; below, the Rāṇī Triśalā expressing her joy at feeling the child leap. Legend, *Śoka harṣa,* 'Sorrow and joy'.
Plate XII.

Folio 48. Nativity of Mahāvīra; the Rāṇī Triśalā reclining with the infant, attended by a maid with fly-whisk. Legend, *Vīra janma mejha snātra*.
Plate XII.

Folio 56. Mahāvīra bestowing alms previous to adopting the monastic life. Legend, *Vīra dāna*.
Plate XII.

Folio 60. Tonsure of Mahāvīra: Mahāvīra seated beneath the Aśoka tree, plucking out his hair, attended by Indra. Legend, *Dīkśā* (Tonsure). Reverse: Mahāvīra in *kāyotsarga posture* 'suffering with equanimity all calamities arising from divine powers, men or animals'—the later represented by a cobra, scorpion, lion, and dog. Legend, *Vīra upasargra,* 'Austerity of Mahāvīra.' [*sic*, *Vīra upasarga,* 'Calamities of Mahāvīra.']
Plate XII.

Folio 64. Samavasaraṇa of Mahāvīra: the Jina seated in the triple-walled four-gated enclosure. Legend, *Jñāna*, 'Attainment of wisdom'.
Plate XIII.

Folio 66. Mahāvīra as a Perfected Being; enthroned as a Siddha, between two trees above the *Siddha śila* [*sic*, *Siddha śilā*]. Legend, *Vīra mukti*, 'Release of Mahāvīra'.
Plate XIII.

Folio 72. Pārśvanātha enthroned: elaborate architectural setting; cobra cognizance on pedestal of throne. Legend, *Pārśva pratimā*, 'Image of Pārśva'.
Plate XIII.

Folio 73. Above, Kamaṭha seated between four fires and understood also to be enduring the heat of the sun, making the penance known as that of the 'Five Fires'. Below, Pārśva rescuing the serpent king Dharaṇa. Legend, *Kamaṭha pañcāgnī*, 'Kamaṭha's practice of the Five Fires'.
Plate XIII.

Folio 75. Pārśvanātha standing in a lake, practising the *kāyotsarga* penance, supported by a *yakṣa* and protected by Dharaṇa with seven expanded hoods, on the occasion of Meghakumāra's assault. Legend, *Pārśva upasargra* [*sic*, *upasarga*].
Plate XIII.

Folio 78. Neminātha enthroned, in elaborate architectural setting; unrecognizable cognizance on pedestal of throne. Legend, *Nemi pratimā*.
Plate XIII.

Folio 79. Above, a bearded man kneeling before the conch of Kṛṣṇa; below, Neminātha overcoming the gods, represented by one four-armed deity. Legend, *Śaṁkha pūrīu harihā ḍholiu,* and in later hand *Śaṁkha purīu* (*habhā*?) *hāthe hī ḍelemo ṅemīnātha-jī*.
Plate XIV.

Folio 80. Above, a bearded man on horseback at a palace or city gate, a woman within. Below, a man with charioteer driving in an *ekka* through a deer park. Legend, *Nemi pasūvāḍ*; in later hand, *Nemīnātha-jī jani* (or, *jāna*) *kare pasūvāḍe āyā che*.

The two pictures seem to suggest the story of king Samtānu related in the *Śatruñjaya Māhātmayam* (*Indian Antiquary*, XXX, 1901, pp. 294-6.) On this supposition, the upper picture would represent Samtānu's meeting with Gaṅga or (Gaṅgeya) driving in an *ekka*. But the legend plainly mentions Neminātha, and the word *pasūvāḍ* can only mean 'cattle-pen'. The pictures are therefore probably connected with Nemi's marriage, the lady in the upper part being perhaps Rājīmatī, while the lower half represents Nemi on his way to Junāgaḍh, where he sees the animals ready to be slaughtered for the wedding feast. Though the animals are not cattle, but deer, they seem to be in a kind of enclosure.
Plate XIV.

Folio 83. Ten Tīrthakaras. Legend, *Tīrthakara 10.*
Plate XIV.

Folio 84. Ten Tīrthakaras. Legend, (*Tīrtha*)-*kara 10.*
Plate XIV.

Folio 88. Ādinātha (Ṛṣabha) enthroned, in elaborate architectural setting, conch cognizance (erroneously) on pedestal of throne. Legend, *Ādinātha pratimā.*
Plate XIV.

Folio 89. Subject not identified. Rider on an elephant, surmounted by a large umbrella of dominion, accompanied by one attendant riding behind. Legend, *Hastī mūrti kākumbha* [*sic, mūrtikā kumbha*].
Plate XIV.

Folio 95. Eleven Gaṇadharas, or apostles, of Mahāvīra or Neminātha, with an Oṃkāra [*sic*, Hrīṁkāra] ideograph. Legend, *Ganadhara* 11.
Plate XV.

Folio 98. Subject not identified (scenes from the life of Ārya Vajra?) A monk seated with a book, before a table, facing a nun who is addressing him, a child in a circle between them; below, a nun rocking a child in a cradle. Legend, *Vaira Svāmi pālaṇūṁ*; also, in later hand, *Vaira Svāmī cehura Svāmi pālakhī*, 'The Swāmi's cradle'. Vaira Svāmi is probably the Ārya Vajra of the Therāvali 4, or 13.
Plate XV.

Folio 100. Subject not identified. A man, and a woman dancing, rocky landscape; the former aiming an arrow at a parrot on a tree. Erotic motif? Legend, ... *nṛtya āṁbāluci*; in later hand, *nṛtya ābāluci*, 'Viewing the dance'.
Plate XV.

The MS. ends with the adoration verses at the close of the 'List of Sthaviras' (only nine of the verses being given, the last concluding *kāsavagutte paṇivayāmi*). The original colophon, *Iti Therāvali Sūtraṁ*, has been defaced.

4

22.364. Manuscript of the *Kalpa Sūtra*, 147 folios, less nos. 16, 29, and 43 (no. 4 imperfect); seven lines to a page, with 39 miniatures. The text is written in black ink with narrow red borders at the sides, the central string holes rubricated but not perforated. The miniatures are painted in gold (a greenish tone is obtained in certain parts by the use of pigment over the gold), black, blue, white, and scarlet. A majority of the miniatures are labelled, and some have faint marginal sketches. Cotton-covered boards (*paṭharī*). (Folio 4, picture broken away.) Dated = AD 1494. Cover dimensions .278 x .127 m., leaves .226 x .109 m.
Ross Collection.

Folio 1. Mahāvīra enthroned, with six attendants; the throne supported by elephants. Lion cognizance.
Plate XV.

Folio 2. Mahāvīra, enthroned, as Guru, teaching, worshipped by two disciples; above and below, the Eight Auspicious Symbols.
Plate XV.

Folio 5. The Fourteen Dreams of the Brāhmaṇī Devānandā (twelve only shown, the sun and moon being omitted). Legend, *14.*
Plate XV.

Folio 8. Indra enthroned, with two attendants. The deity is four-armed: l.r.h. *sūcihasta,* u.r.h. with trident, u.l.h. with elephant goad, l.l.h. with fruit. Legend, *Indra sabhā*, 'Darbar of Indra'.
Plate XVI.

Folio 12. Indra kneeling, in front of his throne, u.r.h. and l.r.h. as before, the two other hands raised in a gesture of reverence (towards Mahāvīra). Legend, *Namokṣuṇakaha,* 'He offers salutation'.
Plate XVI.

Folio 18. Indra enthroned, as at first; Hariṇegameṣī receiving orders, and departing on his errand. Legend, *Indra Hariṇegamesī.*
Plate XVI.

Folio 20. Obverse: Hariṇegameṣī has removed the foetus from the womb of the Brāhmaṇī Devāṇandā, departs. Legend, *Devāṇandā garbho-pahār.* Reverse: Hariṇegamesī brings the foetus to the Kṣatriyaṇī Triśalā. Legend, illegible.
Plate XVI.

Folio 23. Obverse: Lying in of Triśalā [*sic*, Triśalā asleep]; the queen reclining, a maid with a *caurī*. Legend, *Triyadevī*. Reverse: Fourteen Dreams of Triśalā (twelve only, as before; but the sun and moon are seen in the 'Lying in' [*sic*, preceding]).

Plates XVI and XVII.

Folio 34. Seated four-armed goddess (Padmāvatī ?) [*sic*, Śrī], upper hands with lotus flowers, l.r.h. with rosary, l.l.h. with fruit. Legend, *caūdasa jhā* ... pna.

Plate XVII.

Folio 40. Two groups of contesting men: above, boxers with larger gloves, below, wrestlers. Probably the king (Siddārtha) at daily exercise in his gymnaisum. Legend, ... *juddha*.

Plate XVII.

Folio 44. The king's toilet: he looks at himself in mirror, while a woman dresses his long hair. Legend, *mājaṇu*.

Plate XVII.

Folio 46. Four Brāhmaṇas, with long white beards, in two pairs, discussing the dreams. Legend, *svapna-pāṭhaka*.

Plate XVII.

Folio 56. Birth of Mahāvīra: Triśalā reclining, the child by her side, a maid in attendance. Legend, illegible.

Plate XVII.

Folio 57. The Anointment Festival (*abhiṣeka*): Mahāvīra seated on the lap of a deity [Śakra], with two attendants holding water-jars. Affronted bulls above. Legend, *Rāja-sabhā*.

Plate XVIII.

Folio 64. Giving of alms. Legend, *Seva* ... *arā dāna*. The lower of the two Brāhmaṇa mendicants carries a begging bowl (*kamaṇḍalu*).

Plate XVIII.

Folio 66. Like the miniature on f. 1. Legend, *Vīra pratimā*.

Plate XVIII.

Folio 68. Tonsure of Mahāvīra: Indra (represented with only two hands) receiving the royal robes. Legend, *Dīkṣā letā*, 'He receives ordination'.

Plate XVIII.

Folio 71. Samavasaraṇa of Mahāvīra: The usual triple-walled enclosure with four gates; a well and animals in each corner. Legend, illegible.

Plate XVIII.

Folio 73. Ādinātha as Siddha, enthroned above the heavens in Īṣātprāgbhārā; the inverted crescent being the *Siddha silā* or rock of the Perfected. Bull cognizance on throne. Trees at each side and mountains below. Legend, *mukti*.

Plate XVIII.

Folio 80. Mahāvīra as Siddha: similar in all respects to the last, but with lion cognizance on throne.

Plate XIX.

Folio 82. Birth of Pārśvanātha. Legend, *Pārśvanātha*.

Plate XIX.

Folio 83. Above, left, Kaṭha seated between four fires, the sun indicated above, practising the 'Five fire penance': right, Pārśva rescuing the serpent Dharaṇa. Below, subject not identified: a lady (?) on foot followed by a rider (Pārśva?) with attendant on a caparisoned elephant. Legend, *Vāmā devī* (the name of Pārśva's mother). The picture possibly refers to Pārśva's marriage ('Pārśva, arrayed brilliantly, riding a white ele-phant, arrived at the marriage pavilion', *Pārśva-nātha Caritra,* Sarga VI, v. 34).

Plate XIX.

Folio 88. A Jina seated above the *Siddha silā* in the Īṣātprāgbhārā. Apparently a conch cognizance, indicating Neminātha, and if so out of order as Siddha. Legend, *Vā* ... *na*.

Plate XIX.

Folio 89. Pārśvanātha enthroned, with six attendants; the throne supported by elephants. Like no. 1, but the Jina overshadowed by the seven-headed *nāga* Dharaṇendra, and with cobra cognizance on throne. Legend, *Pārśvanātha*.

Plate XIX.

Folio 90. Tonsue of Neminātha. Indra receiving the royal robes. Legend, *Neminātha dīkṣā*.

Plate XIX.

Folio 95. The Twenty Tīrthakaras between Ṛṣabha and Neminātha.

Plate XX.

Folio 99. Ādinātha (?) enthroned, with six attendants. Like nos. 1 and 89, but no cognizance.

Plate XX.

Folio 100. Birth of Ādinātha.

Plate XX.

Folio 107. Two miniatures on obverse of leaf: to left, Mahāvīra with six of his Gaṇadharas (disciples); to right, the remaining six (making twelve in place of eleven). Legend, *11 gaṇa.*

Plate XX.

Folio 123. Above, a monk seated reading from a manuscript [*sic*, with a mouthcloth], instructing two monks standing before him; below, two monks standing before a lion. (Story of Balamitta?) Legend, illegible.

Plate XX.

Folio 124. A monk seated reading from a manuscript [*sic*, with a mouthcloth], instructing a layman (prince?), and monk with a manuscript [*sic* mouthcloth] squatting before him.

Plate XXI.

Folio 142. Like 124. Legend, *Guru.*

Plate XXI.

Folio 143. Like 124. Legend, illegible.

Plate XXI.

Folio 144. A monk seated reading from a manuscript [*sic*, with mouthcloth], instructing two monks, one standing, one kneeling before him.

Plate XXI.

Folio 147. (last). Damaged miniature. Above, two monks with manuscripts [*sic*, mouthcloths]; below, three lay worshippers [two male and one female] and two (or three) monks.

The last five pictures seem to represent Kālakācārya's visit to Sāgaracandra [not possible if MS. does not contain story of Kālaka].

Plate XXI.

Colophons: on ff. 146 and 147 obverse. *Iti Śrī Paryuṣanā Śrī Kalpa Sūtraṁ samāptam ... Śrī Pattana madhye Śrī Kalpa-pustikā likhitaṁ saṁvat 1551 varṣe āṣāḍha māse* ... and on f. 147 reverse, by another hand, imperfectly preserved, *Saṁvat 1674 varṣe māha śudi 2 ... Pattane ... Tātahaḍa gotre, Usavāla jñātīya, Usavāla gacche ... Śrī Kaka Sūri. Tatu śiṣya ... Śrī Tejacamdrāya, Kalpa pustakaṁ pradattaṁ.* ... According to the first colophon the manuscript was written at Pattan (not to be confused with Pāṭan, the well-known Jaina centre of learning), in Gujarāt, in AD 1494. Pattan is perhaps the modern Patti, in the Lahore district of Pañjāb. [No, the reading *Pattane* does refer to Pāṭan in Gujarat!] Most of the Jaina MSS. in the Museum collections were originally obtained from a Jaina priest of Patti; this applies to all except items 5, 7, 13, 14.

5

19.142. Two leaves of a MS. of the *Kalpa Sūtra* and *Kālakācārya Kathā,* nine lines to a page. Prākṛt language, Nandināgarī [*sic*, Devanāgarī] characters, a miniature on each leaf. Gold figures on red ground. Thin paper. MS. dated Saṁvat 1519 = AD 1461.

Leaves .257 x .112 m. Ross Collection.

The MS. is described with an illustration in the Catalogue of *Sculpture, Painting and Drawings of Ancient India.* Kevorkian galleries, New York, 1918.

Six leaves of the same MS. including the last, with dated colophon, are in the Metropolitan Museum of Art, New York, and one in the Fogg Art Museum, Cambridge. [Text still with Kevorkian (1927, Dec.)]

LIST OF MINIATURES

Folio 51. Above, Neminātha bestowing alms on a Brāhmaṇa; below, the tonsure of Neminātha: the Jina is seated (no tree), and attended by Indra. Legend, *Nemi ṭhākaraṇa dīkṣa,* 'Lord Nemi's initiation'.

Plate XXXVI.

Folio 59. Tonsure of Ādinātha: the Jina is seated beneath a tree, and attended by Indra. Legend, Ā*(dinātha) dīkṣā ṭhākar,* 'Lord Ādinātha's initiation'.

Plate XXXVI.

6

17.2279. Manuscript; of the *Kālikācārya Kathā;* nine leaves, nine lines to a page, Prākṛt language, Nandināgari [*sic*, Devanāgarī] characters, with six miniatures. No covers. Early fifteenth century.

Leaves .26 x .11 m. Ross-Coomaraswamy Collection.

This is the MS. C.D. referred to on p. 91 of 'Notes on Jaina Art' (Coomaraswamy, *Journal of Indian Art*, Vol. 16, 1914) where three of the miniatures are reproduced, including one in colour. The colouring is similar to II, M.F.A. 17.2277. The picutres are labelled, but there are no marginal sketches.

The text consists of one hundred and twenty verses, beginning:

Hayapaḍiṇīyapayāvo titthannaikārau
kālānilao
(Ja)yau jayāṇaṁdayaro jugapavaro kālagāro 1.

At v. 5 we get the first few lines of Jacobi's text at the beginning of the verse section:

Yathā caturbhiḥ kanakaṁ parīkṣyate, etc.

but the following portions do not correspond. The last verse reads:

Iya bohiyabahuyanarā, divaṁgayāguruguṇā jugappavarā,
Sirikālagasūrivarā, havaṁtu bhavvāna bhaddakarā. 120.

followed by the colophon, *Iti Śrī Kālikācārya Kathā sampūrṇāḥ.*

This is the Prākṛt version noticed by Peterson. P., *Second report of operations in search of Sanskrit MSS. in the Bombay Circle* (Appendix 1, Cat. of MSS. in the Temple of Śāntināth, Cambay, p. 225), Bombay, 1884.

LIST OF MINIATURES

Folio 1. Conversion of Kālakakumāra; below, the groom returning to the palace with the riderless horse (?). Legend, *Kālikakumarayai.*

Plate XXII.

Folio 2. Kālakācārya as Guru instructing the Śaka king [*sic*, Śaka king with knife and pot; Kālaka telling him to go to India]. Legend, *Śake rājā guru.*

Plate XXII.

Folio 5. Above, Kālakācārya at the kiln, changing the potter's clay to gold, accompanied by the *Shāhi*; below the *Shāhi* with a soldier bearing the gold. Legend, *Raṭavahai.*

Plate XXII.

Folio 6. A Jaina monk, with hands raised in respectful greeting, addressing a lion; three other monks below. Legend, *Balamitta bhaṇai.*

Plate XXII.

Folio 8. Siege of Ujjayinī; slaying of the magic ass. Legend, *Gaddabhie ... vidyā jai.* The archer on horseback is evidently Kālakācārya himself.

Plate XXII.

Folio 9. Above, Kālakācārya in conversation with Indra disguised as a Brāhmaṇa; below, with Indra in his own form, his hands raised in respectful adoration. Legend, *I(ndra ...).*

Plate XXII.

7

21.1673. Manuscript of the *Sālibhadra Carita:* 39 leaves (lacking f. 2), 12 lines to a page, rubricated, with narrow red borders but no indication of string holes with 45 miniatures. In western Hindī.

.252 x .112 m. Marianne Brimmer Fund: from the Nahar collection. The text commences:

Oṁ Duhā:

Sāsaṇa nāyaka samarīyaṁ, barddhamāna jinacaṁda
Aliya bighana dūre hare āpe paramāṇaṁda 1
Sahūko jiṇavara sārikhā paṇi tīratha dhaṇī viseṣa
Pariṇī jete jāī jaṁ, lokanīti saṁpeṣi 2
Dāṇa sīla tapa bhāvanā, śiva pura māraga cyāri
Sariṣā chaṁ soṁ paṇi ihā, dāna taṇo adhikāra 3.
Sālabhadra sukha saṁpadā, pāne dāna pasāi
Tāsu carita vakhāṇatā, pātaka dūra pulāi 4
Tāsu prasaṁga jethaī dhannā-nī puṇi bāta
Sāvadhāna thaī sā bhalo mati karayo vyāghāta 5

Ṭāla. Caupaīnī:

Magadha desa śreṇika bhūpāla, pīta nyāya-kare causāla
Bhāva bheda sūdho sarada ai, jiṇavara āṇa akhaṁḍita vahi͂ 6
Nita navalā karatī nītī khelaṇā mātī rāṇī

and concludes:

Dhanā bharī ṭāla:

Iṇai avasara Śreṇaka paracāvaī, Bhadrā phīra ghari āvai͂, jī:
Paḍilā bhīna sakī prastāvai͂, tiṇa gāṭī prachitāvai, jī. 1.
Sālibhadra Dhanna riṣa-rāya, tāsu namunītā pāyā jī:
Je tapa japa ṣapaka sikāyā, sūdhā sādhu kahāyā, jī: 2. *sā*
Nānā moṭā dukhana ṭāli, kalimala paṁka paṣālī, jī:
Caramasa mai͂ jiṇavara sāṁbhalī sūdho aṅasaṇa pālī jī. 3.
Bārabara sasaṁjama ārādhā, āpa savratha sādhā, jī:
Sara gati karmanikā citavādhī, savārtha siddha lāddhī, jī. 4.
Surā sārai sura bhavana vicālai, paṇi navi nātha nihālai, jī:
Potānau bolyau saṁbhārai, haraṣī tāhu vaiti ṇaikā lai, jī 5.
Savārtha siddha hutā cavana, munīvara nara bhava lahisai, jī:

Mahābī dehai vrata ārdasī, avicala siva sukha varasī, jī. 6.
Prata ṣidhāūnī taṇa phala jāūṇī, bhāva adhaka mana-āūṇī jī:
Aṭṭa laka dāūna samāpo prāūṇī ājita varanī bāūṇī, jī. 7.
Sādha carita kahi vāmana sarasa, tenaie bhaṣīu haraṣaï, jī:
Solaha sai aṭhahattari barasai, āsoja vadi chaṭṭheï divasai, jī. 8.
Śrī Jina Siha-sūri sāmati sāraï, bhaviyaṇa naï upagarai, jī:
Śrī Jina Rāja vacana anusāra, carita kahyau suvicāra jī 9.
Iṇa pari sādhu tanā guṇa gāvai, je bhaviyaṇa mana bhāvai, jī:
Aliya vighana savi dūri palāvai, mana bacata phala pāvai, jī. 10.
Eha sabaṁdha bhavika bhaṇa sai, eka manā saṁbhali sai, jī:
Dukha doha gate dūri iga masai, mana baṁchata phala lahisai, jī. 11. *sā.*

According to the verses of the text numbered 8 and 9 it would appear that this Hindī version was made by Śrī Jina Sihasūri following the version of Śrī Jina Rāja, in saṁvat 1678, equivalent to AD 1621.

Colophon:

Iti śri Sālibhadra tī copaï saṁpurṇaṁ. āriyāṁ-jī Śrī Śrī
Bālā-jī Māhā-satyāṁ-jī Śrī Śrī Lāchāṁ-jī kī tat sīṣyaṇī gaṁgā
likhatāṁ Kīsngaḍh maṭhe samt 18 sa 50 mā tīvā prabā vade sāt
budavāra subha bhavataṁ kīlāṇam astu. Iti Śrī sapurṇaṁ.

According to this colophon, the MS. was written by the pupils of the Reverend Bāla-jī and Lachān-jī at Kiṣaṇgaṛh monastery in Saṁvat 1850 (AD 1793).

This MS. is perhaps a copy of the same text as that named by H.H. Wilson in *Asiatic Researches*, Vol. XVII, p. 245 (with particulars): I am indebted to Dr. F.W. Thomas for this reference. The Western Hindī in which the text is written is often hard to understand. The script is a form of Nāgarī closely related to the Nandi-nāgarī of the Prākṛt texts, with many archaic forms and spellings. *ṣ* is frequently used for *kh*. The forms of the proper names naturally differ from those of the Sanskrit text quoted above in the summary of the story, but in some cases two forms are used side by side, e.g. Śreṇaka and Seṇaka.

LIST OF MINIATURES

Folio 1. Seated Jina. Legend, *Śrī Mahāvīra-jī;* but the bull cognizance implies Ādinātha (Ṛṣabha).

Plate XXIII.

Folio 3. Six niches with figures, representing a city (Rājagṛha) with king, officers, trader, common people and cows. Legend, *Sāhukār nagarī ma baṭhā chai*, 'Leading men are seated in the town'.

Plate XXIII.

Folio 4. Obverse: Dhannā going with her son Saṁgama. Legend, *Saṁgamyo. Reverse, left:* Saṁgama grazing cows. Legend, *Bāchḍā carāva chai*, 'He grazes cows'. *Right:* Dhannā seated, the child on her lap, four women standing. Legend, *Saṁgamyo khīra māga chai*, 'He asks for milk-rice'.

Plate XXIII.

Folio 5. Obverse: Dhannā seated before wicker table fanning a tray of food, a brass churn beyond. Legend, *Khīra ṭhāra cai bhāvanā bhāva chai,* 'She cools the rice-milk'.

Plate XXIII.

Reverse: Same scene, but Saṁgama standing giving the rice-milk to the Jaina ascetic standing facing him. Legend, *Saṁgamyo sāṁdhāna khīra varāva chai,* 'He bestows the rice-milk with devotion'.

Plate XXIV.

Folio 6. Bhadrāmātā reclining, regarding a miniature rice field in the air above her. Legend, *Bhadrāmātā supanu sālaro dekha chai*, 'Bhadrāmātā sees a rice field in a dream'.

Plate XXIV.

Folio 7. Obverse, left: Bhadrāmātā reclining as before, the child on her lap, a maidservant with a fan. Legend, *Sālibhadra janamyo*, 'Nativity of Sālibhadra'.

Right: The same maid offering a vase of flowers to a man on a throne. Legend, *Gobīṁdra seṭha nai dāsī vadhāi deva chai,* 'The servant maid brings the good news to Seṭh Gobīnd'.

Plate XXIV.

Folio 8. Obverse: Bhadrāmātā rocking Sālibhadra in a cradle. Legend, *Sālibhadra palaṇa jhula chai*, 'She rocks Sālibhadra in a cradle'.

Reverse: Marriage of Sālibhadra, bride and bridegroom seated in centre, a Brāhman and sacred fire to left, group of 32 women to right. Legend, *Sālabhadra jī paraṇa chai*, 'Sālibhadra is married'.

Plate XXIV.

Folio 9. Sālibhadra seated with his wife in a pavilion, a deity (Sālibhadra's father) bringing golden caskets. Legend, *Devatā Sālibhadra ka tetīs pei lyāyo chai*, 'The god brings Sālibhadra 33 caskets.'

Plate XXIV.

Folio 10. Bhadrāmātā seated: traders with shawls. Legend, *Bopārī kāṁbal lāyā bhadrā dekha chai*, 'Bhadrāmātā inspects the blankets brought by the merchants'.

Plate XXV.

Folio 11. *Obverse:* Above, Sālibhadra's treasury, with two men seated, and caskets; below, two men with a money bag. Legend, *Goṭhārī koṭhārā khulā chai*, 'The treasurer opens the treasury' (i.e. to pay the blankets).

Reverse: King Seṇaka seated conversing with the merchants. Legend, *Seṇaka rājā vyopāryān bulāyā māga chai*, 'King Senaka asks the merchants for the blankets'.

Plate XXV.

Folio 12. *Upper left:* Seṇaka's messenger before Bhadrāmātā. Legend, *Śreṇaka-jī chaḍīdār sālabhadra ka melyo*, 'Seṇaka's messenger meets Sālibhadra'.

Lower left: Abha Kumāra and Bhadrāmātā. Legend, *Abha Kumāra Bhadrā kani āyo*, 'Abha Kumāra (the king's minister) comes to Bhadrāmātā'.

Plate XXV.

Folio 13. Abha Kumāra and Bhadrāmātā before King Seṇaka. Legend, *Bhadrā Abha Kumāra ka sāthā Seṇaka-jī kana āl*, 'Bhadrā comes to King Seṇaka with Abha Kumāra'.

Plate XXV.

Folio 14. King Seṇaka upon an elephant, proceeding with attendants, in landscape. Legend, Śreṇaka rājā Sālabhadra gharā āva chai, 'King Seṇaka goes to Sālibhadra's house.'

Plate XXV.

Folio 15. *Obverse:* King Seṇaka sitting in the upper story of Sālabhadra's house. Legend, *Śreṇaka rājā cothī bhomakā bīrājyo chai*, 'Seṇaka rājā adorns the fourth floor'.

Reverse: Bhadrāmātā summons Sālibhadra, who is seated in a room with his wives. Legend, *Bhadrāmātā Sālabhadra nai bulāvaṇa nai āyā chai*, 'Bhadrāmātā comes and summons Sālibhadra'.

Plate XXVI.

Folio 18. Sālibhadra presents his son to the king (?). No legend.

Plate XXVI.

Folio 19. *Upper left:* the king seated in the bath, two attendants massaging his arms. *Lower right:* Bhadrāmātā finds the signet ring.

Plate XXVI.

Folio 20. Sālibhadra gives alms. (?)

Plate XXVII.

Folio 21. Gobīnd conversing with his wife.

Plate XXVII.

Folio 22. Gobīnd conversing with two of his wives.

Plate XXVII.

Folio 23. Sālibhadra hearing the doctrine from two Jaina ascetics seated beneath a tree. Legend, *Sālabhadra sādha kan bakhāṇa suṇa chai*, 'Sālibhadra listens to the exposition of the sādhus'.

Plate XXVII.

Folio 24. Sālibhadra taking leave of his mother, Bhadrāmātā. No legend.

Plate XXVII.

Folio 26. *Obverse:* Sālibhadra takes leave of his wives. Legend, *Sālibhadra tīn asatrī chorī*, 'Sālibhadra leaves his three wives'.

Reverse: A lady (one of Sālibhadra's wives) with clasped hands, in night scene with crescent moon and four animals, like jackals. Legend, *Cocī hīranī suṁ ardāsa kara chai*, 'Coci complains to the wild deer'.

Plate XXVIII.

Folio 27. Subhadrā massaging Dhana-jī. Legend, *Dhanā-jī tā mora Subhadrā kara chai.*

Plate XXVIII.

Folio 28. Dhana-jī departing: one of his three wives seeks to detain him. Legend, *Dhanā-jī kī strī palo pakaryau chai*, 'Dhana's wife takes hold of his garment'.

Plate XXVIII.

Folio 29. Dhana-jī standing before Sālibhadra seated with his mother. Legend, *Dhanu-jī Sālibhadra nai teḍabā āyo chai*, Dhana comes under the influence of Sālibhadra'.
Plate XXVIII.

Folio 30. Sālibhadra asks his mother's permission (to depart). Legend, *Sālibhadra māṭā pāsa anumata māga chai,* 'Sālibhadra asks his mother's leave'.
Plate XXVIII.

Folio 31. Sālibhadra' wife tries in vain to prevent his departure. Legend, *Sālibhadra kī astrī palo jhālyo cha(i)*, 'Sālibhadra's wife releases his garment'.
Plate XXVIII.

Folio 32. Sālibhadra sets out, borne in a palanquin, to receive initiation. Legend, *Sālibhadra-jī dīkkhyā levaṇana jāya chai*, 'Sālibhadra goes forth to take *dīkṣā*'.
Plate XXIX.

Folio 33. Sālibhadra and Dhana receive initiation from a saint (Mahāvīra) enthroned between two trees. Legend, *Sālibhadra-jī Dhana-jī dīkkhyā līnī,* 'Sālibhadra and Dhana receive *dīkṣā*'.
Plate XXIX.

Folio 34. Jaina ascetics (Sālibhadra and Dhana) begging. Note the respirators (*mohomatī*), to avoid killing insects by breathing (shown also on folio 23), and the brush (*ughā*) to dust away insects from the path. Legend, *Sālibhadra-jī baharṇana āyā polyau najā bāde*, 'Sālibhadra seeks alms at the gate'.
Plate XXIX.

Folio 35. The same ascetics departing, meeting a woman, Mathitahārikā (present incarnation of Saṁgama's mother), who gives alms. No legend.
Plate XXIX.

Folio 36. Bhadrāmātā and Dhana's mother before Mahāvīra, enthroned. Legend, *Mātā pucha chai*, 'The mothers ask'.
Plate XXX.

Folio 37. Sālibhadra and Dhana die by voluntary starvation. Group of women and King Seṇaka respectfully watching. Legend, *Sālibhadra-jī Dhana-jī saṁtāro karyau chai*, 'Sālibhadra and Dhana accomplish voluntary death by starvation'.
Plate XXX.

Folio 38. Two women mourning. Legend, *Mātā vilā tāpa kare chai*, 'The mothers lament bitterly'.
Plate XXX.

Folio 39. Obverse: Sālibhadra and Dhana in paradise. Legend, *Savāratha siddha devatā huvā,* 'They become Sarvārthasiddha gods'. *Reverse:* with decorative rosettes.
Plate XXX.

8

17.2280. Manuscript of the *Ratan Sār,* 21 leaves, 13 lines to a page, Prākṛt language, Nandināgarī characters, with 4 crude miniatures. No covers. Dated Saṁvat 1663 = AD 1576.

Leaves .265 x 5 m. Ross-Coomaraswamy Collection.

9

17.2281. Manuscript of the *Rāja Prasnīya*, 76 leaves, 1 to 16 lines to a page, Prākṛt language with Sanskrit *ṭīkā*. Nandināgarī characters, no miniatures. No covers, but outer leaves decorated in red. Finely written on thin paper. Dated Saṁvat 1665 = AD 1608.

Leave .265 x .11 m. Ross-Coomaraswamy Collection.

Colophon: *Saṁvat 1665 varṣe ... lekhi: Śrī.*

Extract from *ṭīkā* on last page: *Iti mala(ya)giri viracitā Rā* the body. Paesi claims to have proved the contrary experiment. The book is parallel to the Pāyāsisuthe of the Buddhist canon; and the type is found also in the Buddhist *Milindaprasna*.

The contests have been described by E. Leumann, Oriental Congress, VI, Leiden 1883, III, 2, 490ff.
Plate XXXI.

10

17.2282. Manuscript of the *Sāmudrika Lakṣana*, a work on physiognomy or rhetoric; in Sanskrit. Six leaves, seventeen lines to a page, no miniatures, no covers.

Leaves .275 x .22 m. Ross-Coomaraswamy Collection.

The text commences:

Ādidevaṁ praṇampādau sarvvajñaṁ sarbadarśinaṁ
Sāmudrikam pravakṣyāmi subhagaṁ puruṣastriyo 1.
Pūrvamāyuḥ parīkṣet paścāllakṣaṇaṁevaca

Āyurhīnā narānāryyo lakṣaṇaiḥ
kiṁprayojanaṁ 2.

and concludes

Jṇātavyaṁ vivudhaiḥ strīṇām, lakṣaṇaṁ-
bāpya lakṣaṇaṁ
Kulavṛddhi yaśovṛddhiḥ, lakṣmī bṛddhi
bhāvet yataḥ 49.

followed by the colophon:

Iti Śrī Sāmudrike Lakṣaṇādhyāyaḥ:
graṁthāgraṁtha 277 saṁpūrṇaṁ,

followed by fourteen lines of *mantras*.

11

17.2283. Manuscript of the *Bhava-vairāga śataka*. 8 leaves, 6 lines to a page, Prākṛt language, with Sanskrit *ṭīkā*. Nandināgarī characters, no miniatures. No covers. Finely written on thin paper. Sixteenth century.

Leaves .254 x .11 m. Ross-Coomaraswamy Collection.

Colophon: *Itī Bhava vairāga śatakaṁ samāpṭaḥ b(emi)* (Not to be confused with the well-known *Vairāgya Śataka* of Bhartṛhari).

A hundred verses on the nonentity of phenomena, the vanity of all earthly weal, the sorrow of birth and death, etc., for which the Jaina religion is the only remedy. The text has been published and translated by L.P. Tessitori, in *Giornale della Societa Asiatica Italiana*, 22, 179-211 and 24, 405ff.

Plate XXXII.

12

17.2284. Manuscript of the sixth section of the *Nala-Davadantī*, consisting of two leaves, the outer side of each with coloured decoration. Hindī [*sic*, Old Gujarati] language, Nāgarī characters. Dated *Saṁvat solaḥ tihuttaraiṁ* [*sic. tihattaraiṁ*], i.e. 1673=AD 1616.

Leaves .242 X .104 m. Ross-Coomaraswamy Collection.

The latter part of the *Kathā Kośa* (trans. C.H. Tawney, London, 1895) contains a lengthy version of the story of Nala and Damayantī: the present MS. mentions different names and seems to belong to an older and different recension, if, indeed, it has any connection with the story apparently indicated by the name—the contents appear to be merely edifying. It consists of 15 *caupāīs* and a lengthy colophon, part of which is hardly decipherable:

Commencement:

Sakala jaina guru pranamuṁpāyā,
vāgadeva mujha karahu pasāyā
Gāisu āhu kumara riṣirāyā, jiṇa muni pālī
pravacana māyā 1.
Sakala sudāvā hoï vadhāvā, āha. kumara
muṇivara guṇa gāvā. Āṁkaṇī
Magadha desa tribhuvani viṣyātā, pura
vacasaṁ tajyāṁ racyoï viṣyātā
Vasaï sāmāyakā nāma kuvaṁvī (?), savala
citraṁ māyā naviṭaṁtr
Dharmaghoṣa guru āyā nāṇī, vadi suṇaï
desaṇa jiṇa vāṇī.

Extract from the colophon:

Dhala dasamī gītā chandniḥ, Sudharmā
Sāmi paraṁparā:
Chandra kula Vayara Sāmi sākhi, Kotika
gaṇa Gaccha Kharatarāü:
bhaṭṭārakā subhāṣi, yuga para dhāna
Jiṇacaṁdra prathama
śiṣya siromaṇī: jasu Gotra Rīhaḍa nāma
paṁḍita Sakalacaṁdra
prasidha ghaṇi: tasu sīsaya bhaṇaī
Samayasūṁdara
upādhyāyaiṁ vācanacām.
Reja Harṣanandana prathama śiṣyanaiṁ
ādaraiṁ. 1.
Gotra Golacha ...
Saṁghamaiṁ dīpatā Kharatara Gaccha
siṇagāra, sinagāra, dharma taṇā
dhuraṁdara deva guru rāgī ghaṇūṁ.
Rāyamalla-putra-ratna Amipāla
Khettasī Netasī taṇūṁ. Rāja Sītā sabhatī
javi hunskiṇa Netasī āgraha
karī. Caüpaī kīdhī Samayasūṁdara Nala
Davadaṁtī caritasa. 2.
Saṁvat solaḥ tihuttaraiṁ māsa vasaṁta
Ānaṁda nagara manohara meḍataü.
Jiṁhāvā supūjya Jiṇade Vāsapūjya tīrtha-
kara prasādaṁ
Gaccha Kharatara ... yuga para dhāna
Jinasiṁha Sūri sadaguru ....
Samayasūṁdara Kīyaü āgraha Netasī ...
Caüpaī nalada davakerī catura māṇasa
citavasvī. 3.
Iti Śrī Nala Davadaṁtī saṁbamdhe ṣaṣṭā
khamdaḥ samāptaḥ. Śubham bhavatu,
Lūṇāvāsa madhye.

From which it appears that Samaya sundara, disciple of Sakalacandra and guru of Hariṣanandana, wrote this poem in 1673 Saṁvat, at the instigation of Netasī, son of Rāyamalla, Luṇāvāsa monastery of the city of Ānanda.

The date *solaḥ tihuttaraiṁ* must be read as *solaḥ tihattaraiṁ*, giving Saṁvat 1673, equivalent to AD 1616. Jinasiṁha Sūri of the Bṛhat-

Kharatara Gaccha died in Saṁvat 1674. Ānanda is the modern Ānand, chief town of the Khaira District of the Bombay Presidency.

Plates XXXIII and XXXIV.

13

21.1664. *Stotra* in praise of Jinas, in Sanskrit. Single leaf of text written on one side only in red and white Nāgarī characters on a black ground. Dimensions, .264 x .12 m.

Marianne Brimmer Fund.

14

21.1665. *Stotra* in praise of Neminātha, in Sanskrit. Single leaf of text, written on one side only in Nāgarī characters on a red ground. Dimensions, .263 x .119 m.

Marianne Brimmer Fund.

Colophon (not wholly legible):

Iti Śrī Paṁḍita kṛtaṁ Śāli
Nemināthastotraṁ sampurṇaṁ ...
mūlodharmmo jinoktaṁ.

15

17.2295. Painting on cotton, representing the Jina Pārśavanātha enthroned, with deities, saints and symbols in the surrounding compartments. Probably fifteenth century.

Dimensions, .30 x .31 m. Ross-Coomaraswamy Collection.

Described and reproduced in Coomaraswamy ('Notes on Jaina Art', *Journal of Indian Art*, Vol. 16, 1914).

The central figure is drawn over a square of gold leaf, in the manner of MSS. M.F.A. 17.2277 and 2278, the colours used being scarlet (background), yellow (for flesh, etc.), crimson, pink, blue, green, black, and white. The cloth has been primed before painting. Spots of sandal paste on the chief figures show that the picutre has been used as a cult object. Originally folded in nine, with a *nandiyāvartta* diagram at the back. Iconography:

1. Śrī Pārśvanātha enthroned in a *mandir.*
2. Samavasaraṇa of Śrī Pārśvanātha.
3. 'Pañca-pad': five Oṁkāra ideographs, and five Siddhas, above the *Siddha-śilā*. These five persons probably represent the 'Pañca-puruṣa' (whose significance in Jaina mythology is un-known to me: but see Blumhardt, J.F., *Catalogue of Hindi, Hindustani, and Panjabi MSS. in the British Museum*, 1899, p. 4).
4. The god Indra [*sic*, a goddess.]
5. The Nāga Dharaṇendra.
6. The Yakṣīṇī Padmāvatī.
7. The goddess Padmāvatī (or Ambikā?) [*sic*, Ambikā]
8. Suddharma Swāmi (?) (successor of Gautama Swāmi).
9. Not identified.
10. Gautama Swāmi (Mahāvīra's successor as spiritual leader of the Jaina community).

Plate XXXV.

16

17.2296. Drawing representing Śrī Pārśvanātha enthroned: cobra (*nāga*) cognizance. Dimensions, .064 x .128 m. Ross-Coomaraswamy Collection.

17

17.2297. Painting representing Śrī Ṛṣabha enthroned: bull cognizance. Dimensions, .074 x .090 m. Ross-Coomaraswamy Collection.

18

17.2298. Drawing representing Śrī Ṛṣabha enthroned in a *mandir*: bull cognizance. Dimensions, .113 x .288 m. Ross-Coomaraswamy Collection.

Plate XXXVI.

19

17.2299. Painting representing Kunthanātha enthroned: goat (*chāga*) cognizance.

Inscribed: *Kunthanātha-jī 17.*

Dimensions, .128 x .197 m. Ross-Coomaraswamy Collection.

20

17.2300. Painting representing Śrī Arahanātha enthroned: *nandiyāvartta* cognizance.

Inscribed: *Arahanātha-jī 18.*

Dimensions, .127 x .193 m. Ross-Coomaraswamy Collection.

21

17.2311. Painting representing Abhinandana-Nātha, with monkey (*kapi*) cognizance.

Inscribed: *Śrī Abhinandana-jī 4.*

Dimensions, .115 x .153 m. Ross-Coomaraswamy Collection.

Plate XXXVI.

MISCELLANEOUS DRAWINGS

22

17.2285. The Fourteen Dreams of the Rāṇī Triśalā. Coloured drawing.

Dated equivalent to AD 1627.

Dimensions, .252 x .105 m. Ross-Coomaraswamy Collection.

Iconography: upper row, from left to right.

(1) Elephant (*hastī*), (2) Bull (*ṛṣabha*), (3) Lion (*sīha*), (4) Lakhmī, (5) Garlands (*phulnīmalā*), (6) moon (*candamā*), (7) Sun (*Sūrya*);

Lower row, from left to right...

(8) Banner (*dhvaja*), (9) golden vase (*purṇakalasa*), (10) Lotus lake (*Mānasarovara*), (11) Sea of Milk (*samudra*), (12) Heavenly mansion (*vimāna*), (13) Jewel-heap (*ratan*), (14) Smokeless fire (*niradhuma-agni*).

Each of the items labelled in Nāgarī characters: there is also one line of inscription giving the date Saṁvat 1684 (= AD 1627) and place Campāvatī (probably near Jodhpur).

Plate XXXVII.

23

17.2286. The Fourteen Dreams of the Rāṇī Trīśala. Coloured drawing. Seventeenth century.

Dimensions, .24 x .107 m. Ross-Coomaraswamy Collection.

Iconography; upper row, from left to right.

(1) Elephant, (2) Bull, (3) Sun, (4) Moon, (5) Golden vase, (6) Lotus lake, (7) Heap of gems;

Lower right, from left to right:

(8) Lion, (9) Garland, (10) Banner, (11) Centre panel) Lakṣmī, (12) River or sea, (13) Mansion, (14) Fire.

Plate XXXVII.

24

17.2287. The Eight auspicious objects (*aṣṭamaṅgala*) and the Fourteen Dreams of the Rāṇī Triśala: reverse with miscellaneous sketches. Uncoloured drawing.

Dimensions, .315 x .195 m. Ross-Coomaraswamy Collection.

25

17.2288. Four leaves of crude sketches. Nineteenth century. Ross-Coomaraswamy Collection.

26

17.2289. Illustration to the *Sālibhadra caritra:*

Painting; three architectural compartments. In the centre Sālibhadra and Dhana seated on a throne, conversing with Bhadrāmātā who stands before them; to right and left, the thirty-two wives of Sālibhadra. Cf. 17.1673, f. 8 with a group of 27 women. With labels in Nandināgarī character. At the back is written a list of the Fourteen Dreams of the Rāṇī Triśalā. Eighteenth century.

Dimensions, .274 x .120 m. Ross-Coomaraswamy Collection.

The legends above the three central figures read: *Bhadrāmāttā chai, Sālabhadra Seṭh chai, Dhano nāmai bahaneü.*

Plate XXXII.

27

17.2290. Fragment of painting representing a man applying sectarian marks to his forehead. Perhaps Rajput. Early seventeenth century.

Dimensions, .08 x .05 m. Ross-Coomaraswamy Collection.

Plate XXXVI.

28

17.2291. Outer leaf of a MS. with decoration: reverse with painting of a Jaina priest worshipping the vision of Sarasvatī, who is four-armed and carries a book and *vīṇā*, and rides on *haṁsa*. The priest waves a *caurī* and carries a bowl: behind him a flowering tree. Seventeenth to eighteenth century.

Dimensions, .215 x .107 m. Ross-Coomaraswamy Collection.

Plate XXXII [*sic*, XXXVIII].

29

17.2292. Painting, representing Śrī Kṛṣṇa on lotus seat: four-armed, with lotus, chank, and mace. Perhaps Rajput. Seventeenth to eighteenth century.

Dimensions, .056 x .044 m. Ross-Coomaraswamy Collection.

Items 17.2293 and 17.2294 are by the same hand.

30

17.2293. Painting, representing Rāma and Sītā enthroned, attended by Lakṣmaṇa and Hanuman. Perhaps Rajput. Seventeenth to eighteenth century.

Dimensions, .067 x .046 m. Ross-Coomaraswamy Collection.

31

17.2294. Painting, representing two men seated, one with a *sitār*, the other reading or singing from a book.

Perhaps Rajput, Seventeenth to eighteenth century.

Dimensions, .569 x .046 m. Ross-Coomaraswamy Collection.

32

22.706. Hrīṁkāra *yantra*. A diagram of a squatting human figure within the monogram Hrīṁ: dated equivalent to AD 1705.

Dimensions, .403 x .578 m. Gift of Ananda K. Coomaraswamy.

The uppermost enclosed area reads:

Me svahā. Oṁ Śṛiṁ Klīṁ nomo arihamtāṇaṁ namo siddhānāṁ namo āpa asya yantra prabhāva. sarva manuṣyāsaṁ strīyā sarva rājā navāyaha:

Text six lines from the bottom begins:

Vi(krama) saṁvat 1762 and concluded *sarva siddhi guru kī ajnā kura.*

Various feminine deities (Caṇḍikā, Sāradā, Padmāvatī, Gomukha, etc.) and represented as having their seat in the parts of the body.

The Hrīṁkāra is a monogram symbol associated with Pārśvanātha and according to Jaina interpretation is composed of the letters *ha* (meaning Parśvanātha), *ra* (meaning Dharaṇendra), and *ī* (meaning Padmāvatī). (Burgess, J., 'Papers on Śatruñjaya and the Jains', *Indian Antiquary*, XIII, 1884, p. 279.)

Plate XXXIX.

INDEX OF REGISTRY NUMBERS

Registry Number	*Catalogue Number*	*Plate Number*	*Page*
17.2276	1	....	40
		II	41
		II	42
		III	43
17.2277	2	....	43
		IV	45
		V	46
		VI	46
		VII	47
		VIII	48
		IX	49
		X	49
17.2278	3	...	49
		XI	50
		XII	50
		XIII	51
		XIV	52
		XV	53
17.2279	6	....	58
		XXII	59
17.2280	8	...	66
17.2281	9	...	66
		XXXI	67
17.2282	10	....	67
17.2283	11	....	67
		XXXII	68
17.2284	12	...	68
		XXXIII	69
		XXXIV	69
17.2285	22	XXXVII	72
17.2286	23	XXXVII	72
17.2287	24	....	72
17.2288	25	....	73
17.2289	26	XXXII	73
17.2290	27	XXXVI	73
17.2291	28	XXXII	73
17.2292	29	....	73
17.2293	30	....	74
17.2294	31	....	74
17.2295	16	XXXV	70
17.2296	15	....	71
17.2297	17	....	71
17.2298	18	XXXVI	71
17.2299	19	....	71
17.2300	20	....	71
17.2311	21	XXXVI	71
19.142	5	XXXVI	58
21.1664	13	....	69
21.1665	14	....	69
21.1673	7	....	60
		XXIII	62
		XXIV	62
		XXV	63
		XXVI	64
		XXVII	64
		XXVIII	65
		XXIX	65
		XXX	66
22.364	4	....	53
		XV	54
		XVI	54
		XVII	54
		XVIII	55
		XIX	56
		XX	56
		XXI	57
22.706	32	XXXIX	74

PLATE I

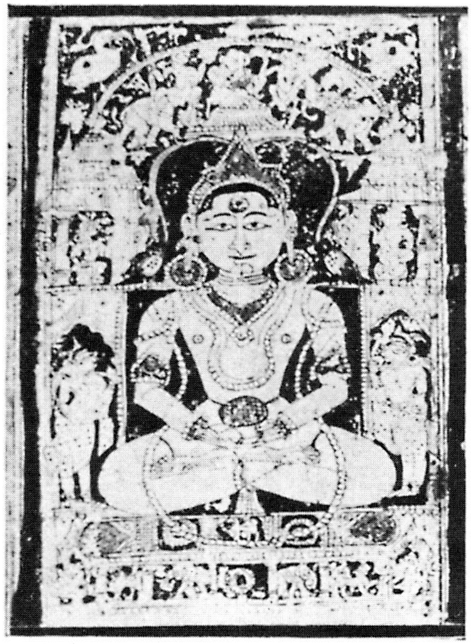

FOLIO 1

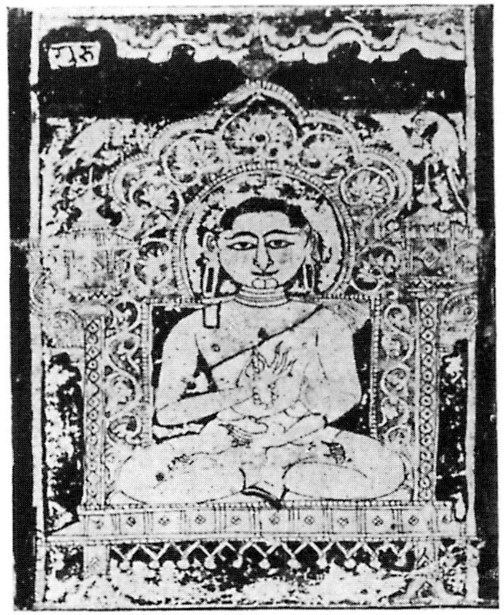

FOLIO 2

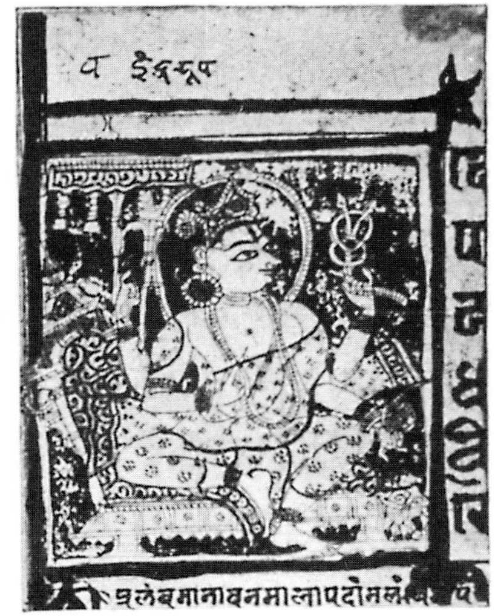

FOLIO 6

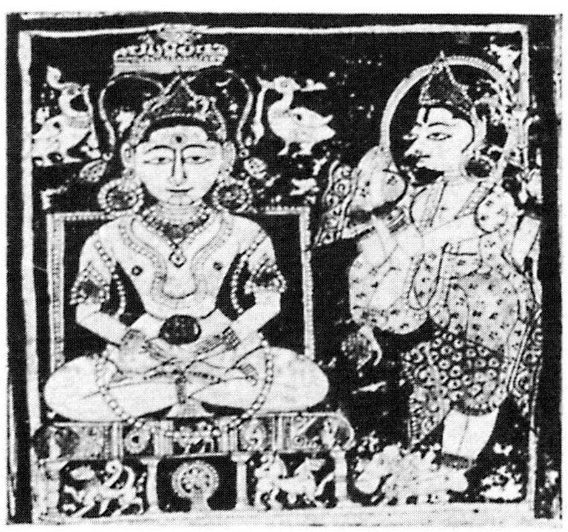

FOLIO 9

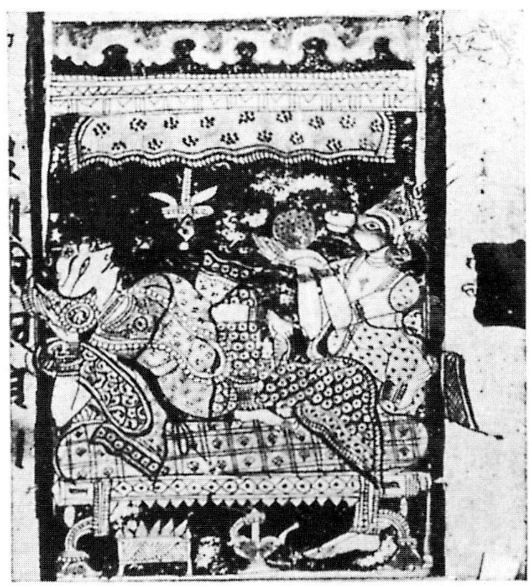

FOLIO 15

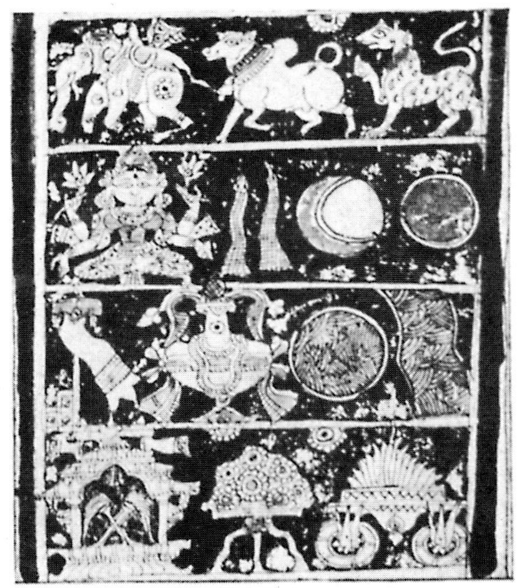

FOLIO 34

1. (17.2276)

PLATE II

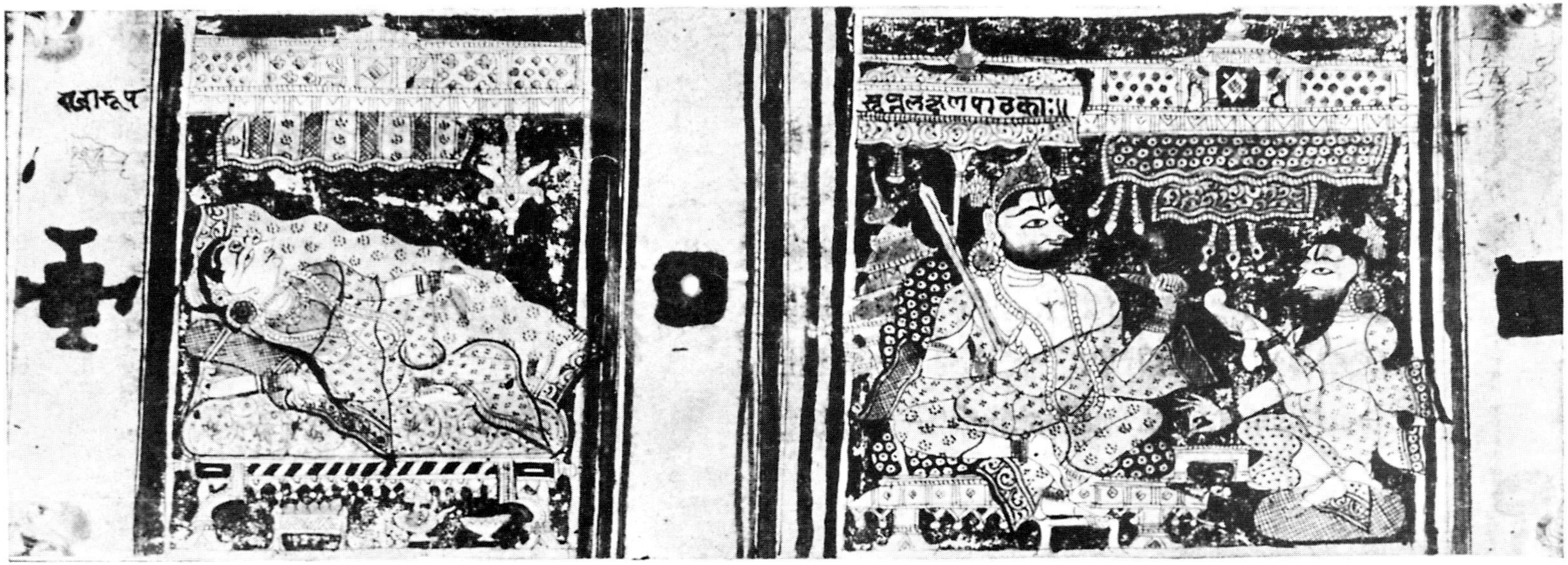

FOLIO 36

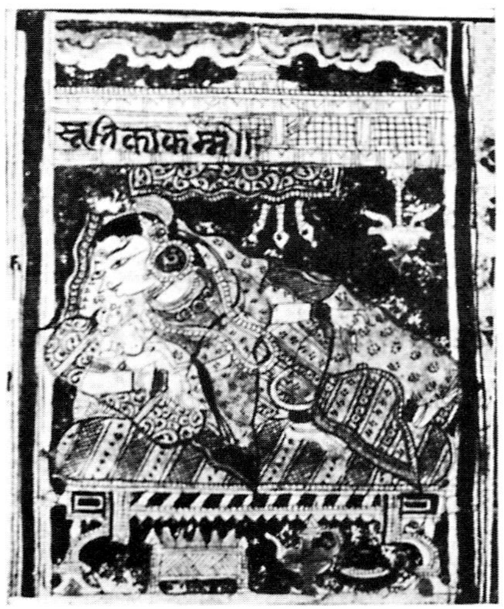

FOLIO 41

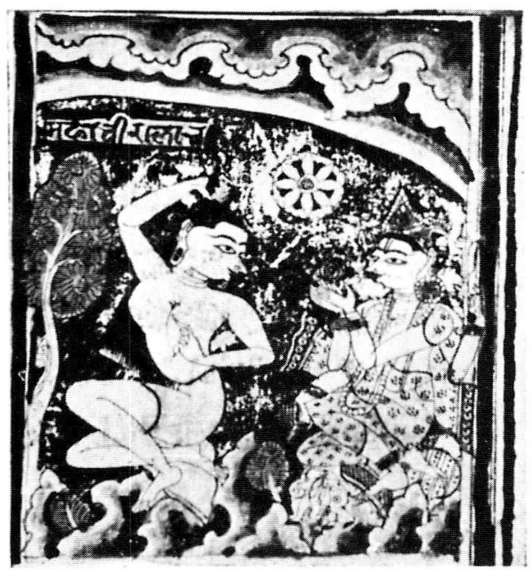

FOLIO 49

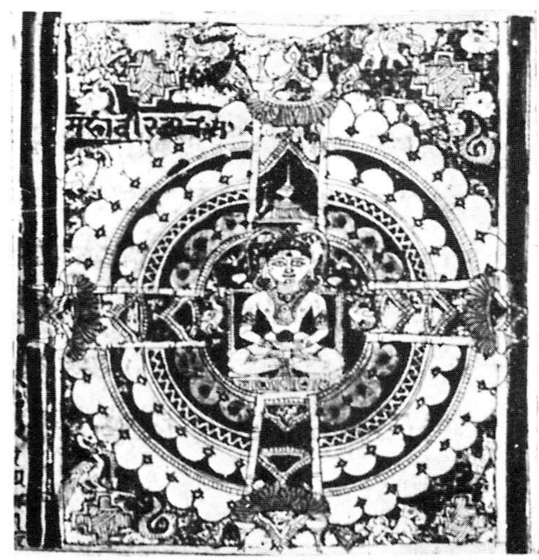

FOLIO 53

1. (17.2276)

PLATE III

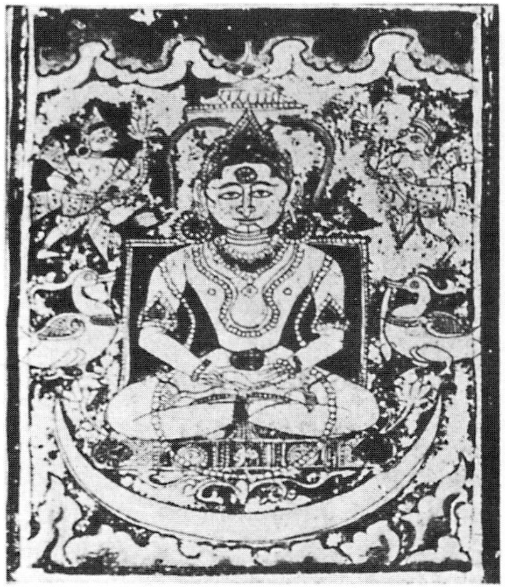

FOLIO 55

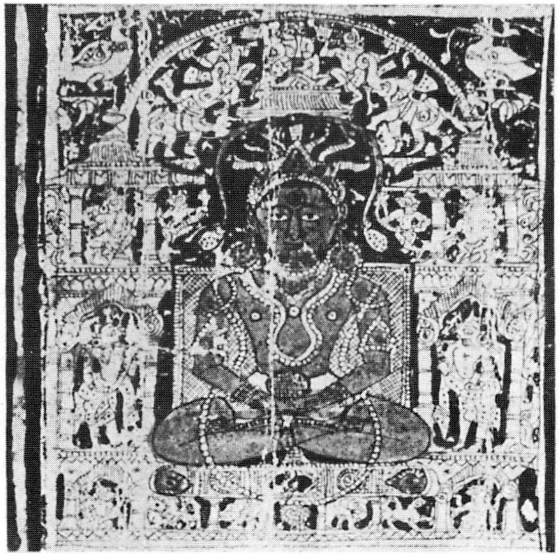

FOLIO 59

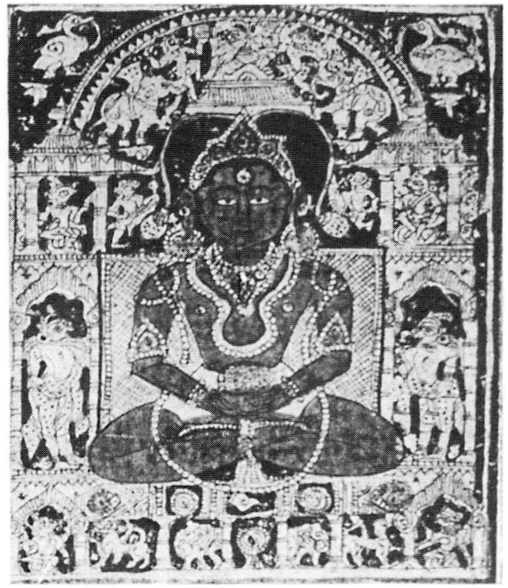

FOLIO 66

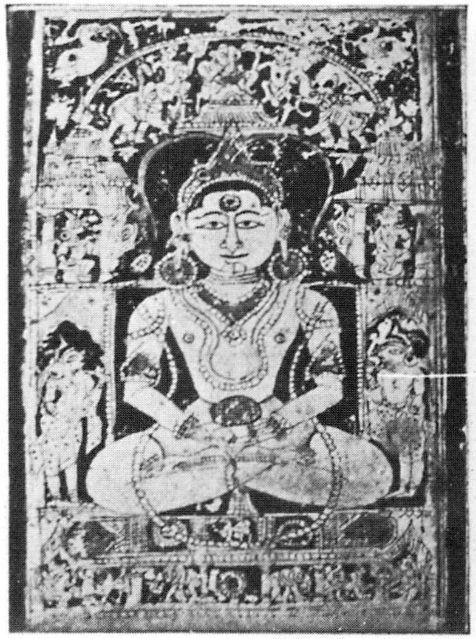

FOLIO 72

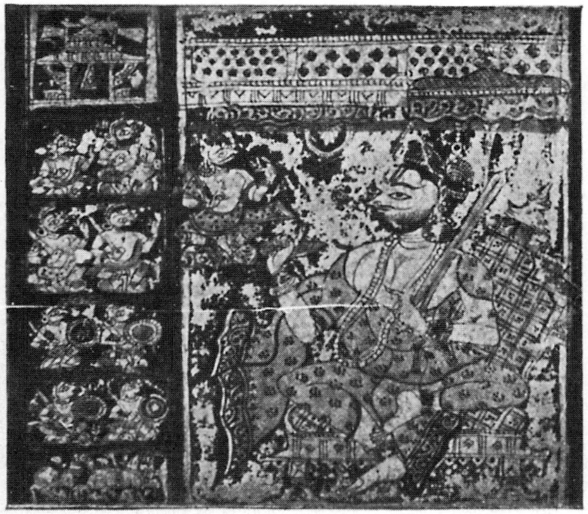

FOLIO 100

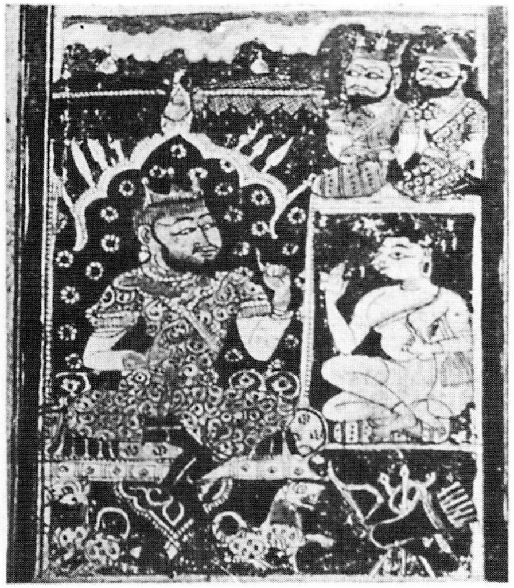

FOLIO 100

1. (17.2276)

PLATE IV

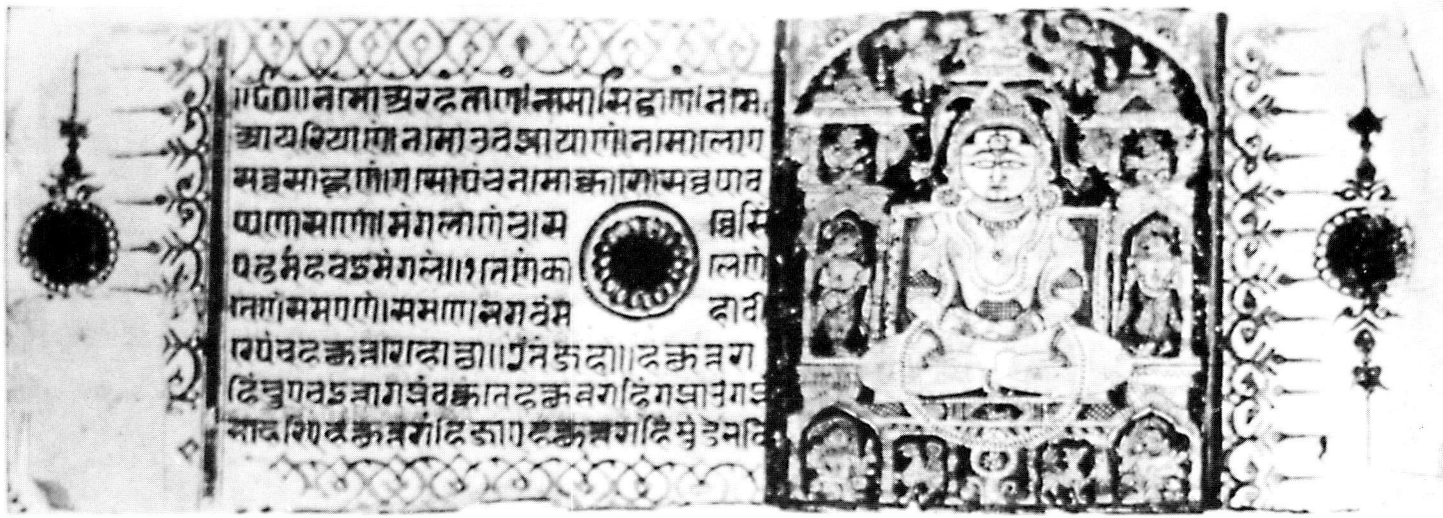

FOLIO 1

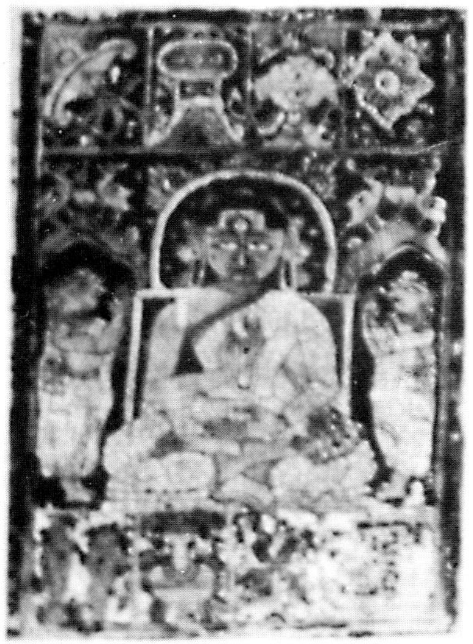

FOLIO 2

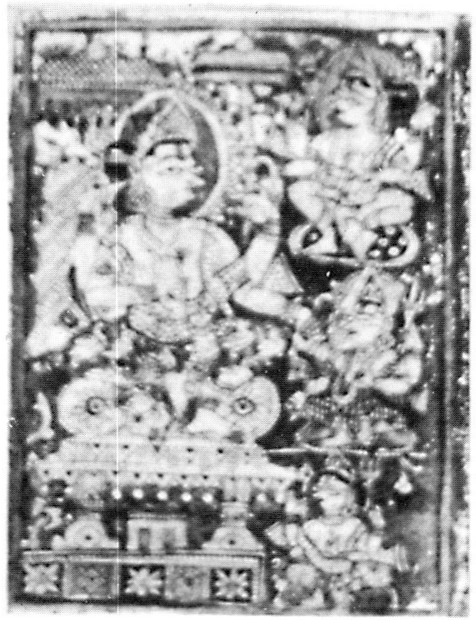

FOLIO 5

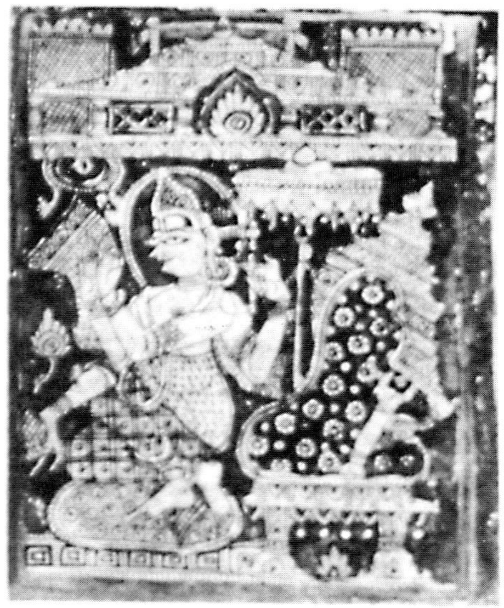

FOLIO 6

2. (17.2277)

PLATE V

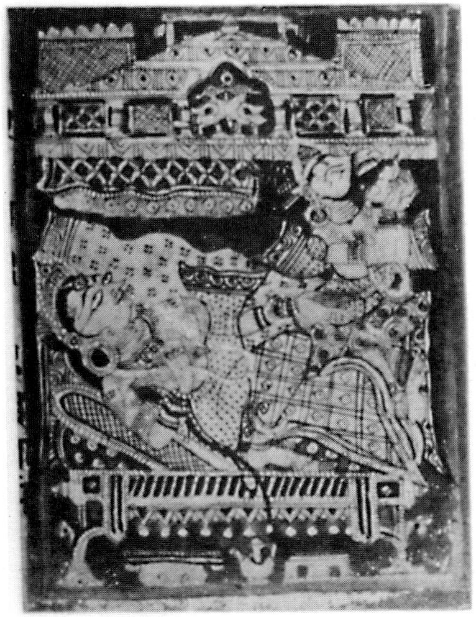

FOLIO 10

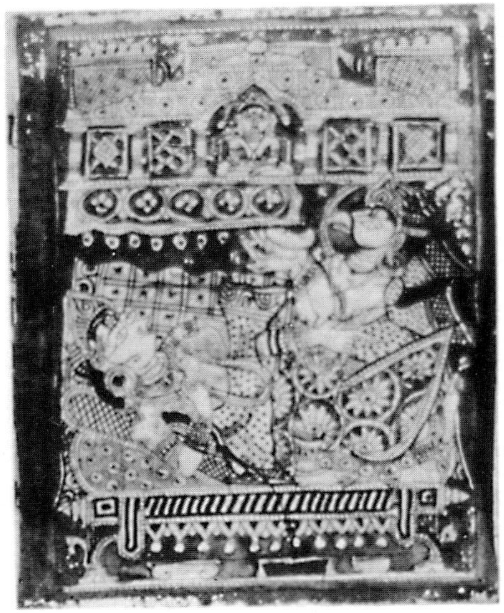

FOLIO 11

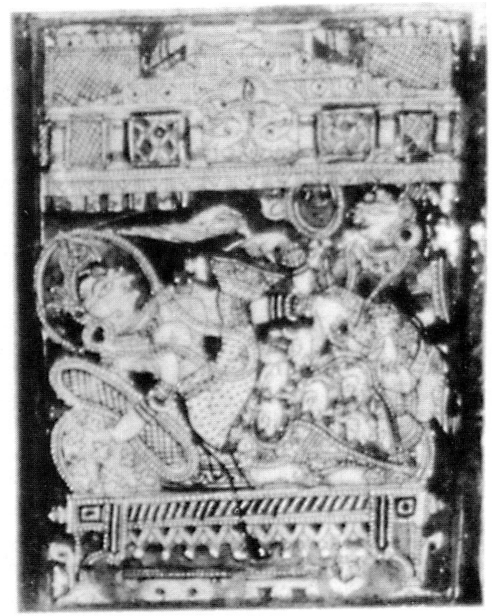

FOLIO 12

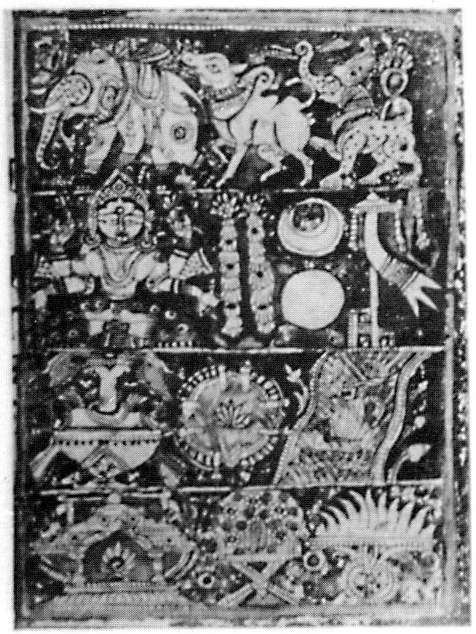

FOLIO 13

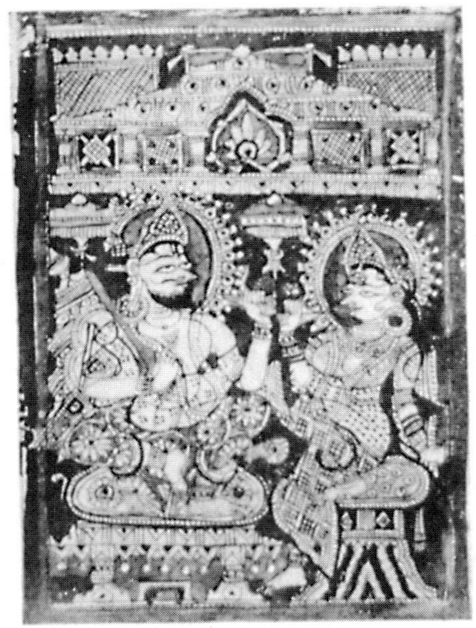

FOLIO 19

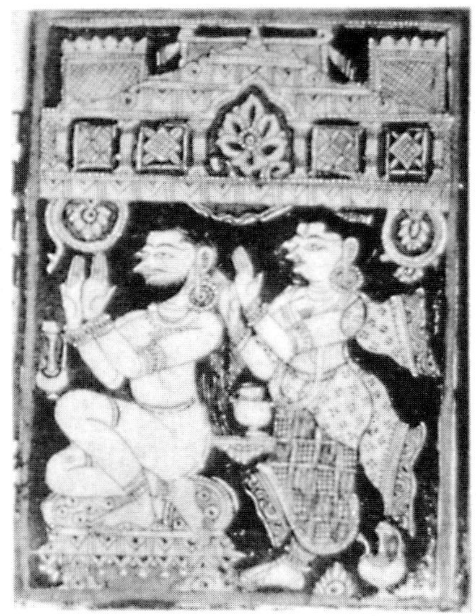

FOLIO 21

2. (17.2277)

PLATE VI

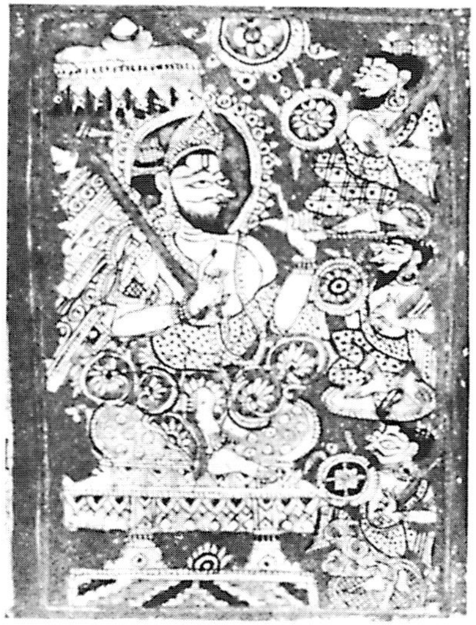

FOLIO 22

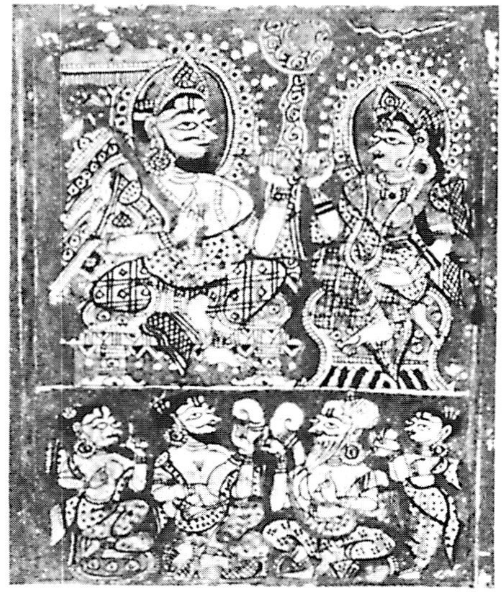

FOLIO 23

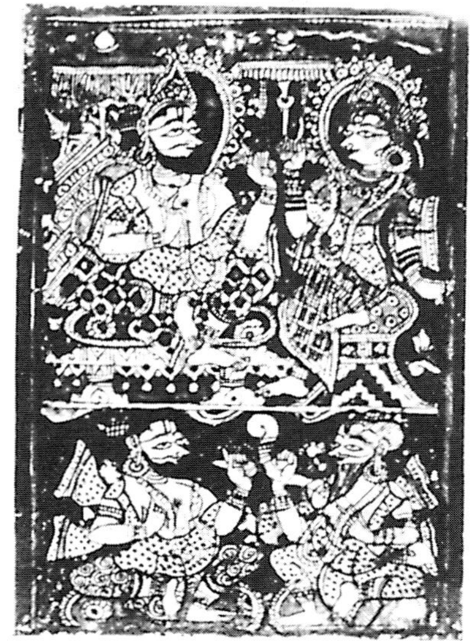

FOLIO 24

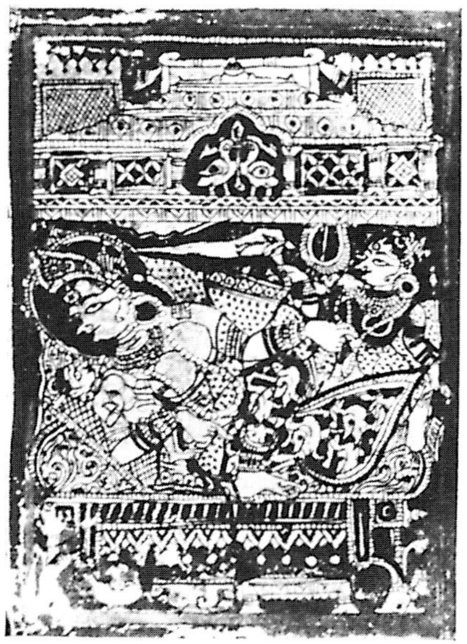

FOLIO 28

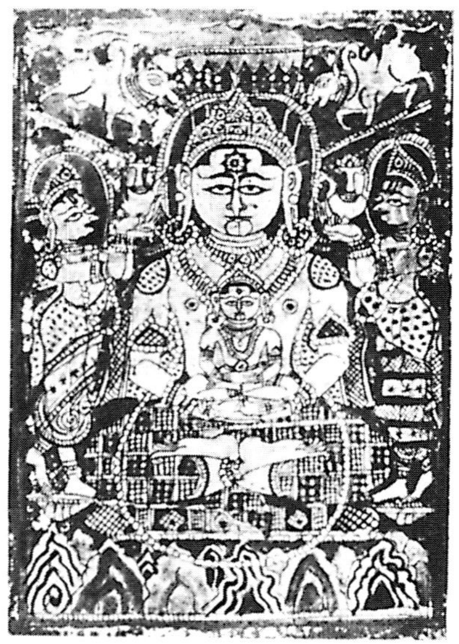

FOLIO 29

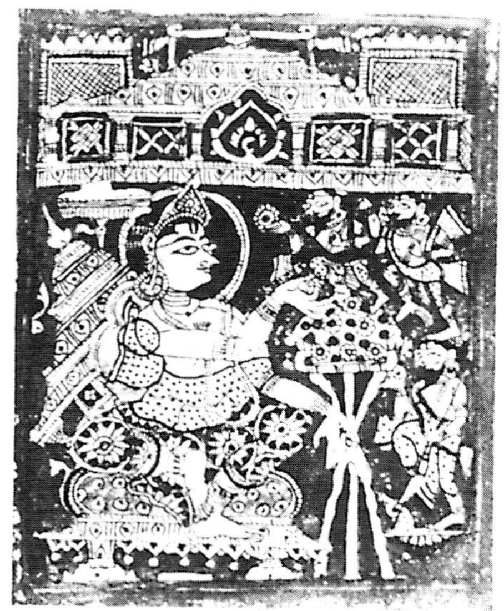

FOLIO 32

2. (17.2277)

PLATE VII

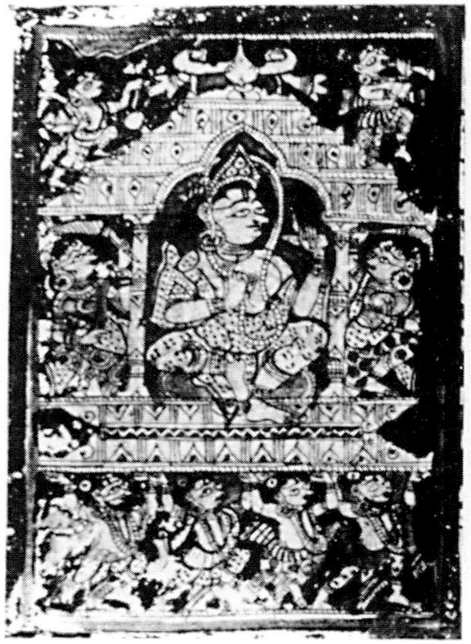

FOLIO 33

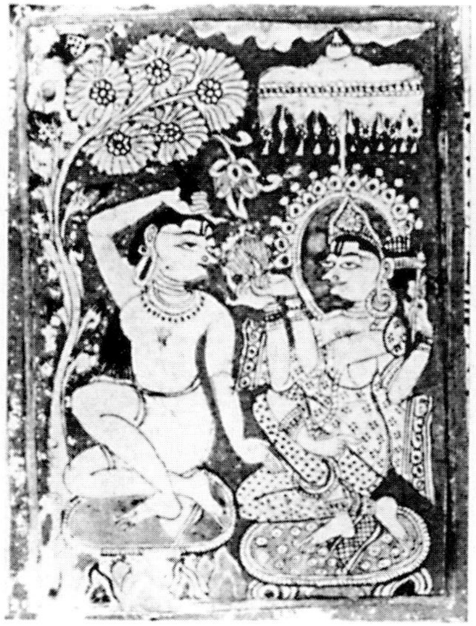

FOLIO 34

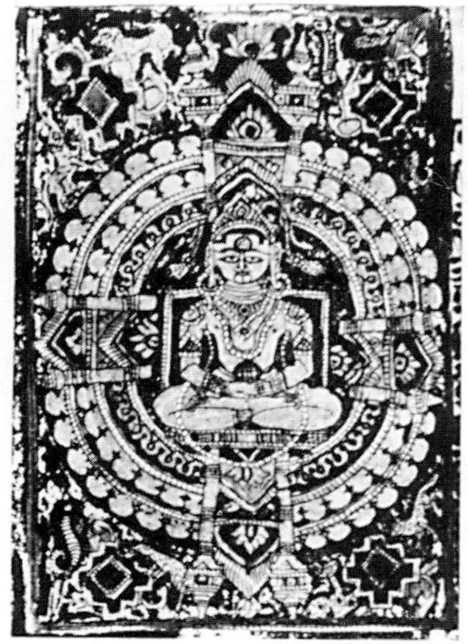

FOLIO 37

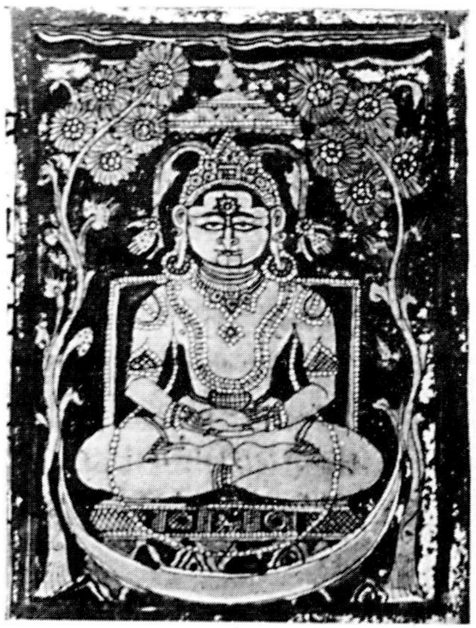

FOLIO 38

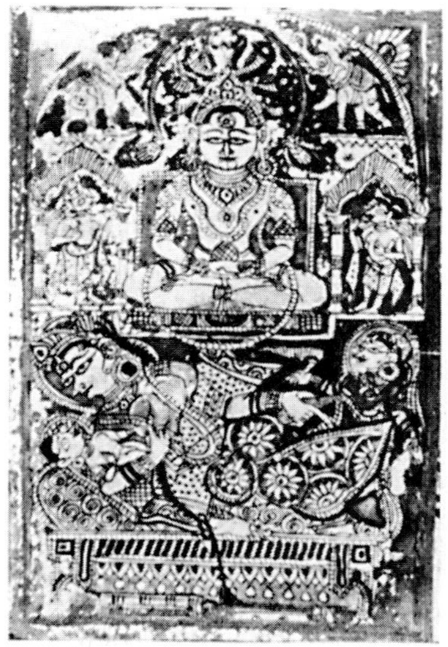

FOLIO 41

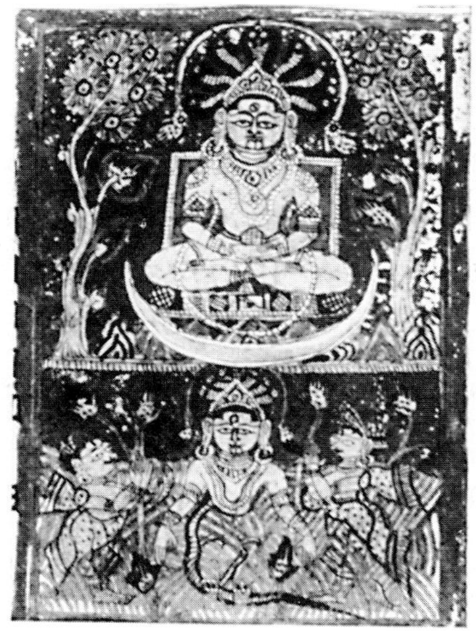

FOLIO 44

2. (17.2277)

PLATE VIII

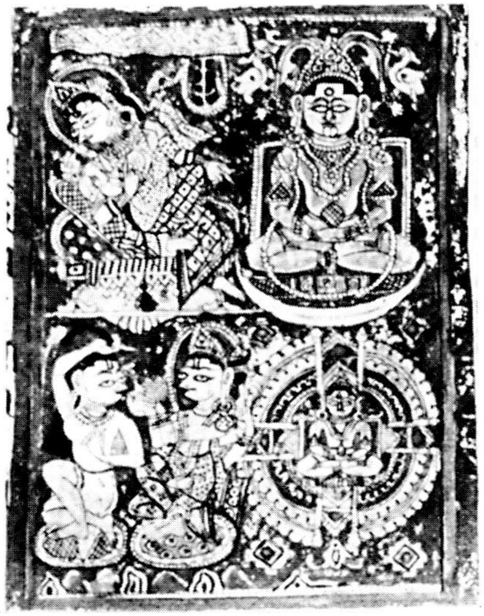

FOLIO 47

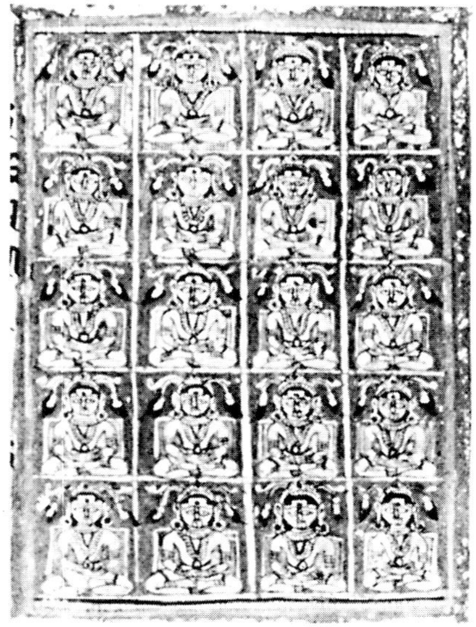

FOLIO 48

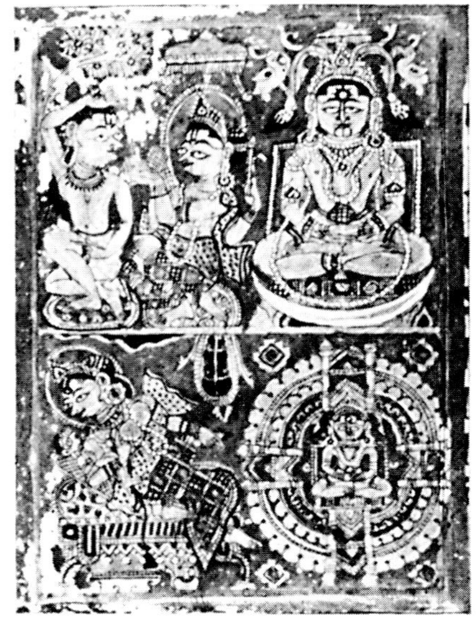

FOLIO 50

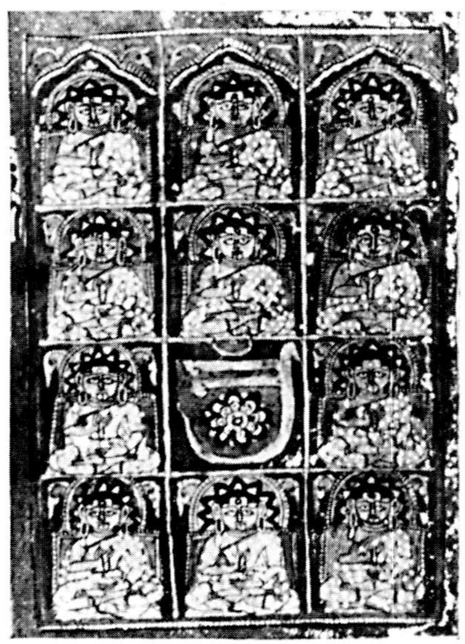

FOLIO 54

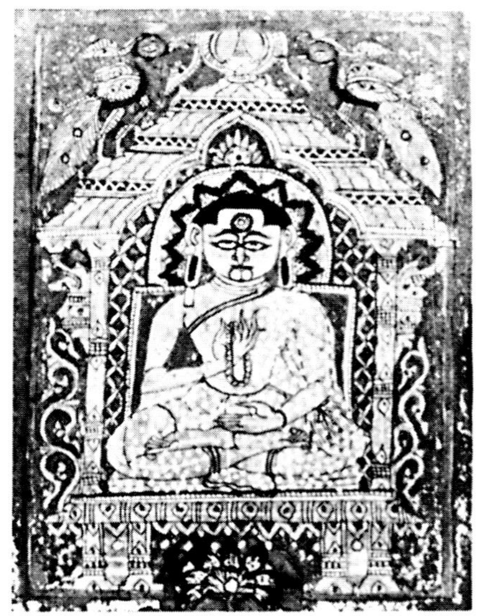

FOLIO 61

2. (17.2277)

PLATE IX

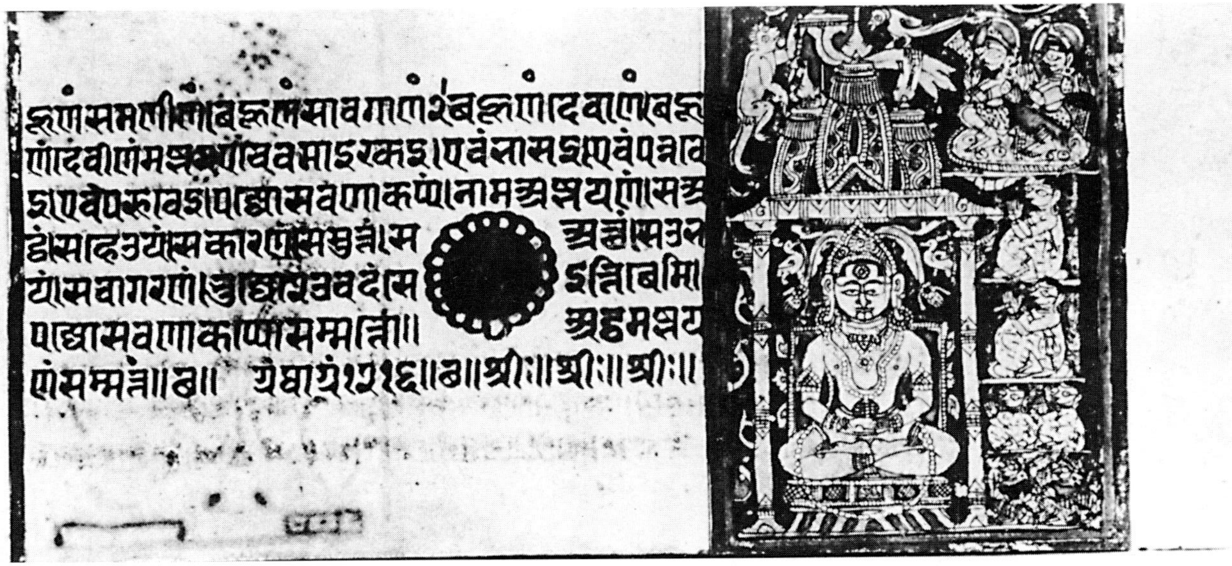

FOLIO 72

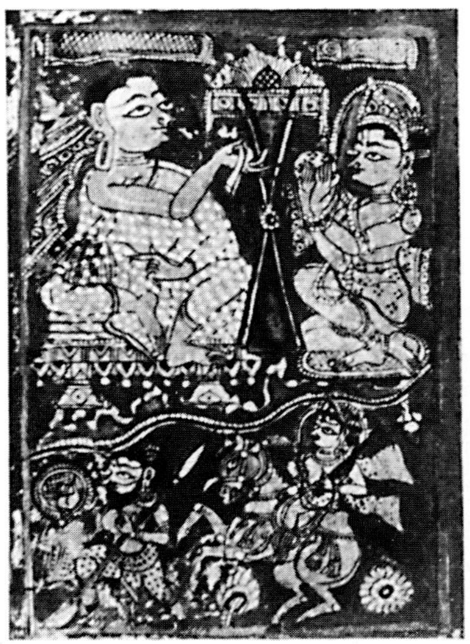

FOLIO 72

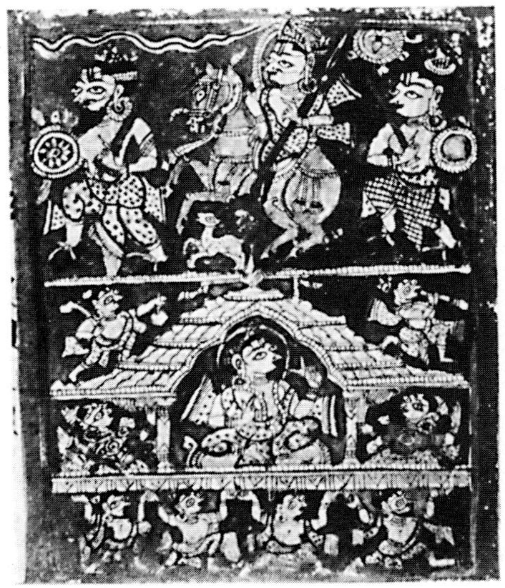

FOLIO 73

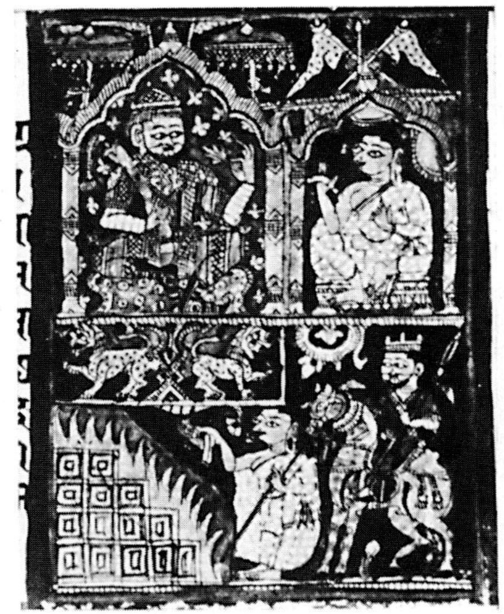

FOLIO 74

2. (17.2277)

PLATE X

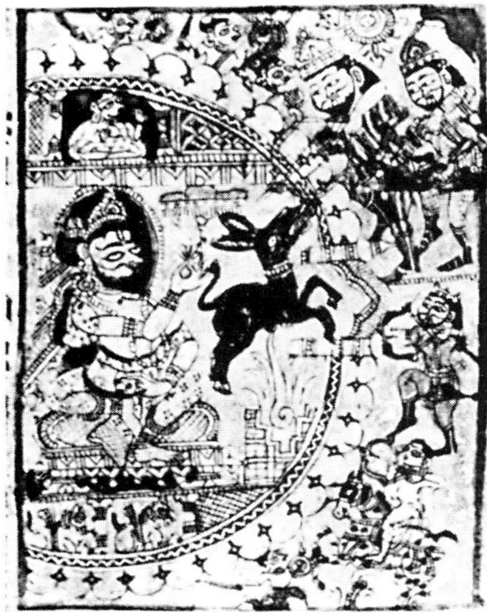

FOLIO 75

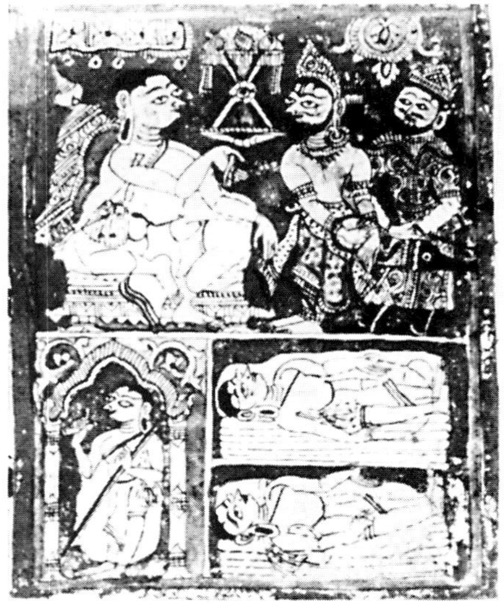

FOLIO 76

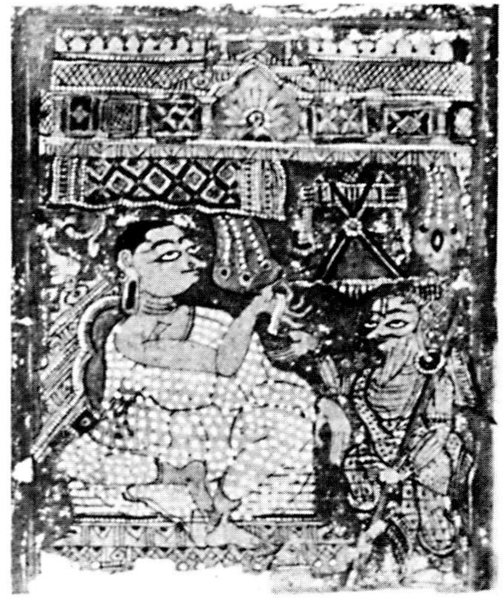

FOLIO 78

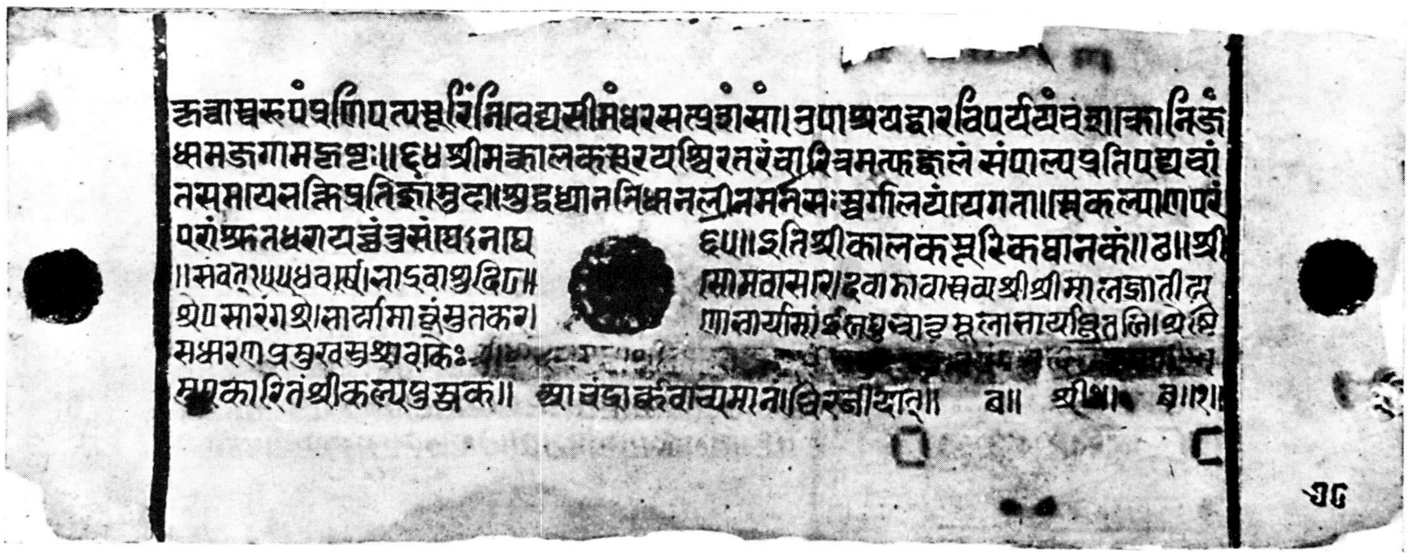

FOLIO 78

2. (17.2277)

PLATE XI

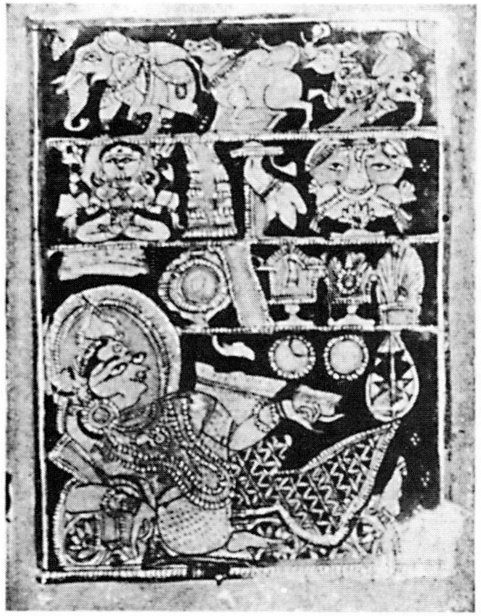

FOLIO 4

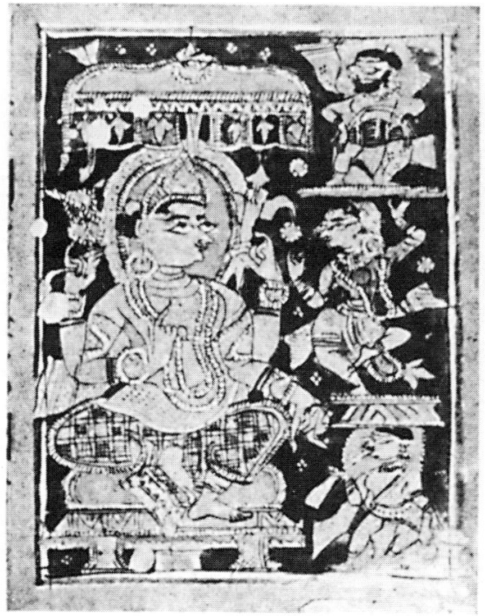

FOLIO 8

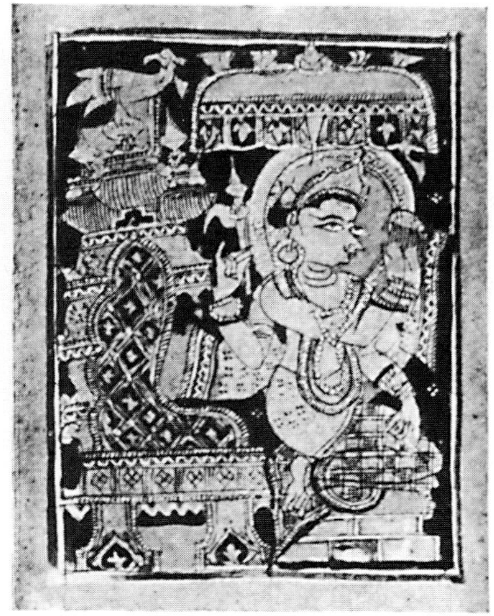

FOLIO 10

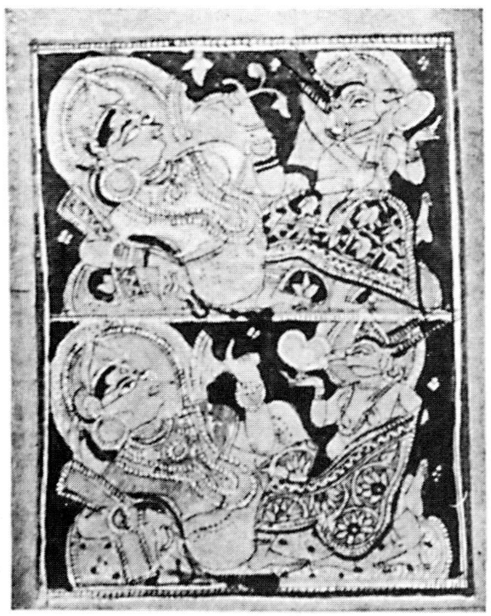

FOLIO 17

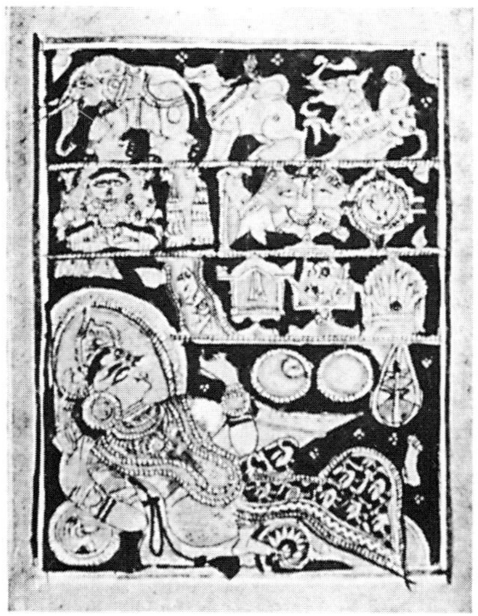

FOLIO 21

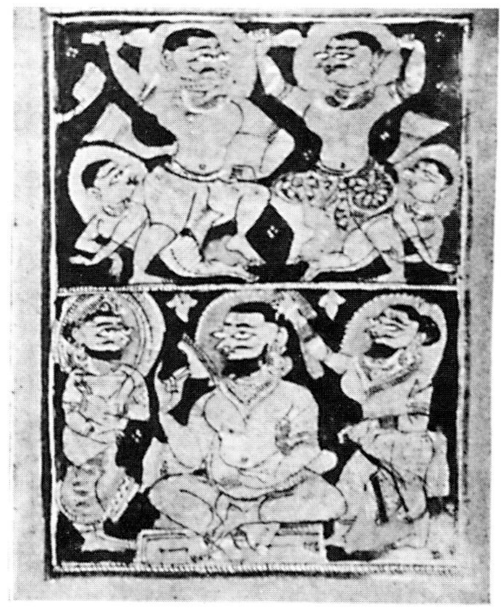

FOLIO 35

3. (17.2278)

PLATE XII

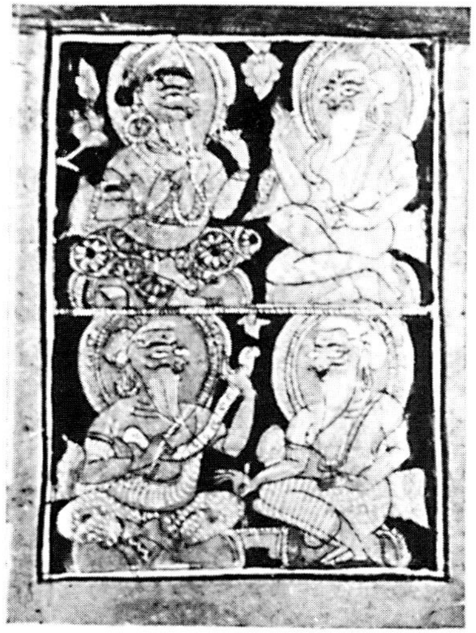

FOLIO 39

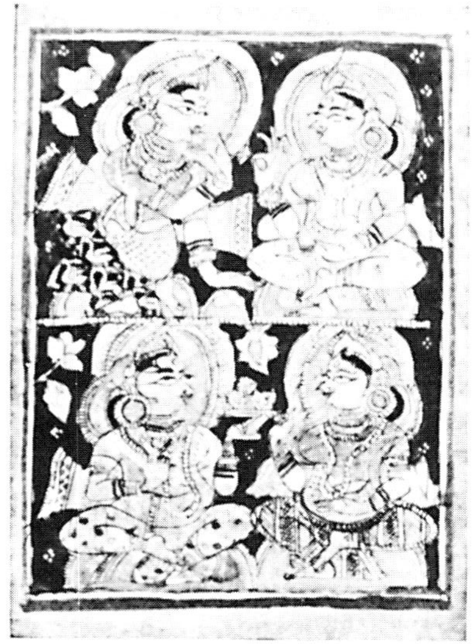

FOLIO 46

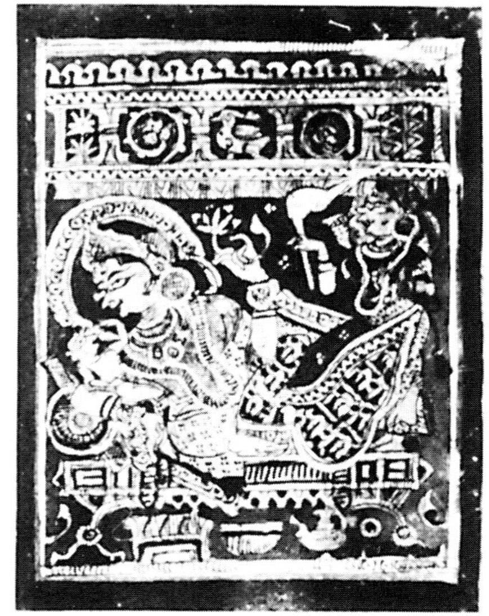

FOLIO 48

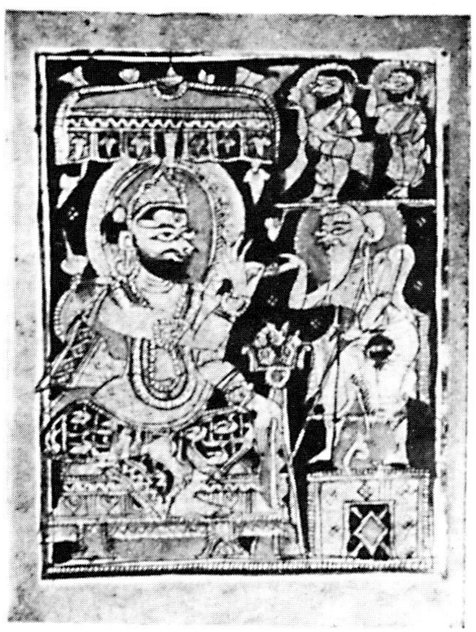

FOLIO 56

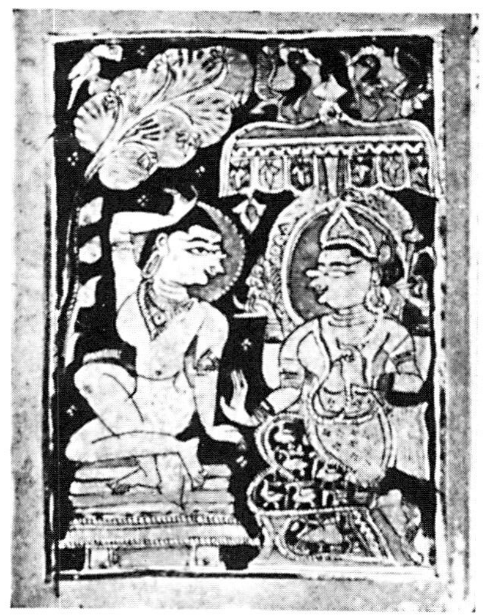

FOLIO 60

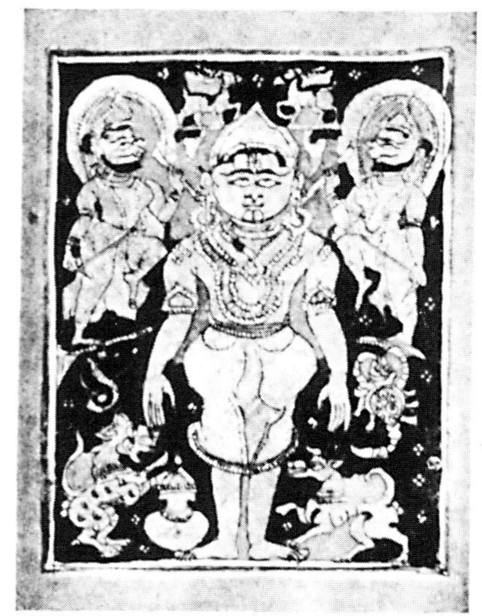

FOLIO 60

3. (17.2278)

PLATE XIII

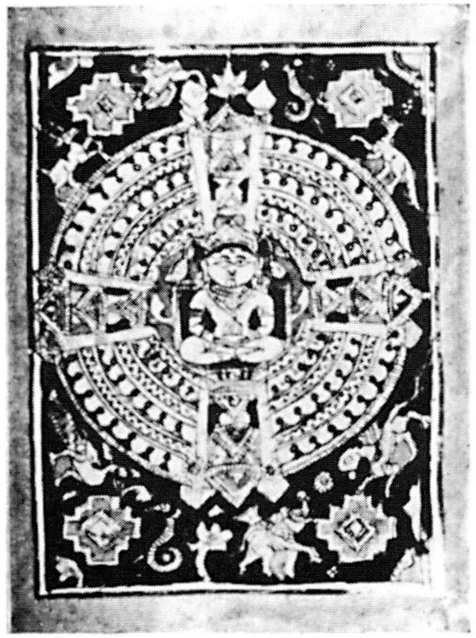

FOLIO 64

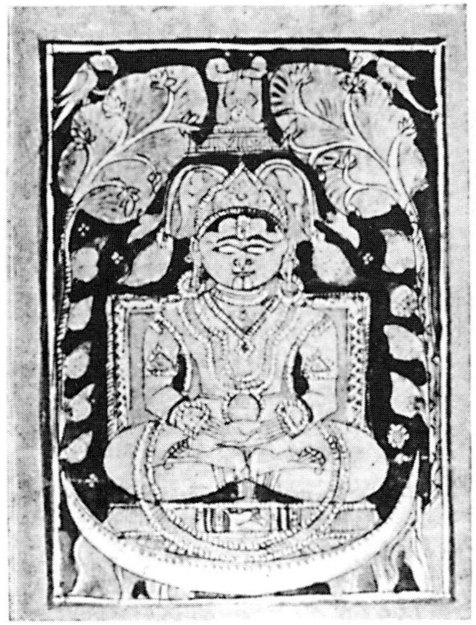

FOLIO 66

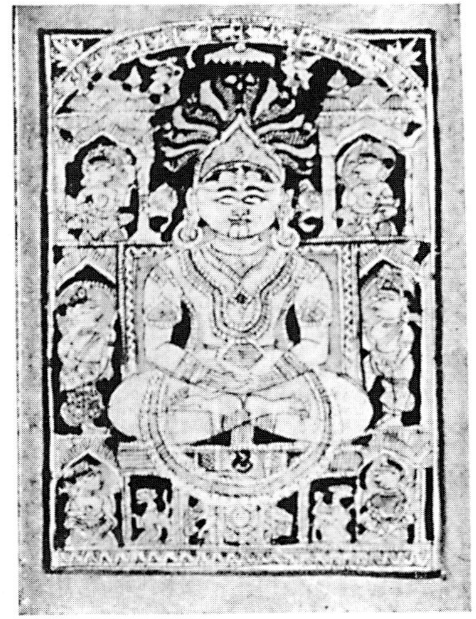

FOLIO 72

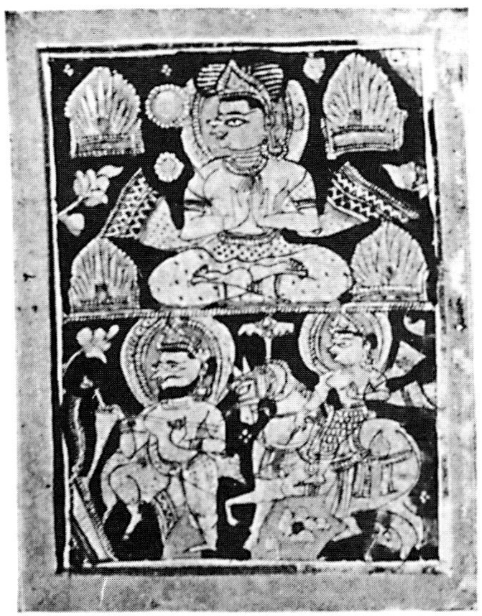

FOLIO 73

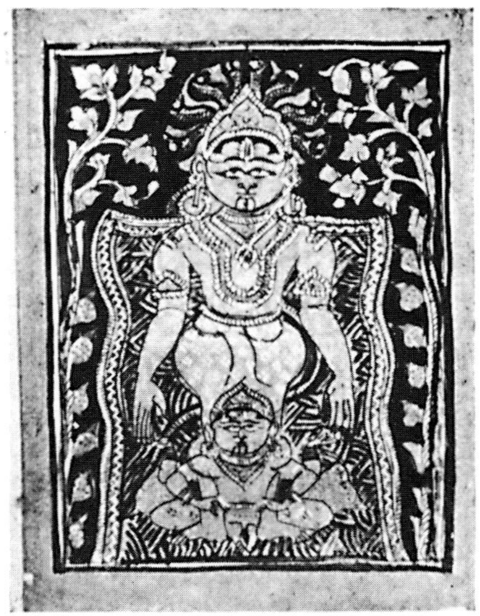

FOLIO 75

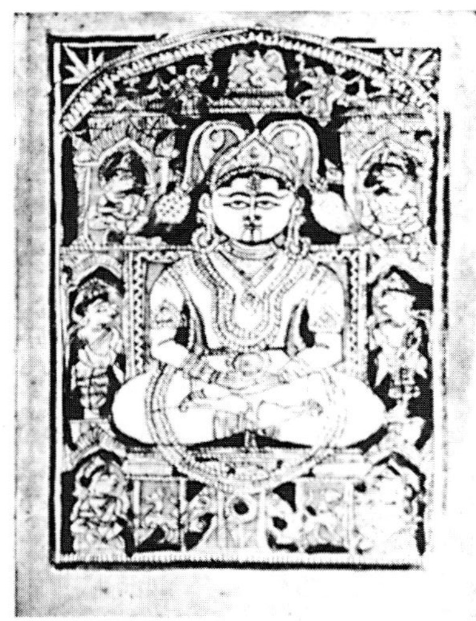

FOLIO 78

3. (17.2278)

PLATE XIV

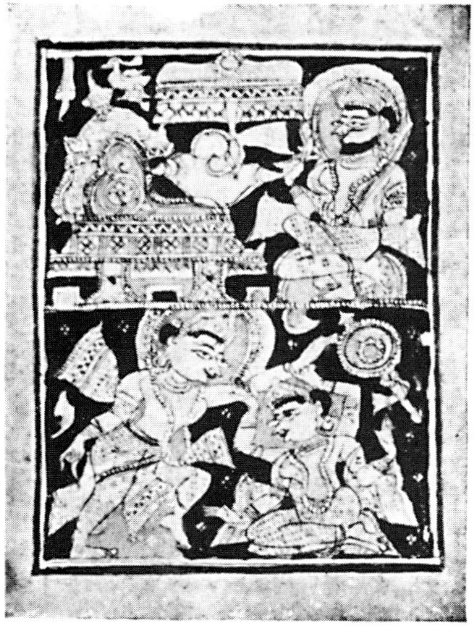

FOLIO 79

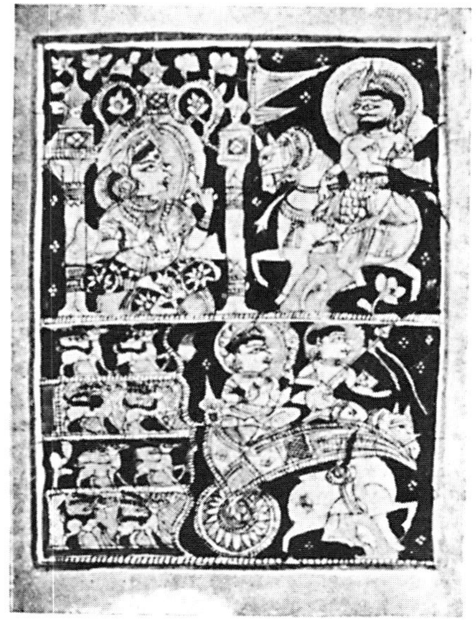

FOLIO 80

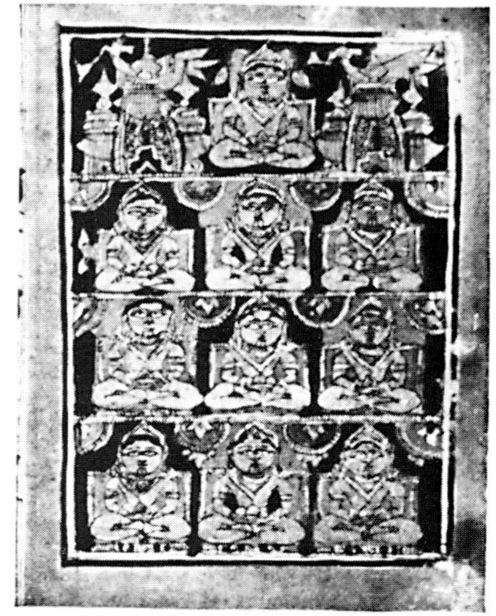

FOLIO 83

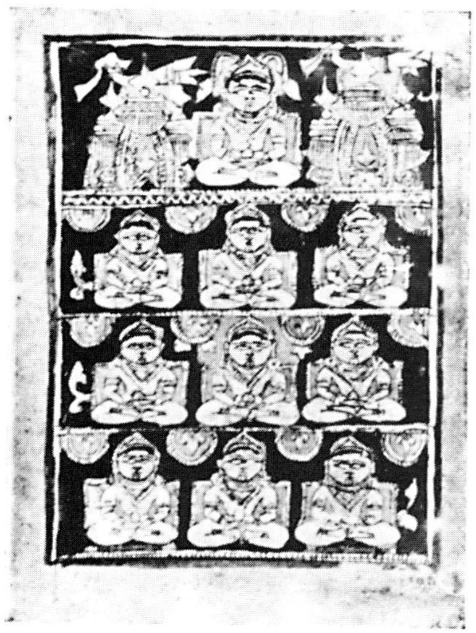

FOLIO 84

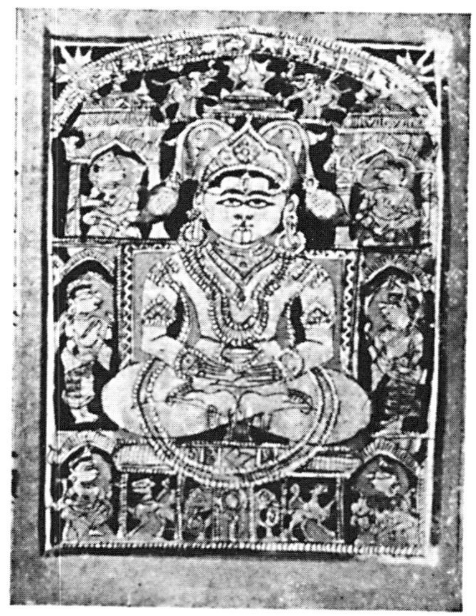

FOLIO 88

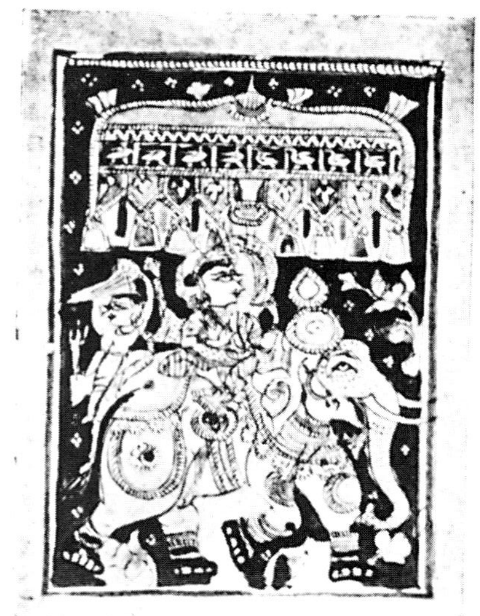

FOLIO 89

3. (17.2278)

PLATE XV

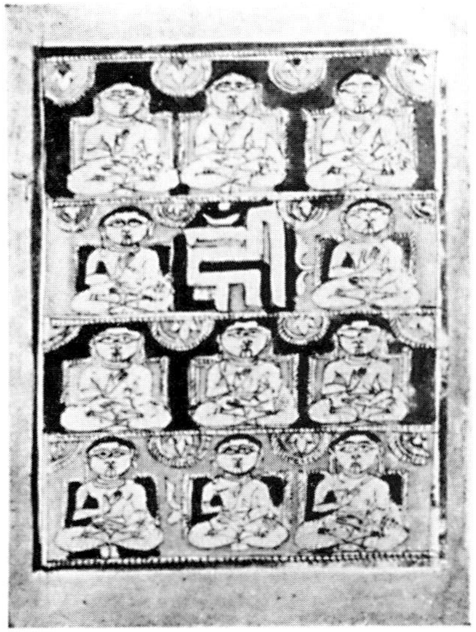

FOLIO 95

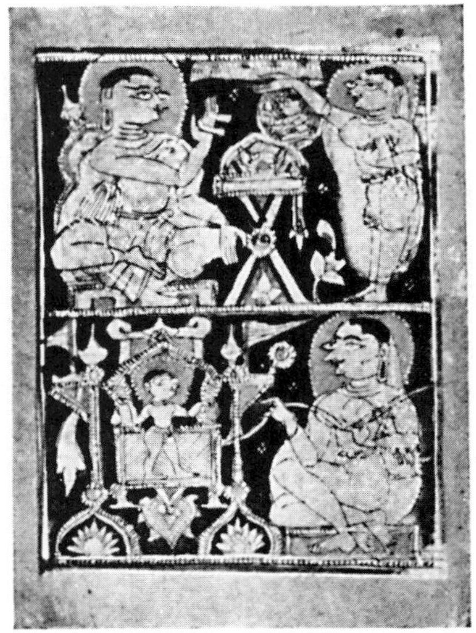

FOLIO 98

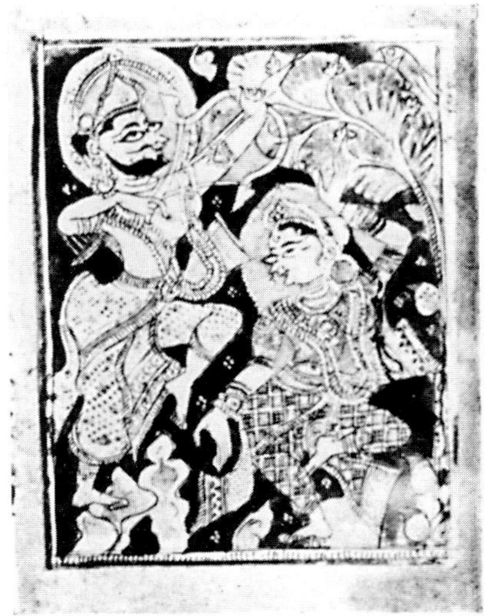

FOLIO 100

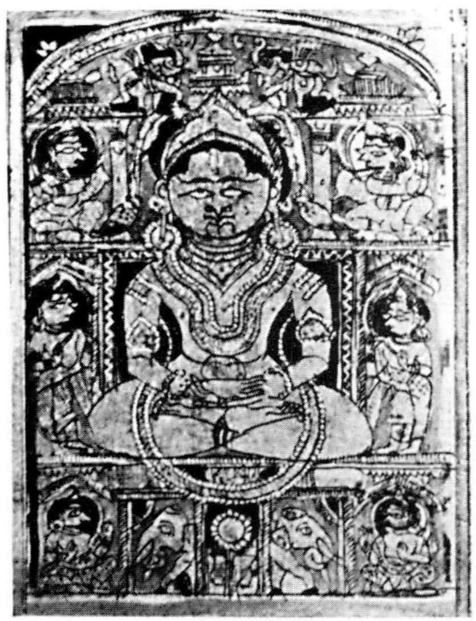

FOLIO 1

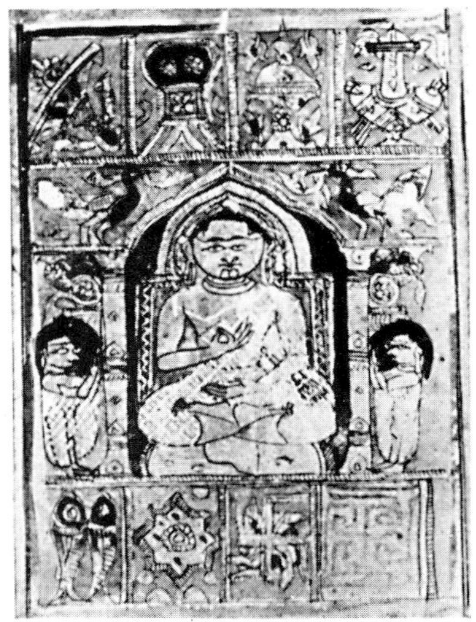

FOLIO 2

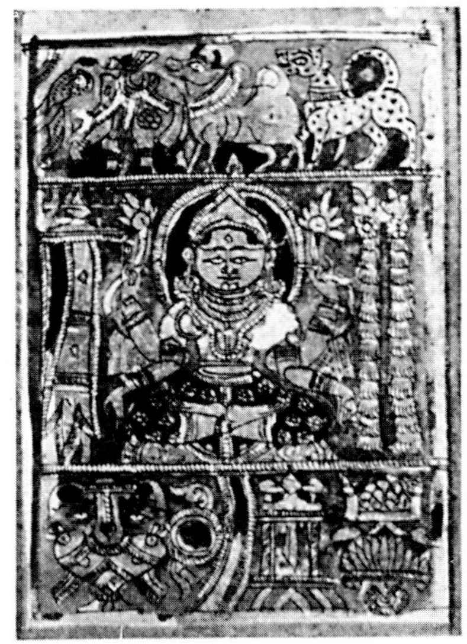

FOLIO 5

3. (17.2278) and 4. (22.364)

PLATE XVI

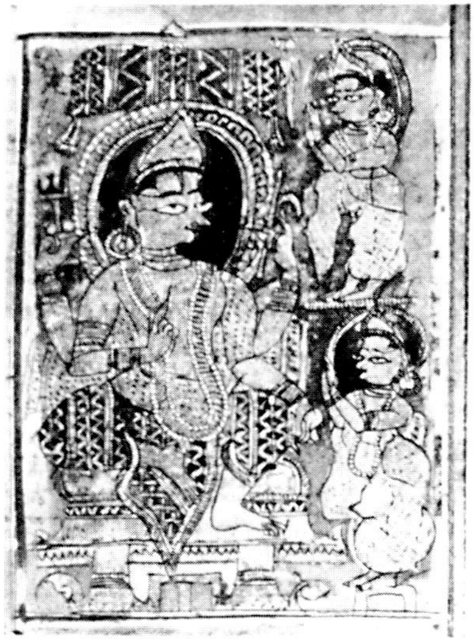
FOLIO 8

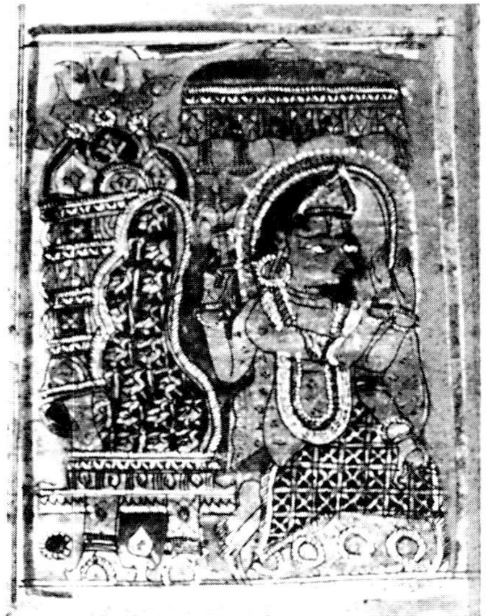
FOLIO 12

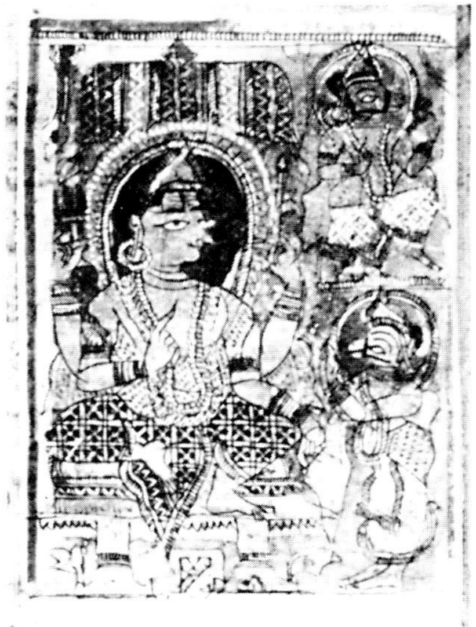
FOLIO 18

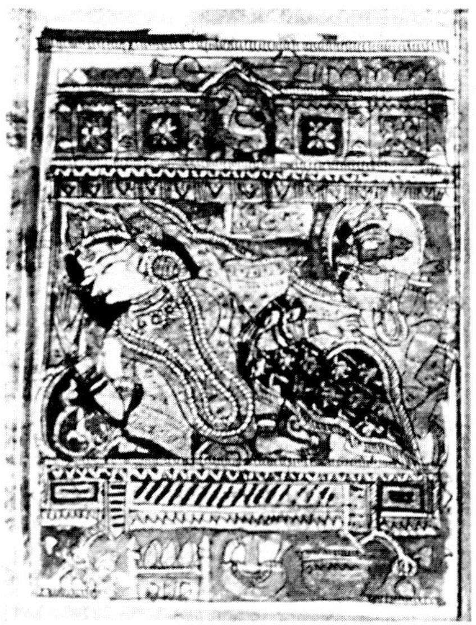
FOLIO 20

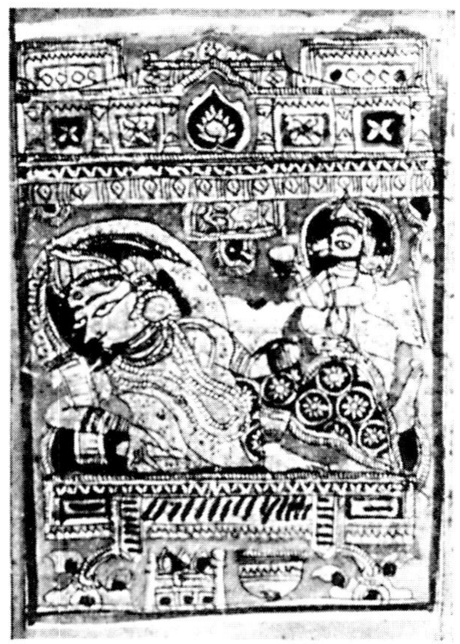
FOLIO 20

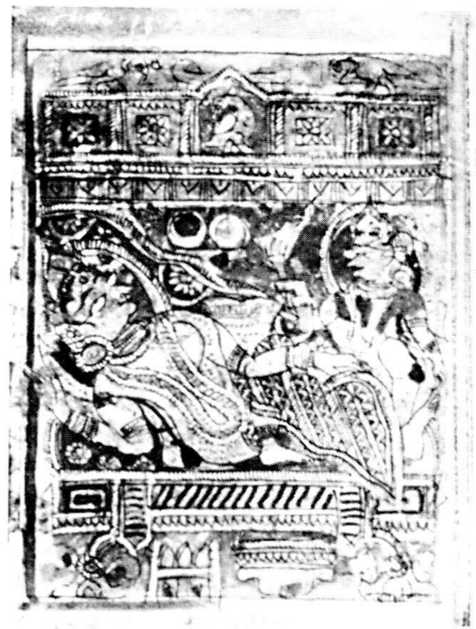
FOLIO 23

4. (22.364)

PLATE XVII

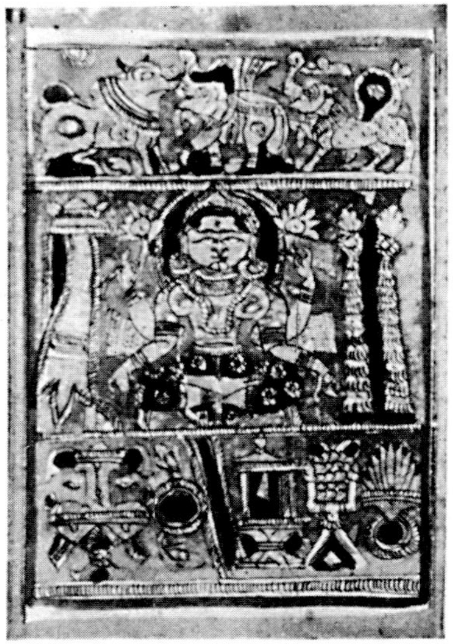

FOLIO 23

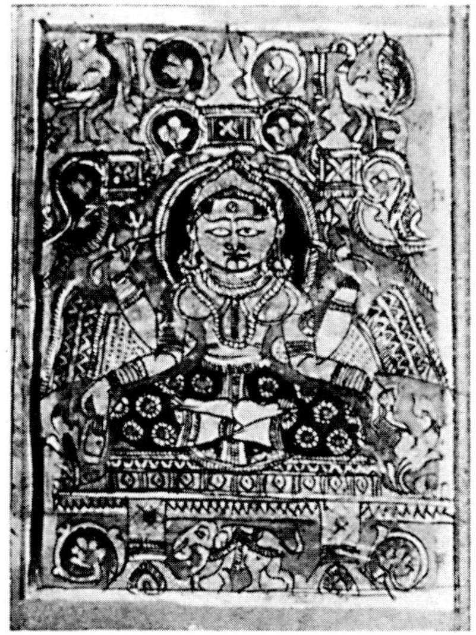

FOLIO 34

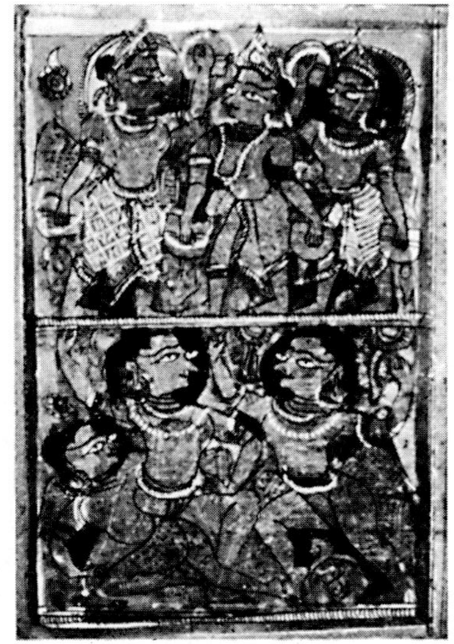

FOLIO 40

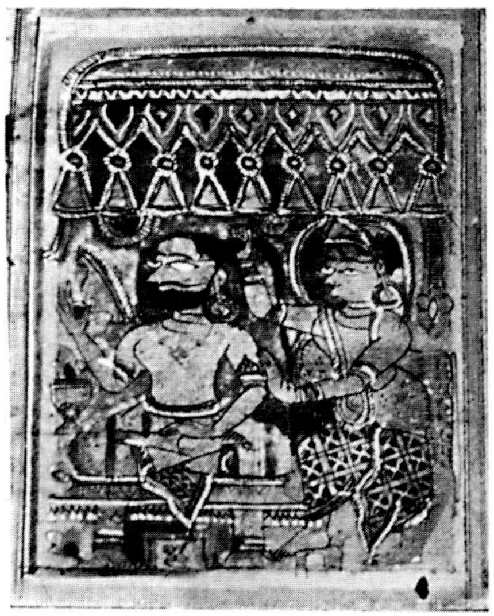

FOLIO 44

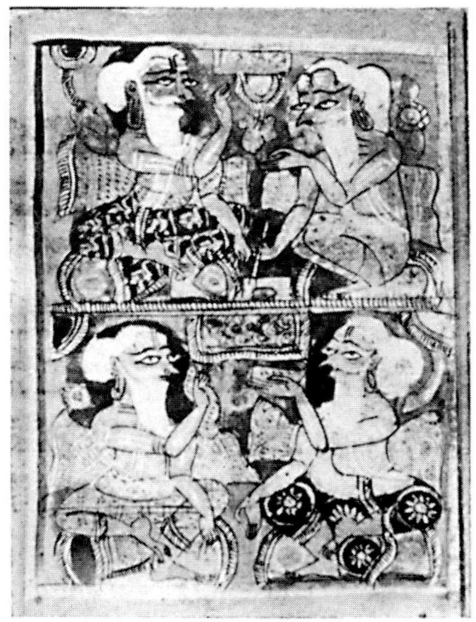

FOLIO 46

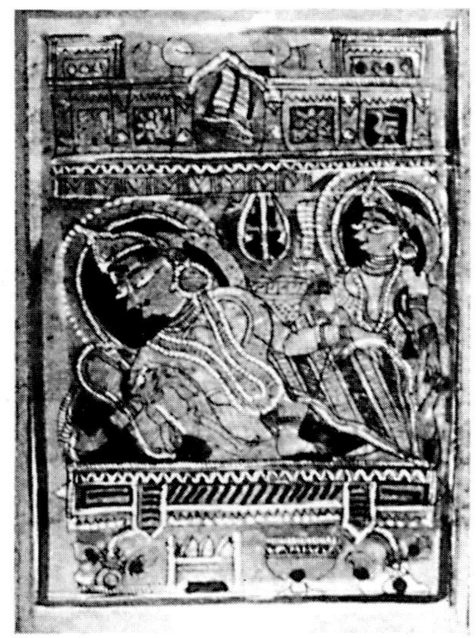

FOLIO 56

4. (22.364)

PLATE XVIII

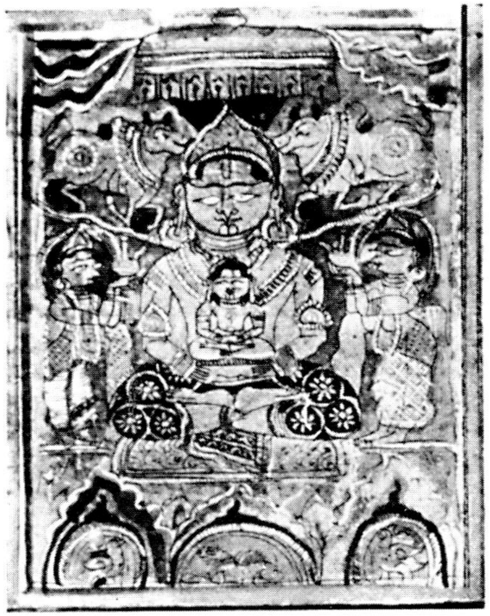
FOLIO 57

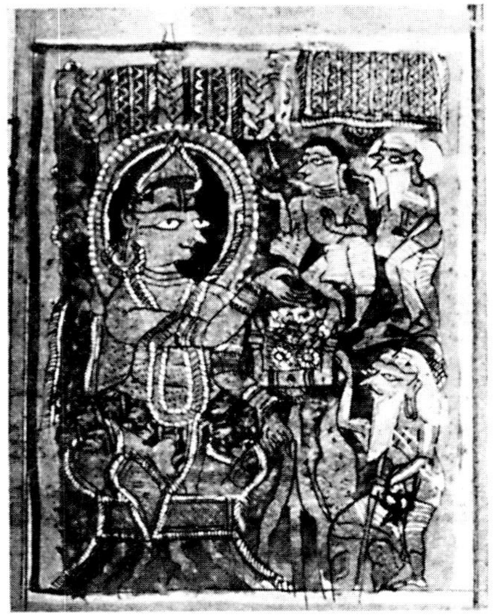
FOLIO 64

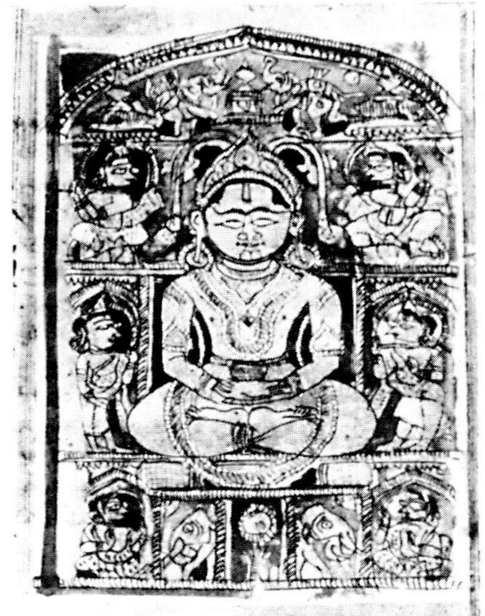
FOLIO 66

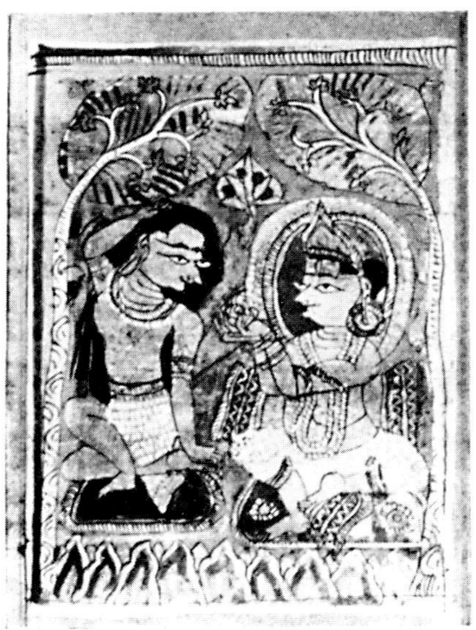
FOLIO 68

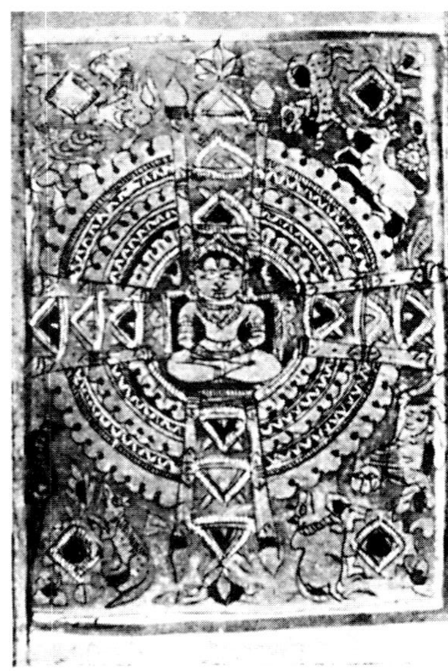
FOLIO 71

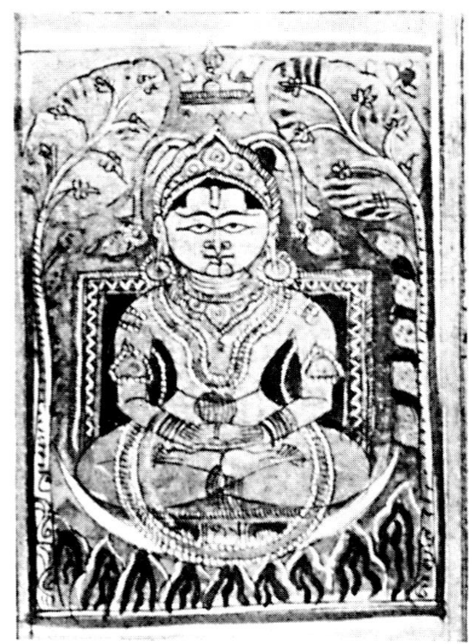
FOLIO 73

4. (22.364)

PLATE XIX

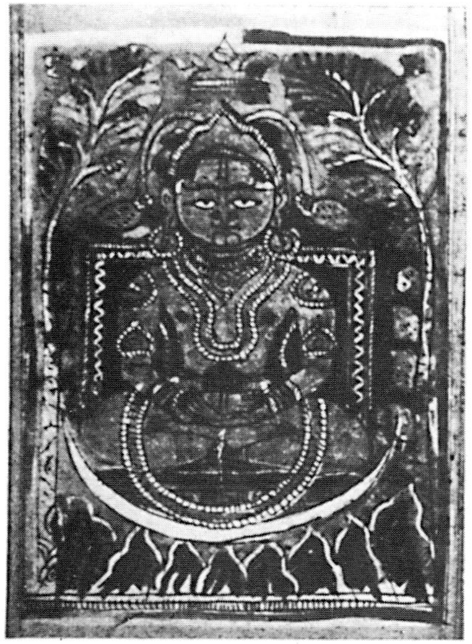
FOLIO 80

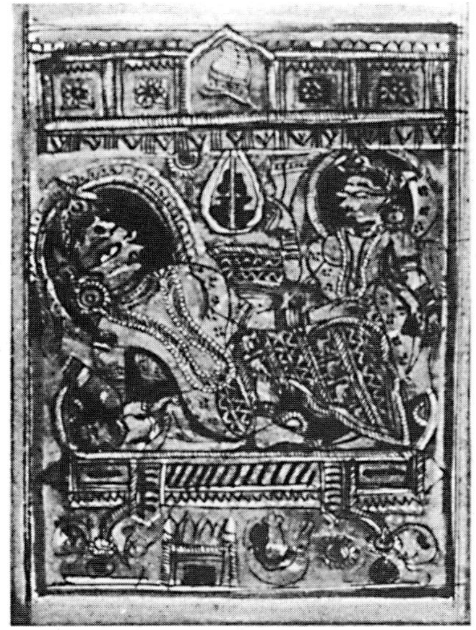
FOLIO 82

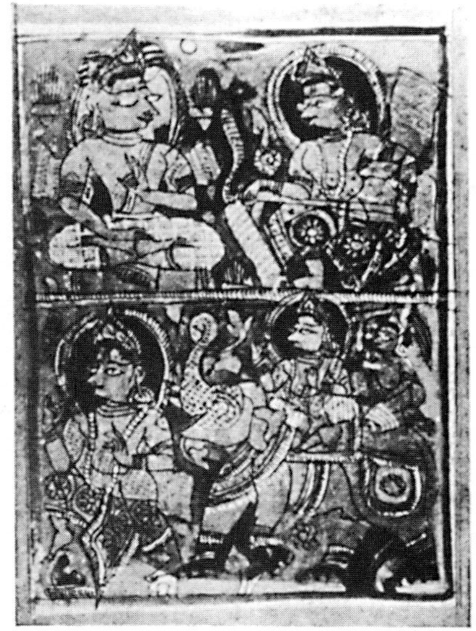
FOLIO 83

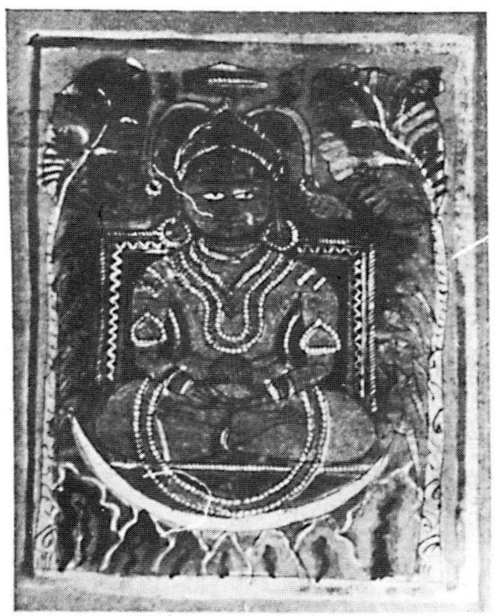
FOLIO 88

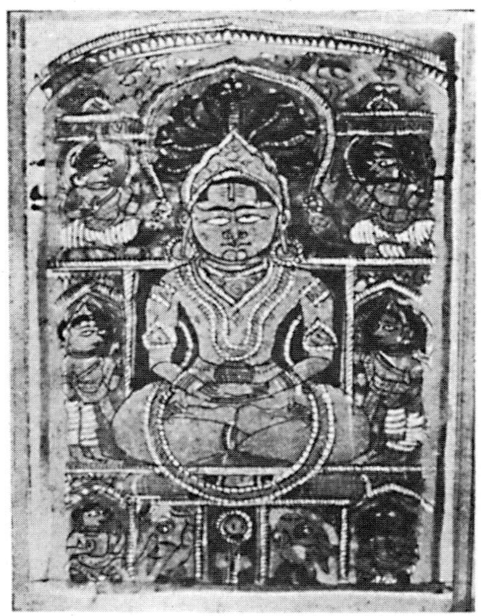
FOLIO 89

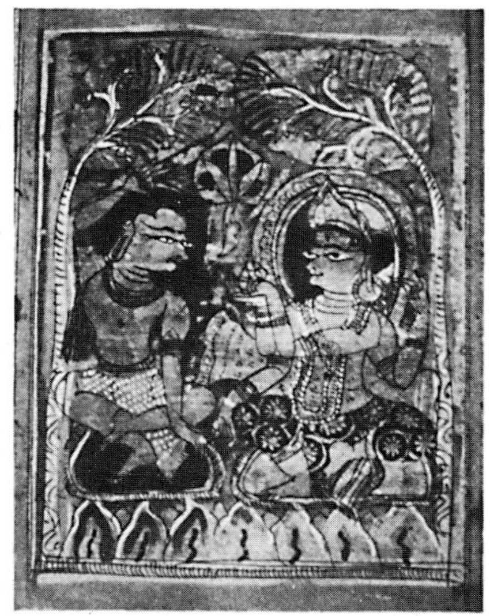
FOLIO 90

4. (22.364)

PLATE XX

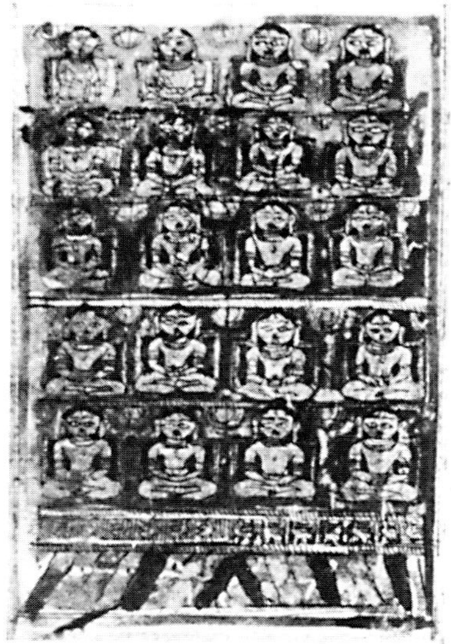

FOLIO 95

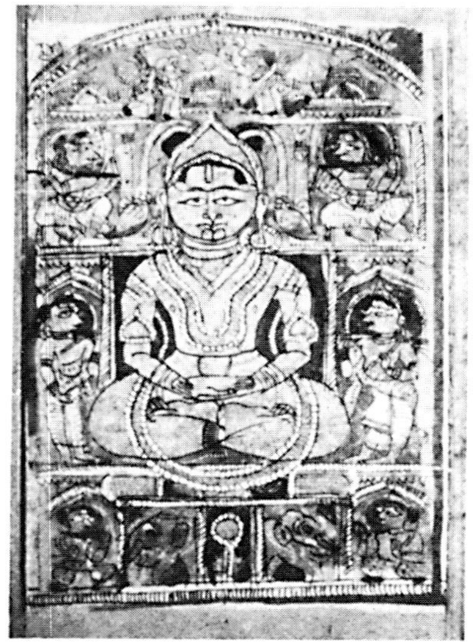

FOLIO 99

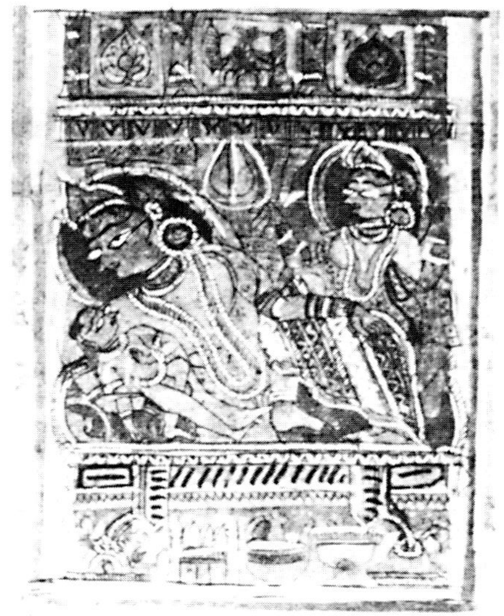

FOLIO 100

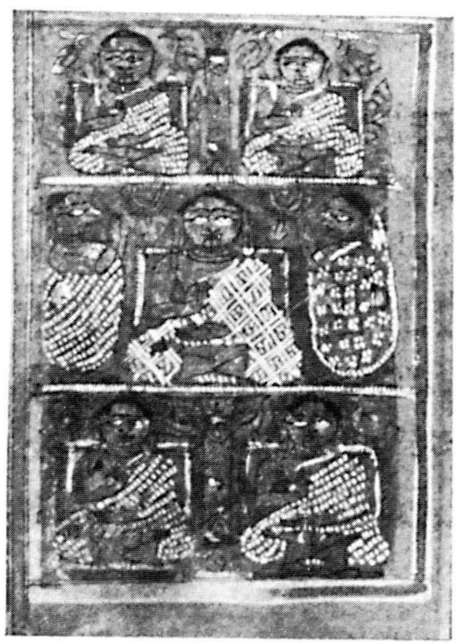

FOLIO 107

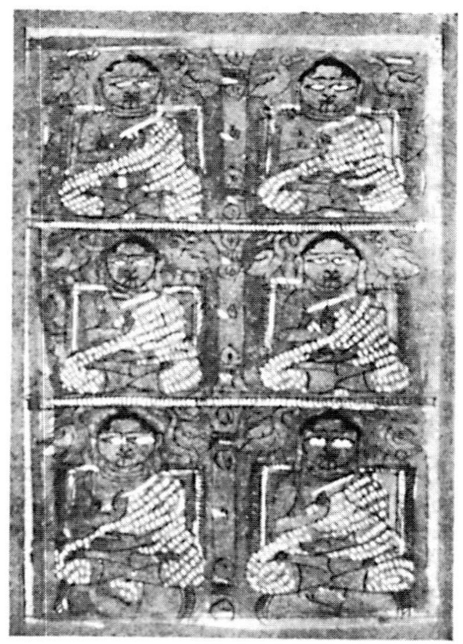

FOLIO 107

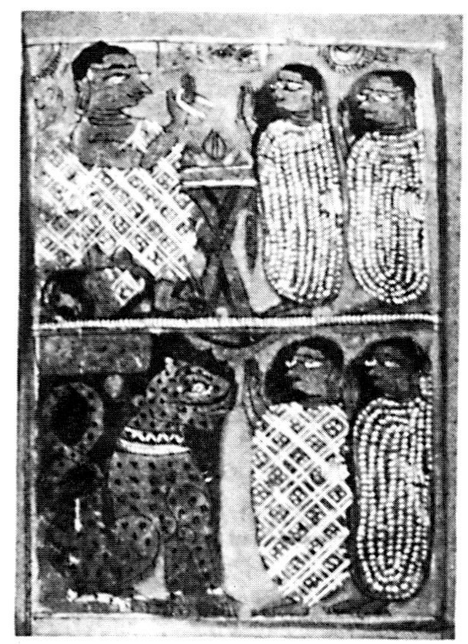

FOLIO 123

4. (22.364)

PLATE XXI

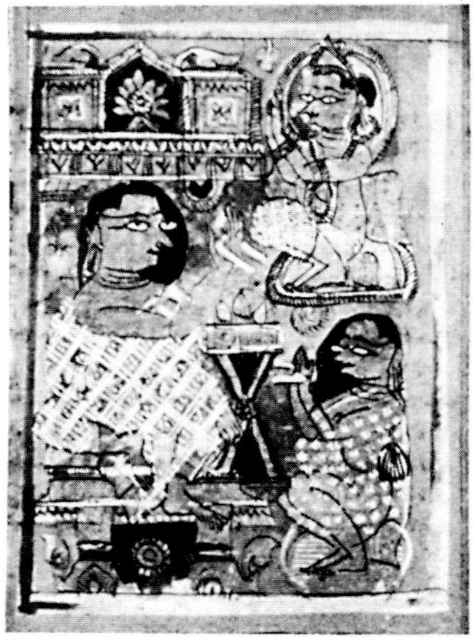

FOLIO 124

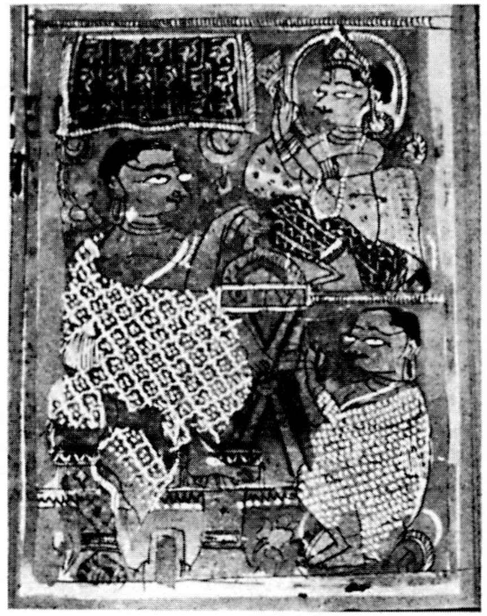

FOLIO 142

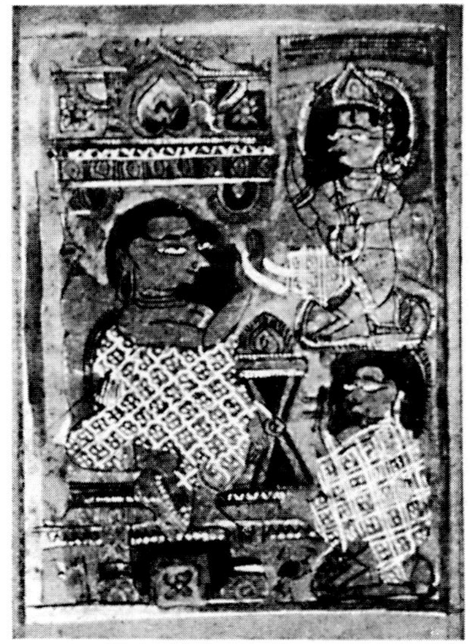

FOLIO 143

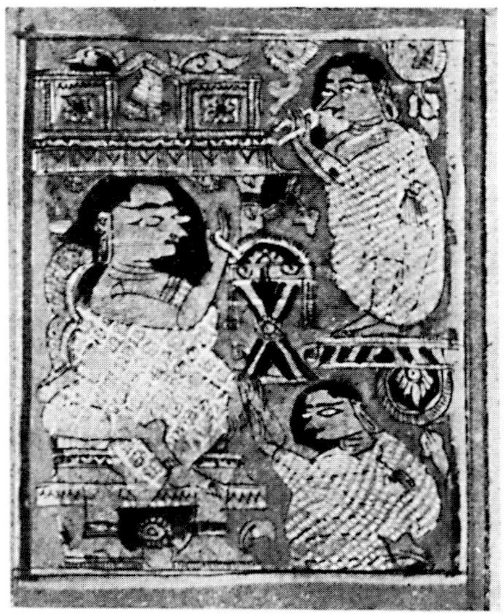

FOLIO 144

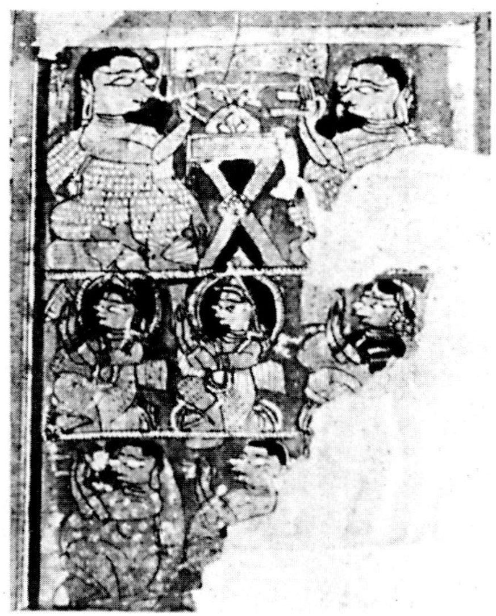

FOLIO 147

4. (22.364)

PLATE XXII

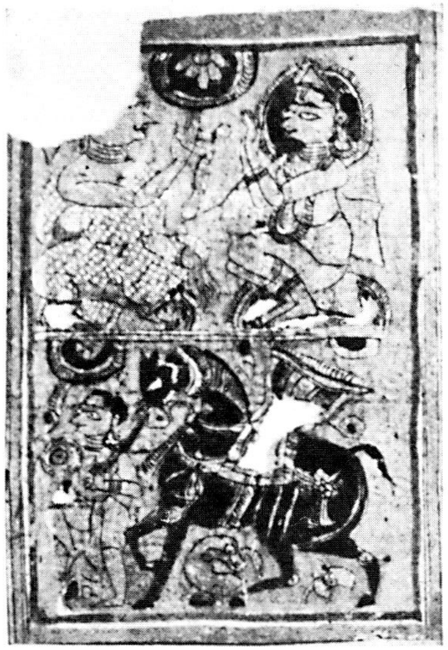
FOLIO 1

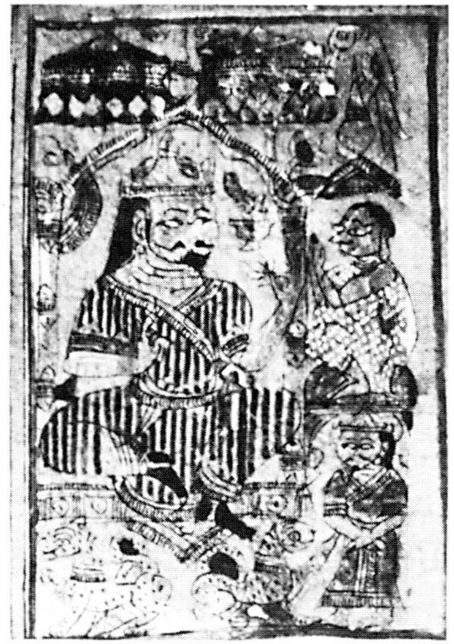
FOLIO 2

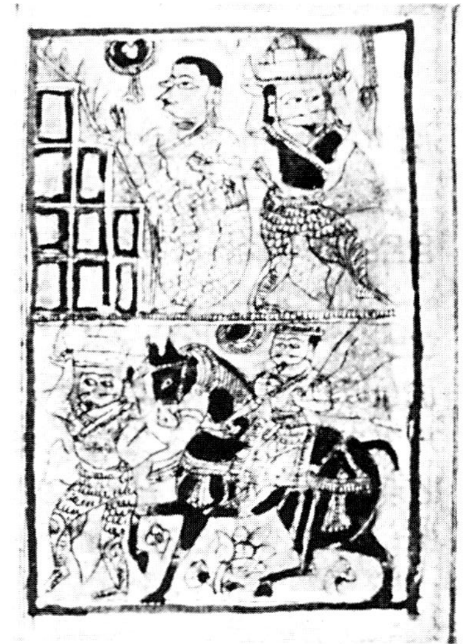
FOLIO 5

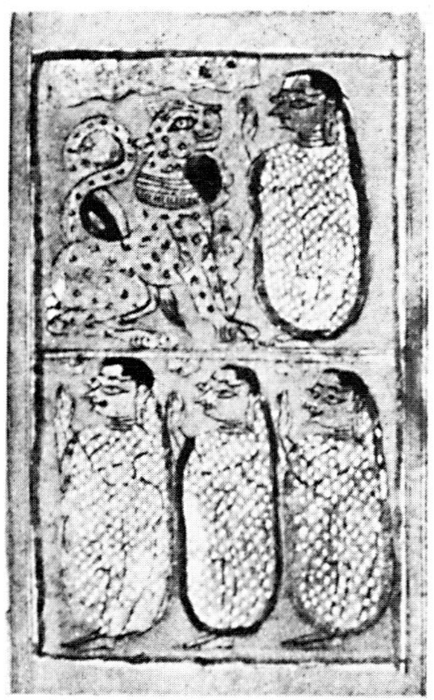
FOLIO 6

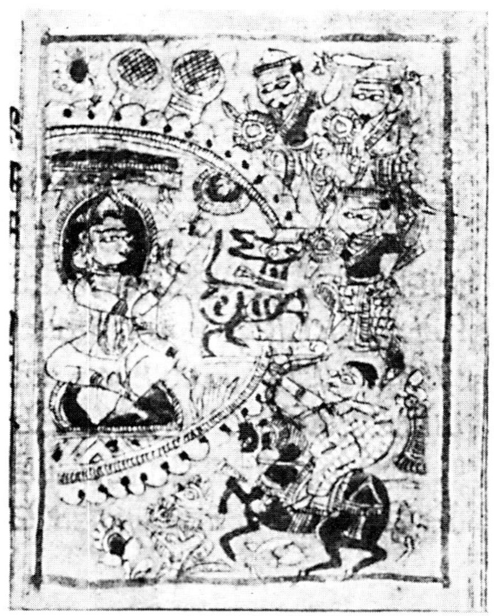
FOLIO 8

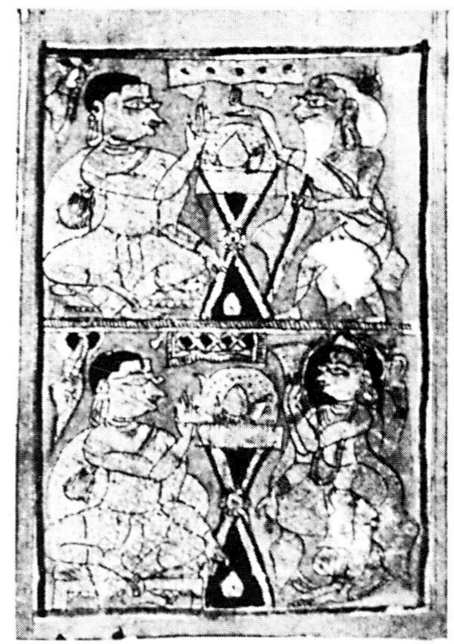
FOLIO 9

6. (17.2279)

PLATE XXIII

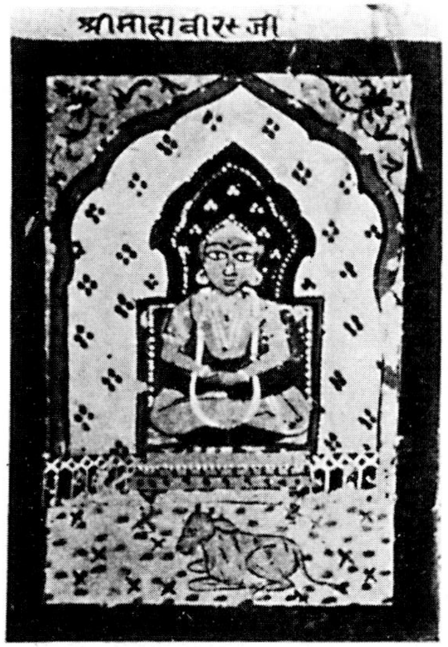

FOLIO 1

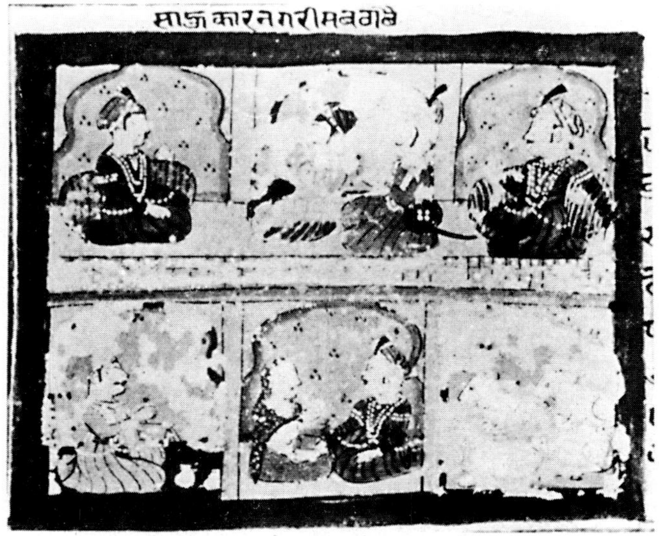

FOLIO 3

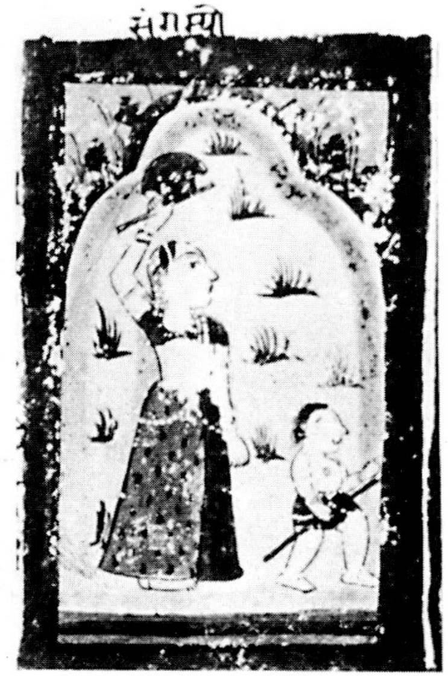

FOLIO 4

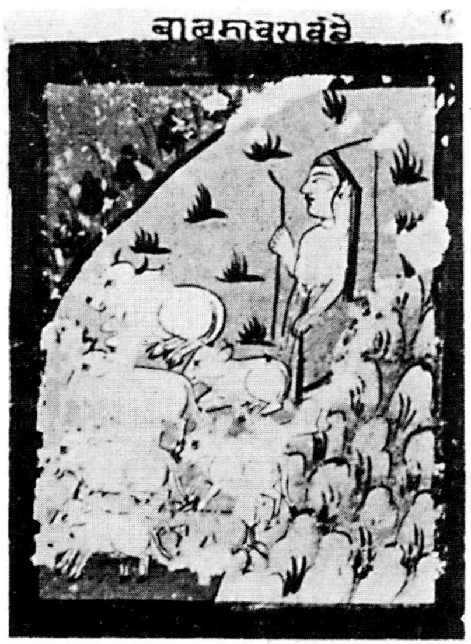

FOLIO 4

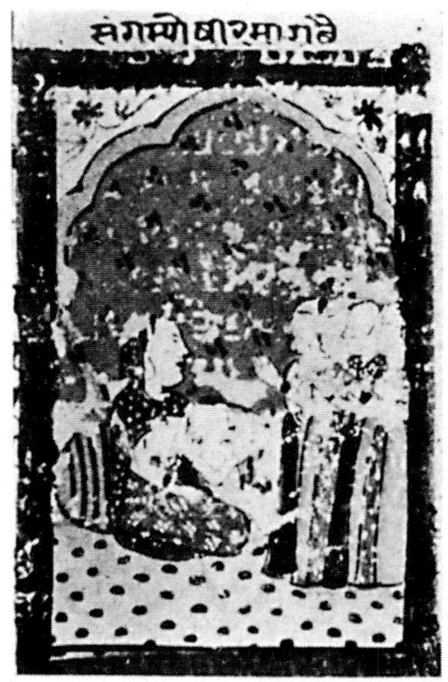

FOLIO 4

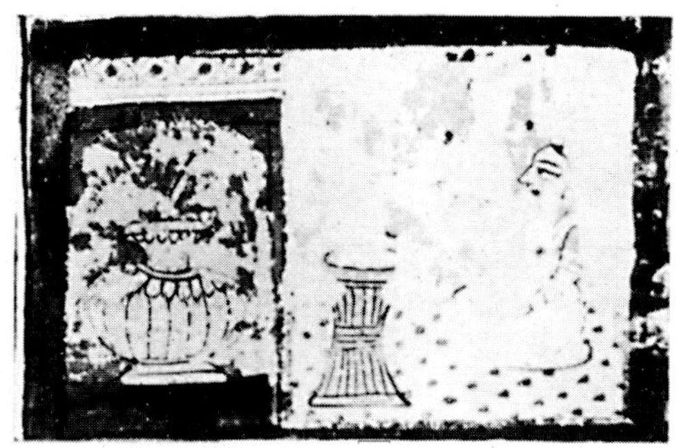

FOLIO 5

7. (21.1673)

PLATE XXIV

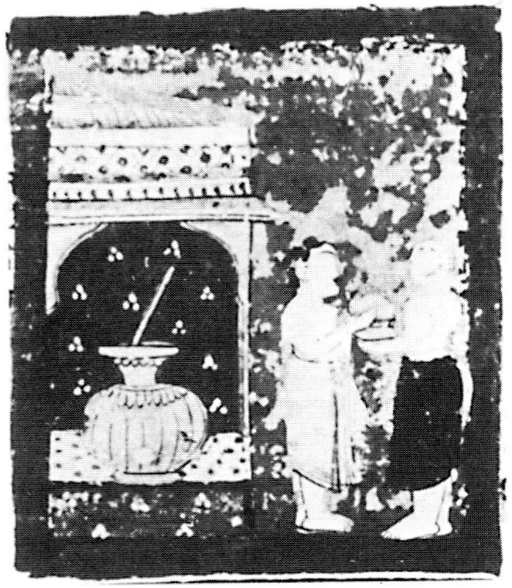

FOLIO 5

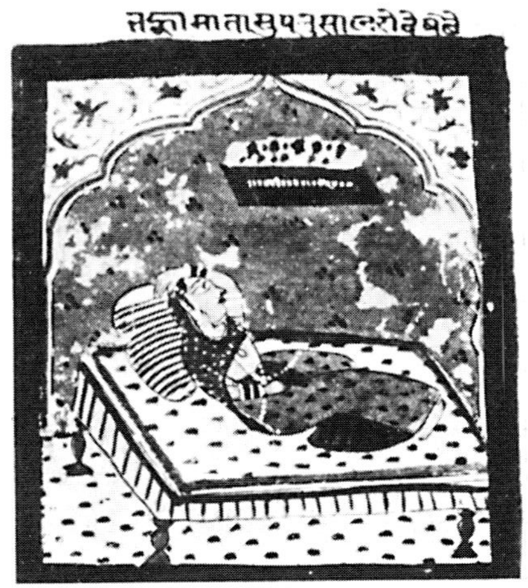

FOLIO 6

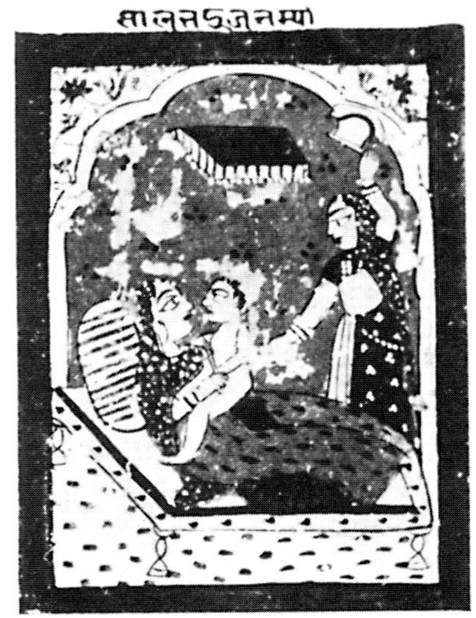

FOLIO 7

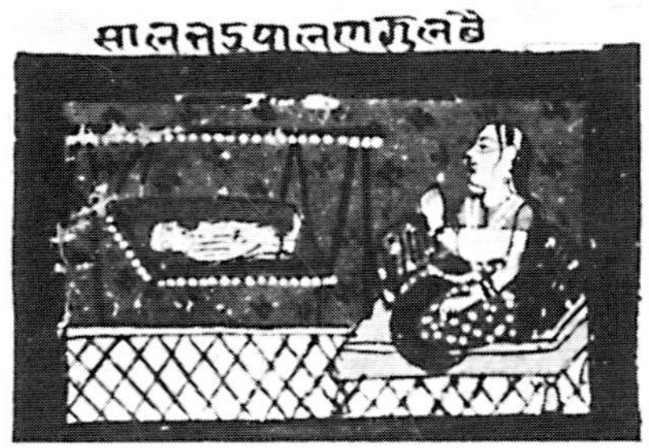

FOLIO 8

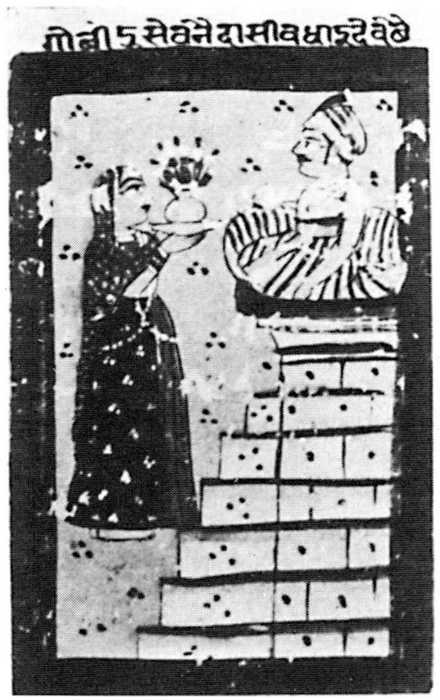

FOLIO 7

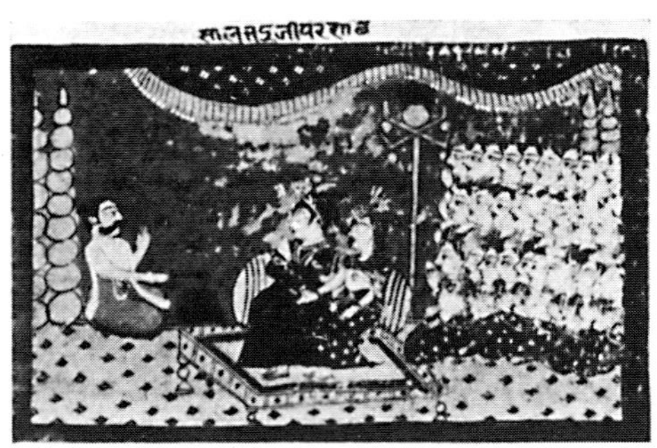

FOLIO 8

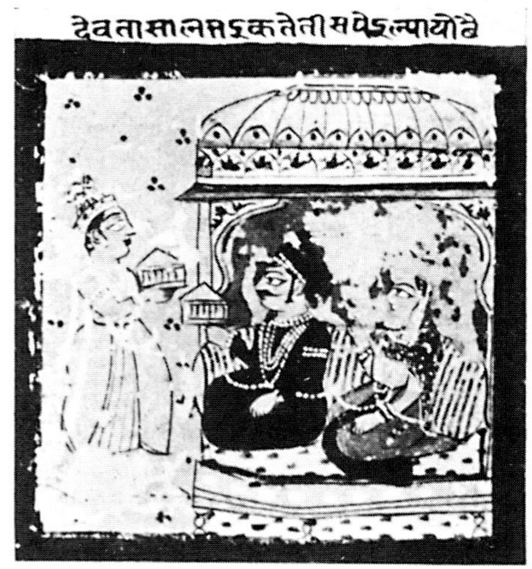

FOLIO 9

7. (21.1673)

PLATE XXV

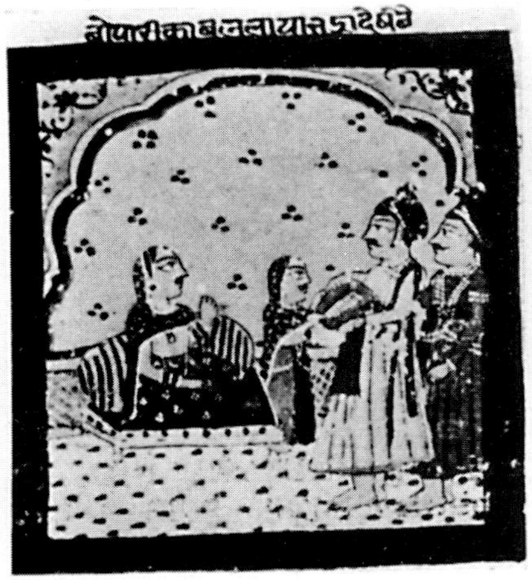

FOLIO 10

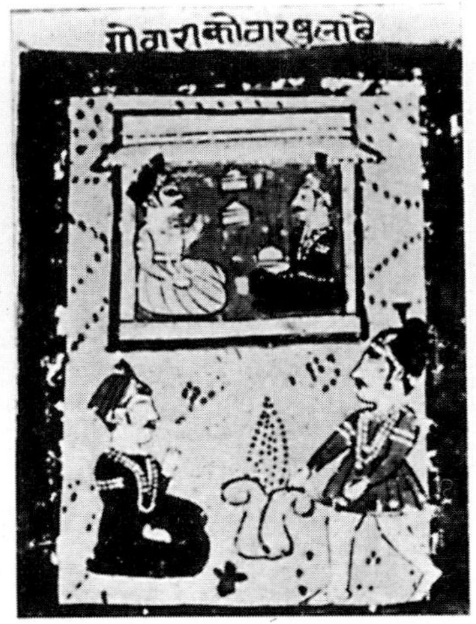

FOLIO 11

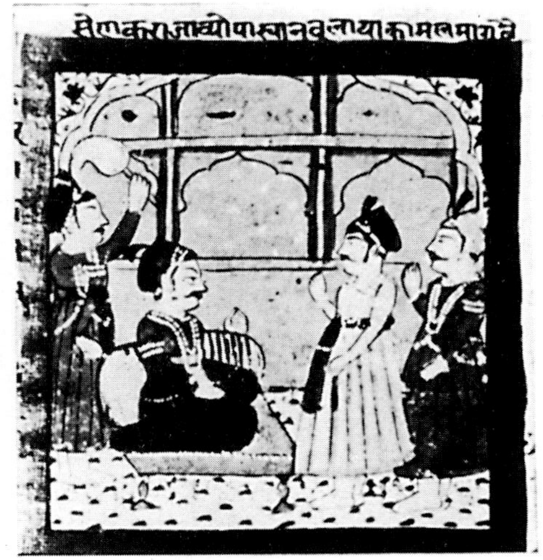

FOLIO 11

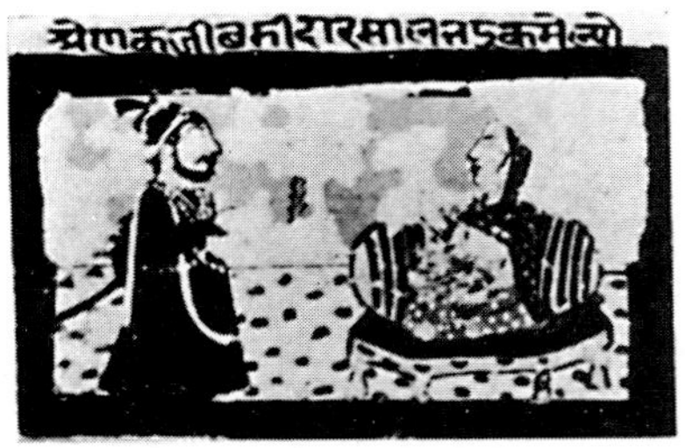

FOLIO 12

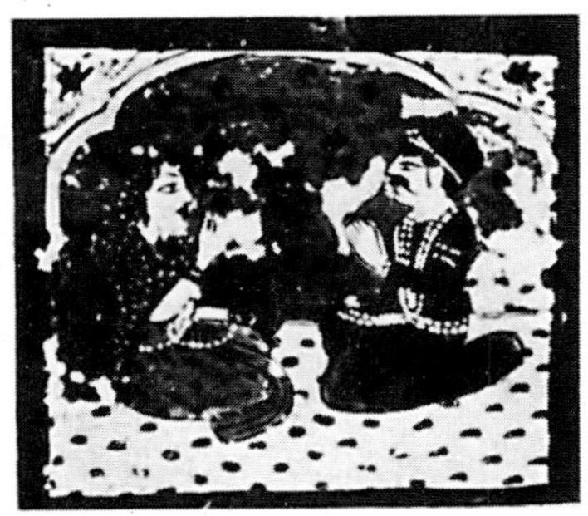

FOLIO 12

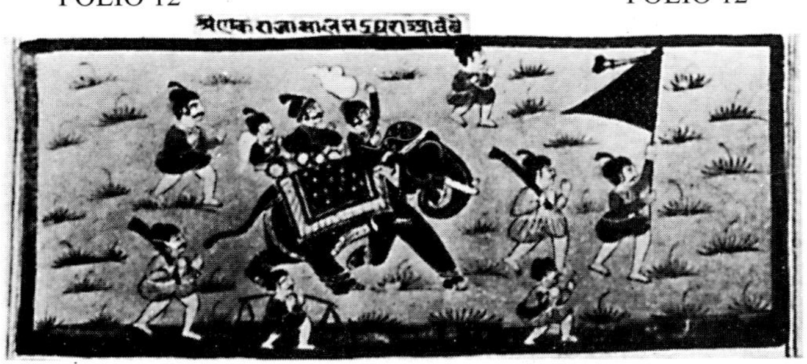

FOLIO 14

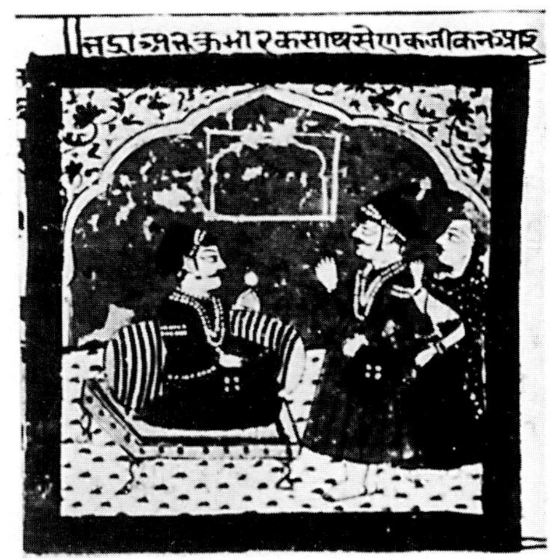

FOLIO 13

7. (21.1673)

PLATE XXVI

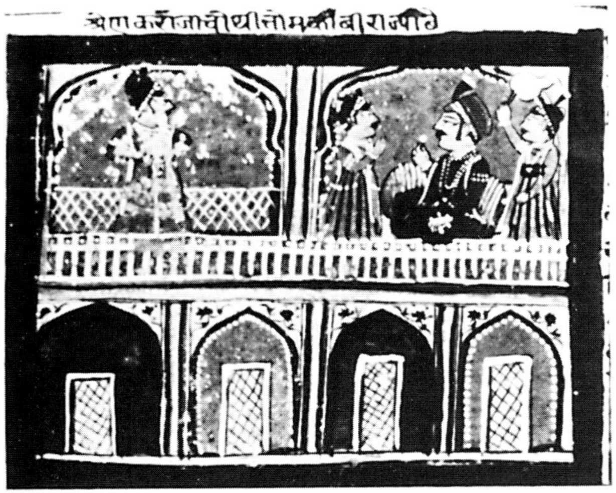

FOLIO 15

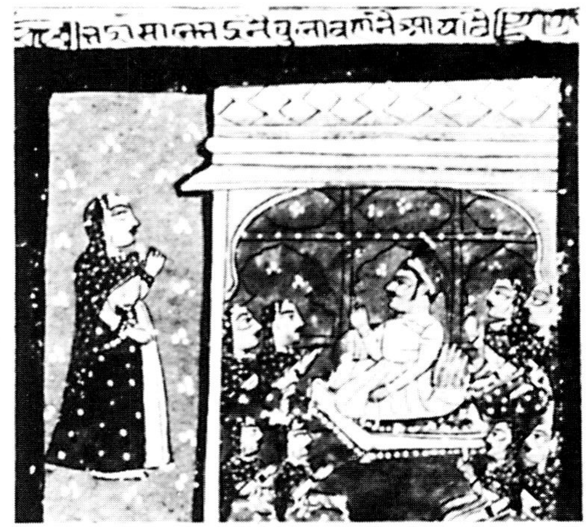

FOLIO 15

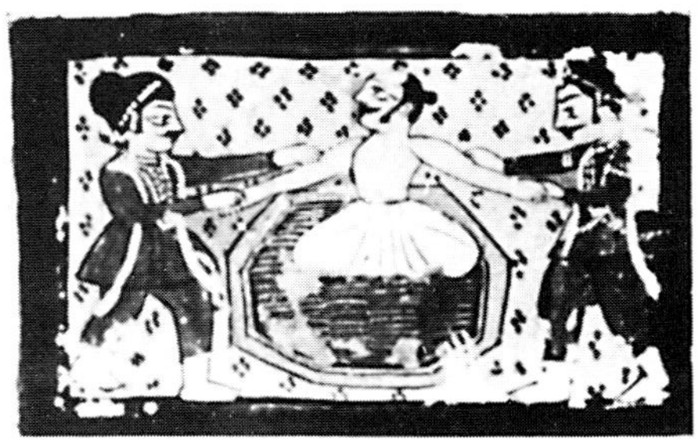

FOLIO 19

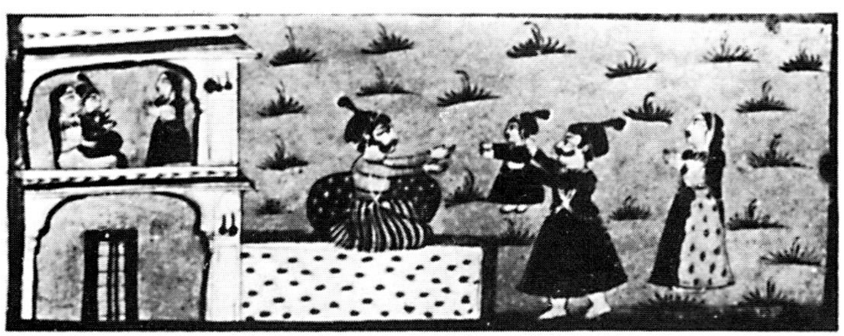

FOLIO 18

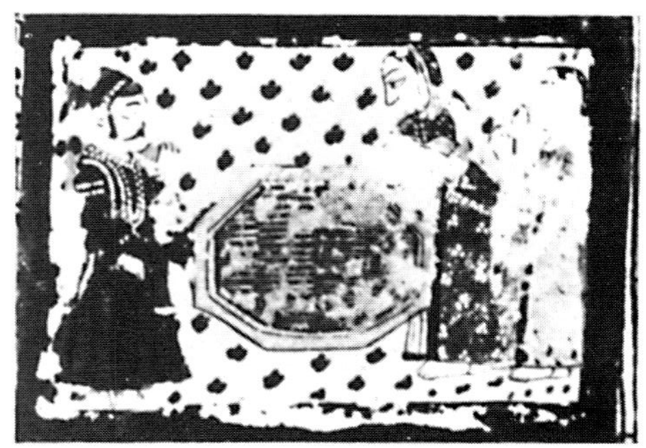

FOLIO 19

7. (21.1673)

PLATE XXVII

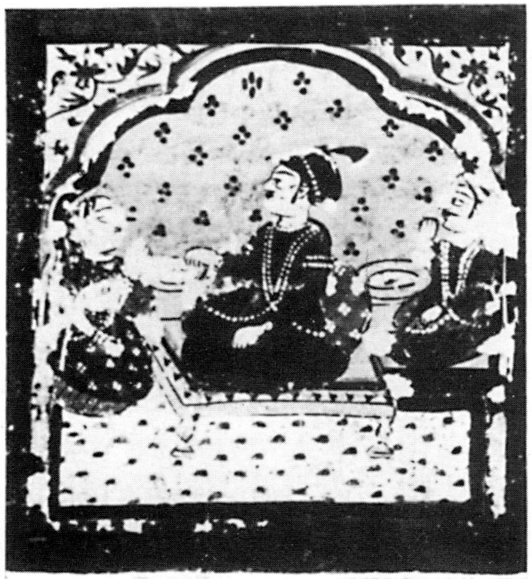

FOLIO 20

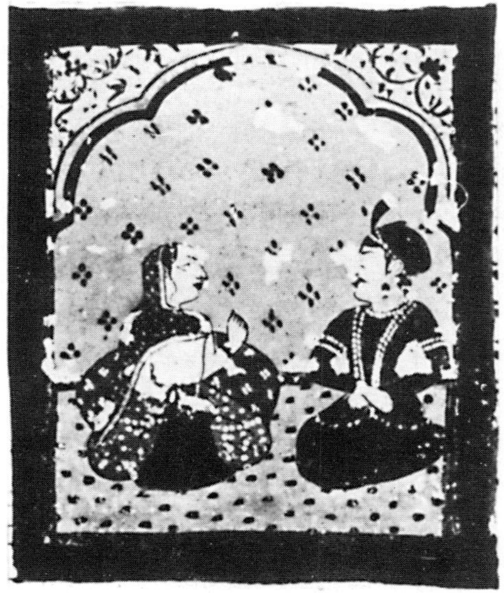

FOLIO 21

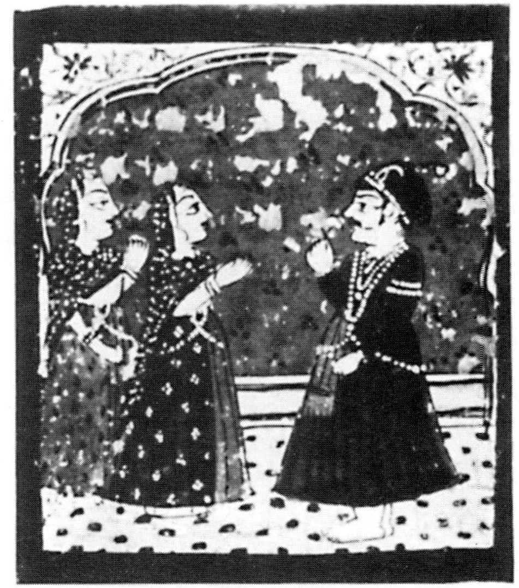

FOLIO 22

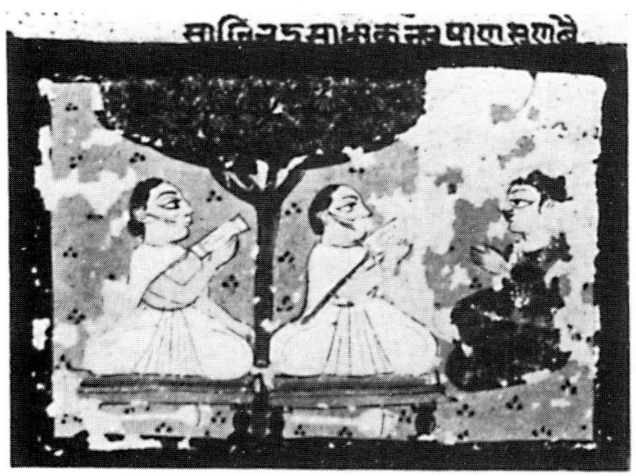

FOLIO 23

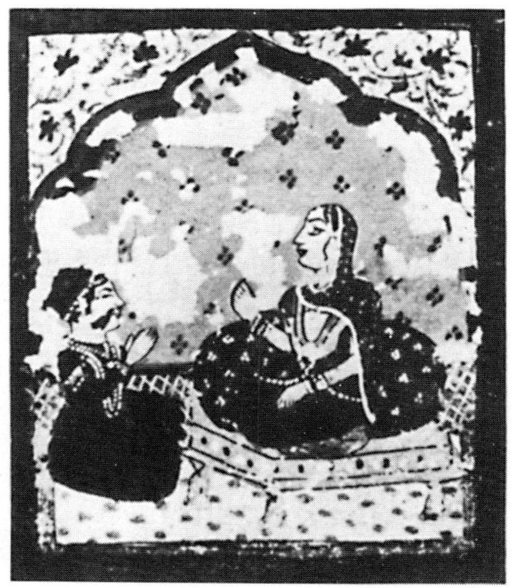

FOLIO 24

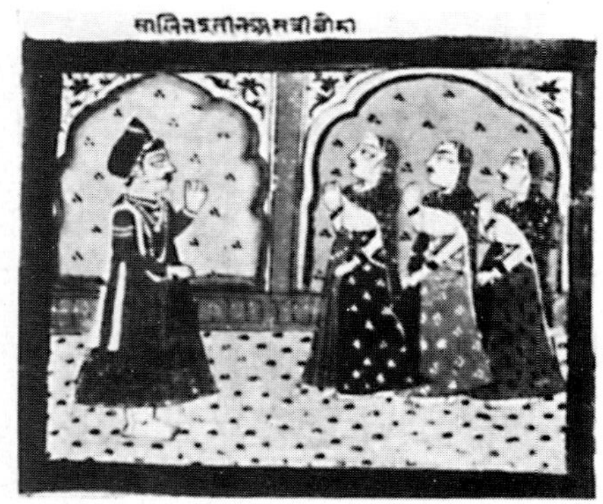

FOLIO 26

7. (21.1673)

PLATE XXVIII

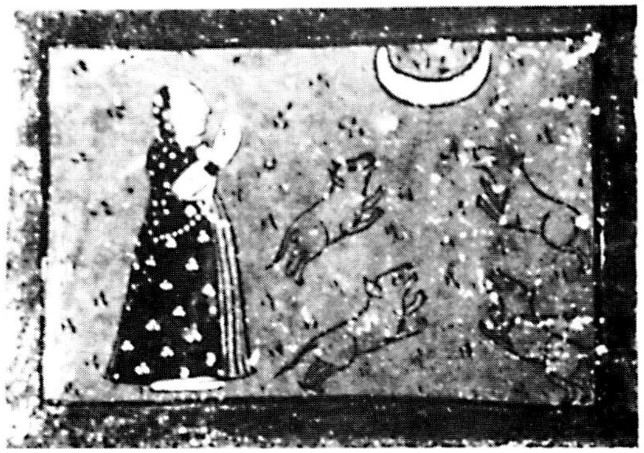

FOLIO 26

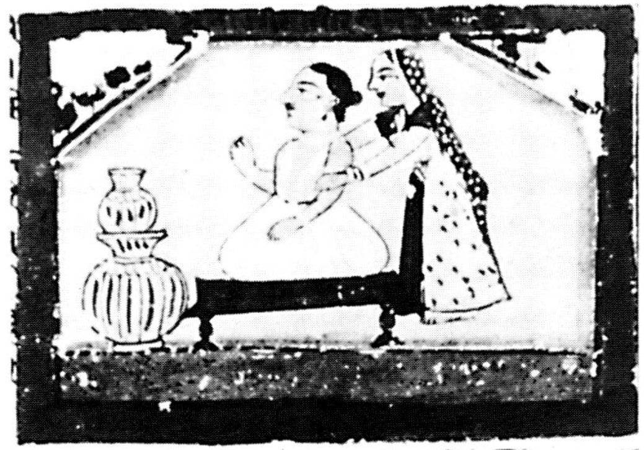

FOLIO 27

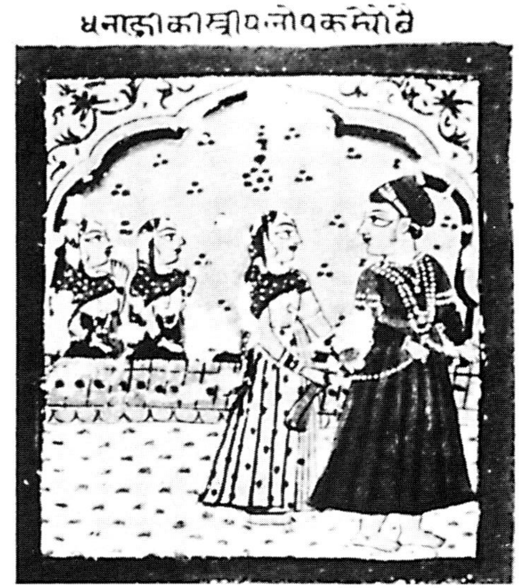

FOLIO 28

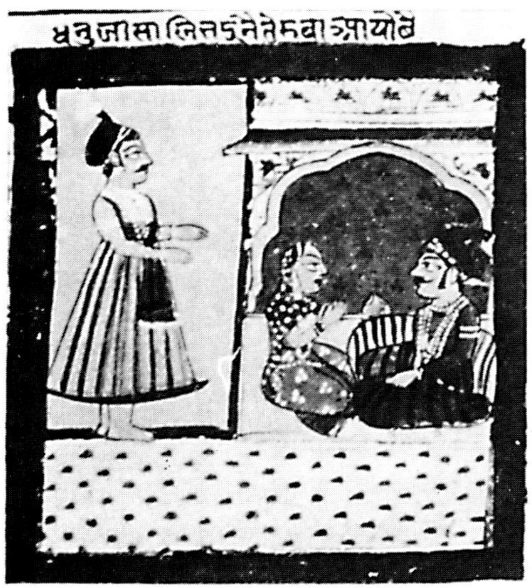

FOLIO 29

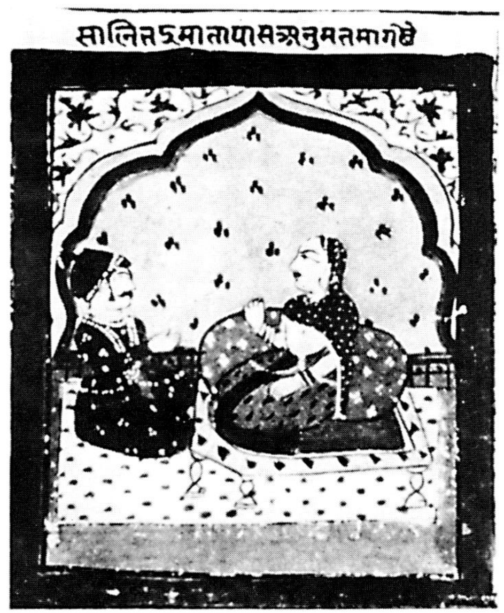

FOLIO 30

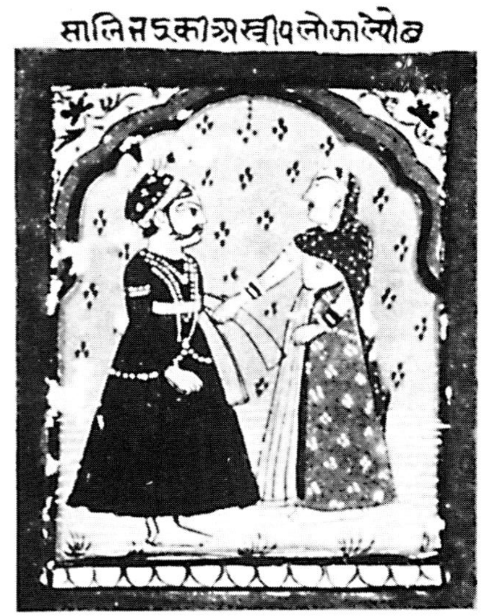

FOLIO 31

7. (21.1673)

PLATE XXIX

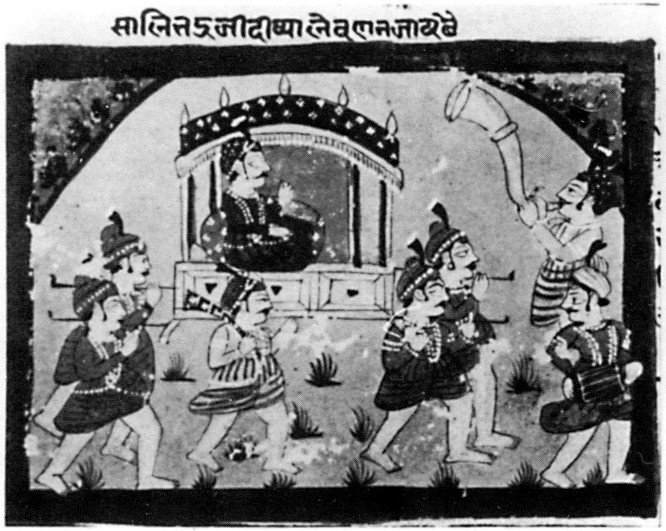

FOLIO 32

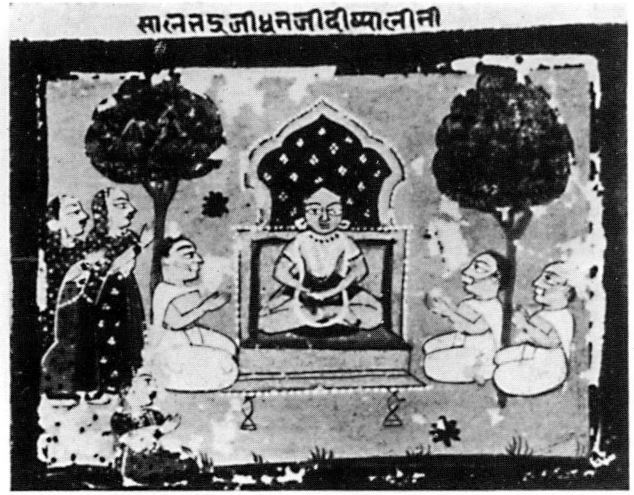

FOLIO 33

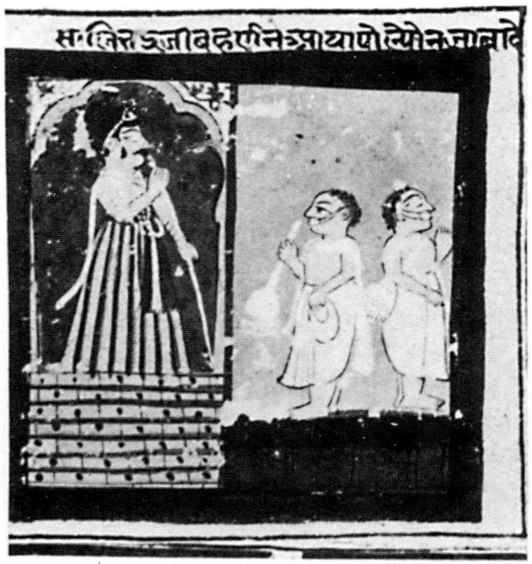

FOLIO 34

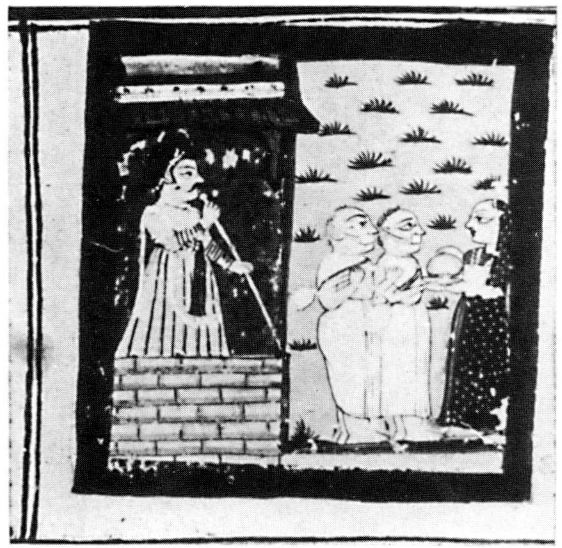

FOLIO 35

7. (21.1673)

PLATE XXX

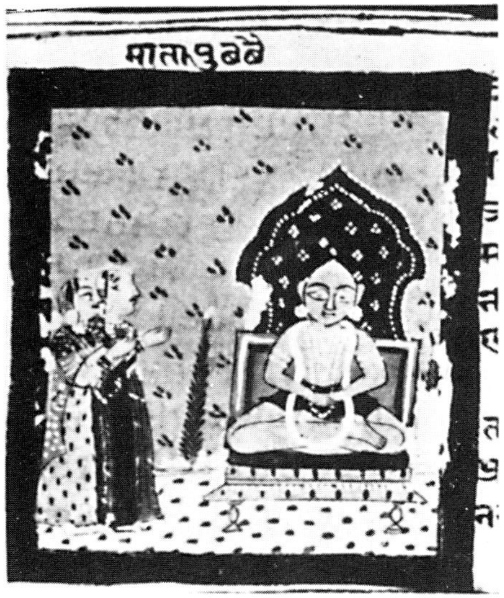

FOLIO 36

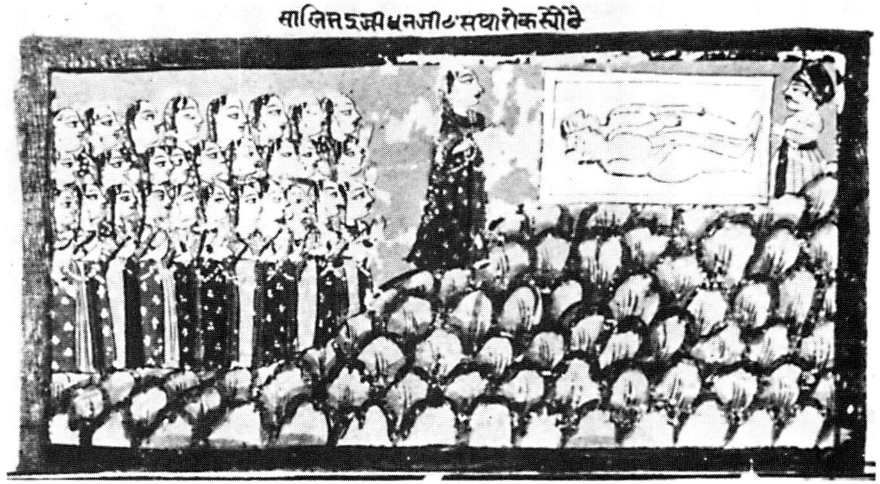

FOLIO 37

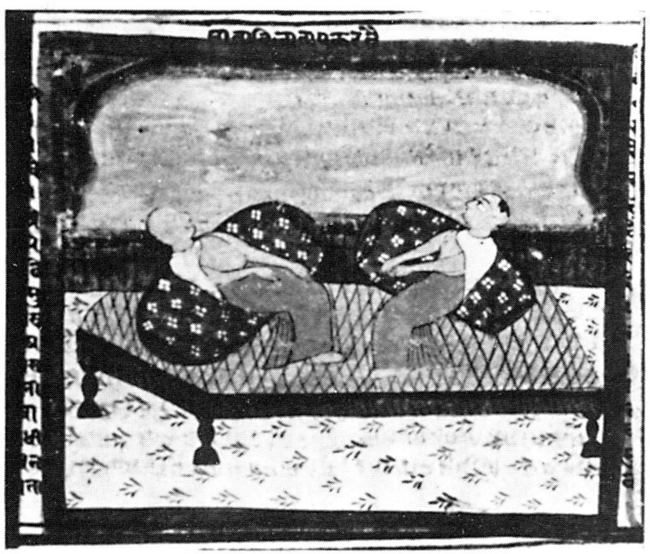

FOLIO 38

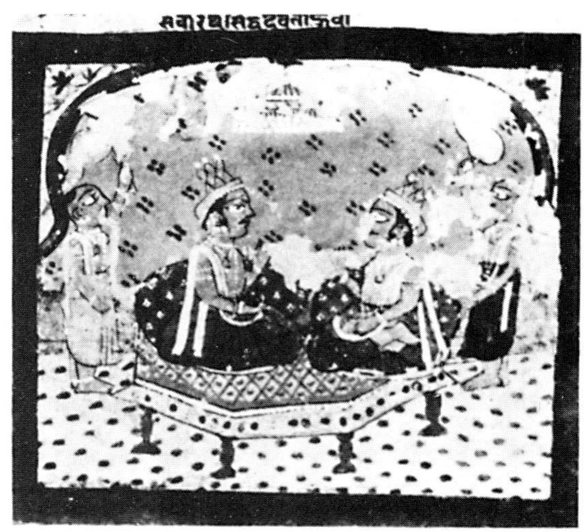

FOLIO 39

7. (21.1673)

PLATE XXXI

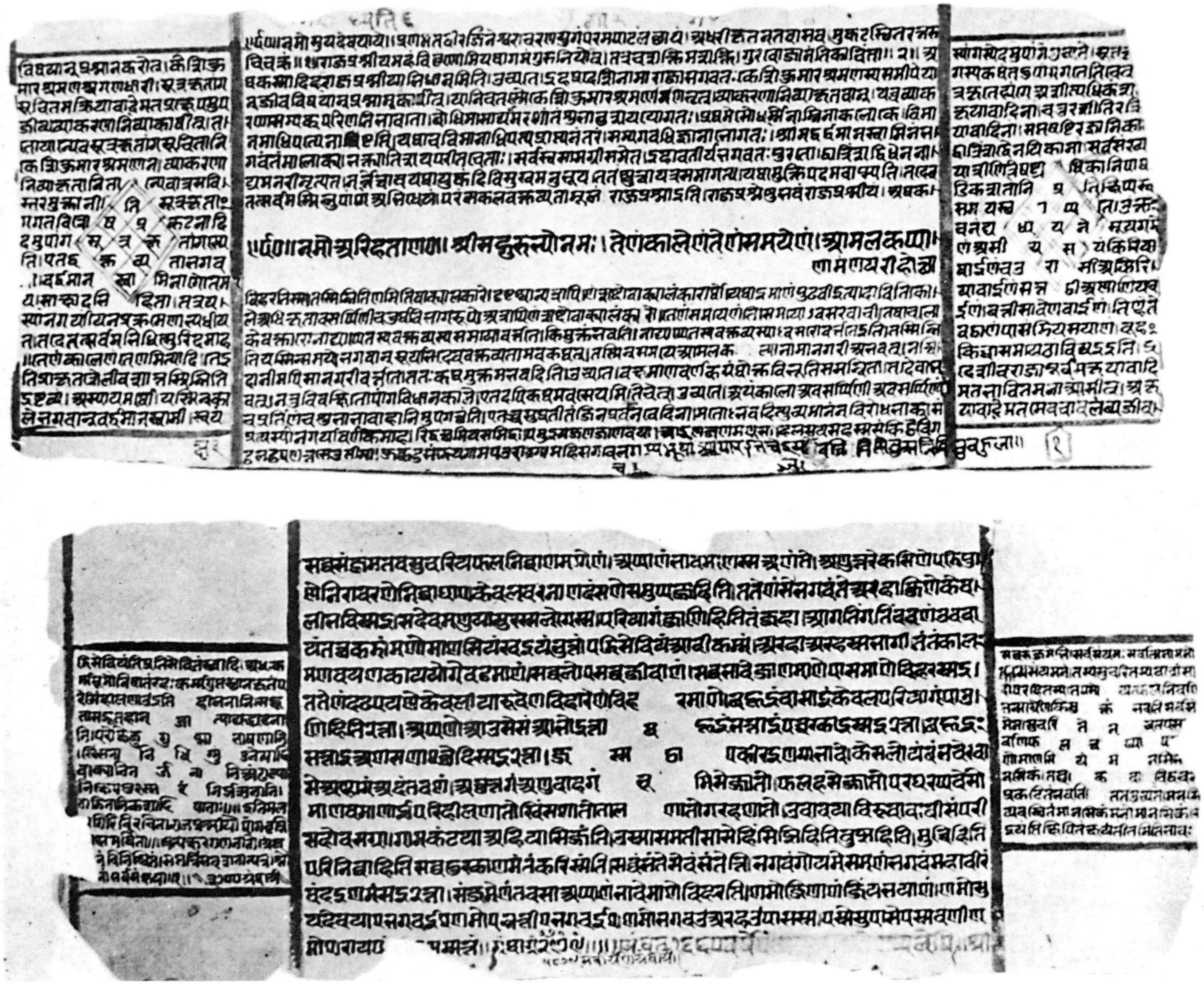

9. (17.2281)

PLATE XXXII

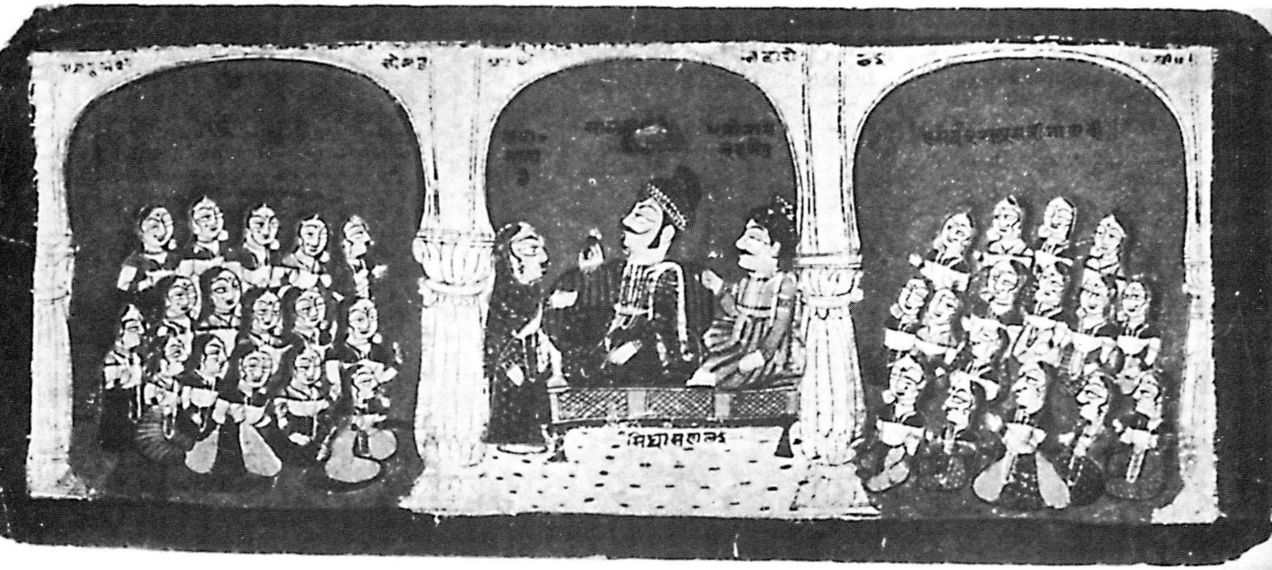

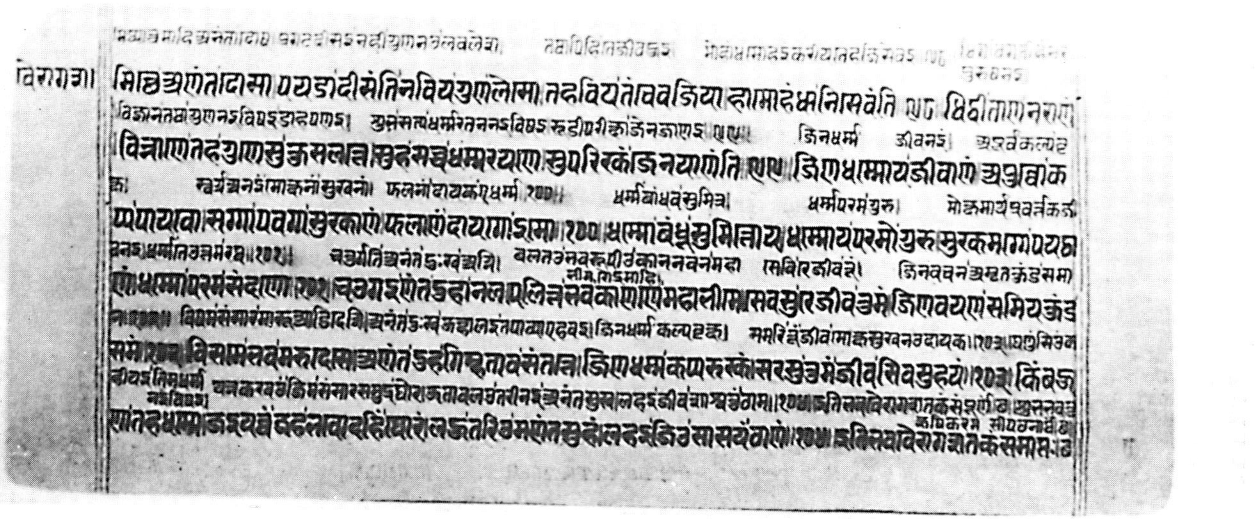

26. (17.2289) and 11. (17.2283)

PLATE XXXIII

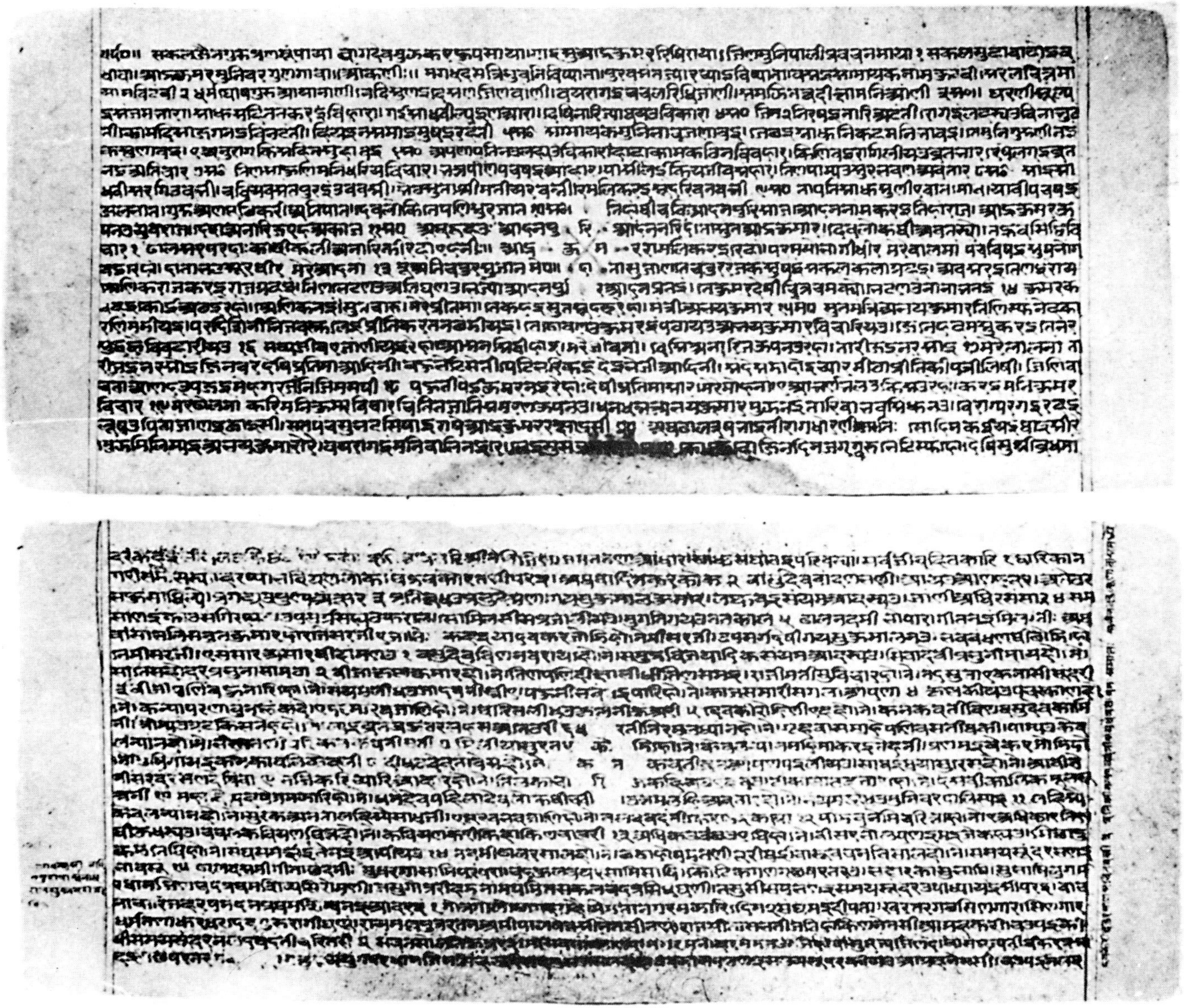

12. (17.2284)

PLATE XXXIV

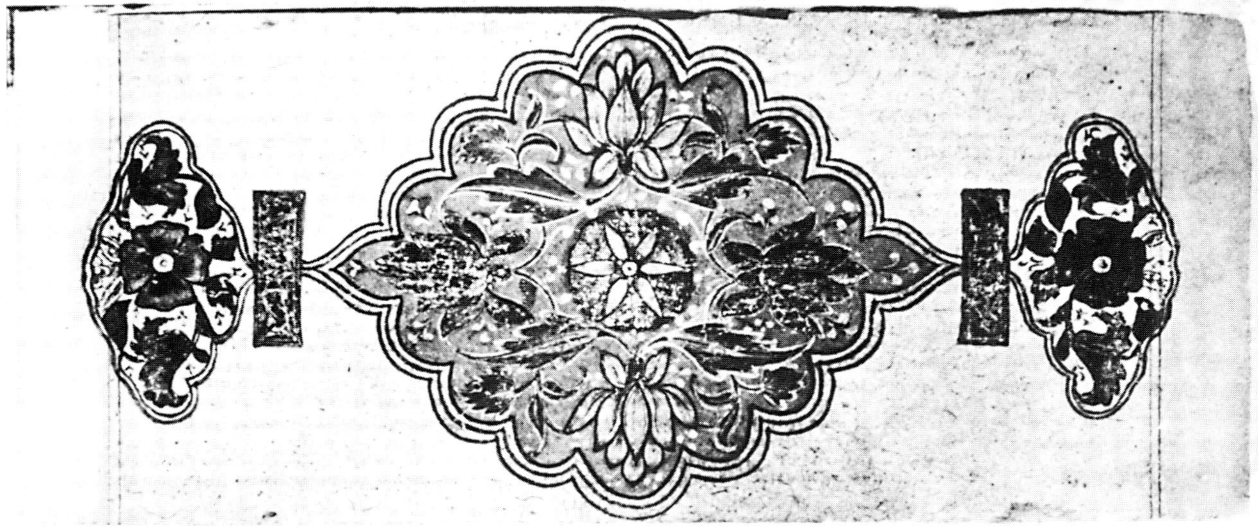

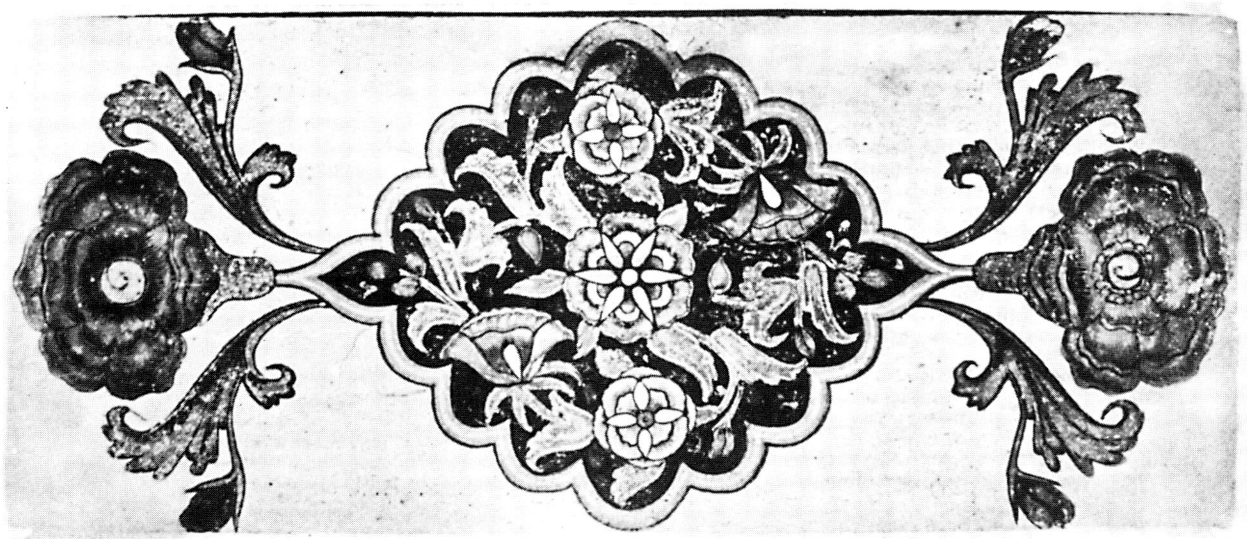

12. (17.2284)

PLATE XXXV

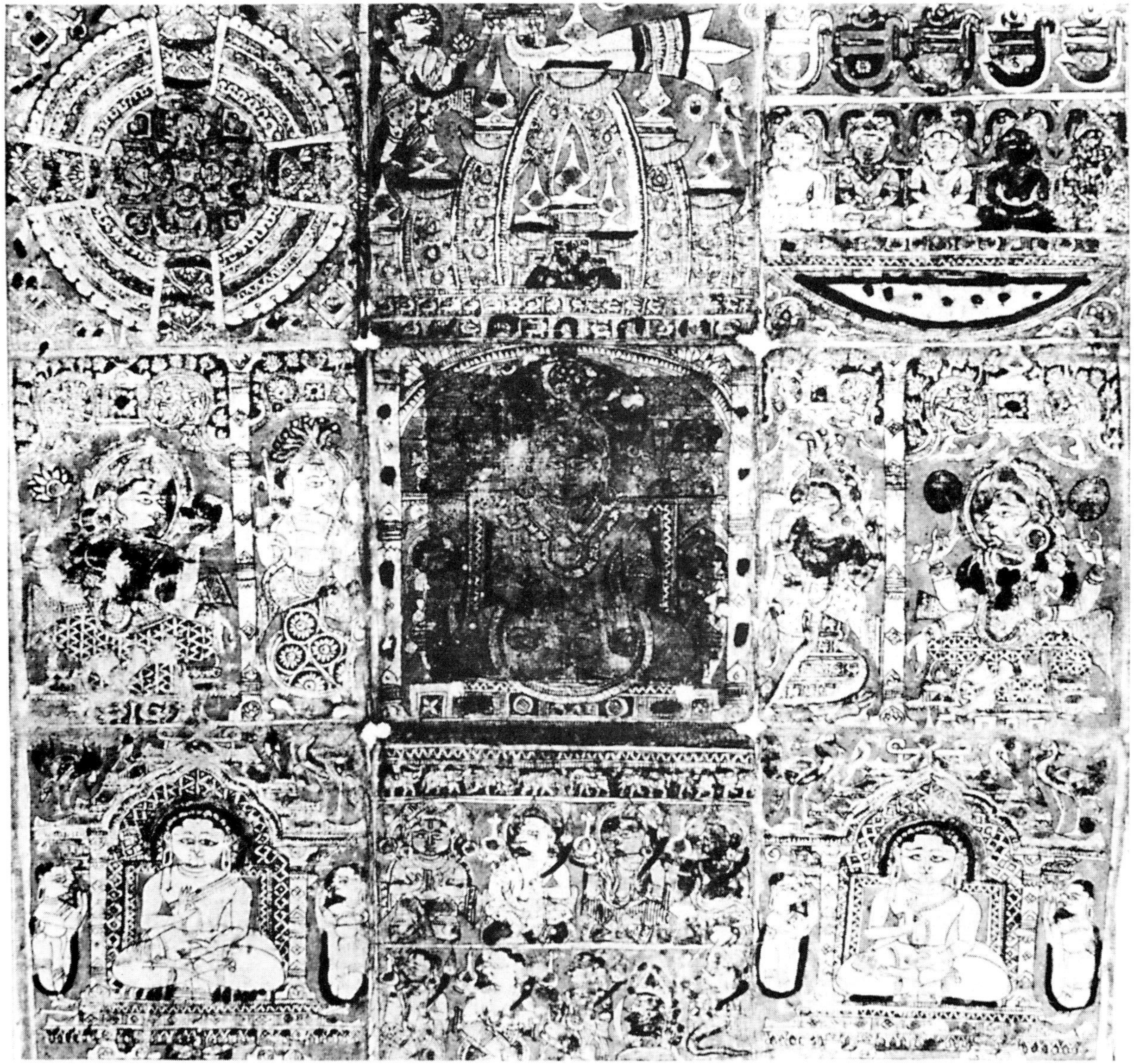

15. (17.2295)

PLATE XXXVI

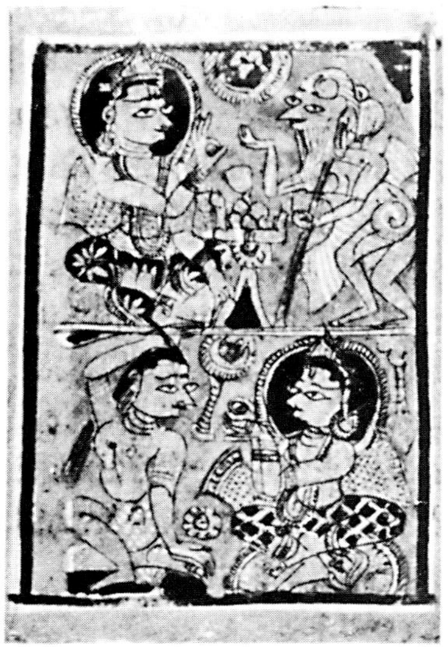

5. (19.142) FOLIO 51

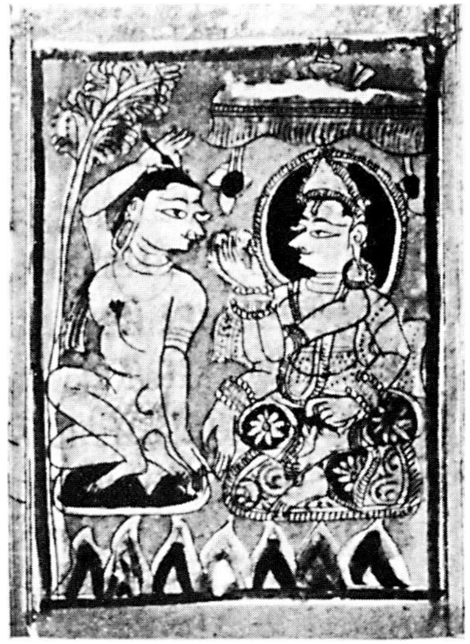

5. (19.142) FOLIO 59

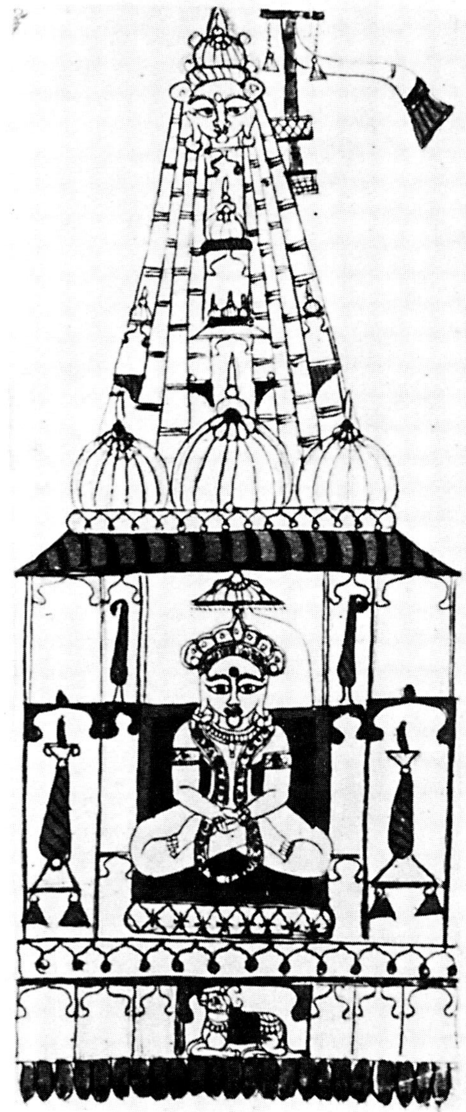

18. (17.2298)

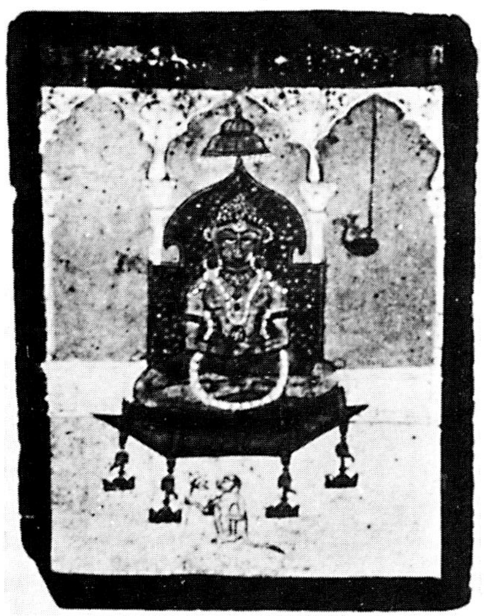

21. (17.2311)

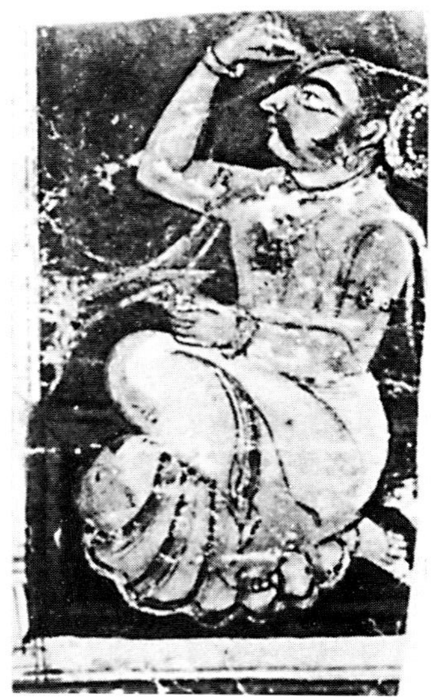

27. (17.2290)

PLATE XXXVII

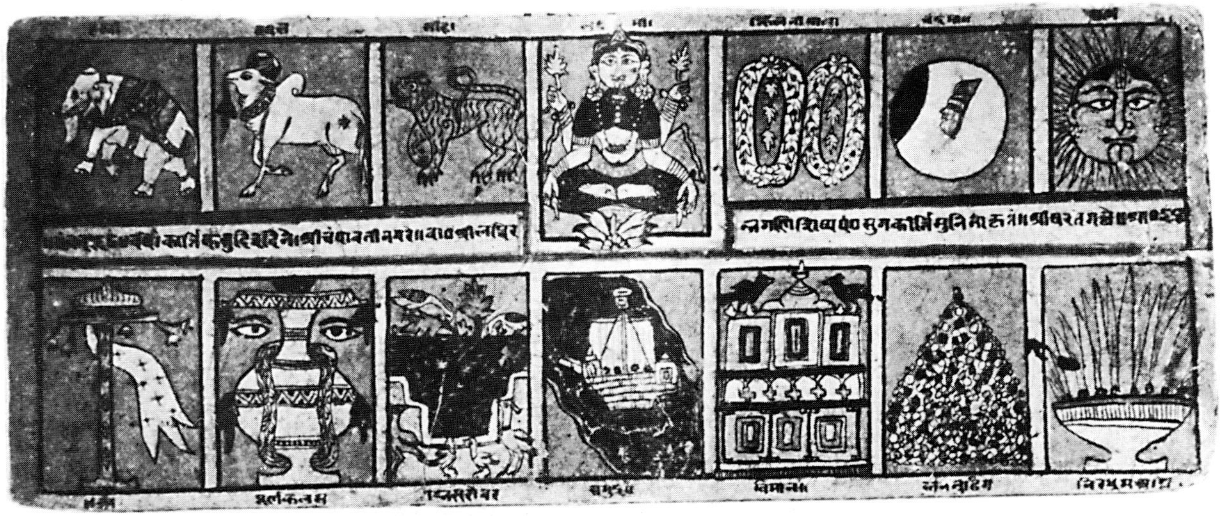

22. (17.2285)

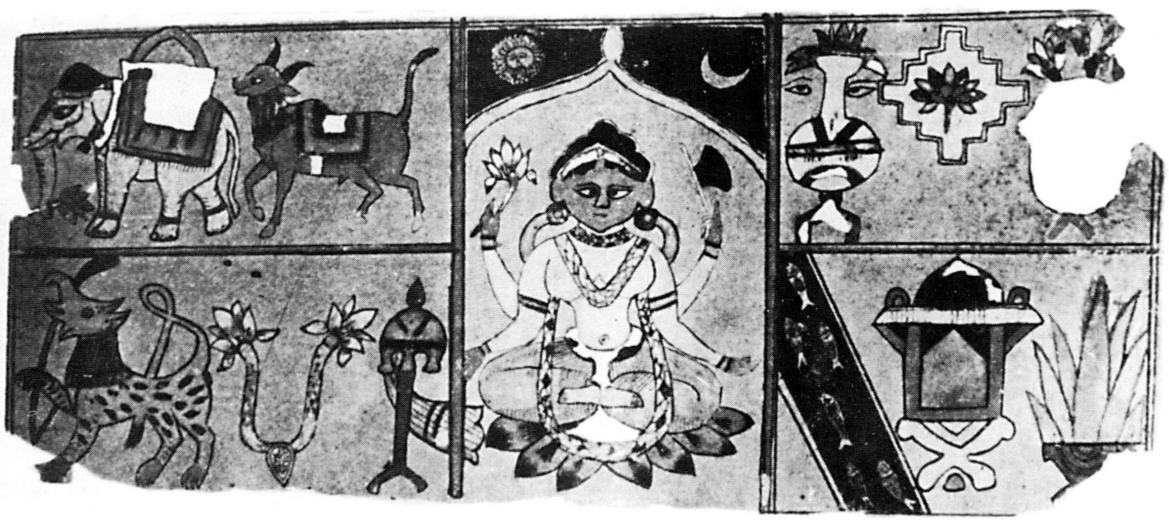

23. (17.2286)

PLATE XXXVIII

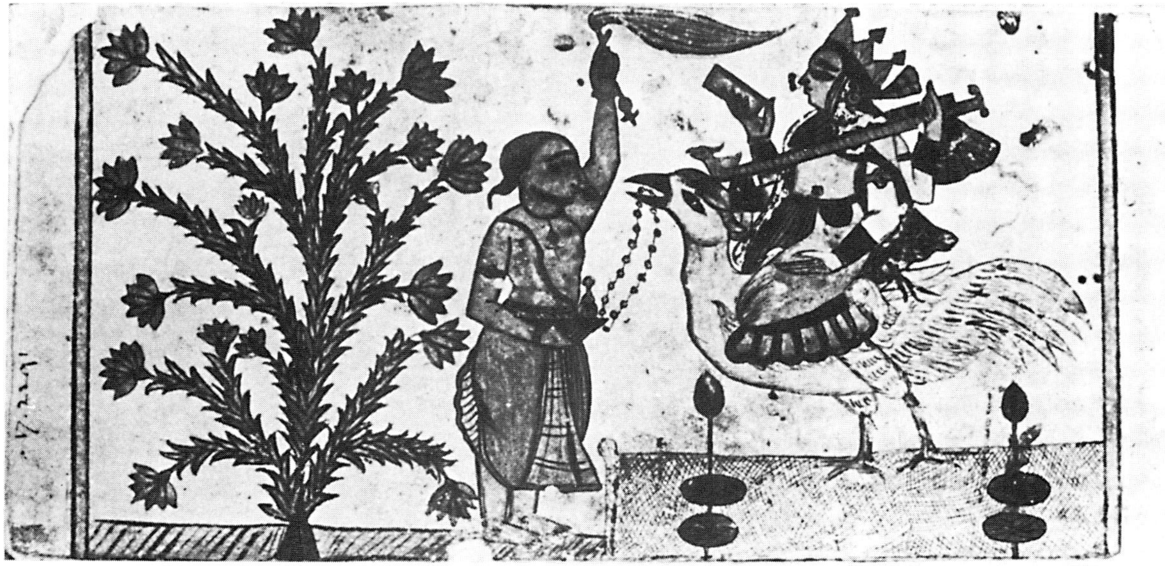

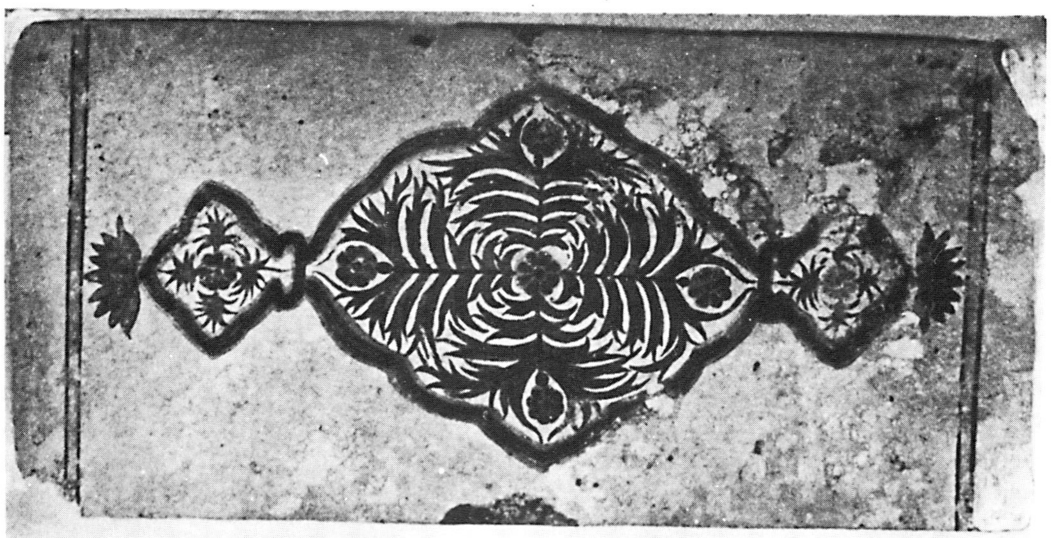

28. (17.2291)

PLATE XXXIX

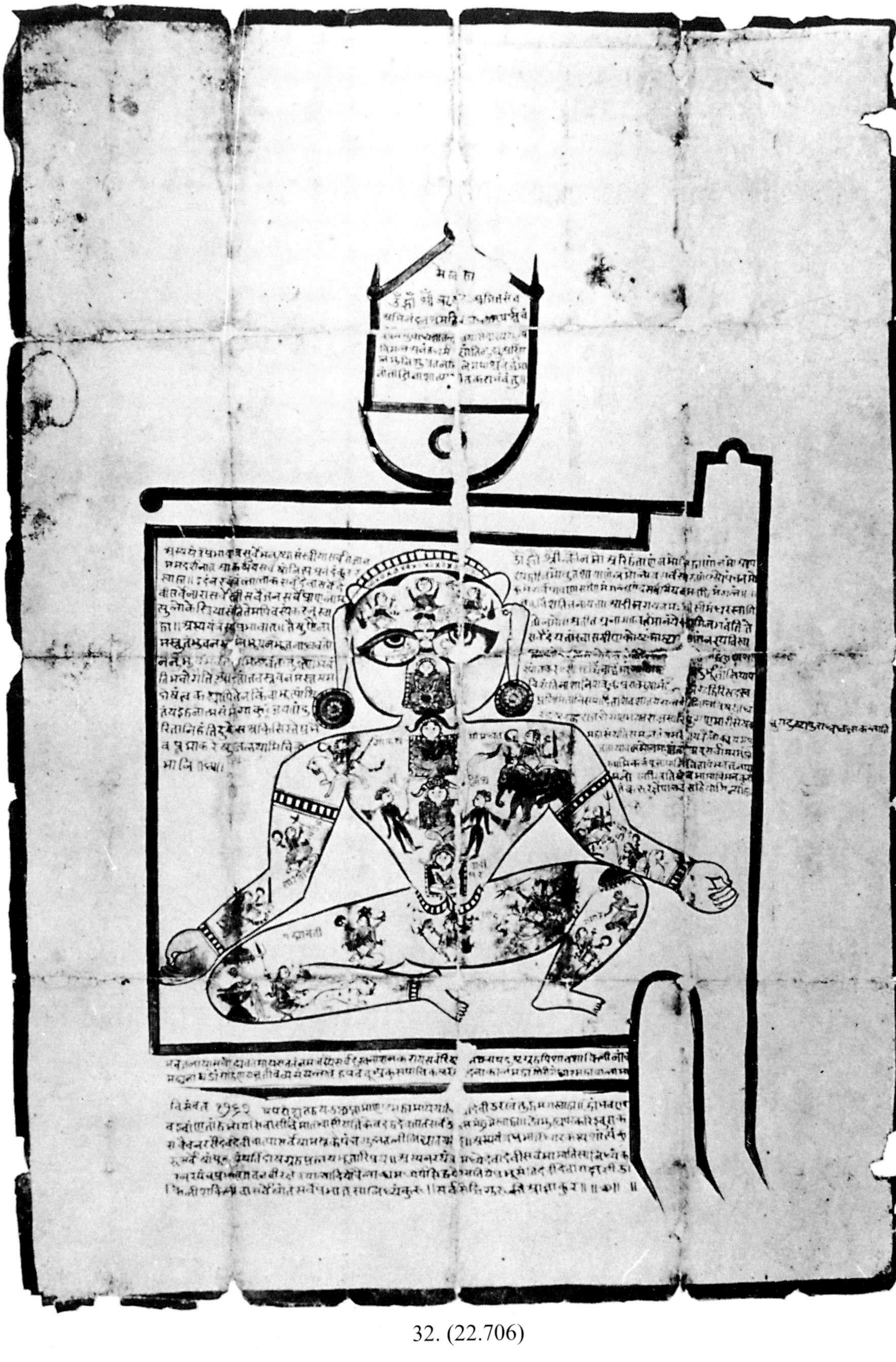

32. (22.706)

History of Indian and Indonesian Art

Part IV
Early Mediaeval, Mediaeval, Rajput Painting and Later Arts and Crafts

[The following are extracts from Part IV, relating directly to Jaina art.]

MEDIAEVAL: FROM AD 900:
PĀLA, CĀḶUKYA, COḶA,
RĀJPUT, & c.

[p. 106]
The nomenclature of the mediaeval architecture presents considerable difficulty. In any case, a sectarian classification, such as that which forms the main defect of Fergusson's work, is quite misleading. For just as in the case of sculpture, there are no Buddhist, Jain or Brāhmaṇical *styles* of architecture, but only Buddhist, Jaina and Brāhmaṇical buildings in the Indian style of their period.

[pp. 111-13]
The Jaina temples at Mount Ābū are deservedly famous.[1] These take their name of Dilvāṛa from the adjoining village, situated at a height of 4000 feet on an isolated hill in Southern Rājputāna; the group consists of four temples, of which the most important are those of Vimala Shā and Tejahpāla, respectively ca.1032 and 1232. They are constructed entirely of white marble, quarried in the plains below, and carried up the steep hill by infinite labour. These are domed shrines with pillared halls. As Cousens remaks 'the amount of beautiful ornamental detail spread over these temples in the minutely carved decoration of ceilings, pillars, doorways, panels, and niches is simply marvellous; the crisp, thin, translucent, shell-like treatment of the marble surpasses anything seen elsewhere, and some of the designs are veritable dreams of beauty. The work is so delicate that ordinary chiseling would have been disastrous. It is said that much of it was produced by scraping the marble away, and that the masons were paid by the amount of marble dust so removed. The two great domical ceilings are the most remarkable feature (Fig. 221); all the fretted marble is deeply undercut, and in the centre there hangs a great carved pendant. It must not be supposed that all this work is overwrought; this is rather one of those cases where exuberance is beauty. It will be understood, of course, that all the figure sculpture is necessarily in the same key, each individual figure being but a note in the whole scheme, not a profound invention to be separately studied. The same applies even to the images of the Jinas in this period; each is severely simple, but all are alike in representing nothing more than the skilled realization of a fixed formula. Just a millennium had passed since the setting up of Friar Bala's Bodhisattva at Sārnāth: not one of the mediaeval craftsmen could have created a work of like intensity, but had such a thing been possible, such a figure would have completely destroyed the unity of any mediaeval shrine. Under these circumstances it is not a fault, but a virtue in the craftsman that he could not, if he would, have achieved what have been utterly inappropriate to his design.

There is another and even more picturesque Jaina *tīrtha* or place of pilgrimage at Taraṅga, not far from Siddhapur, with a temple of Ajitnātha, built by Kumārapāla. The most remarkable of such *tīrthas* however, are the great temple cities—cities not built for human habitation, but consisting of temples alone—picturesquely situated on the hills of Girnār in Kāṭhiāwāḍ and Śatruñjaya or Pālitāna in Gujarāt.[2]

[1]D.R. Bhandarkar, 'Some Temples in Mt. Abu', *Rupam*, 3, 1920. H. Cousens, *The Architectural Antiquities of Western India*, London, 1926.

[2]For Girnār and Śatruñjaya, & c. See J. Fergusson, *A History of Indian and Eastern Architecture,* 2nd ed., London, 10; and H. Cousens, op. cit.

At Girnār the great temple of Nemināthа is certainly older than 1278 when it was repaired; another, built by the brothers Tejahpāla and Vastupāla, founders of the second temple at Mt. Ābū above referred to, dates about 1230. The former stands in a colonnaded court of some seventy cells, the latter is a triple shrine arranged in Cāḷukyan fashion about a central hall. At Śatruñjaya the total number of shrines, in eleven separate enclosures, exceeds five hundred. Some date back to the eleventh century, the majority range from 1500 to the present day. One of the largest is the temple of Ādinātha in the Kharataravasī Taluk, built by a banker of Aḥmadābād in 1618; this is a shrine of two storeys, with a well proportioned *śikhara,* and with a verandah of which the pillars bear capitals richly carved with figures of musicians and dancers. A small shrine built by the Nagar Seṭh, or Head of the Guilds of Aḥmadābād in 1840, is a pillared hall of unique design, with external verandahs; the floor is divided by twelve piers into nine smaller squares, those of the angles having domed roofs, those of the centre and sides being crowned by towers; the five principal icons represent sacred mountains. Other picturesquely situated Jaina temple groups are found at Rāṇpur (especially the Gaumukha temple, AD 1438) in Jodhpur State, and Parasnāth in Bengal.

[pp. 118-21]

The chief seat of the Jainas in Southern India, Śravaṇa Beḷgoḷa, Hāsan District, Maisūr, contains innumerable shrines, some being situated in the village itself, others on the two hills, the Cikka and Doṭṭa Beṭṭas. The term *beṭṭa* is applied to a special form of shrine consisting of a courtyard open to the sky, with cloisters round about and in the centre a colossal image, not of a Tirthaṃkara, but of a saint. By far the most remarkable of these is the great image of Gommaṭeśvara on the Doḍḍa-beṭṭa hill, fifty-seven feet in height, thus one of the largest freestanding images in the world. It was set up, or rather, carved *in situ*, for Cāmuṇḍa Rāja about AD 983. The saint, who was the son of the first Tīrthaṃkara, and resigned his kingdom to become an ascetic, is represented in the immovable serenity of one practising the *kāyotsarga* austerity, undisturbed by the serpents about his feet, the ant-hills rising to his thighs, or the growing creeper that has already reached his shoulders. Another figure at Ilivālā is over twenty feet in height. There exist also statues to Bharateśvara, the saint's brother. The treatment is very formal.

Ordinary temples known as *bastis* and containing images of Jinas are likewise abundant at Śravaṇa Beḷgoḷa, most of them being in Coḷa-Drāviḍa style and dating from the eleventh or twelfth century. At least two metal images of about the same date are still in private possession in the village; an example from the same district is illustrated in Fig. 234. The Jaina *maṭha* or monastery in the village is decorated with paintings of scenes from the life of certain Tīrthaṃkaras and Jaina kings.[3]

A more peculiar type of Jaina temple is represented in Kannaḍa (Kanara) country below the *ghāṭs* especially at Mūdabidri near Mangalore. The style belongs to the time of the kings of Vijayanagar, and is characterized by its sloping roofs of flat overlapping slabs, and a peculiar kind of stone screen enclosing the sides, recalling a Buddhist railing. The nearest analogy for the sloping roofs is found in the Himālayan forms, and some authors have assumed a connection of style between Kannaḍa and Nepāl; more likely similar conditions have produced similar forms, the Kannaḍa roofs being well adapted to the excessive rainfall below the *ghāṭs.*[4]

[3]For Śravaṇa Beḷgoḷa see R. Narasimachar, *Inscriptions at Śravaṇa Belgola,* Epigraphica Carnatica, II, 2nd ed., Bangalore, 1923. The Jaina image, figure 234 has been published by Hadaway in *Rūpam*, 17, 1924. Other early Jaina bronzes include one published by Nahar and Ghose, *Epitome of Jainism,* and one in the Barton Museum, Bhavnagar, examples of later date are common, cf. Coomaraswamy, *Catalogue of the Indian Collections in the Museum of Fine Arts, Boston, Part II: Sculpture,* pp. 142-5; S. Hadaway, 'Notes on Two Jaina Metal Images', *Rūpam*, 17, 1924; Luard, in *Journal of Indian Art*, Vol. XXI; Rivett-Carnac, in *JIA*, Vol. IX; T.H. Hendley, in *JIA*, Vol. XVII, 1916; Narasimachar, loc. cit., & c. The painting in the Jaina *maṭha* at Śravaṇa Beḷgoḷa is illustrated by Narasimachar, Pl. XLVIII. Another example of a southern Jaina painting, of uncertain date is preserved on the ceiling of a Jaina temple at Kāñcīpuram (Fig. 256); another, ascribed to the eleventh century at Tirumalai, N. Arcot District (*Epigraphia Indica*, IX, 229).

[4]Cousens, *The Architectural Antiquities of Western India,* London, 1926, p. 34, and Cousens, *The Chalukyan Architecture of the Kanarese Districts,* announced; J. Fergusson, op. cit., Vol. II, pp. 75ff; *Archaeological Survey of India, Annual Report*, 1914-15, pt. 1, d. 9.

Figures of Gommaṭeśvara are not found in northern India. But there is a series of rock cut temples, and colossal images at Gwāliar. Most of the excavated shrines are mere niches containing the statues, all of which represent Tīrthaṃkaras, the largest being fifty-seven feet in height.[5]

Strictly analogous to the mediaeval painting of Bengal and Nepāl is that of the illustrated manuscripts of the Gujarātī school. Here too we have a series of constantly repeated compositions, varying only in unimportant details, and clearly indicating a long precedent tradition. As before, the pictures form square panels of the height of the page, occupying spaces left for them in advance by the scribe, and in many cases the subjects are identified by brief legends. In accomplishment, and in detachment from all preoccupation with effect or with emotion, they rank indeed, although represented by examples of later date, above the works of the Eastern school. With one exception, to be referred to below, all the Gujarātī works are illustrations of Jaina texts, and in almost all cases of the *Kalpa Sūtra*, a work dealing with the life of Mahāvīra and certain other Tīrthaṃkaras, and another poem, the *Kālikācarya* [*sic*] *Kathā*, which is an edifying tale describing the faithful dealings of the holy monk Kālika [*sic*] with the wicked king Gardabhilla.[6]

Only one example of an illustrated *Kalpa Sūtra* on palm leaf is known, dated equivalent to AD 1237 and now preserved in a *bhaṇḍār* at Pāṭan.[7] Several examples on paper, dated in the fifteenth century are known, others undated, and others of later date.[8] The paper manuscripts reproduce the form of the old palm leaves, the illustrations being arranged in the same way (Fig. 255). It is indeed characteristic of the illustrated manuscript in India, that the picture bears no organic relation to the page, and merely occupies a space (*ālekhya sthāna*) left unfilled by the scribe for the purpose; in all probability scribe and painter were always different persons. The style is one of pure draughtsmanship; the colour is indeed brilliant, but it is the outline that establishes the facts, and this outline, though exceedingly facile and almost careless, is very accomplished, and very legible. In many cases the execution might well be called brilliant, and this applies as much to the tiny thumb-nail indicatory sketches in the margins as to the finished miniatures. The variety of scenes and circumstances represented is very considerable, and the pictures afford valuable information on contemporary, or more probably, considering the conservatism of the style, earlier than fifteenth century manners, customs and costumes.

Another document of the same school is a manuscript of the Gujarātī poem, *Vasanta Vilāsa* (Fig. 257), now in the possession of Mr. N.C. Mehta. Quite exceptionally, this manuscript is in the form of a scroll, verses of the text alternating with the painted panels, seventy-nine in number, by which it is fully illustrated. The poem describes the pomps and glories of the Spring, and the paintings, in consequence are all of a lyrical character, and as such unique in the Gujarātī school. In point of style, they are absolutely identical with those of the religious manuscripts, and may have been executed by some of the very same artists. The *Vasanta Vilāsa*, was written, according to the colophon, at Aḥmadābād in the year AD 1415.[9]

It may be remarked that all the Gujarātī painting exhibits marked peculiarities in the delineation of the human form, the most conspicuous being those of the three-quarter profile position, in which the further eye protrudes unnaturally, and the long pointed nose projects beyond the outline of the cheek. The expansion of the chest, moreover, is so much exaggerated, that it is often difficult to distinguish a man from a woman. Of these peculiarities the bulging eye and projecting

[5]Fergusson, op. cit., Vol. II, p. 48.

[6]For full descriptions and illustration of paintings in Jaina manuscripts see Hüttemann, 'Miniaturen zum Jinacaritra', *Baessler-Archiv*, Band IV, 2; Coomaraswamy, *Catalogue of the Indian Collections of the Museum of Fine Arts, Boston, Part IV: Jaina Paintings and Manuscripts;* H. Von Glasenapp, *Der Jainismus*, Berlin, 1925.

[7]Nahar and Ghose, *Epitome of Jainism*, 1914, pp. 696, 706.

[8]Beside those in Boston, there are good examples in the Indian Office Library and in the British Museum, London, in the Museum für Vœlkerkunde and the State Library, Berlin, in the Freer Gallery, Washington, U.S.A., and in the collections of P.C. Nahar, and A. Ghose, Calcutta, and of P.C. Manuk, Patna, as well as others in the Pāṭan *bhaṇḍārs*.

[9]N.C. Mehta, 'Indian Painting in the Fifteenth Century', *Rūpam*, 22-3, 1925; O.C. Gangoly, 'Vasanta Vilāsa, A New Document of Indian Painting', *Ostasiatische Zeitschrift*, 2, 1925.

pointed nose are met with already in the eighth century frescoes of Elūrā (Fig. 196); Gujarātī painting is no doubt a continuation of the early western style, referred to by Tāranātha as that of the 'Ancient West', the Rāṣṭrakūṭa and perhaps Paramāra frescoes of Elūra representing an intermediate stage in the development. The wall paintings of Śravaṇa Beḷgoḷa and Kāñcīpuram referred to above, are of course, in another and southern (Drāviḍa) style.

PLATE LVII

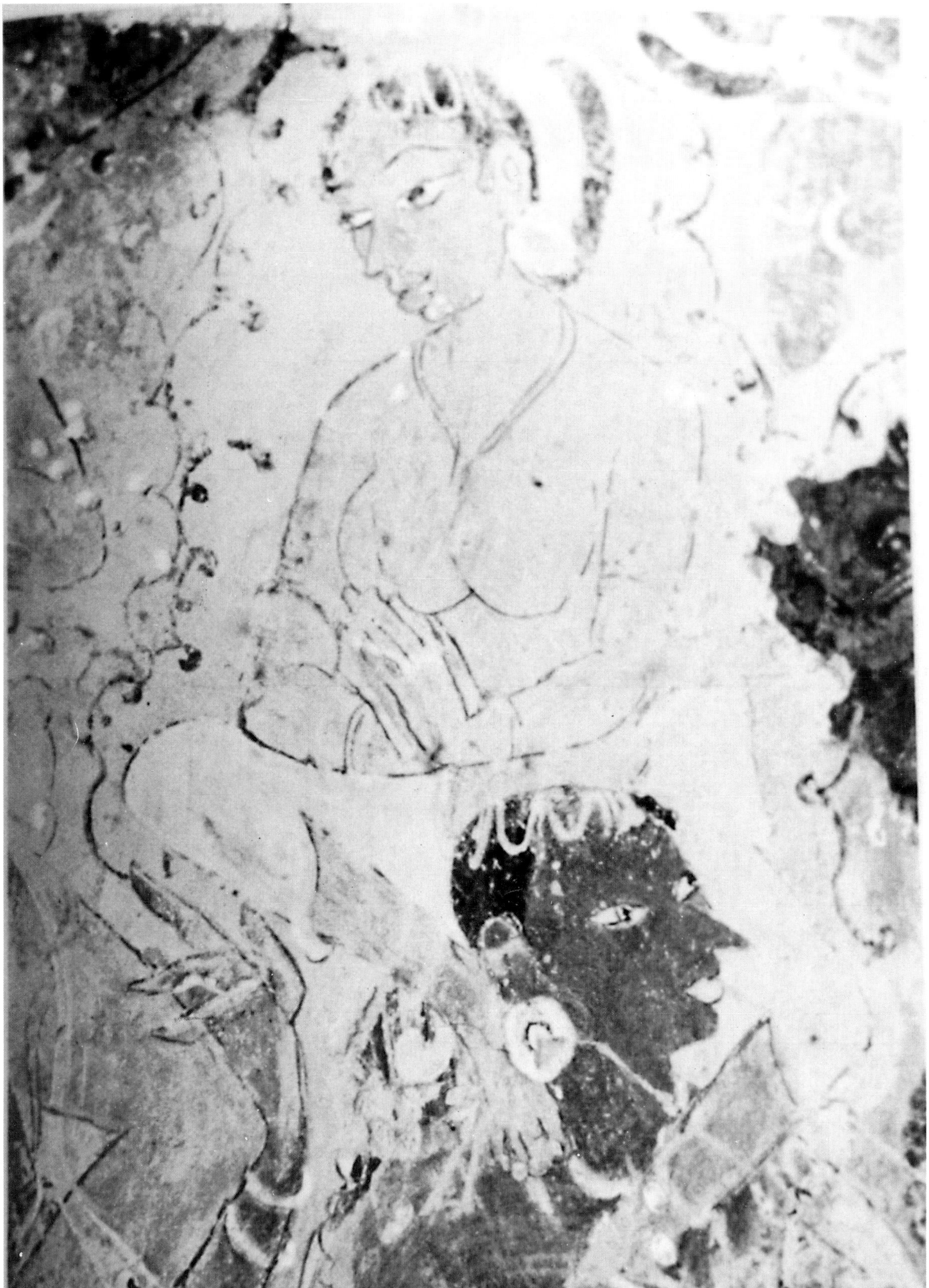

196. Lakṣmī, ceiling painting, Kailāsa, Elūrā, detail; eighth century.

Early Mediaeval (Rāṣṭrakūṭa)

PLATE LXVIII

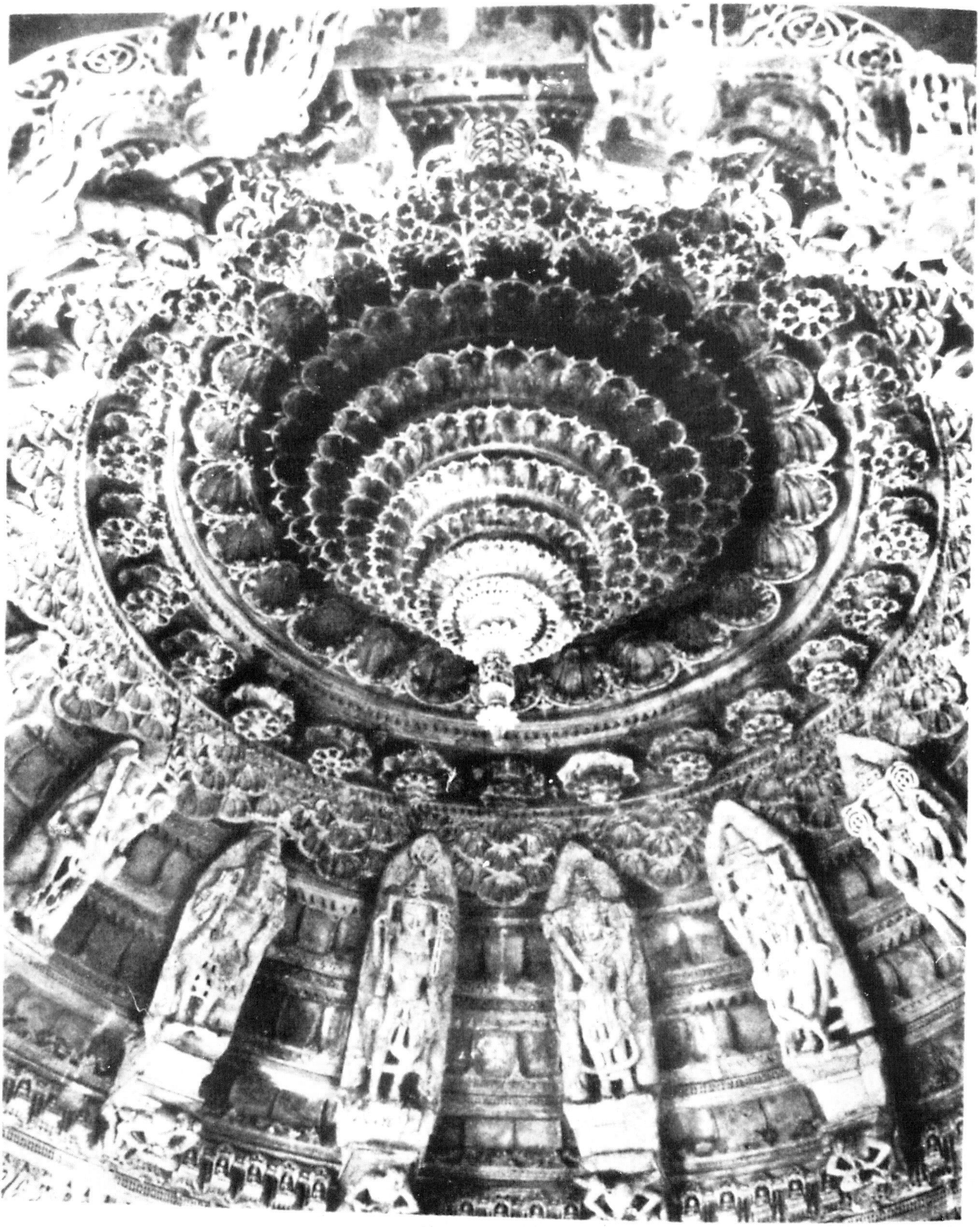

221. Tejahpāla's temple, Dilwāṛa, Mt. Ābū, ceiling; AD 1232

Mediaeval

PLATE LXXII

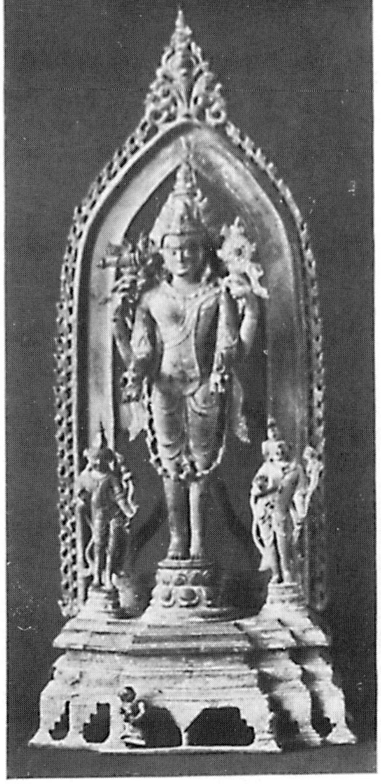

231. Viṣṇu, bras, Sagardighi; eleventh century. Calcutta.

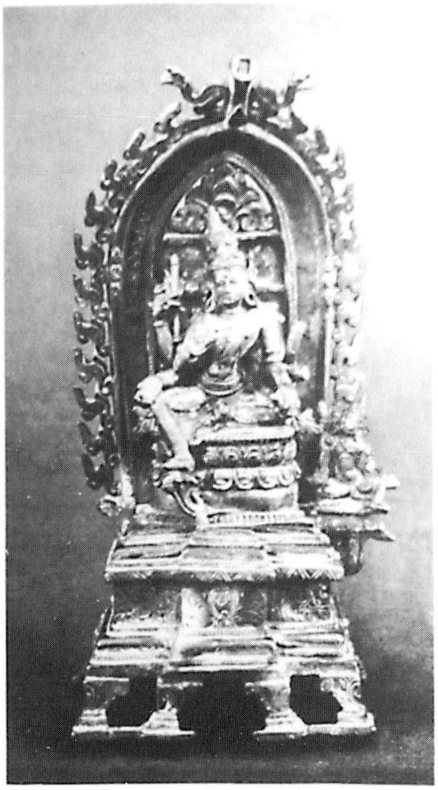

232. Bodhisattva, bronze, Kaśmīr? tenth century. Srinagar.

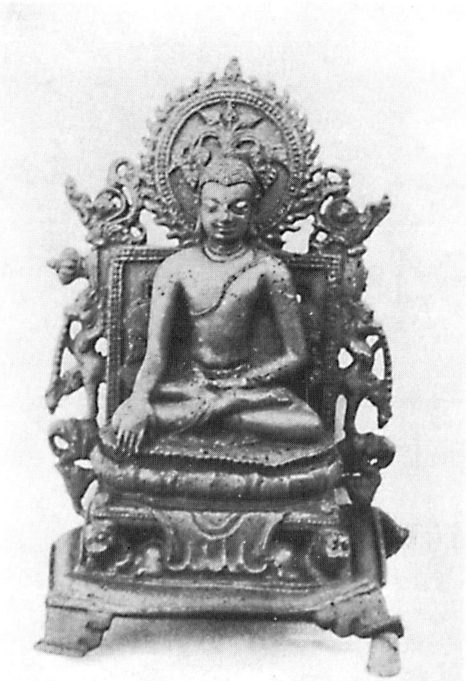

233. Buddha, bronze, Nālanda; tenth century. Nālandā.

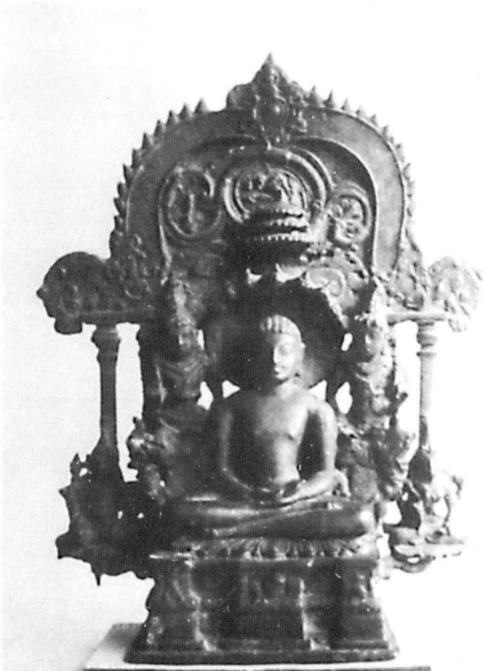

234. Pārśvanātha, Kannaḍa; tenth century. Kay Collection. Madras.

Mediaeval (Pāla and Cāḷukya)

PLATE LXXX

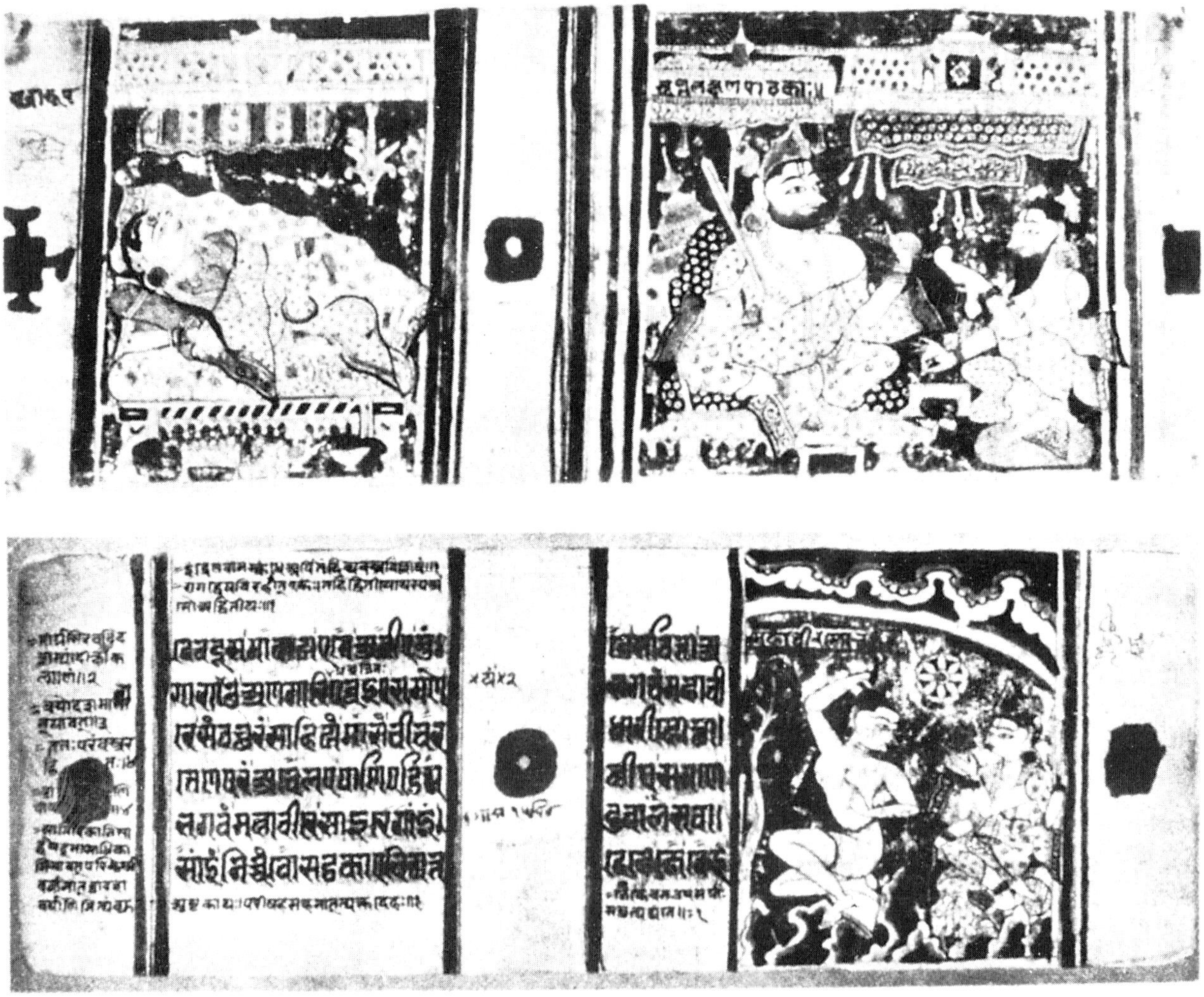

255 a and b. The leaves of a manuscript of the *Kalpa Sūtra*, Gujarātī, fifteenth century. Boston.

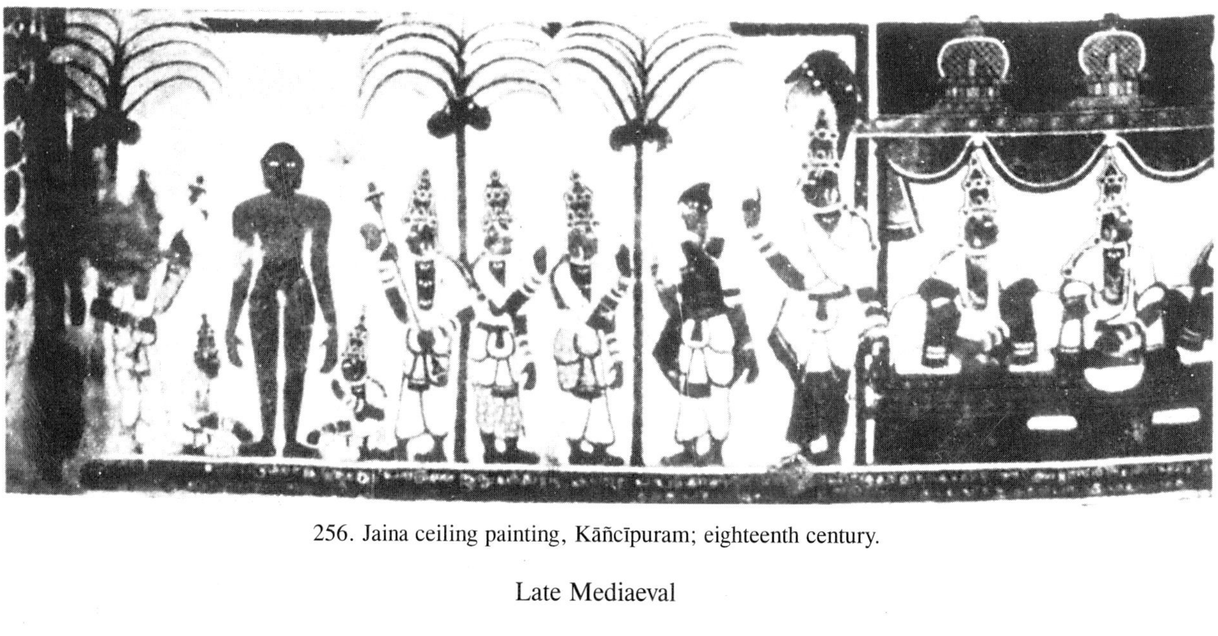

256. Jaina ceiling painting, Kāñcīpuram; eighteenth century.

PLATE LXXXI

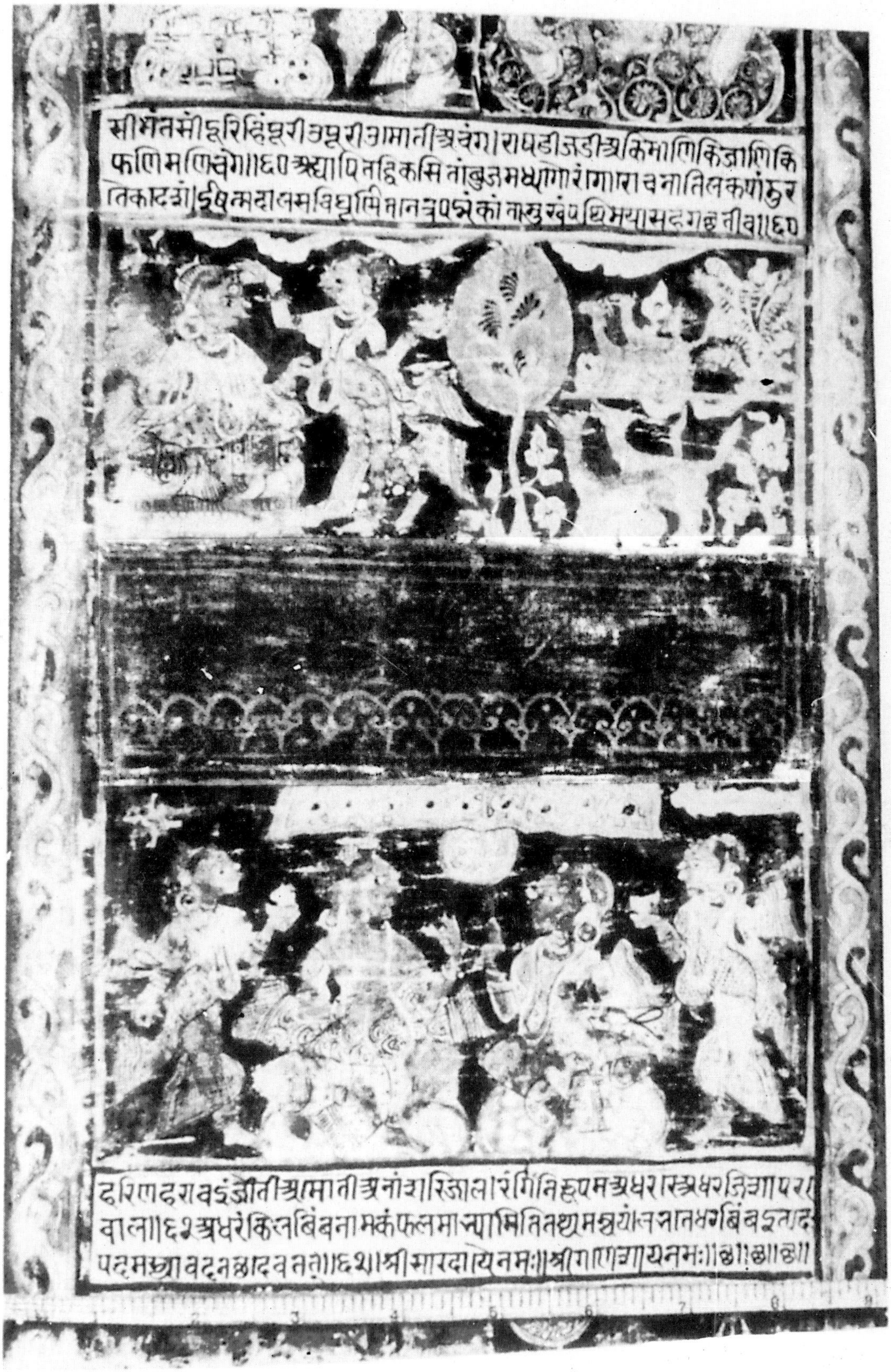

257. Part of a manuscript of the *Vasanta Vilāsa*, Gujarātī; AD 1451
N.C. Mehta Collection.

'The Conqueror's Life' in Jaina Painting: Explicitur Reductio Haec Artis Ad Theologiam[1]

Professor Brown and Mr. Ramachandran have provided us with authoritative and almost exhaustive denominative accounts of the iconography of Jaina painting, in western and southern India.[2] It has long been recognized that as compositions and in symbolism the illustrations of the lives of the Jainas [*sic*] or 'Conquerors' are by no means contemporary inventions, but rather slightly varying recensions of archetypal formulae of which the date of fixation can hardly be determined for want of documents. In this respect the Jaina compositions correspond to those of folk art, which are evidently the lineal descendants of types of an unknown and in this case certainly a very remote antiquity. In this connection, it is the purpose of the present article to call attention to certain characteristics of the Jaina formulation, as to which there can be said what is also true of Indian iconography generally, viz., (1) that the formulation is in hardly any detail a private property of the sect that makes use of it, and (2) that ultimate explanations can only be found in the Vedic metaphysical tradition, and/or cognate traditions. In other words, the miniatures are not merely illustrations of the life of this or that one of the twenty-four Tīrthaṁkaras (virtually, 'pontifices') but in the last analysis are illustrations of a universal 'Book of Genesis' (*bhāva vṛtta, jātavidyā*) or cosmogony. In this respect, of course, what can be said of the pictures is equally true of the texts which they 'illuminate' in more than one sense.

As in the parallel case of Buddhism, Jaina heterodoxy, although it involved a formal rejection of Vedic tradition, changes nothing essential in the primordial conception of the procession of an eternal avatar; what takes place, so far as the 'Conqueror's life (*jinacaritra*) is concerned, is a partial, and only very partial rationalization of the underlying 'myth',[3] which is now narrated as if its logical sequences had been a series of historical events taking place at stated times and places. It may be granted, of course, that the story told may have had an historical equivalent in this sense, that all of history repeats a primordial pattern. But supposing it be possible

[1] i.e. in which the arts are referred to that science in which they are more eminently present, as are effects in their cause. The form of the sub-title is suggested by St. Bonaventura's Opusculum de reductione artium ad theologiam, a translation of which will appear as Part III of my Mediaeval Aesthetic, in the Art Bulletin, in due course. The peculiar propriety of our procedure in the present, Jaina, connection, will be apparent by reference to Hemacandra's *Triṣaṣṭiśalākāpuruṣacaritra,* I, 1, 648ff. where in a description of those who are considering a painting, the first place is given to those 'versed in Holy Writ' (āgama-vit), whose judgment is based on the picture's agreement with the 'meaning of Writ' (āgamārthāvisaṁvādi), the second place to the 'very pious' persons who delight in the representations (bimbāni) of the holy personages as such, third place to the 'technical experts' who criticize the draughtsmanship, and fourth to those 'others' who are charmed by the colours. These points of view correspond approximately to the well known classification of references as respectively anagogic (paramārthika), moral, allegorical, and literal. In the present article, the reader is invited to consider Jaina painting from the first of these points of view, that of the āgama-vit, the vidu, ya evaṁ vidvān.

It should perhaps be explained that 'reduction' does not mean 'diminution'; reduction, literally 'leading back', or 'reference', is always 'to a superior species', as for example when we speak of 'reducing potentiality to act'.

[2] W.N. Brown, *Miniature paintings of the Jaina Kalpasūtra*, Washington, Smithsonian Institution, 1934; T.N. Ramāchandran, *Tiruparuttikuṇṛam and its temples*, Madras, Government Press, 1934. I take this opportunity to endorse Professor Brown's suggestion (*JAOS*, 54, 440) that Ramachandran somewhat postdates the earlier paintings at Tiruparuttikuṇṛam.

[3] For what is to be understood by a 'myth' see Guénon, 'Mythes, Mysteres, et Symboles', Le Voile d'Isis, No. 190, 1935.

to abstract from the story told, by elimination of all its 'miraculous' elements, a circumstantial reference, that by no means represents the full intention (vera sentenzia) of the 'narrative'. The deity indeed assumes a 'human nature' in the beginning, but that 'has nothing to do with time', and is far from implying that he becomes however great 'a man'. In other words, it is precisely the miraculous features of the story, which if subtracted from the written or visual narrative would leave us with nothing but the faintest shadow of 'biography', that represent its essence. The miraculous legend is not, or need not be, historically true as having taken place and as taking place always.

Jainism, like Buddhism, reflects a revolt of the temporal power (*kṣatra regnum*) against the spiritual power (*brahma, sacerdotum*).[4] This revolt is prefigured as a possibility in the figure of Indra, the Vedic Lucifer and prodigal son who takes possession of the paternal treasures and extroverts the power and the glory of the interior kingdom. But whereas in *RV.* Indra acts for the most part as Agni's vassal, exercising a delegated power (*RV*,[5] X, 52, 5, imitated in the *Rājasūya, ŚB.* V, 3, 5, 27 f. and V, 4, 3, 3, f.), and thus in legitimate relation to, and as protector of, the spiritual operation (*vratapā, 'fidei defensor'*). At the same time, there is presented another possibility. This possibility, latent in principio, is realized in Indra's *Vaikuṇṭha* form: 'maddened by pride in his own heroic-energy and deluded by the magic of the Titans' (*svena, vīryeṇa darpitaḥ ... mohito'suramāyayā,* BD. VII, 54 f.) he attacks the Angels, and has to 'awakened' (*buddhvā*) before he returns to his allegiance. As maddened, deluded, and torpid his status is thus satanic, Lucifer has been darkened, and is then Satan.[6] This satanic possibility is necessarily realized in the due course of history, where it is represented by an actual revolt of the temporal power, such as is reflected in Jainism and

[4] Already in the Upaniṣads, kings are sometimes made out to have been the instructors of Brahmans.

[5] Abbreviations; *ṚV.* (or when no indication is given), *Ṛg Veda Saṁhitā; AV., Atharva Veda Saṁhitā; VS. Vājasaneyi Saṁhitā; AB., Aitareya Brāhamaṇa; ŚB., Śatapatha Brāhmaṇa; BD. Bṛhad Devatā; BU., Bṛhadāraṇyaka Upaniṣad; KS., Kalpasūtra, Jinacarita; D., Dīgha Nikāya; S., Saṁyutta Nikāya; Sn., Sutta Nipāta; J., Jātaka; SP., Saddharma Puṇḍarīka; JA. Journal Asiatique; JRAS, Journal Royal Asiatic Society; JAOS, Journal American Oriental Society; ZDMC, Zeitschrift der Deutschen Morgenländischen Gesellschaft; MASB, Memoirs Asiatic Society of Bengal.*

[6] Not to be confused, of course, with the Dragon, whom as Lucifer Indra has already overcome, but in his likeness; 'Hell' being a reflection of the Divine Fire, the 'Outer Darkness' a reflection of the Dark Ray, or wrath, and sundered from it by the width of the entire universe. In Pl. XXXVIII, Fig. 3, for example, the Serpent is not the Devil, but Death. In the same way in Buddhism, Māra (as Mṛtyu, 'Death', as Gandharva, 'Eros') is by no means Satan (as pretended by Przyluski, in *JA.* CCX, 1927, p. 122). Death is the Father, Life the Son; between whom there is an aeviternal opposition (*vyādhi*) *ab extra*, and an eternal at-one-ment (*samādhi*) *ab intra*. It is the destiny (*artha*) of every Hero to wrestle with the Father (the 'unfriendly father', *RV.* 1, 117, 17 and VI, 44, 22, or conversely 'unfriendly' son, X. 124, 2), to conquer Death; and when his course is run, not indeed to 'die', but to become our Father Death, cf. *BU.* 1, 2, 7, '*so punar ekaiva devatā bhavati mṛtyur eva, apa punar mṛtyuṁ jayati, nainam mṛtyur āpnoti*', 'He becomes again the Only Angel, even Death, he has defeated repeated death, death gets him not.' Death and Love unify (hence *ekaṁ bhū,* causative 'to slay', intransitive 'to die') and are immortal; Life divides (*pradhvansayan, AA.* III, 2, 3), Life comes and goes. Varuṇa, Mṛtyu-Gandharva, *nirguṇa brahman, amṛta: Mitra, āyus, Agni Vaiśvānara, martya.*

Neither must the occasion of Indra's fall be confused with his well known '*kilbiṣāṇi*', in which 'guilts' are included all those acts of violence, robbery, and deceit which are connected with the primordial act of procession. The distinction is sharp. The *kilbiṣāṇi,* things that must be done, and are actually done, by 'infallible necessity' (*necessitas infallibilitatis*); the pride and delusion which are the occasion of the fall are indeed inevitable and may be foreseen, but their actuality is a matter not of infallible but of 'affective necessity' (*necessitas coactionis*) and in the category of voluntary sin. More exactly, the acts of divine procession are in themselves altogether sinless and insofar as the proceeding power 'does not eat of the tree' but merely 'looks upon it' (*abhicākṣīti,* i.e. beholds the world picture as in Śaṅkara, Svātmanirūpaṇa, 96) remain immaculate; but insofar as the proceeding power 'eats of the tree' (*pippalam ... atti,* I, 164, 20) these are the acts of original sin, and as such forecast the subsequent pride and delusion (*darpa, moha*), their reward is death, and hence the prayer, 'Release us from the Father's property, from the fetter of Death, from all the angels' sin' (*muñcatu ... varuṇyād uta yamasya paḍbīṣāt devakilbiṣāt,* X, 97, 16).

As may been, Satan is not from the Indian point of view irredeemable; it is similarly understood in Islam that Iblīs will be restored at the end of time. This is also implied in the Christian formulation that the fallen angels are 'fallen not in nature but in grace'.

Buddhism, and can be recognized in every historical cycle.[7] We find in Jainism and Buddhism an emphatic assertion of the superiority of the *regnum* (*kṣatra*), and this in contemporary history coincides with the rule of such kings as Aśoka who are not of the divine lineage, but in the proper sense of the words 'tyrants' and 'usurpers', and as might be expected ardent patrons of those very heterodox faiths which justify the substitution of moral qualification for that of a 'character imprinted' by initiation. That a tyrant may be personally virtuous and courageous is not to the point here made. Whether virtuous or vicious, the tyrant is not ruling by divine right or according to the Supreme Law (Vedic *ṛta* and *dharma,* Pali *dhamma*), but in accordance with a personally good or evil will, and either way all kinds of irregularity are permitted.[8] What has been said above may seem to have been a digression, but has been necessary because it is precisely the expansion of a double heresy, at the same time spiritual and political, that can alone explain at once the rise of the heterodox sects themselves (in which the older myths are rationalized and humanized), and that of the patronage to which we owe the greater part of the monuments of early Indian art (in which the now pseudo-historical conceptions of the eternal Messiah are illustrated). It is then and therefore precisely at this point that an aniconic imagery and ritual procedure are first subordinated to the felt necessity for a more anthropomorphic symbolism, illustrative of the 'gospels' (*caritra*, etc.) in which the 'lives' of the Conquerors are related. That is also what took place in a somewhat different way at the close of the Middle Ages in Europe, 'classical' representation encroaching upon 'celtic' form, but with this distinction that whereas in Europe the ideal of the static figure before long altogether supplanted that of the kinetic form,[9] in India the concept of form continuously controlled even the figural representation, and has retained control until quite modern times; in India, the humanistic (as distinguished from the normally humane) point of view asserting itself only in Mughal painting in the sixteenth century, and elsewhere not before the still very recent surrender of Indian artistic orthodoxy to European sentimentality. One may say that the principles of art are preserved in India today only by the illiterate, for whose conservative ignorance we cannot be sufficiently thankful.

Notwithstanding, then, that the records of early Jaina art are far less complete than those of early Buddhist art, we can confidently attribute a first fixation of its dominant conceptions to a period antedating the beginning of the Christian era, and contemporary with the growth of the canonical literature. Apart even from the type of the seated Illuminate, common to Jainism and Buddhism, and known for both at least from the Kuṣāna period, there has long been known a relief from Mathurā,[10] having on one side a representation of the goat-headed genius Bhagavā Nemeso in the inscription (Hariṇegamesī in the *Kalpasūtra*), and on the other a dancing scene representing no doubt the music of Indra's court, as in Pl. XXXIII, Fig. 1; the theme of this slab is then that of 'Indra's command', and it may

---

If it is nevertheless said that Satan is beyond redemption, a reconciliation of the contrary dicta can be made as follows: in any temporal order there must always and inevitably be found a Satanic power, an Antichrist, but it by no means follows, nor can it indeed be, that in aeonic sequences this satanic power will be always individually the same. Satan's status from this long point of view is, like that of other angels (*devas*), rather that of a function than an individual property.

[7] In Europe, for example, at the close of the Middle Ages. The revolt of the temporal power is naturally followed by that of the economic power or bourgeoisie (the rise of merchant kings and accompanying colonial expansion in India, the rise of capitalistic industrialism in Europe), and this in turn by that of the manual or proletarian power (contemporary democracy in India and Europe, leading either to communism or to fascism).

[8] Aśoka is a 'genius', with all the liabilities of genius; the kingdom does not survive him; cf. Alexander, Akhenaton, Akbar and some more modern dictators, good or evil as the case may be. The work of genius cannot endure; it is always distorted by the followers and imitators. Work, on the other hand, that is devoid of idiosyncrasy, being conformed to the Eternal Law (*ṛta, dharma*), remains perpetually efficacious. What is indicated here in connection with politics, is equally applicable in the field of art.

[9] A masterly study of the European sequence in which the ideal of kinetic form is gradually superseded by that of the static figure, see A. Gleizes, Vers une conscience plastique, La Forme et l'Histoire, Paris, 1932.

[10] V.A. Smith, *Jaina Stupa of Mathura,* 1901, Pl. XVIII (misprinted XVII in Brown, loc. cit., p. 15). For other Kuṣāna representations see C.J. Shah, *Jainism in Northern India*, 1932, Pl. XXVI.

be remarked that representations of Indra's court and those of the actual commission entrusted to Hariṇegamesī are similarly closely associated in the illustrated manuscripts of more than a thousand years later date.[11]

The representations in Jaina Mss. of the *Kalpasūtra* story of the transference of the Conqueror's embryo from the womb of the Brāhmaṇī Devānandā to that of the Kṣatriyānī Tisalā (Triśalā) are very well known, and are again illustrated here in Pl. XXXIII, Fig. 2. It is by no means without sufficient reason that Indra is so much concerned in this matter of his namesake's, Mahāvīra's nativity. For the Jaina Conqueror's birth is analogically a birth of Indra himself, or what amounts to the same thing, of Indrāgnī, Indra and Agni being 'twins' (*RV.* VI. 59, 2, etc.), or again in other words, a birth of Indra as the Sun a resurrection of '*sol invictus*', '*il summa sol*'. The epithets Mahāvīra, 'Great Hero' and Vardhamāna, 'Waxing, or waxen, big', are propria of Indra (e.g. mahāvīra, *RV.* I, 32, 6; *vīratama* ... *nṛṇām* III, 52, 8; *pravṛddha,* IV, 18, 1; *vavṛdhāna,* V, 2, 12). Indra and Agni, or Indrāgṇī (king and priest, cf. Harihara), are born like every messianic hero, of two different mothers, of unlike aspect but kindred nature. In Christianity, for example, these are presupposed in the orthodox doctrine of the dual birth, temporal and eternal: the eternal mother being 'that nature by which the Father begets',[12] and from which the Son takes on that 'human nature that has nothing to do with time'; the temporal mother the Virgin Mary from whom he takes on human flesh, in V, 2, 2 Buddhist Mahā Māyā, Jaina Devānandā, Vaiṣṇava Devakī and Śaiva Satī, Kālī; the latter to Vedic 'Dawn' and 'Mother-Earth', Sūryā,[13] the handmaid[14] V, 2, 2, Saraṇyū's 'savarṇā', Indra's second mother Vikuṇṭ hī (daughter of Prajāpati, *BD.* VII 49-50), Buddhist Pajāpatī, Jaina Tisalā, Vaiṣṇava Yośodā[15] and Śaiva Pārvatī, Gaurī. The *Kalpasūtra* story of the Conqueror's nativity and corresponding illustrations reproduce with an almost literal fidelity *ṚV.* I, 113, 1-3 where Night 'when she hath conceived for the Sun's quickening, yields the place of birth (yoni) to Dawn', and I. 124, 8, where 'sister to more excellent sister yields the place of birth' (yoni).[16]

II

We pass on to a consideration of the fourteen prognostic dreams which are similarly transferred

[11] For examples of manuscript illustrations, and references to the literatures dealing with the complex figure of Hariṇegamesī, see Brown, loc. cit., pp. 14-18 and Figs. 5-15. The Manuscript Ha. described by Brown, p. 3, and from which he reproduces numerous subjects, is now in the Museum of Fine Arts, Boston (M.F.A. 35.38). My interpretation of the Mathurā relief is the same as Brown's but independent. In Brown's Fig. 13, it seems to me that the river separates earth from heaven; that the four-armed figure to right is that of Indra; and that the seated figure above is that of Śrī, (and thus 'in a more excellent way' that of Tisalā herself), the upper register in fact combining what is separately shown in Pl. XXXV, Figs. 3 and 4. The structure below to the left, which indeed looks like a kiln recurs in Pl. XXXV, Fig. 2 and may well represent a ghāṭ.

[12] St Thomas, *Sum. Theol.*, I, q. 41, a. 5 c, the Son of God being 'a natural son', bi, III, q. 32, a. 1. c., begotten 'by a vital operation from conjoint principles' (ib. I, q. q7, 1. 2).

[13] As distinguished from 'the other' (*anyām*) in X, 85, 21-2.

[14] *Peṣī*, the sense of which as referring to one who is second and subordinated to the Queen (*mahiṣī*) is clear enough from the context. A rendering as 'handmaid' is justifiable on the assumption that peṣī is from *piṣ* 'to grind', viz., in this connection, to 'grind corn', whence the sense of 'servant' or 'handmaid'.

[15] Foster-mother (not knowing that the child is not her very own) in the Vaiṣṇava story; as Yaśodharā, bride in the Buddha legend, but either way 'Dawn' (Uṣas, *yaśasvatī* in *RV.* I. 79, I and X, 11, 3).

[16] Cf. *RV.* III. 2, 2 and 11, 'He became the son of two mothers ... he was quickened in unlike wombs and was born as a bull or lion' (*ubhe sa mātror abhavat putraḥ* ... *sa jinvate jaṭhareṣu* ... *citreṣu nānadat,* etc.); Gopatha Brāhmaṇa, I, 33 'Two wombs, one generation' (*dve yonī ekam mithunam*); or as expressed by St Thomas, *Sum. Theol.* III, q. 35, a 5 ad 3, 'on the part of the child there is but one filiation in reality, though there be two in aspect.' In connection with Professor Brown's Fig. 14, a small correction may be made. For while it is true that 'in this art eyes are regularly represented open, no matter what the circumstances', it is not out of place that Devānandā's eyes should be open in this particular case, for Hariṇegameṣī is leaving, and it is expressly stated (*KS.* 31) that after the embryo had been removed, Devānandā 'woke up' (*paḍibuddhā*). As to this matter more generally, it may be observed that sleep or waking are indicated by the positions of the hands, as may be seen by a comparison of Professor Brown's Figs. 16 and 17.

from Devānandā to Tisalā. We shall not attempt to deal with all these in equal detail, but will say that all are characteristic prefigurations of the 'Great Hero' (mahāvīra) about to be born, the Sun about to rise. Agni is called a bull, in countless Vedic texts, and sometimes a lion, e.g. in I. 95, 5, 'when he is born, they (Heaven and Earth as Agni's parents) attend the lion lovingly' (*siṃhaṃ prati joṣayete*). The dream of a pure white elephant[17] (*KS.* 33, Pl. XXXIII, Fig. 3, Brown Fig. 21) not only parallels Mahā Māyā's prognostic dream of the birth of the Bodhisattva, but recalls *RV.* IV, 16, 14, where Indra, assimilated to the Sun, is compared to an elephant (and lion); cf. also *AV.* III, 22, I, invoking 'that elephant glory (varcas) that came into being from Aditi's body' and ib. 4-5, 'whatever splendour is the Sun's and the Titan-elephant's may that much elephant-glorious Indra-power (*indriyam ... hastivarcasam*) be congruent (*saṃ gacchasva*) in me'.[18]

In the vision of Śrī (Pl. XXXV, Fig. 4, Hg. folio 27, Brown Fig. 24) the goddess mother is seated as usual on a lotus that rises from a lotus lake (*pauma ddaha*, *KS.* 36, *padma hrada = puṣkariṇī*); the two lotus flowers mentioned in the text are held in her hands, but the *'disā ga'iṇḍoru pīvara karabhisiccamāṇim'* are omitted. The lotus lake is the same as the Milky Sea that is the subject of another dream, cf. Lakṣmī's epithet *'ksīrasāgara-sutā'*; Brown's Fig. 13, upper register, being precisely a combination of Pl. XXXV, Figs. 3 and 4. The vision of Śrī is really one of Tisalā herself in a glorified likeness, as Dawn and Mother Earth, Indrāṇī, etc., just as the representations of the Sirimātā in Buddhist art, although not strictly speaking 'nativities' are nevertheless 'maternities'. It may be added that in the Śrīsūkta,[19] which may be regarded as the principal authority for the Gaja-Lakṣmī type in art,[20] Śrī is referred to as the mother of sons, all of whom can be regarded

[17] Analogous to Tisalā's and Mahā Māyā's dreams of a white elephant is Vāmā Devī's vision of a snake crawling on the edge of her bed on the night of Pārśva's conception, who is so named because the snake (*sarpa*) entered her body from the side (*pārśva*, from *parśu*, 'rib'), as related by Devendra in comment on the Uttarādhyāyana, see Charpentier in *ZDMG.* 69, 1915, p. 35; that the snake 'crawled on' (*paḍisappantam = pratisarpantam*) manifestly constitutes an *'ati sarpaṇa'* like that by which the procession of Arbuda, the son of Kadrū, is effected in *AB.* VI, 1, cf. *ṚV.* IX, 86, 44 where Soma *'ahir na jūrṇam ati sarpati'*, 'as the serpent, over-creeps inveteration', i.e. is rejuvenated and born. Cf. *ṚV.* X, 86, 23, 'Parśu, daughter of Manu' and VIII, 6, 46 'Tirindira, child of Parśu'; even Indra's lateral birth (*pārśvāt*, V, 2, 2), prototype of Siddhārtha's in the Buddha legend, is at the same time a birth 'from Parśu'. As Manu's daughter, Parśu is Iḍā, Maitrāvāruṇī, Mother-Earth, etc., through whom he, Manu, begat the 'children of men' (*SB.* I, 8, 8-11). It is in the same way that Eve, who is the Man's Adam's 'rib', becomes the mother of all living (*Genesis*, III. 31), begotten in her by him. If it is not expressly stated that Pārśva, who entered his mother's side as a snake (as may be seen in the miniature reproduced by Brown, loc. cit., Fig. 89, upper register) was also born from her side, as might be expected per *analogiam,* there is nothing to prevent us from assuming a lateral birth in his case or that of any other of the 'Conquerors', which would accord with a rule that is not merely Indian, but universal, cf. for example, Rustam's birth by Caesarian operation, where the myth has been rationalized. The case of Jesus corresponds to that of Pārśva in that the texts are not explicit; in any case his birth is understood to have taken place 'without opening the passage' (St Thomas, *Sum. Theol.* III, 35, 6) and in Hieronymus (*Ad Jovinianum*, I, 42) is actually assimilated to the Buddha's 'to whom a virgin gave birth from her side' (*buddam ... a latere suo virgo generarit*).

[18] Cf. *RV.* X, 14, 8 *saṁ gacchasva tanvā suvarcā* (in connection with resurrection).

[19] Scheftelowitz, *Die Apokryphen des Ṛgveda,* Breslau, 1906, pp. 72-80, and 'Śrīsūkta', in *ZDMG.* 75, 1921, pp. 37-50.

[20] I take this opportunity to call attention to one of the many well known correspondences of Sumerian with Vedic formulation. That in the Gaja Lakṣmī compositions, Śrī-Lakṣmī is laved by heavenly streams pured out by the Dikpāla elephants from jars held in their trunks corresponding to the lustration of 'the "hand-maid of the Moon-god" when in pain she bore the divine calf Amarga' (Langdon, *Semitic Mythology,* pp. 96-7). In Vedic texts the 'divine calf' is always Agni, and the Theotokos never herself a solar, but always a lunar principle, an Asurī. The same may be observed in Christian iconography where the Virgin Mary, Mother of God, is often represented as standing or seated in the crescent of the moon, the light of the sun proceeding from the child in her arms. More strictly speaking, Aditi as the eternal mother in 'avinābhāva' union with the father, as nature to his essence, is altogether pythoness and titaness; Aditi as the temporal (aeonic) Mother, Earth and Dawn, Serpent Queen and Radiant Beauty (Śrī Lakṣmī), although the daughter of the Sun (Dante's 'O Virgin Mother, daughter of thy son') is Night and pythoness by mother-right, only 'changing her skin' and becoming 'sun-skinned' when she becomes the Bride and Milch-

as forms of Agni, Kardama for example corresponding to Purīṣya, and Ciklīta (identified with Jātavedas in the following khila) with the '*anaddhā-puruṣa*'. Agni made of clay and employed in the Agnicayana ritual (*VS.* XI, and *ŚB* VI, 3, 3, 4, and 4, 4, 14).

The case of the dream of the Fire is even more transparent, and of particular interest here on account of the magnificent illustration in Mr. Heeramaneck's Ms. Hg., folio 34, Brown loc. cit. Fig. 33, here reproduced in colour, Pl. XXXIV. In the text, *KS.* 46, 'She saw a fire in vehement motion, fed with very brilliant oil and mead (*mahughaya-parisiccamāṇa= madhu-ghṛta-pariśicyamāna*), smokeless[21] and crackling. The mass of its flames, rising one above the other made as it were a network, and here and there the tips of the quivering flames scorched as it were the very sky (*ambaraṁ va ... payantaṁ = ambaram iva ... pacat*, cf. *RV.* X. 45, 7, *śukreṇa śocisā dyām anakṣan*). The great fire is blazing on a mountain. As being fed with oil and mead or honey, this is in any case a sacrificial fire; and both in this respect and as being kindled on or from the mountain, answers to countless Vedic accounts of the first kindling of Agni, for example I, 13, 3-5 '*(agniṁ) madhujihvaṁhaviṣkṛtam ... barhir ... ghṛtapṛṣṭ ham'*, and I, 93, 6, '*amanthād (agniṁ) pari śyeno adreḥ'*. In the smaller representations of the Fire, in miniatures in which all of the Fourteen Dreams are seen together, it is always shown as burning actually upon an altar (vedi), of the type familiar on Kuṣāṇa coins.

Tisalā sees also the Milky Sea (*khīroya sāyaram = kṣīra-sāgaram*) 'with its waters spreading in all directions, its wind-driven billows rushing to and from the shore, lashed to foam by the monsters of the deep, with the mighty roar of Gaṅgā-eddy (*gaṅgāvarta*)', etc. (*KS.* 43, abbreviated). The picture, Pl. XXXV, Fig. 1, Hg. folio 32, Brown Fig. 30, shows us more than this. Here is the dangerous River of Life, with its near and farther shores, and a '*mumukṣu*' waiting on the bank, eager to board the Ship of Life, the Sun-ship, floating on the stormy waters.[22] The mast of this ship is the axis of the universe, cf. *Daśakumāracarita,* introductory verse, 'mast of the ship of the earth, axis of the Zodiac' (*kṣaunī-nau-kūpa-daṇdda ... jyotiścakrākṣa-daṇḍa*), and the 'one foot' of the Sun, who as the watcher in the crow's nest surveys the universe (*abhi yo viśvā bhuvanāni caṣṭe, RV.* VII, 61, 1 and parallel passages). An altogether analogous representation is that of the 'mansion of the Sun', illustrated from an Alpana painting in A.N. Tagore's *Bāṅglār Vrata*, Pl. 99.[23]

'Then she saw a banner (*dhayam=dhvajam*) supported by a golden staff', etc. (*KS.* 40-1) as represented in Pl. XXXV, Fig. 2, Brown Fig. 28, Hg. folio 31. The corresponding Vedic '*ketu*', 'banner', is always the referent for Agni, Indra, or the Sun, and of the separation of light from darkness, cf. I, 129, I, where in the beginning 'there was no "*ketu*" of day and night', whereas in X, 103, 11, Indra is called upon for aid in battle with the Titans when the 'flags are gathered' (*saṁṛteṣu dhvajeṣu*), and when the Sun is risen 'his banners (*ketavaḥ*), his rays, are seen abroad amongst the kindreds, like shining fires' (*AV.* XIII, 2, 16), cf. Song of Solomon, VI, 4, 'Terrible as an army with banners'; in the *Daśakumāracarita*, l.c., 'the staff of the banner of the river of life' (*kṣaradamara-sarit-ketu-daṇḍa*) is again an aspect of the axis of the universe.[24]

---

cow by whom all things are brought forth and from whom all milk their nature. For all this see my 'Darker side of Dawn', Washington, 1935; and with *RV.* X. 85, 24, f. compare St Bernard, *Cominica Prima post Octavum Epiphaniae,* II, 2, 'Christ will present his bride, whom he loved in her baseness and all her foulness, glorious with his own glory, his Church without spot or wrinkle.' It may be added in connection with the Vedic equivalence of Dawn and Mother-Earth (here represented by Śrī, established on her lotus-ground) that in Sumerian doctrine also Mother-Earth, 'the mother of mankind', is 'heavenly lady' and the 'light of heaven' (Langdon, *Semitic Mythology,* pp. 12, 91).

[21] Cf. *Kaṭha Up.*, IV. 3, *puruṣo ... jyotir iva adhūmakaḥ.*

[22] Cf. for example, *RV.* VII, 88, 3, 'Where I with Varuṇa embarked, drove out our bark into mid-ocean, rode on the crests of the waves, there let us swing in the easy-riding swing'; *AV.* XII, 2, 47, 'Mount this ship of Savitṛ's, let us cross over'; *ŚB.* II, 3, 3, 14-15, 'This ship is heavenwardbound' (*naur ha vā eṣā svargyā*).

[23] The chevron running down the mast is a lightning motif, and can be recognized also in the Alpana painting. In the latter, the 'world' (represented by the circle or square) and the 'earth-ship' below it, and by which the Sun's one foot is supported (*pratiṣtha*), are separated; in the Jaina miniature combined to form an 'ark' with its 'beasts' (*paśavaḥ*).

[24] The axis of the universe has many aspects in one and the same, as well as in cognate traditions. Beside

For the lotus lake (*puṇḍarīya, KS.* 42 = *puṇḍarīka*) cf. *ṚV.* X, 107, 10, where the place in which Indra's nuptials with the Guerdon (Dawn) are to be consummated is 'like a lotus-lake' (*puṣkariṇīva*), and X, 142, 8 'Let there be pools and lotus-lakes' (*puṇḍarīkāṇi*). The resonant abode (*vimāna*) of light (*KS.* 42, Brown Fig. 31) corresponds to the Vedic 'chariot of light' (*jyotiratha*), wherein Agni, Indra, and all the deities proceed.

'The brimming vase (*punna kalasa, KS.* 41 = *pūrṇa kalśa, pūrṇa ghaṭa*) abode of Lakṣmi, with its bunch of lotus' (*kamala-kalāva=kamala kalāpa*) is perhaps the most familiar of all auspicious symbols throughout the history of Indian art. It is precisely as the abode of Śrī-Lakṣmī as well as by itself that the brimming vase appears repeatedly in early Buddhist art, for example at Sāñcī.[25] Examples are illustrated here in Pl. XXXV, Fig. 2 (to lower right) and Pl. XXXVI, (a large and admirably executed painting on cotton, unfortunately badly worn). It is, however, a peculiarity of Jaina art that this '*punna kalasa*', the Vessel of Plenty, is regularly provided with eyes, and thus indeed animated. This form of the symbol has been discussed by Hüttemann (Baessler Archiv, IV. 1914, pp. 52-3) and by Brown, loc. cit., p. 12. According to Hüttemann: Die Vase ist das Symbol des vollkommensten Wissens, des '*kevalañāṇa-daṃsana*'. Brown suggests that the vase=cloud, and that the eyes are 'a vestigial representation of the sun', and cites *AV.* XIX, 53, 3, where 'a Full Vessel is set up in Time'. A similar symbol is constantly employed in Mesopotamian art[26] where it is always the source of two flowing streams (Vedic *dvidhārāḥ*). The brimming and inexhaustible vessel, then, is a representation of the Fountain of Life, and as a symbol seems to say 'Let Soma never lack, that giveth rest' (*somasya śambhuvaḥ*, I, 105, 3), 'May that unfailing spring (*utsam ... akṣitam*) that the Maruts milk (*duhantaḥ*) be ever available' (VIII, 7, 16); it is the 'reservoir' (*kośam*, VIII, 72, 8) and 'inexhaustible well (*avatam ... akṣitam*) of Soma', ib. 10-11. It is indeed just as a '*pūrṇa kalaśa*' that the reservoir of Soma is represented under Varuṇa's protection, at Bādāmī.[27]

It is moreover precisely in this connection that the eyes, which could in any case be regarded as Varuṇa's eyes, whether the Sun (X, 88, 13, and X, 129, 7) or Sun and Moon (*akṣī divas*, I, 72, 10 and implicit in V, 62, 8), can best be explained, viz., as 'the eyes of Soma, by which eyes of ours we see the Golden (Sun, or Germ)' (*somasya svebhir akṣabhiḥ*) I, 139, 2); as to which 'eyes'[28] a fuller explanation is given in *AB.* II, 32, 'The eyes of the Soma-pressings are the silent praise (*tuṣṇīṃ-śaṅsa= orationes secretae*). ... He who is a comprehensor of this, he by means of the eyed Soma-pressings reaches the light-world. The silent praise is the eye of the Sacrifice but though the silent praise is actually one, it is uttered twice, so that the one eye may be a pair of eyes.[29]

These more fully documented explanations are by no means contradictory of those suggested

---

the aspects mentioned above there may be cited also those of the staff of the umbrella of cosmic dominion, that of the axle-tree of the chariot of light (the wheels of which are Heaven and Earth), that of the stem of the rose or lotus that represents the Mother of God, that of the Soma-stalk (*RV.* IX, 74, 2), and that of the Śiva-liṅgam. The axis is also the trunk of the Tree of Life, the sacrificial post (*yūpa*), the vertical (*stauros*, Skt. *skambha*) of the Cross, and the Islamic qutb. All things are figured (*ārpita, AV.* X, 7, 32) in this axis.

[25] Not indeed as a nativity, but perhaps as a 'maternity', cf. my notice of Foucher's Iconography of the Buddha's Nativity, in *JAOS*, 55, pp. 323-5.

[26] E.D. Van Buren, *The Flowing Vase and the God with Streams*, Berlin, 1933.

[27] My *Yakṣas*, II, Washington, 1931, Pl. 45, Fig. 1. A large variety of forms of the brimming vase are illustrated in this tract, with discussion, pp. 61-4.

[28] The 'eyes' in I, 139, 2 are those of contemplation (*dhī*) and intellect (*manas*), terms which correspond again with Sun and Moon (Cf. *BU.* 1, 3, 14 and 16, and *ŚB.* X. 3. 3. 7). The text reads actually: *somabhiṣ cana manasā svebhir akṣabhiḥ somasya svebhir akṣabhiḥ*, 'With contemplations and with intellect, the eyes of Soma, by which our eyes', etc., and there can be no doubt that Grassmann is right in taking '*cana*' here as '*bejahende*'.

[29] An analogy can be recognized in the ocelli painted on the bows of Indian ships, and ancient ships elsewhere, whereby these ships are as it were animated and assimilated to the Sun-ship and the living (*ātmanvat*) ships of the Aśvins. Inasmuch as the two sides of the ship (*naumaṇḍe, ŚB.* II, 3, 3, 15=*bhittī*, cf. *naumaṇḍa* in *JB.* I, 125, *naurmaṇḍapa* in *Bauddha. ŚS.*, sometimes mistranslated 'rudders'), like the two wheels of the chariot of light, correspond to *bṛhat* and *rathantara, āhavanīya* and *gārhapatya*. Heaven and Earth, the two eyes must be those of the Sun and Moon. For illustrations, see J. Hornell, Indian boat designs, *MASB.*, Calcutta, 1920.

by Hüttemann and Brown, whose interpretations, taken together, in the same way demonstrate for this symbol a significance both physical and spiritual.[30]

III

Turning now from the prefiguring dreams to their realization, we shall consider two more, and by no means the least informative of the types of Jaina illustrations. Plate XXXVII reproduces a remarkable picture of the 'Fortunate Sunrise' (*śrī sūryodaya* is the marginal annotation) of the morning following the night of Tisalā's dreams and actual conception. 'He, the thousand-eyed (i.e. all seeing) maker of the day, shining in his radiance, awakened the groups of lotuses (i.e. the 'grounds of all the worlds). When in due season the Angel of Day had arisen and by the blows of his hands the darkness was expelled, they the Kṣatriya Siddhatta[31] rose from his bed' (*sayaṇijjao abbhuṭṭhei, KS. 59 = śayanīyā abhyuttiṣṭhati*). That is in effect a description of the First Sunrise in the beginning of days (*agre ahuān*) so often celebrated in *ṚV.*; that Siddhattha 'rises from his couch' is more than a simple daily awakening, it is the resuscitation of the Father in the Son, in accordance with the Vedic conception of linear descent, in which the son becomes the 'father's father' (*pituṣpitṛ*) as well as his 'own son', or grandson, '*tanūnapāt'*, for Agni, indeed is kindled by Agni (I, 12, 6). That sunrise and that sun are indeed the same as those of the corresponding hour when the Great Hero has been actually born and the 'universe is resplendent with one light' (*KS.* 97, cf. *jyotir jyotiṣām* 'light of lights', *ṚV.* I, 113, 1; *jyotir ekam bahubhyah,* 'one light for many', I, 93, 4; *ekaḥ sūryah,* 'one Sun', VIII, 58, 2, etc., and similarly J.I. 76, *ekobhāsā ahesum*) which is the manifestation of the Conqueror in the worlds.[32] In the miniature, to cite Professor Brown, 'the bright golden ball of the sun, with first a blue and then a white rim against a red background (cf. *KS.* 59, "the inhabited world was, as it were, dipped in saffron"), is just above a variegated mountain peak.' That is mount Meru, Vedic '*parvata, adri*', 'The rock of ages', *adrim acyutam,* VI, 17, 5, whence the cattle (potentialities unrealized) are freed, the Rock (*aśman*) whence flows the River of Life, '*aśmanvatī, sarasvatī*', *ṚV.* passim; the Himavat of *KS.* 36, and Meru 'around which the Sun for ever circles', *KS.* 39.[33] It is upon this same Meru that Indra performs the Conqueror's lustration (*abhiseya = abhiṣeka* described in *KS.* 97-9), which is not

[30] A similar dual application of all symbols (actually, the distinction of *karma* from *jñāna kāṇḍa*) is highly characteristic of the Vedic tradition, and therefore no more than might be expected in the present case. The same holds good for the analogous Vessel in the Grail tradition, where the Chalice is at the same time a food-provider and a manifestation of the highest truth. The designation of Soma as *śambhū,* rendered by 'that giveth rest' is significant in this connection; for this 'rest', from one point of view, is that which is coincident with the attainment of desire, and from another is the peace of liberation from desire, inasmuch as we no longer desire, but rather love, what we possess.

[31] In the Buddhist legend, Siddhārtha is the name of the Son. In either case the goal (*artha*) attained is that foreseen by Agni, X, 51, 5, 'That was the goal (*etam artham*) I, Agni, wotted of. Note in this connecton that the Buddha's corresponding Hesitation (*Brahmasaṁyuttam, S.* I, 138 f.) is like Agni's really a trepidation—'It was foreseeing hurt (*vihiṁsa*) that I did not utter the Eternal Law.' In both cases the unitary principle 'shrinks from' the division (extension, crucifixion) inseparable from procession; both express the thought, 'May this cup be taken from me'; both assume their task.

[32] The release of prisoners and remission of debts (*KS.* 102) in accordance as it is with Indian custom at the 'birth of a royal heir', corresponds in reality to the Harrowing of Hell on the occasion of the Bodhisattva's Awakening, *J.* I, 76, and this is really a 'release from what is Varuṇa's, from Yama's hobble, from all original sin' (*ṚV.* X, 97, 16). That it is the Indian custom to release prisoners, etc., at the birth of a royal heir affords an admirable example of 'regularity', as this term is employed technically in connection with 'agibilia': The pattern of an orthodox society is, just as much as its ritual where everything is done 'in imitation of what was done in the beginning' exemplary, and precisely therefore 'regular' (*ṛtvya, dharmya*). Exogamy, for example, 'depends' upon the principle that the Theotokos is never a Devī, but always an Asurī, i.e. in origin, though she becomes, a Devī by her marriage, just as a woman becomes a 'member' of her husband's family.

[33] The mountain corresponds to the Buddhist gṛdhrakūṭa, 'Vulture Peak', cf. *SP.* XV, 10, 'I have never left this Vulture Peak.' That Indra is the officiant corresponds not only to the Brahmanical part he also plays as Agnīdh when he brings the strew for the Bodhisattva's Throne of Awakening (*bodhi-pallaṁka* = Vedic vedi), but equally to his position in *RV. passim*, as officiant at the First Sacrifice, where he obtains his title of 'Hero'.

merely a natal bath and baptism, but a royal initiation (*rājasūya*)[34] as represented in Pl. XXXVIII, Fig. 1; and also, one cannot doubt, the same as the mountain upon which, again with Indra officiating, the Conqueror's sacerdotal initiation (*dīkṣā*) is effected, as represented in Pl. XXXVIII, Fig. 2. Both of the characters thus formally communicated and imprinted are the Conqueror's by divine right, as they are those of every Messiah born in the '*genealogia regni dei*'.[35]

[34] According to which Indra's *vīrya* is linked with that of his namesake, in the manner described in *ŚB.* V, 4, 2, 8-9, citing *VS.* X, 20. It should be noted that *vīrya* is 'heroism' not merely in the sense of 'bravery', but as the 'whole virtue' of the 'Hero', his 'manhood' (not 'humanity') in every sense, and as 'virility', including the 'seminal virtue' (cf. Bühler's rendering of *vīrya* by 'seed' in his translation of *Manu,* I, 8). It is then as much by his vivifying power as by his bravery that the Hero conquers Death, and awakens these that are asleep.

[35] It is remarkable and not without its ironies, that both of the Conquerors, both Great Heroes (Buddhist and Jaina), despite the vehement assertations of Kṣatriya superiority that have been made, abandon the household life, receive a sacerdotal initiation (which is also a 'second birth'), and play the parts of the priestly and omniscient Agni, that of the Brahman who 'jītavidyāṁ vadati', *ṚV.* X, 71, 11; the abandonment of the household life (*abhinikkhamana*) is precisely the translation of Agni from the *gārhapatya* to the *āhavanīya* altar. The superiority of knowledge to action, that of intellectual to physical operation, which is of the essence of Brahmanical and of all other orthodox doctrines, is freely admitted; the Kṣatriya as such, the man of action as such, is treated as a mere worlding. And this is carried so far that one may say that in Buddhism and Jainism, the position of the *kṣatra*, the *regnum*, although nominally exalted, is actually degraded. What corresponds in Europe is the replacement of the concepts of purity and regularity by those of Puritanism and moralism. The sensibility that is in a measure proper to the *regnum* (as distinguished from the *sacerdotum*), now unrestrained and overreaching, becomes a sentimentality, or in other words materialism, characteristically expressed in an undue contempt of the world, no longer seen as a theophany. On the other hand, the doctrine of a due proportion of the outer to the inner life is maintained in both the orthodox developments of Vedic tradition, respectively Vaiṣṇava (*karma yoga*, Kṣatriya initiation) and Śaiva (*jñāna yoga*, Brāhmaṇa initiation). In other words, the Indian rejection of Buddhism was normative, in the same sense that the 'Thomist revival' (considered apart from the bigotry of some of its exponents) is normative at the present day.

We consider next the representation of an apparently trivial episode of the 'enfances', based on Hemacandra's *Triṣaṣtiśalākāpuruṣ acaritra, parva* 10, summarized by Brown, loc. cit., p. 32 in connection with his reproduction of the same miniature, our Pl. XXXVIII, Fig. 3. A deity unnamed in this text, but in whom we have previously recognized Death (*mṛtyu*),[36] is jealous of the Great Hero's virtue (*vīryam,* virile power),[37] and upon an occasion when the latter is at play[38] with his companions, 'assumed the form of a serpent and appeared at the foot of a tree', just as Māra in the Buddha legend appears at the foot of the Tree of Awakening. All but the Great Hero are terrified and run away (as Indra is similarly deserted in his conflict with Vṛtra, *ṚV.,* VIII, 96, 7; *AB.* IV, 5, etc., and the Bodhisattva in his conflict with Māra, J.I, 72). Presently the serpent assumes the form of one of the boy companions, and is no longer recognized; all set about to climb the tree; the winner is to have the privilege of riding on the backs of the losers. Mahāvīra naturally reaches the top first, and there 'shines like the Sun above Mt Meru', while his companions hand below as 'branch-creatures', i.e. like birds or monkeys. Expressed in Vedic terms, the Great Hero has defeated Death, and as the Solar Eagle rests on the topmost branch of the Tree of Life, while below him are all creatures, nested in its branches; as in *ṚV.* I, 164, 22, 'It is in that tree that all the eagles taste the mead, abide, and make their nests; at its top, they say, the fig is sweet, which none may reach who knoweth not the Father',

[36] *MFA Bulletin,* No. 197, p. 38, q.v. I have since discovered (Ramachandran, loc. cit. p. 117) that the story is also told in the *Śrī Purāṇa* (Vol. IV) and in the *Vardhamāna Purāṇa,* and that here the name of serpent is given there as Saṁgama, i.e. Death, cf. *ṚV.* X, 14, 1, where Yama is *saṁgamano jananām.* The episode is illustrated amongst the older paintings at Tiruparuttikuṇṛam, see Ramachandran, Pl. VII, Fig. 1.

[37] It is precisely by his 'virile-energy' (*vīryeṇa,* II, 11, 5) that Indra (*mahāvīra* in I, 32, 6) overcomes the serpent, Ahi, who is also Vṛtra, Death, etc.

[38] 'Play,' sc. *līlā*; cf. *ṚV.* IX, 20, 7 where Soma goes, 'playfully' (*krīḷuḥ*) to his sacrificial death; X, 3, 5 where Agni's flames are 'playful'; X, 85, 18 and 42, *krīḷantau;* X, 79, 6 *akrīḷan krīḷan;* and twenty-five other Vedic uses of root krīḷ, and the 'stag at large' in VII, 87, 2; and Eckhart's 'Eternal playing of the Son ... there has always been this play going on ... eternally before all creatures ... sport and players are the same' (I, 148).

cf. also *PB.* XIV, I, 13 where it is a matter of climbing a tree, and the question is put, 'Those who ascend to the top of the great tree, how do they fare thereafter?', and answered 'Those who have wings fly away, those without wings fall down'; on climbing the tree, cf. also *PB.* IV. 7. 10. and *JUB.* I. 3 and III. 13.

IV

Let us consider, in conclusion, no longer the explicit references of the paintings, but the manner in which these references are made. In the miniature last discussed, an example may be seen of the method known as 'continuous narration' or 'continuous action', defined in Professor Brown's words as 'the portraying in one composition of two or more scenes from the same series'. Taking first the right hand half of the picture, we see Mahāvīra alone, carrying a 'hockey-stick',[39] and before him the Serpent, coiled about the Tree (in a fashion suggestive of Christian representation of the Fall, where indeed the 'situation', viz., 'in Eden', is the same, although the 'event' is different; Mahāvīra's right hand is extended, perhaps about 'to pick up the snake like a piece of rope and throw it to the ground'. There is no indication of a climbing contest (which seems to be implied by the figures of the two companions in the upper register of Brown's Fig. 67); the Snake is not represented as climbing in competition, for its is in the form of one of Mahāvīra's playmates, and not 'propria persona', that the Snake competes. Then considering only the left hand side of the picture, and ignoring the Serpent, but not the Tree (which still defines the 'situation') we see the Great Hero, nimbate as before, but now having won the forfeit, riding on the back of one of the companions, or more probably on the back of the Serpent, on the shoulders of Death, still in the assumed person of one of the companions.[40] In the same way in Brown's Fig. 106, the painter 'combines two moments of the narrative ... the urging by Krishna's wives and the urging by Krishna himself' (Brown, loc. cit., p. 46).

The method of continuous narration is not of course specifically Jaina, nor even specifically Indian, but rather simply 'primitive'. In Pl. XXXVIII, Fig. 4 we adduce an excellent example from a Buddhist source of the second century BC, i.e. antedating by more than a millennium and a half the Jaina miniatures that have been discussed above. In this Buddhist relief the Nāga Erakapatra is shown three times in one and the same composition,[41] first as a seven-headed serpent in its own watery home, then in human form with serpent hoods, still in the waters, but in an attitude of worship, and finally in this second form kneeling beside the altar and tree that represent the Buddha.

Here, then, is a method of narration ... possible in visual art, but difficult in words[42] according to which a succession of events is actually represented in spatial simultaneity. The method contrasts with that of a now much more familiar and 'realistic' type of art in which a strictly momentary condition, rather than a continuous act of being, is depicted. The limiting concepts are on the one hand that of the 'world-picture' (*jagac-citra*)[43] in which all that belongs

[39] For discussion of this motif, see Brown, loc. cit. p. 32. The representation in contemporary Western Indian Vaiṣṇava paintings the stick is like a polo-stick, and probably served as a herdsman's crook as well as for play.

[40] In the conclusion, the Serpent again assumes a terrible ophidian form, but is defeated in conflict, does reverence to Mahāvīra, and retires to its own place. Here the equivalence to Krishna's *Kāliya-damana* is evident.

[41] For the story see *JRAS.* 1928, pp. 629/30. The type of the seven-hooded, or sometimes three-hooded Nāga of Indian iconography is the protean serpent dragon (Ahi-Vṛtra-Viśvarūpa) whose seven-rayed head becomes by sacrificial transformation Agni, or the Sun with his seven rays, or Seven Suns that light the Seven Regions. Similarly the Sumerian Mushussu, seven-headed dragon slain by Ninurta, and as Langdon remarks (*Semitic Mythology,* p. 130) 'it would be remarkable if this entire Indian and Iranian legend was not ultimately Sumerian'. The same applies to the slaying of a polycephalous Hydra by Herakles (really a conflict of the Son with the Father), cf. Frankfort, 'Gods and myths on Sargonid seals', *Iraq,* I, 1934, p. 19. Erakapatra's procession is an *ati sarpaṇa* in the sense already explained, see also my Darker Side of Dawn, Washington, 1935, and 'Angel and Titan, a study in Vedic ontology', to appear in *JAOS* immediately.

[42] Possible, however, when words employed not as signs but as symbols are pregnant with many meanings; such a use of words tending towards the concept of the single Word (vāc) by which and in which the divine intellect (*manas*) expresses and creates all things, cf. *RV.* VIII. 24. 7 *viśvāni viśvamanasaḥ*. 'Oṁ' is a 'continuous narrative'.

[43] Śaṅkarācārya *Svātmanirūpaṇa,* 96; *Genesis,* 1, 31; etc.

to every where and every when takes place immediately and is seen at a single glance without duration or spatial analysis; and on the other, that of the static glimpse of what takes place at a single moment in a given time sequence and in a given place determinable geographically. These limiting concepts are then of two entirely different 'nows'; in one case the now of eternity, in the other a dateable now; and in the same way, concepts of two entirely different 'heres', one that is everywhere, the other local. Evidently, the continuously narrative art tends rather to the representation of the now of eternity apart from temporal and spatial extension, than to the now envisaged by the painter of effects and of events.

In this respect the visual art again reflects a point of view that is unequivocally expressed in the Vedas, that of the real immediacy of all the happenings that may seem to be described as taking place in succession. We have treated of this elsewhere in an article entitled Eternal Creation in the *Ṛg Veda*,[44] and shall do so now more briefly. That the divine life is uneventful is indicated in *ṚV.* by the constant use of the historical present; by the constant employment of such words as '*sadya*',[45] '*makṣu, muhur*', and '*nu*' in the sense 'immediately' and not at any one time more than another; and by explicit statements contradicting from the '*jñāna kāṇḍa*' and '*paramārthika*' point of view the reality of those 'events' that are related elsewhere in the form of 'myths' and 'legends' (*ākhyāna, itihāsa*) and, from the literal-minded (*karma-kāṇḍa* and *pratyakṣa-priya*) point of view ... that of the lowest level of reference ... may seem to have actually 'taken place'.

That *RV.* deals as stated above only with a timeless act of being will be illustrated here only briefly. Taken together, the three citations next following assert the simultaneity of the Conception, Nativity, and Mission: III, 29, 3 'No sooner impregned than bare the Bull' (*sadyaḥ pravitā vṛṣaṇamajana*); IV, 7, 10 'No sooner born than he displayed his vital-power' (*sadyaḥ jātasya dadṛśānam ojas*); X, 115, 1 'No sooner born than instant waxed and went on his great errand' (*yadi jījanad ... nu vavakṣa sadyo mahi dūtyam caran*). In the same way it is said that all of Indra's famous battles are merely works of imagination, as true and no more true today tha they were in the beginning, as true and no more true here than at the outermost limits of space: 'All that they call thy battles, Indra, are indeed nothing but thy Magic (*māyetsā te yāni yuddhāni āhuḥ*), neither hast thou, any foe today, nor hast thou ever had in time past' (X, 54, 2, cf. VI, 18, 12); 'It is by thy speculation that thou art most slayer of the Dragon' (*dhiyā ... vṛtrahantamaḥ,* VIII, 24, 7).[46] It is the cutting edge of the 'tongue' by way of 'axe' that 'hews' (*takṣ*) the wood of which the world is made (e.g. I, 20, 2 *vacoyuja tatakṣa manasā*), by way of spade that digs up Agni (*ŚB.* VI, 3, 1, 34 and 4, 1, 5). The creation, in other words in noumenal and nominal, a matter of nomenclature (*nāmadheya*), that is to say of ideas only, of all those forms (*nāmāni*) that Varuṇa knows speculatively (*dhiyā*), mirrored, that is to say, in that world-picture of which we spoke above.

The actus primus (*ārambha*) of the human artist (*mantrin, śilpin,* etc.) is in the same way a contemplation (*dhyāna*), the actus secundus or servile operation (*karma, vrata*) an imitation (*anukaraṇa*) of this vision (*tad dhyātam*) seen as if in a mirror (*pratibimbavat*), i.e. 'speculatively'. We can hardly wonder then that the result should be in some degree comparable to the world-picture, to some extent and as far as possible a representation of things *sub specie aeternitatis* apart from time and space. The same thing can be recognized in the technique of vertical projection, perspective à cheval, the 'bird's eye' view of things, which is so characteristic of Jaina painting and Indian art generally as well as of other traditional arts. For it is again the Sun, Varuṇa's 'eye', Agni as Mitra '*uṣarbudh*', the Buddha as 'eye in the world' (*cakkhuṁ loke, D.* II, 158, S. I, 138, *Sn.* II, 9, 6,[47] the Sun who is most eminently 'equestrian', and is the 'bird' that sees the world-picture (*viśvam abhi caṣṭe,*

[44] To appear in the *Vedanta Kesari*, Ramakrishna Memorial Number; and in French, in Le Voile d'isis.

[45] Literally, 'today', 'this day'. Cf. Eckhart and others, '*hodie est eternitas*'.

[46] In other words, the whole of *RV.* is an 'arrangement' of God, who is variously named according to his manifestations (V, 44, 6), whom being One they subdivide mentally (X, 114, 5, cf. III, 19, 4 and VIII, 58, 1), the Sacrifice by which he is extended (X, 90, 6) and discriminated (X, 90, 14) being essentially eternal, and (like the Christian Sacrifice, the Mass) only accidentally connected with time, for 'He has once for all done what is inimitable as long as the sun and moon alternately shall rise' (X, 68, 10, Macdonell's translation).

[47] *Sn.* III, 9, 6, *bhagavan buddhacakkunā lokaṁ volokesi.*

etc. *RV.* I, 164, 44, II, 40, 5, VII, 61, 1, X, 85, 18, etc., *Kaṭha Up.* V, II)[48] spread out (*uttānam, prathitam*) like a map without horizons (*aparimāṇa, aparidhi*), and not as one sees who stands below and gazes horizontally, where 'distance' is obscured by 'foreground'.[49]

We are not by any means suggesting that the methods of continuous narration and vertical projection were devised in order to be the presentation of a vision of things apart from time and space, but rather that things seem apart from time and space, in '*dhyāna*' Vedic '*dhi*' could not have been otherwise represented. One could not merely by an arbitrary and 'archaistic' imitation of the method repeat its implications; the thing must 'proceed from within, moved by its form'. The modality of 'primitive' art is not a 'style' adapted by a process of reasoning to a given content, but concreated with its content, just as whatever is created in the likeness of a given form is not an imitation of a preexisting form, but, 'concreated' with its form, by which it is informed.[50]

It has thus been demonstrated what is the ultimate content of Jaina art, and that its stylistic formulae are not merely appropriate to, but inseparable from the expression of this content, and as a matter of infallible necessity. All this will apply with equal validity to the interpretation of the iconography and techical formulae of other than Jaina Indian arts, none of which can be profoundly understood apart from their roots in Vedic symbolism; and will apply in the same way to all other orthodox arts, Christian or folk art for example. For the burden and idiom alike of all such orthodox art has been continuously transmitted in accordance with the 'universal and unanimous tradition' (*sanātana dharma, philosophia perennis,* etc.) of which the ultimate source is a 'revelation' (*śruti,* etc.) received in the beginning from the Light of Lights.

LIST OF ILLUSTRATIONS

Plate XXXIII, Fig. 1. Indra's court. Ms. Ha., now Museum of Fine Arts, Boston, No. 35. 38; Fig. 2. Hariṇegamesī leaving Devānandā. M.F.A., Boston, Ms. No. 17. 2277; Fig. 3. Tisalā's dream of the White Elephant. Ms. Hg., Heeramaneck collection.

Plate XXXIV. Tisalā's dream of the Fire. Ms. Hg., Heeramaneck collection.

Plate XXXV. Fig. 1. The Milky Ocean. Ms. Hg., Heeramaneck collection; Fig. 2. Tisalā's dream of the Banners, and the Brimming Vase. Ms. Hg., Heeramaneck collection; Fig. 3. Tisalā's dream of the Lotus Lake, Ms. Hg., Heeramaneck collection. Fig. 4. Tisalā's dream of Śrī-Lakṣmī. Ms. Hg., Heeramaneck collection.

Plate XXXVI. The Brimming Vase, Painting on cotton, fifteenth century, M.F. A. No. 33. 679.

Plate XXXVII. The Glorious Sunrise. Ms. Ha., M.F.A. No. 35. 38.

Plate XXXVIII. Fig. 1 Mahāvīra *abhiṣeka;* the child is seated in Indra's lap, on Mt Meru. Ms. Fr., Freer Gallery; Fig. 2. Mahāvīra's *dīkṣā,* Indra officiating. M.F.A., Boston, Ms. No. 17.2277: Fig. 3. Mahāvīra and the Serpent, Saṁgama. Ms. Ha., M.F.A. No. 35. 38. Fig. 4. The Procession of Erakapatra Nāgarāja. Bharhut, ca. 175 BC. Calcutta Museum.

[48] *Kaṭha Up.,* V. 11, *Sarvalokasya cakṣuḥ.*

[49] The solar point of view (*darśaṇa*) is not only a hieratic, but also the royal point of view, as distinguished from the plebeian point of view implied by horizontal perspective; the Sun being husband of the Earth stretched out below him (*uttānam bhūmim,* X, 27, 13 and X, 142, 5) in the same way that a king is the husband of the earth (bhūpati).

[50] The familiar doctrine of the inseparability of content and style has been expressed as follows: 'The idea of a work is in the mind of the operator as that which is understood, and not as the image whereby he understands' and 'Creation does not mean the building up of a composite thing from preexisting principles, but it means that the composite is created so that it is brought into being at the same time with all its principles' (St Thomas, *Sum. Theol.,* I.q. 15, a. 2 c and q. 45, a. 4 ad 2). This may seem at first glance to contradict what applies to the artist's servile operation (actus secundus), in which an essential form first seen intellectually is subsequently imitated in material. But it must be understood that a form (idea, *nāma*) cannot be seen as such, in *samādhi* the form is indistinguished from the intellect itself, in se and *per se* the form has no independent existence; as soon as the form is envisaged by the intellect, in *dhyāna, pratibimbavat, pratyakṣata,* and thus objectively, as a model to be imitated, it is already an embodied form, a composite of form and aspect (*nāma, rūpa*); indivisibility of content (nāma) and style (rūpa) in the material object made by art reflects the indivisibility of content and style in what is already as 'art in the artist' a 'concept', *per verbum in intellectu conceptum,* begotten by manes on *vāc*, not an absolutely immaterial form, but a formulation.

PLATE XXXIII

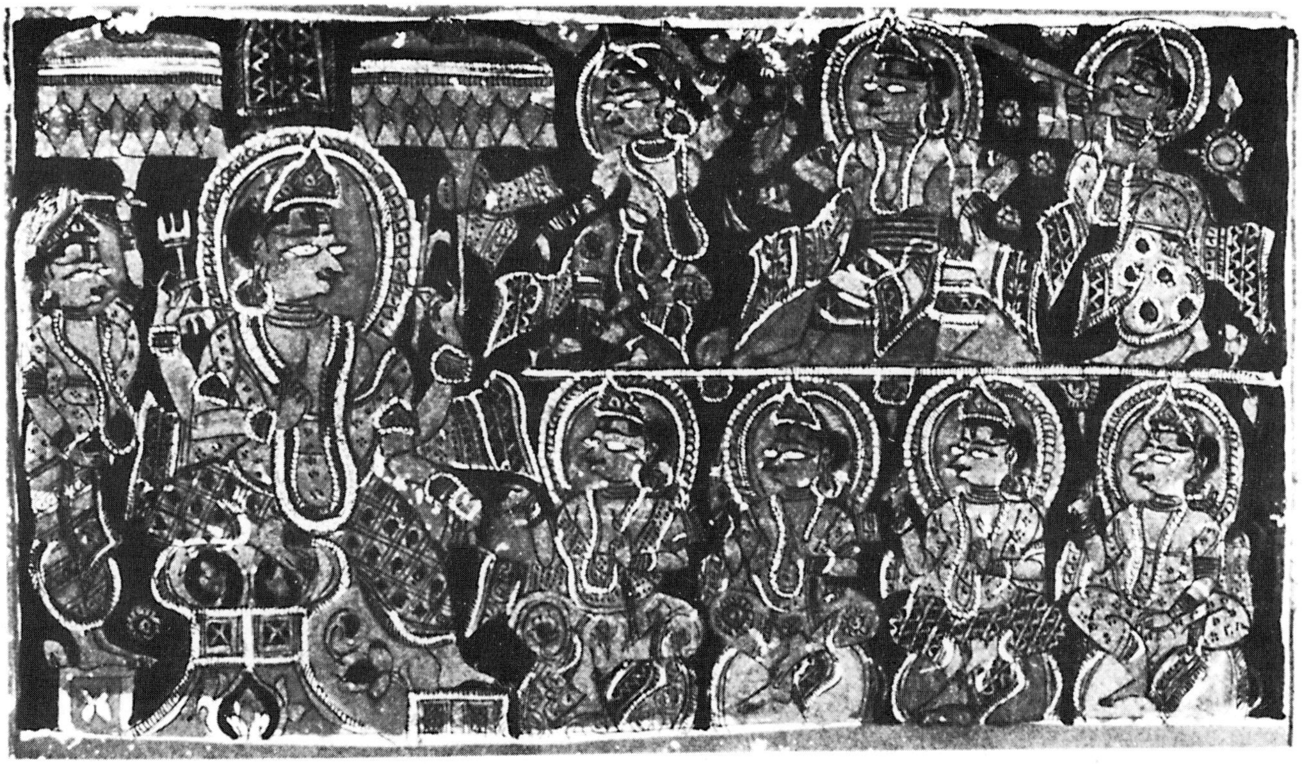

Fig. 1

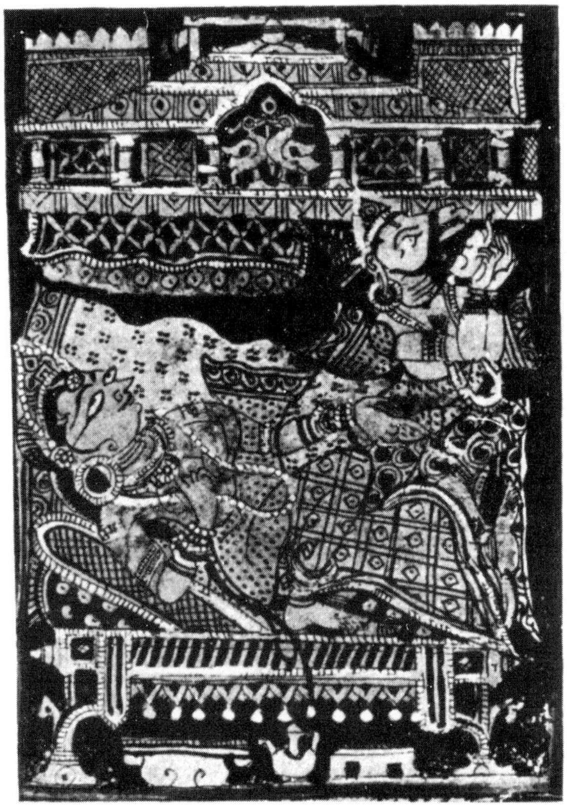

Fig. 2

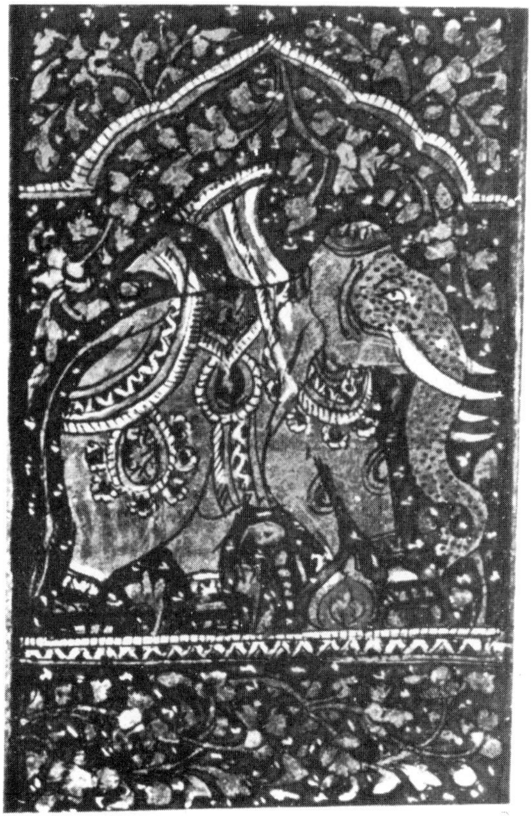

Fig. 3

PLATE XXXIV

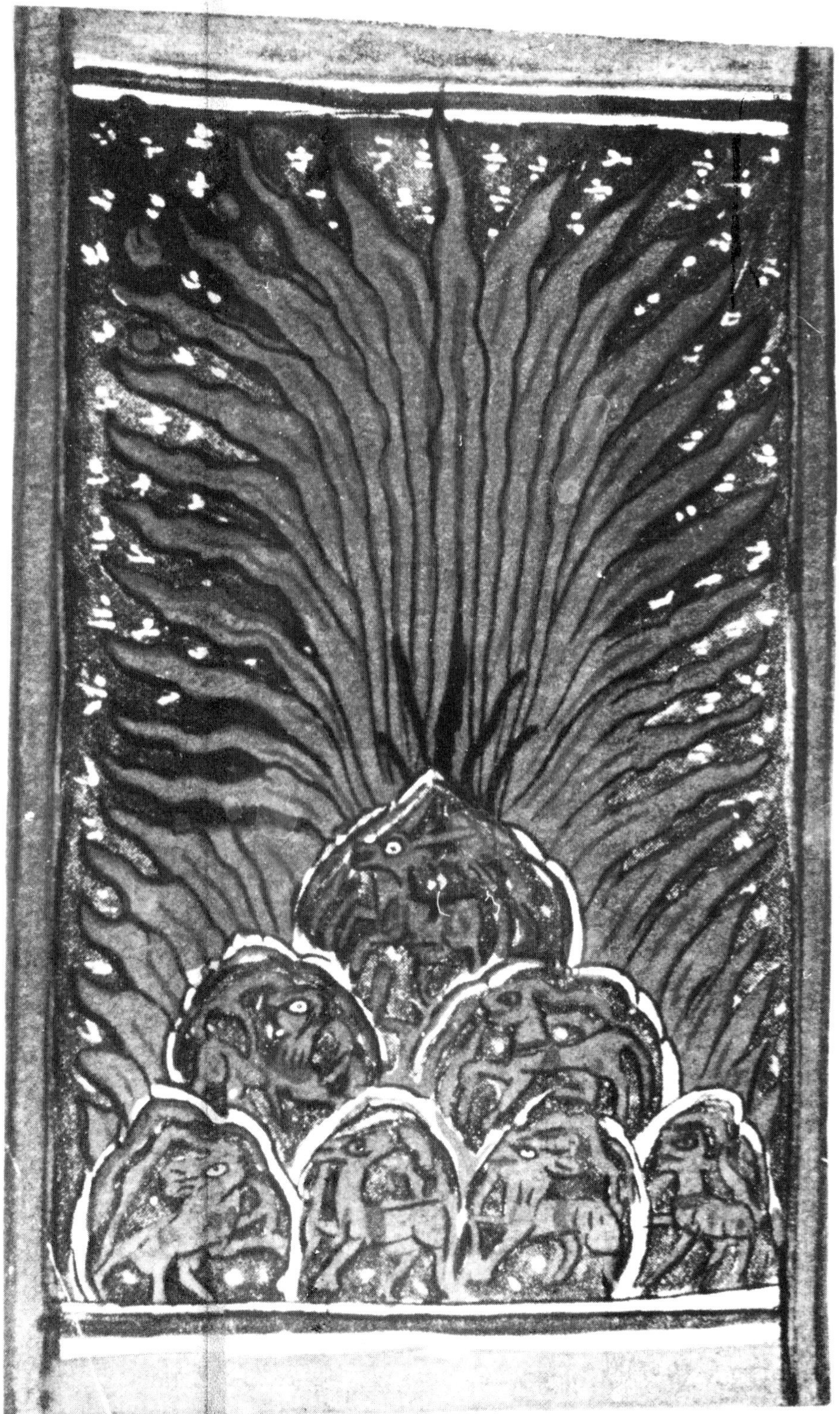

Fig. 2

PLATE XXXV

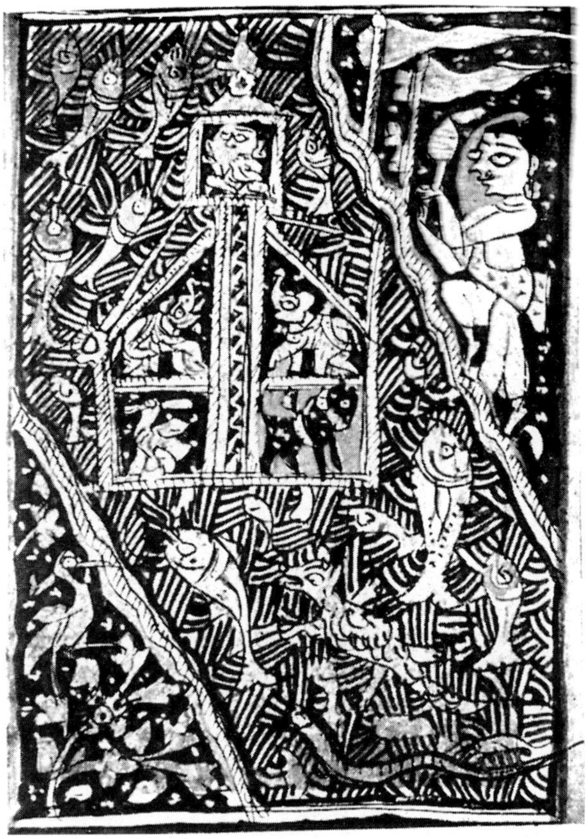

Fig. 1

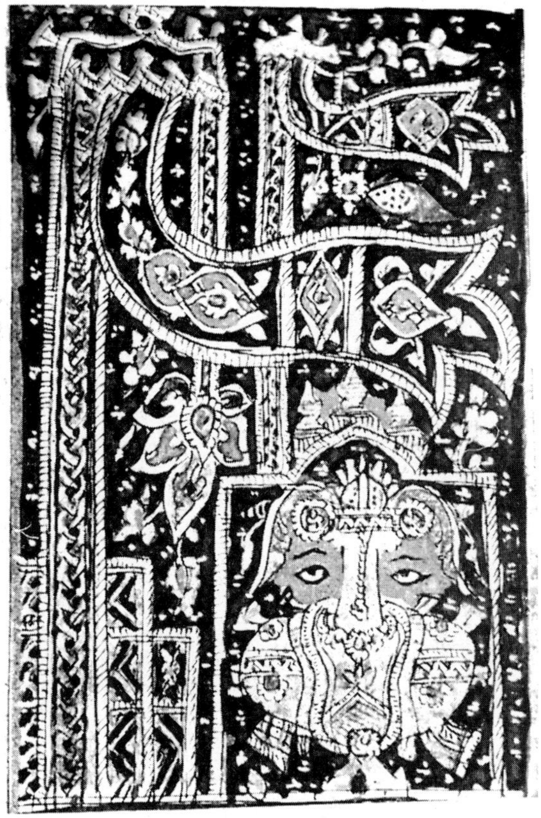

Fig. 2

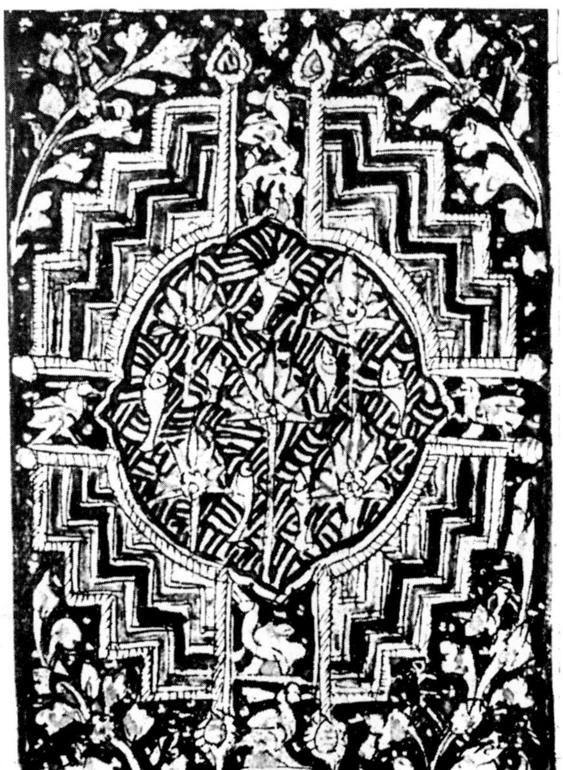

Fig. 3

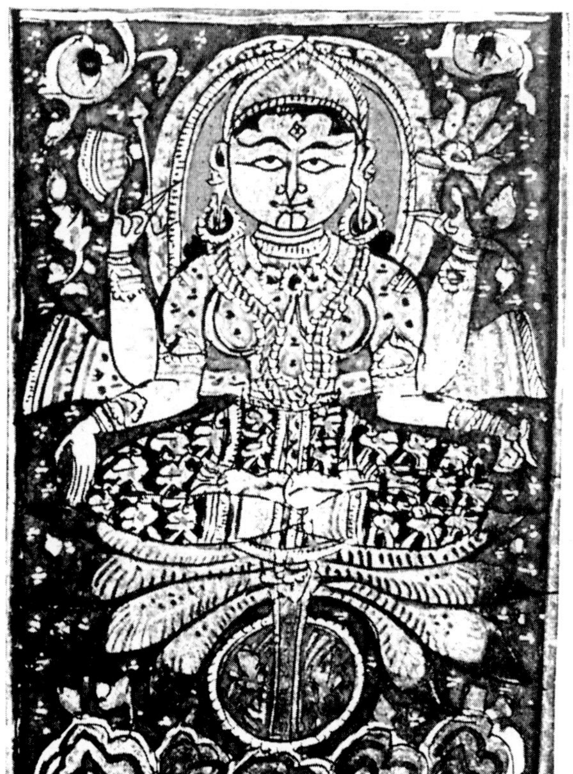

Fig. 4

PLATE XXXVI

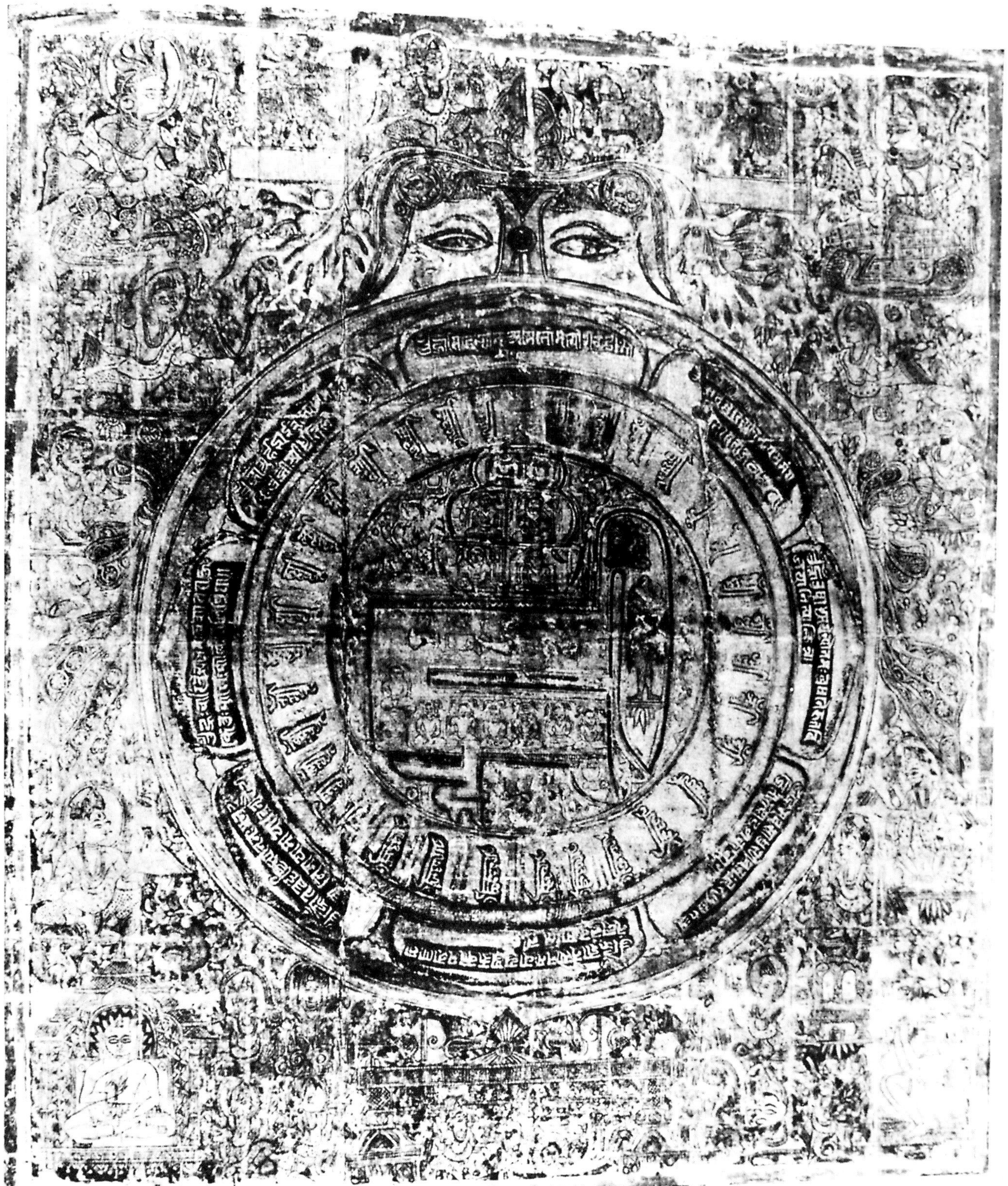

PLATE XXXVII

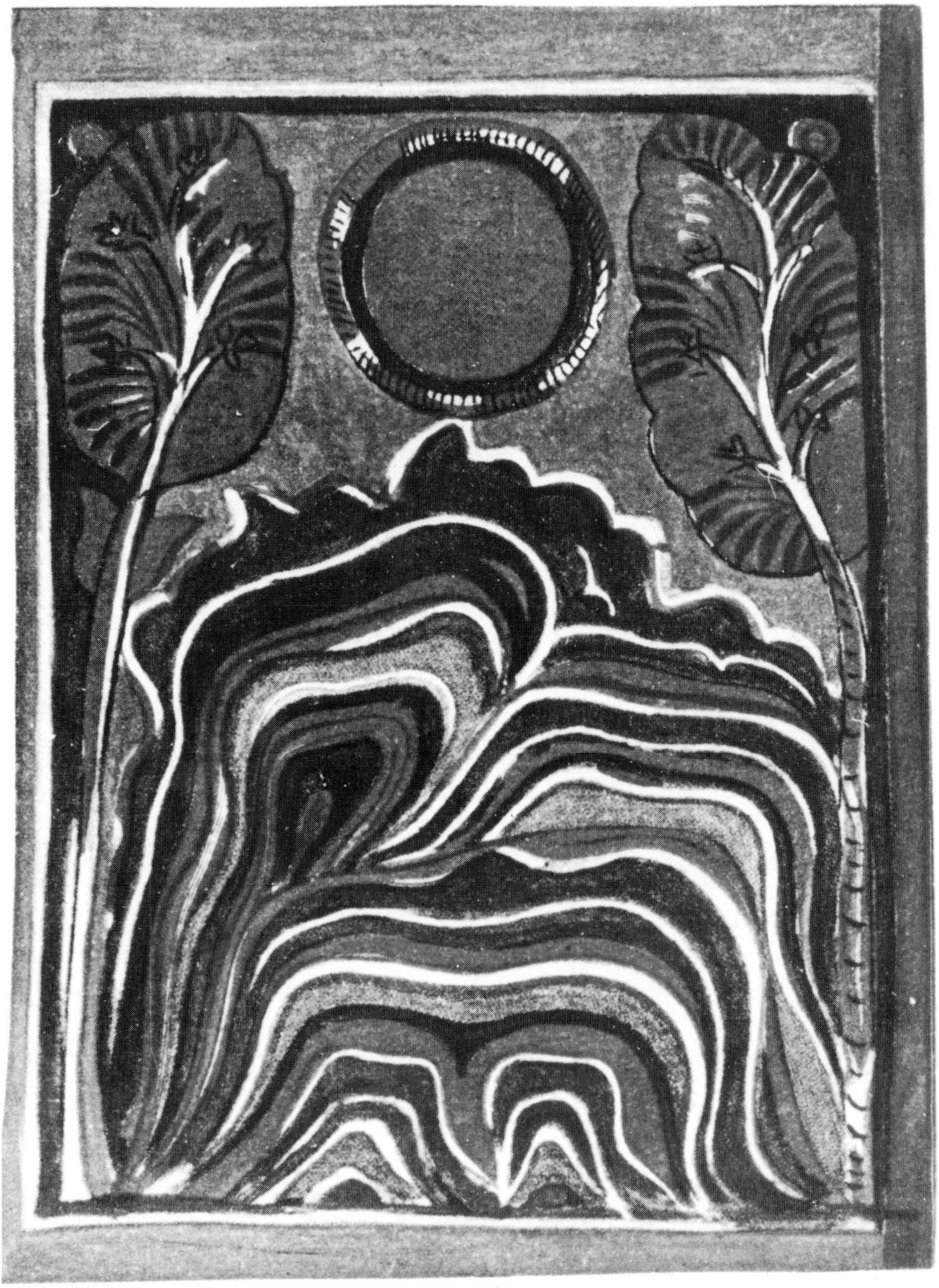

PLATE XXXVIII

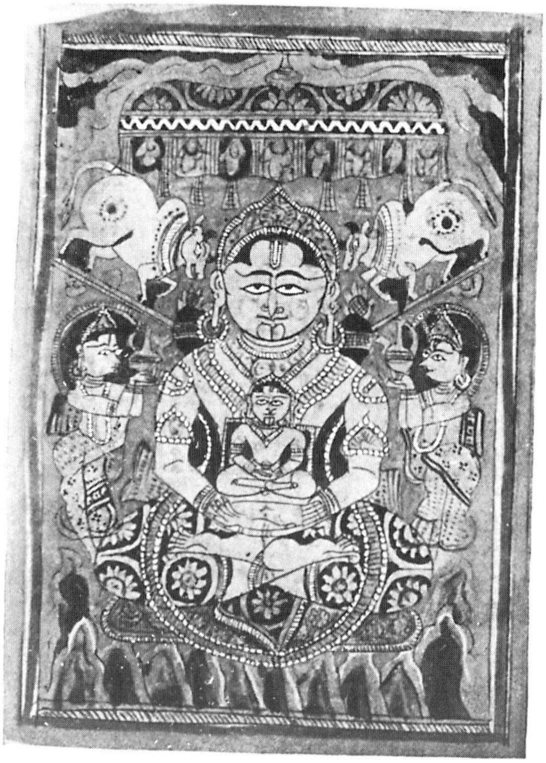

Fig. 1

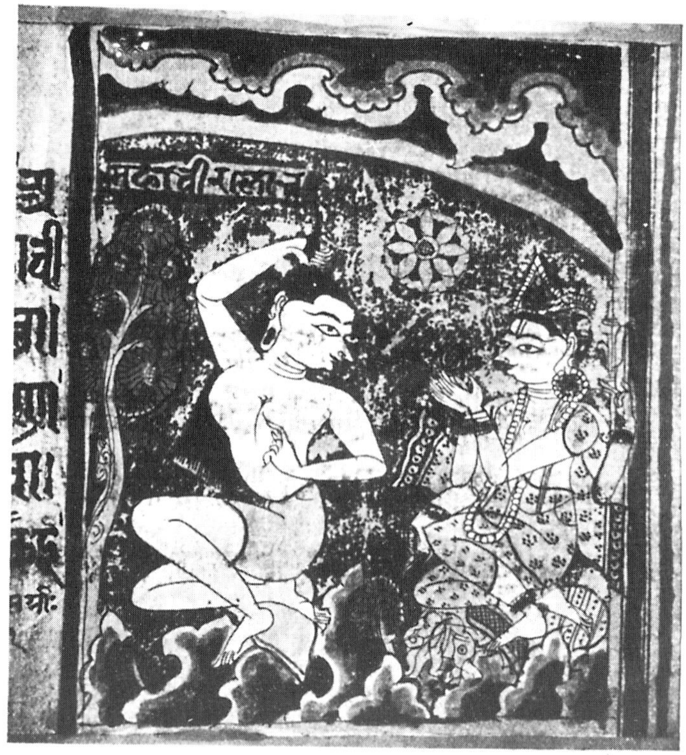

Fig. 2

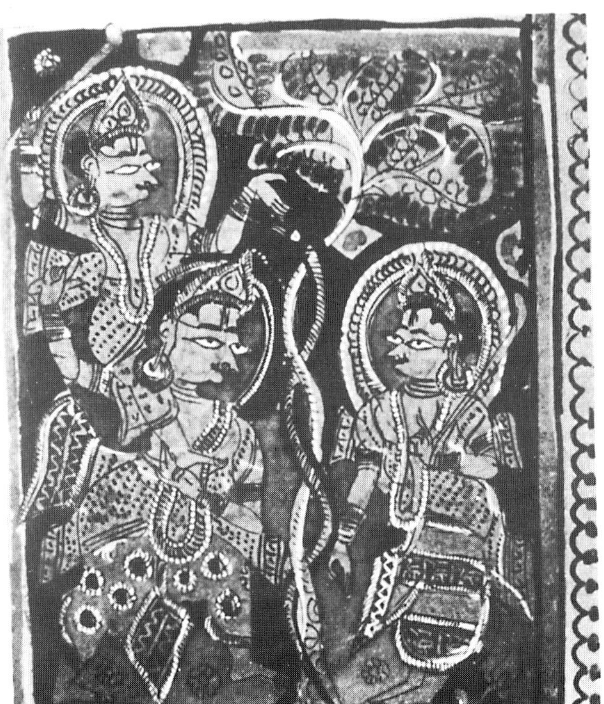

Fig. 3

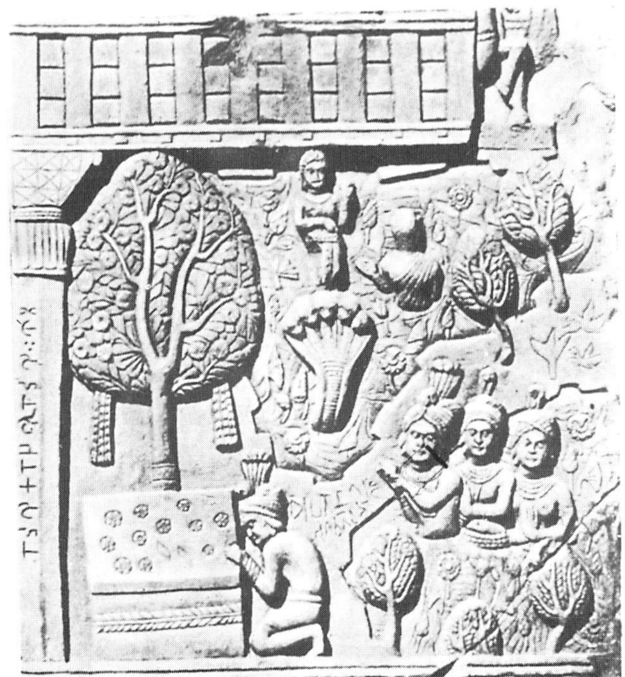

Fig. 4

Notes on Jaina Art

I. INTRODUCTION

This paper forms a contribution to our knowledge of Jaina painting and minor arts, concerning which nothing has yet been published except the valuable *Miniaturen zum Jinacarita* (Miniatures illustrating the Lives of the Jinas) published by Dr. Hüttemann in the 'Baessler Archiv' for last year (Band II, heft 2, 1913). The paintings are not only very important for the student of Jaina iconography and archaeology, and as illustrating costume, manners and customs, but are of equal or greater interest as being the oldest known Indian paintings on paper, and representing an almost hitherto unknown school of Indian art, based like Rajput painting on the old traditions, but carrying us back at least a century and a half further than the oldest available examples of Rajput pictures. It is, indeed, probable that when the Jaina libraries of Western India are made more accessible, they will be found to contain illustrated manuscripts still older than the beginning of the fifteenth century.

The paintings and the minor arts of the Jaina libraries are here regarded chiefly as documents of Indian art. In order, however, to make them fully comprehensible, it is necessary to preface the description and illustration of the actual paintings by a short account of Jainism and of the legends of Mahāvīra and Kālakācārya, which are the main subject of the pictures.

II. JAINISM[1]

The sixth century BC in ancient Indian was the central period of an age of intellectual dissatisfaction, scepticism and psychological experiment. The great monuments of this age are the Upaniṣads, the teachings of Buddha, and the teachings of Mahāvīra. All these documents reflect the movement of thought, mainly of Kṣatriya origin, which endeavoured to penetrate more deeply than of old the meaning of life, and in a manner scarcely contemplated by the old Vedic theologies, and certainly not achieved by their ritual.

We are here concerned only with the religion founded by Mahāvīra, the Great Hero, the Jina, the Conqueror. From correspondences in Jaina and Buddhist tradition it is practically certain that Mahāvīra, otherwise called Vardhamāna (Jṇātiputra) is identical with the Nigaṇṭha Nātaputta who is referred to in Buddhist texts as the leader of a rival sect in the time of the Buddha himself. Thus the founder of Jainism, like the Buddha, taught in the fifth century BC.

What he taught, and the manner of his teaching, also closely paralleled the doctrine and ministry of Buddha. Jainism is essentially an ethical philosophy intended for ascetics, the Nigaṇṭhas, 'Freed of all Bonds', who leave the world to dedicate their whole lives to the search for truth, and its proclamation. They practised a more severely ascetic rule than that of the Buddhists. As in Buddhism, however, there was also recognized a laity, who without renouncing the world, still adhere to the Jaina doctrines, and support the Jaina mendicants. The members of the lay community, if they could not reach the highest goal, could still walk on the path towards it.

Though retaining one and the same body of doctrine, the Jaina community as a whole was early divided into two parts, the Digambaras, 'Clothed with the sky', whose ascetics wear no clothing whatever, and the Śvetāmbaras, who are 'Clothed in white', and who alone possess an order of nuns. The Jaina teaching, like that of Buddha, takes for granted the Brāhmaṇ doctrines of Karma (Deeds, causality) and Saṃsāra (the Ocean [of] Rebirth). Its highest goal is Nirvāṇa or Mokṣa, the setting free of the individual from the Saṃsāra. The means to this end are the three Jewels of Right Knowledge, Right Faith, and Right Walk. Just what the Buddha is to the Buddhists—originally a man like other men, who nevertheless by his own power has attained to omniscience and freedom, and out of pity for suffering mankind teaches to them the way of salvation which he has found—that is the Jina

[1] This section is largely based on *The Jainas*, by J.G. Bühler, and J. Burgess (London, 1903); and on the various publications of Jacobi, elsewhere cited.

to the Jains. The Jina, the Conqueror, is variously known as Kevalin (Omniscient), Buddha (Enlightened), Mukta (Delivered), Siddha (Perfected), Arhat (Adept), and Tīrthakara, 'the Finder of the Ford' through the Ocean of Rebirth. The last title alone is peculiar to the Jains, all the others belonging to the common usage of Brāhmaṇas and Buddhists as well as Jains.

The Jains definitely differ from the Buddhists in the details of their cosmology, and more important, in the fact that they postulate a *place* of purity beyond the heavens, to which place the perfected souls depart at death, nevermore to return. This place, however, is described as *aloka*, a non-world, and thus in its significance corresponds to the Buddhist 'Void' and the unconditioned Brāhmaṇ of the Brāhmaṇas.[2] Nevertheless, the liberated Jina, probably through the influence of lay sentiment and the growth of *bhakti* (loving devotion), came in later times to be regarded as god, to whom prayers might be addressed, who might be represented in images and worshipped in temples, and who may even be spoken of as the Creator. The Jains also differ from the Buddhists, and differed from the outset, in their much greater stress on asceticism, often of an extreme character, and in their exaggerated care for animal life.

Later Jaina tradition further added to the historical individual who founded the order, twenty-three preceding Jinas, of whom the first (Ṛṣabha) is said to have lived more than a hundred billions of oceans of years ago.

While the Buddhist community no longer exists in India, except in Nepal and Ceylon, but is represented throughout Eastern Asia, the Jains have survived in India to the present day, but have not established adherents abroad. The Jainas are to be met with in nearly every large Indian town, chiefly amongst the merchants. They have been politically, and are still economically powerful. To them the architectural splendour of many of the cities of Western India is largely due; as likewise, that of the great temple cities of Śatruñjaya and Girnār, and the beautiful temples at Mount Abu. They now occupy an important position chiefly in Gujarat, Rajputana and the Panjab, and also in Kanara.

In course of time the Jaina community achieved (or condescended to) a more systematic organization. 'There came into existence monuments, monasteries and schools. To this development of a cult corresponded a literary, scientific and artistic activity, of which the earliest results brought the doctrine into fixed forms. Probably most of the original canonical Jaina literature thus took shape early in the third century BC. Bhadrabāhu, the author of the *Kalpa Sūtra* (Lives of the Jinas, particularly Mahāvīra) is stated according to Jaina tradition to have died 170 or 162 years after Mahāvīra himself (528 BC according to Jaina tradition); that is to say, Bhadrabāhu died 358 BC. The *Acārāṅga Sūtra*, which confirms the traditions of the *Kalpa Sūtra* regarding the life of Mahāvīra, is the first of the eleven *aṅgas* or sections of the canon of the third century. All this literature was probably in the main handed down orally until the time of the Council of Valabhi (454 or 467 AD), when new redactions were prepared and the method of teaching novices from books was substituted for purely oral instruction. At that time, and even subsequently, additions may have been made. In any case, it is certain that the *Kalpa Sūtra*, including the main account of the life of Mahāvīra, 'has been held in high esteem by the Jainas for more than a thousand years' (Jacobi, S.B.E. XXII, liii). The oldest available manuscript of the *Kalpa Sūtra* is here spoken of as MS. I.O., from which illustrations are reproduced in Figures 3, 5, 9, 12, 45, 50, 51. An MS. commentary dated 1307 AD is also known. But no doubt the contents of the manuscripts have been handed down substantially in their present form at least from the fifth century AD.

III. LIFE OF MAHĀVĪRA AND OTHER JINAS[3]

At the close of his allotted period of existence in heaven, where he had dwelt for twenty ages subsequent to his last incarnation, Mahāvīra, the last of the Tīrthakaras, took conception in the womb of Devānandā, the wife of the Brāhmaṇa Ṛṣabhadatta, in the town of Kuṇḍagrāma (probably a suburb of Vaiśālī, capital of Videha or Mithilā, the modern Tirhut.

[2] The idea of a place to which departed perfected souls go, is probably a later materialistic interpretation. In the same way, even the Buddhists occasionally reckon Nirvāṇa as a local 'place of departed Buddhas', situated above the heavens (Copleston, *Buddhism in Ceylon*, ed. 2, p. 245). Cf. R.F. Johnston, *Buddhist China*, 1913, p. 97.

[3] Condensed from the *Kalpa Sūtra*, translated by Jacobi, Sacred Books of the East, Vol. XXII.

[Fig. 9] That night the Brāhmaṇī Devānandā lay in fitful slumber, between sleeping and waking, and she dreamt fourteen auspicious and blessed dreams, to wit: of an elephant, a bull, a lion, the lustration (of Lakṣmī), a garland, the moon, the sun, a flag, a vase, a lotus pool, an ocean, a celestial mansion, a heap of jewels, and a flame. She awoke from these dreams happy and contented; and firmly fixing the dreams in her mind, she rose from her couch. Neither hasty nor trembling, but with the even gait of a royal swan, she sought the Brāhmaṇ Ṛṣabhadatta and greeted him. Then she sat down in a rich state chair; calm and composed, with folded hands, she related to him the dreams. He saw that they foretold a son; beautiful and perfect and clever, who would become acquainted with all branches of scripture, grammar and science. She accepted the interpretation, and he and she rejoiced together.

[Fig. 10] Meanwhile Śakra (Indra), wielder of the thunderbolt, rider of Airāvata, wearing robes as spotless as the pure sky, and trembling earrings of bright gold, sat on his throne in the council hall Sudharman in heaven. He who is ruler of heaven and all the gods of heaven and earth, was then enjoying the divine pleasures, such as music and playing and story-telling. He likewise surveyed the whole land of Jambudvīpa (India) with his all-embracing gaze, and he saw that Mahāvīra was conceived in the womb of Devānandā. Trembling with delight, he rose from his throne, and descending from the jewelled footstool, he cast his seamless robe over his left shoulder and advanced in the direction of the Holy One. [Fig. 11] Then he knelt and touched the ground with his head thrice, and joining the palms of his hands, raised them above his head and said: 'Reverence to the Saints and Blessed Ones, the Masters, the Path-makers (Arhats, Bhagavats, Ādikaras and Tīrthakaras), the perfectly enlightened ones; to the highest of men, the lions amongst men, the lotus-flowers of humanity; to the highest in the world, the guides of the world, the lights of the world; the givers of safety, of life and of knowledge; the givers and preachers of law; the possessors of boundless wisdom and intuition; the conquerors and the saviours; those who have reached a stainless and undying bliss whence there is no return, those who have conquered fear. Reverence to the venerable ascetic Mahāvīra, last of the Tīrthakaras, whom the former Tīrthakaras foretold. I here adore the revered one whom I see, may he from there see me.' So saying, Śakra bowed again and returned to his throne.

It immediately occurred to him that it never had happened nor ever could happen that any Arhat, Cakravartin or Vāsudeva had taken birth in a low or degraded or in any Brāhmaṇ family, but only in noble families of pure descent. 'This is the first time that an Arhat has taken conception in an unworthy family;[4] however, it has not yet happened that one has ever been born in such a family. I shall therefore cause the venerable ascetic Mahāvīra to be removed from the Brāhmaṇical quarter Kuṇḍagrāma and from the womb of the Brāhmaṇī Devānandā, and to be placed as an embryo in the womb of the Kṣatriyāṇī Triśalā, wife of the Kṣatriya Siddhārtha; and the embryo of the Kṣatriyāṇī Triśalā to be placed in the womb of the Brāhmaṇī Devānandā'. [Fig. 12] Thus reflecting, he called Hariṇegamesi, the commander of his infantry; he instructed him as aforesaid, to exchange the embryos, and to return and report the execution of the command.

Hariṇegamesi bowed and departed, saying: 'Just as your Majesty orders.' He descended from heaven towards the north-eastern quarter of the world, and assumed a material form; and so he passed with the high swift movement of a god, over continents and oceans, till he reached the town of Kuṇḍagrāma and the house of the Brāhmaṇa Ṛṣabhadatta. There he bowed eight times to Mahāvīra, and cast the Brāhmaṇī Devānandā into a deep sleep, and all her retinue; [Fig. 13] removing all that was unclean, he brough forth what was clean, and placed the embryo of the venerable ascetic Mahāvīra in the womb of the Kṣatriyāṇī Triśalā, and the embryo of the Kṣatriyāṇī in the womb of the Brāhmaṇī Devānandā. [Fig. 14] And having so done, he returned whence he came. With the high swift movement of a god he passed over oceans and continents and reached the heavens and the throne of Śakra, and reported the fulfilment of the command. This befell on the eighty-third day after conception, in the middle of the night.

[Fig. 15] On that night the Kṣatriyāṇī lay on her couch, twixt sleeping and waking, in her bower, whereof the walls were decorated with pictures, and the ceiling painted; the chamber was fragrant with the scent of flowers and perfumes, and the couch was covered with a

[4] That is to say, so regarded by the Jains, whose philosophy and membership, like that of the Buddhists, was primarily of Kṣatriya origin.

mattress of a man's length, with pillows at head and foot, raised on both sides and hollow in the middle, covered with a cloth of figured linen, hung with red mosquito nets, and furnished with all the comforts of a bed, such as flowers and sandal powder. [Figs. 16, 17] Then there came to her the fourteen auspicious and delightful dreams that the Brāhmaṇī Devānandā had formerly dreamt, to wit: a great lucky elephant, marked with auspicious signs, and four-tusked; a lucky bull, whiter than the petals of the white lotus, sleek and well-proportioned, foreboding innumerable happy qualities; a playful beautiful lion, whiter than a heap of pearls—his tail waved, and his beautiful tongue came out of his mouth like a shoot of beauty; Śrī, the goddess of beauty, seated on a lotus, laved by attendant elephants; a garland of *mandāra* flowers hanging down from the firmament, incomparably fragrant, and haunted by swarms of bees; the moon, white as the milk of cows, or as a silver cup; the great red sun, whose thousand rays obscure the lustre of all other lights; a green flag, fastened to a golden staff, with a tuft of soft and waving peacock feather; a full vase of gold, filled with water-lilies; a lake of lotuses, resorted to by swans and cranes and ducks, pleasing to heart and eye; the ocean of milk, beauteous as Lakṣmī's breast,—a splendid and a pleasant spectacle as its waters tossed in moving, ever-changing, excessively high waves, traversed by porpoises and whales; a heavenly mansion of a thousand and eight columns, decked with gold and gems, hung with pearl garlands and decorated with various pictures, filled with music like the sound of heavy rain, perfumed delightfully and full of light; a heap of splendid jewels, high as Meru, illumining the very firmament; and a smokeless, crackling fire, flaming high as if to scorch the very heavens. From these auspicious, happy dreams the Kṣatriyāṇī Triśalā awoke, and all the hair on her body rose up in joy. She rose from her couch, and neither hasty nor trembling, but with the gait of a royal swan, she sought the couch of the Kṣatriya Siddhārtha, and spoke to him with pleasant, gentle words, and with his leave she sat on a chair of state, inlaid with precious stones in various patterns. She related the fourteen dreams, and asked her lord what they might portend. He foretold that she would give birth to a son, who would establish the fame of their family: a beautiful boy who should be acquainted with all branches of scripture, grammar and science, and become a lord of the earth. Then the Kṣatriya and Kṣatriyāṇī rejoiced together; and Triśalā returned to her own couch, and waked till morning, least these good dreams should be counteracted by any bad dreams following.

At daybreak, Siddhārtha called for his servants, and ordered them to prepare the hall of audience. He himself went to the royal gymnasium and practised exercises, such as jumping, wrestling, fencing and fighting, till he was wearied. Then he was well shampooed; and when he was refreshed, he entered the bath-room. [Fig. 18] That was an agreeable chamber; it had many a window, and the floor was covered with mosaic of precious stones. He seated himself on the bathing stool, inlaid with gems, and bathed himself with pure scented water. Then he dried himself with a soft towel, and donned a new and costly robe, with jewels, rings, and strings of pearls. He seemed like a tree granting all desires. [Fig. 19] A royal umbrella was held above him, as he proceeded from his bath and took his seat in the hall of audience, surrounded by chiefs and vassals, ministers, merchants and masters of guilds, knights and frontier-guards—a very bull and lion amongst men. On the one side of the throne he had set eight chairs of state; and on the other a curtain, figured with various pictures, was drawn towards the inner rooms of the palace; and behind this chair was placed a jewelled chair of state for the Kṣatriyāṇī Triśalā. Then Siddhārtha sent for the interpreters of dreams; and they, bathing and donning clean court robes, came from their houses and entered Siddhārtha's palace, and saluting him with folded hands they took their seats on the chairs of state. Meanwhile Triśalā took her seat behind the curtain. [Figs. 20, 21] Siddhārtha recounted the dreams to the interpreters, and they after consideration and discussion, replied to him: 'O beloved of the gods, there are thirty Great Dreams enumerated in our books, and of these, those who dream fourteen dreams are the mothers either of Universal Emperors or of Arhats; and hence the Kṣatriyāṇī, having seen fourteen, will be the mother either of a Cakravartin or of a Jina.' The king Siddhārtha gladly accepted this interpretation and dismissed the interpreters with gifts; and the lady Triśalā returned to her own apartments, neither hasty nor trembling, but with the even gait of a royal swan, glad and happy.

Now from the moment when the venerable ascetic Mahāvīra was brought into Siddhārtha's family, their wealth and their liberality and popularity increased daily; and on this account it was decided to name the child Vardhamāna, the Increaser.

While still in the womb, the venerable ascetic Mahāvīra made the resolution not to pluck out his hair and leave the world during the lifetime of his parents.

[Fig. 20] During the remaining time of her pregnancy, the Kṣatriyāṇī Triśalā guarded herself from all sickness, fear and fatigue, by suitable food and clothing and pleasant diversions and occupation, frequently resting on soft couches, and thus bearing her child in comfort. [Fig. 22] And after the lapse of nine months and seven and a half days, in the middle of the night, when the moon was in conjunction with the asterism Uttaraphālguni, Triśalā, perfectly healthy herself, gave birth to a perfectly healthy boy.

[Fig. 23] That night was an occasion of great rejoicing; the universe was resplendent with one light, as the gods and goddesses descended and ascended, and great was the noise and confusion of the assembly of gods. These gods—the Bhavanapati, Vyantara, Jyotiṣka and Vaimānika—appeared to celebrate the feast of inauguration (*abhiṣekha*) of the Tīrthakara's birthday. Siddhārtha proclaimed a ten days festival in his city, of remission of taxes, almsgiving, and so forth. On the twelfth day there took place a royal banquet, and it was announced that the boy's name would be Vardhamāna.

[Fig. 25] Beside this he is called Śramana, or Ascetic, because he is without love and without hate; and because he stands fast in midst of dangers and fears, and patiently bears hardships and calamities, and is indifferent to pleasure and pain, obedient to a chosen discipline, he is called Mahāvīra, the Great Hero, by the gods.

Mahāvīra dwelt in Videha thirty years, before his parents departed to the world of the gods; and then only, with the permission of his elder brother and the great men of the kingdom, he fulfilled his vow. The Laukāntika gods appeared to him, saying: 'Victory to thee, O bull of the best Kṣatriyas! Awake, reverend Lord of the World! Establish the religion of the law which benefits all living beings in the whole universe!'

[Fig. 24] Mahāvīra had already perceived that the time for his Renunciation (*niskramana*) had come. He made a suitable distribution of all his wealth. This distribution of gifts occupied a whole year, at the end of which time, the four orders of gods, descending from heaven, proceeded to the abode of Mahāvīra. As they arrived in the Kṣatriya quarter of Videha, Śakra (Indra) descended from his chariot, and went apart; and he created by magic a divine pedestal (*deva-chaṃda*) with a throne and footstool. Then proceeding to the venerable ascetic Mahāvīra, Śakra circumambulated him thrice from left to right, and placing him upon the throne, bathed him with pure water and precious oils, and robed him in the lightest of figured muslins, and garlands of pearls and precious gems. Then the god again created by magic a splendid planquin called *candraprabhā* (moon-radiance), adorned with pictures and bells and flags, and provided with a throne; it was conspicuous, magnificent and beautiful.

After completing a three days fast, the ascetic Mahāvīra ascended the throne and took his seat in the palanquin; in front it was borne by men, and by the gods behind,—the Suras and Asura, Garuḍas and Nāgas. Its movement was accompanied by the sound of musical instruments in the sky and upon the earth: and thus it proceeded from the Kṣatriya quarter of Kuṇḍapura along the highway towards the park called Jñātri Khaṇḍa. Just at nightfall the palanquin came to rest upon a little hillock beside an Aśoka tree: Mahāvīra descended, and took his seat beneath the tree, with his face towards the East. He removed his ornaments and fine clothes; and tearing out his hair in five handfuls, he obtained *dīkṣā*, entering upon the homeless life of a friar, adopting the holy rule, and vowing to commit no sin. At the same time he donned a divine garment, which he accepted from Śakra, who received the rejected ornaments and fine clothes and removed them to the Ocean of Milk.[5] At the moment of Mahāvīra's obtaining *dīkṣā*, the whole universe of men and gods became suddenly perfectly silent and motionless, like the figures in a picture.

[5] Thus, according to the *Acārаṇga Sūtra* and the pictures. Another MS. states that the ornaments, etc., were received by Vaiśramaṇa (who is never represented in the pictures). The *Kalpa Sūtra,* though it mentions the divine robe, and thus implies the presence of a divine donor, distinctly states that Mahāvīra was quite alone when he obtained *dīkṣā*; this must be understood to mean that no other human being was present. See also descriptions of the pictures; and the discussion by Hüttemann, loc. cit. pp. 68-70.

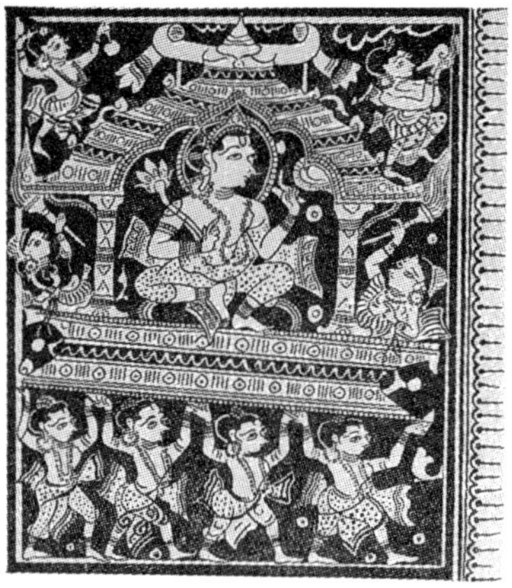

a

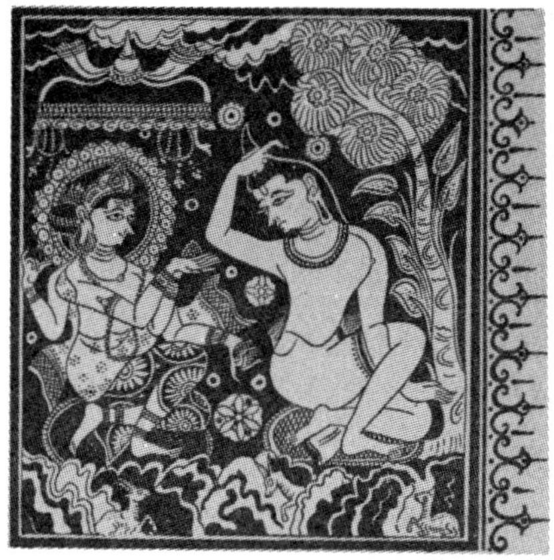

b

Illustrations from the Berlin MS. IC 2367 of the Museum für Völkerkunde, after Hüttemann, *Miniaturen zum Tinacarita*, Baessler Archiv, 1913.

a. Mahāvira carried by the gods in a palanquin. Cf. MS. C.B., folio 33 (labelled *Śibikā*)
b. The *Dīkṣā* of Mahāvīra. Mahāvīra, seated beneath an Aśoka tree, plucks out his hair, while Indra (Śakra) offers him a divine robe. Cf. Figs. 1, 26.

Mahāvīra obtained the degree of knowledge called *Manahparyāya*; and he resolved to neglect the care of his body for twelve years, bearing with equanimity all pleasures and pains, whether arising from divine powers, from men or from animals. The twelve years duly passed in blameless wandering, the practice of religious discipline, and the patient endurance of pain and pleasure. It was in the thirteenth year that Mahāvīra, seated in deep meditation beside a *śāl* tree, near the town Gṛmbhikagrāma, attained to Nirvāṇa, and the unobstructed, infinite and supreme knowledge and intuition of a *Kevalin* (syn. *Jina*, *Arhat)*. Then he became aware of all states of gods or men or demons, whence they came and whither they go, their thoughts and deeds; he saw and knew all circumstances and conditions of the whole universe of living things.

[Figs. 27, 28] When the venerable ascetic Mahāvīra had thus reached the highest intuition and knowledge, the time had come for him to teach the doctrine of the Jinas. To this end the gods prepared for him a *samavasaraṇa,* and entering this by the eastern gate, he took his seat upon the throne, and taught the Divine Law to gods and men.

During a period of nearly thirty years following, Mahāvīra wandered to and fro, spending the rainy season in different cities, founding a great community of monks and lay votaries, and teaching the five great vows, the doctrine of the six classes of living beings, and so forth. [Figs. 3, 29] At the end of that time, in the town of Pāpā, the venerable ascetic Mahāvīra died, cutting asunder the ties of birth, old age, and death, becoming a Siddha, a Buddha, a Mukta, one who is finally released, never more to return, entering the paradise of perfected souls (Īṣat-pragbhāra), above the world and beyond the heavens of the gods. [Fig. 39] The *Kalpa Sūtra* further states that Mahāvīra had nine Gaṇas and eleven Gaṇadharas, i.e. nine companies or orders of monks, established by eleven teachers, his disciples.

The *Kalpa Sūtra* proceeds to give the lives of the Jinas Pārśva, Ariṣṭanemi or Neminātha, and Ṛṣabha and a list of the twenty Tīrthakaras who lived between the ages of Neminātha and Ṛṣabha. The life-stories of Pārśva, Neminātha and Ṛṣabha are identical in nearly all respects with that of Mahāvīra, with only a difference of the names of their parents, and a few other particulars. The lives of these Jinas are illustrated in the pictures in a comparatively summary fashion, while the remaining twenty are usually represented in a single illustration.

[Figs. 30-2] A special legend is, however, attached to Pārśva, and accounts for the canopy of seven snake-hoods always represented above his head in pictures and sculptures. It is said that a *deva* of the name of Meghakumāra (Cloud-prince) attacked the Arhat with a great storm, whilst he was engaged in practising the *Kāyotsarga* austerity (exposure to all weathers): very much as Māra attacked the Buddha at Bodh-Gayā. And just as the *nāga* Mucalinda, whom Buddha had benefited in a former life, then came to protect him by spreading his hoods above his head, so the *nāga* Dharanendra and his consort the *yakśiṇī* Padmāvatī, whose lives had been restored by the Jina in a former existence, now came to protect him, the former spreading his many hoods over the head of his benefactor, the latter holding over him a white umbrella.

IV. SUMMARY OF THE STORY OF KĀLAKĀCĀRYA[6]

I. Birth; II. The Dethronement of Gardabhilla

There was a town in Bhāratavarṣa, named Dharāvāsa. The king of that town was Vajrasiṃha, and his chief queen was the peerless Surasundarī; they had a son expert in every science, and he was named Kālakakumāra. One day he was returning from a drive and saw a Jaina priest preaching in the mango park. He approached the monk, bowed, and listened; and was converted and joined the order, to his father's great grief, together with a numerous company of princes. When he had completed his religious studies, his teacher established him as head of the order in his own stead. With five hundred monks he proceeded to Ujjayinī, and there remained for some days, preaching. Meanwhile there also arrived a party of pious nuns, amongst whom was the beautiful and devout Sarasvatī, Kālakācārya's[7] younger sister.

Gardabhilla, king of Ujjayinī, passed that way, and seeing Sarasvatī, desired her, and carried her off against her will, calling out to her brother for help. Kālakācārya remonstrated with the king, saying that if he set a bad example, law and order would be destroyed, and so forth; but in vain. The infatuated king was not to be persuaded. For a blind man does not see what is visibly before him; but one blinded by passion sees what does not exist—lotus blossoms the moon's disk, and a whole catalogue of beauties, where in sooth exists naught but unclean flesh.

Kālakācārya summoned the fourfold Synod; but that also was vain, and Kālakācārya made a vow, either to drive the king out of his kingdom, or himself to go the way of those who are the enemies of the faith and destroy piety. So saying, the Wise One reflected that he must have recourse to cunning, since the king was brave and powerful, and expert in ass-magic (*gaddhabhīe mahāvijjāe*). He dressed himself as a madman, and frequented cross roads and market places, calling out 'If Gardabhilla is king, what of that? If his zenana is fair, what of that? If I go begging, what of that? Or if I sleep in a deserted house, what of that?' When the townsfolk heard the Wise One crying out in this way, they said 'Alas, the king must be committing some sin, since Kālakācārya, the refuge of the virtuous, has deserted his Order and wanders in the town a madman; alas! alas!'

When the ministers heard that all the folk of the city blamed the king in this fashion, they said to him, 'Sire, do not so, but set free the nun, since great harm is coming of it; and he who injures the monk, plunges himself into a sea of misfortune.' But the king was wrath, and recommended them to reserve their exhortations for their grandmothers. They were astounded, and murmured, 'Who can restrain the ocean when it overflows its banks?'

[Figs. 4, 44, 49] Now the Wise One left Ujjayinī and went to the land of the Śaka clan. The princes are there called Shāhis, and their overlord the Shāhan Shāhi. Kālakācārya remained at the court of one of the Shāhis, and brought him under his power by means of *mantras* and *tantras*. One day when the Shāhi was talking with the Wise One, the door-keeper announced the messenger of the Shāhan Shāhi. He was brought in and gave the king a present, a sword sent by his master. Thereat the Shāhi's face darkened like the sky before rain. Then the Wise One reflected: 'I see a strange thing; for when servants receive an honorable gift from their masters, they are wont to be glad like peacocks at the sight of clouds. I will enquire what this may mean.' When the messenger had departed, the Wise One asked the Shāhi why he was thus downcast at receiving a mark of favour from his master. 'Honorable sir', he replied, 'that was not a sign of favour, but of anger. When he is wrath with us he sends a sword, and we must slay ourselves therewith, and since he is mighty, his commands must be obeyed.' The Wise One enquired, 'Is he angry only with thee, or with others also?' The Shāhi answered, 'He is angry also with the ninety-five other Shāhis, since the sword bears the number 96.' The Wise One said, 'If so, do not slay thyself.' But the Shāhi replied,

[6] Based on the translation by Jacobi, Zeitschrift der Deutschen Morgenländischen Gesellschaft, Vol. XXXIV, 1880, p. 247 *seq.*

[7] i.e. Kālaka, formerly *Kumāra* (prince), now ācārya (*adept*).

'Then he will destroy our whole race; but if I am dead he will spare others. The Wise One said, 'If so, send a messenger to the other princes, to say that we shall set out for Hindustān.' The messenger was sent and the ninety-five Shāhis appeared. Then the first Shāhi asked the Wise One what was to be done next. He replied, 'Cross the Indus with an army and baggage, and go to Hindukadeśa.'

So they did and came to Surāṣṭra. Then it was the rainy season; so they parceled out the land and remained there while the roads were impassable. Then came Spring with his white lotus flowers, like a king with white umbrellas; when white herons are to be seen like white clouds before the first rains; honoured by flamingoes like a Jina by famous kings; when rivers are clear as good men's thoughts, the heavenly regions bright as the words of skilful poets, the welkin free from earthly stain as the body of the highest ascetic; when the *saptacchada* trees are decked with flowers as *munis* are decked with virtue; when the nights are gay with stars; when earth shines bright with all her fields of ripe corn, beloved of the proud bellowing bulls and happy herdsmen; when by night the bosom of the earth, as it were, is bathed in a stream of moonray-nectar; when travellers are led astray by the sweet songs of the careful farmers watching the green rice-fields; when the *cakravāka* wakes to the accomplishment of his dreams of love.

When Kālakācārya beheld such prowess of the Spring, he spake to the Shāhis, for the fulfillment of his wishes, saying, 'Ha! why do ye idle here?' They said, 'Tell us what to do.' The Wise One answered, 'Capture Ujjayinī, the bulwark of Mālwā; there shall ye find good living.' They answered, 'With a good will, but we have no resources, for we brought with us nothing more than bare necessities.' [Fig. 46] So the Wise One with magic powder changed all the potter's stuff to gold, and said, 'Take this for your needs.' They set out accordingly for Ujjayinī.

When Gardabhilla heard of the enemy's approach, he marched forth and met them on the borders of his country and joined battle. He was defeated and his army dispersed like clouds before the wind. He dew back into his city with the remnants of the army. The victors laid siege, and made daily assaults. One day when they were storming the fort, they saw that it was empty; and they asked the Wise One what this might mean. He replied, 'Today is the eighth, when Gardabhilla fasts and practises his ass-magic, go see if there be a she-ass anywhere upon the walls.' They saw that there was an ass, and showed it to the Wise One. He said, 'When she makes a great outcry on the accomplishment of Gardabhilla's rites, immediately every creature two- or four-footed in our army will fall to the ground with blood pouring from his mouth. Take, therefore, all that are two- or four-footed and withdraw two miles from the walls; but give me a hundred and eight accomplished bowmen.' So they did.

The Wise One said to the bowmen, 'When the ass opens her mouth to speak, stop her mouth with arrows before she utters a sound; for if she does so, we may shoot never more. Therefore wait in patience, with bows drawn to the ear.' [Fig. 47] So did they. They stopped the ass's mouth with a hail of arrows, so that it could not utter any sound; and the magic beast fell dead outright. The Wise One ordered his men to take the army prisoner; they stormed the walls and entered Ujjayinī. [Fig. 48] Gardabhilla was captured alive and brought in chains to the Wise One's feet. He said, 'Shameless and vile wretch and evil-doer, soon art thou despoiled of power. So have we done because thou didst shame a nun unwilling, and didst contemn the Synod. He who robs a nun of honour, sets a fire at the root of the welfare of the Jaina faith. Long, indeed, shalt thou whirl about in the *samsāra,* suffering many ills and the more so in this life than any other. Scourging, imprisonment and disgrace are the flowers of the tree of resistance to the Synod. Thou dost not merit that we should parley at all with thee; yet out of pity, since we see thee branded with the burden of many sins and surrounded by the flames of the fire of grief, we speak once more. Go thou and do a bitter penance according to thy sins, if by any means thou mayest cross the ocean of distress.' When Gardabhilla of the evil deeds heard the Wise One speak thus, his very soul grew pale, and he departed thence in misery. Dying in his wanderings, he wanders still in the ocean of rebirth.

Then the princes appointed him as Shāhi whom the Wise One chose, and themselves enjoyed dominion as his vassals. Since they were of the Śaka race, they are called Śakas, and thus began the Śaka dynasty. After a time there arose a king of Mālwā called Vikramāditya, who overthrew the Śakas; gloriously did he reign and rule, and he established his own era. When a hundred and thirty-five years of the Vikrama era had passed, this Śaka king established an era of his own. This explains the Śaka era. Kālakācārya re-established his sister in the pure practice of religion, and himself became the teacher of the Śakas.

V. KĀLAKĀCĀRYA AND INDRA

Once on a time the king of the gods (Śakra or Indra), his shining form decked with long garlands, broad of chest, his arms stiff with splendid bracelets and arm-rings, ear-rings dancing on his cheeks, crowned with a shining diadem bright with the rays of rare gems, gazed upon the world; and he saw the Jina Sīmandhar-swāmi in Purva Videha, in the assembly of the religious. At once he bowed towards him. While he from his place listened to the Jina's teaching, the latter chose the Nigoda rule as the subject of his discourse. When he had heard all, Indra was astounded, and clutching his splendid locks, with eyes wide opened, he exclaimed: 'Honoured Sir, is there in Bhāratvarṣa (India), in this Dussamā age, any one who can thus exactly expound the Nigoda?' The Jina replied: 'O venerable god, there is in Bharata one Kālaka who understands the Nigoda even as I have expounded it.'

[Fig. 51] When the Lightning-wielder (Śakra) heard this, he proceeded thither in the disguise of an aged Brāhmaṇa, and with respectful greeting asked the Wise One: 'Honoured Sir, be good enough to expound the Nigoda rule, according to the teaching of the Jina of your day, for I long greatly to hear it.' The sage replied in sweet and clear tones: 'Since thou hast this curiosity, O fortunate one, listen attentively.'

After hearing the exposition, Śakra (Indra), to test the monk's wisdom, enquired: 'If it be allowed, pray tell me how long I should have to live if I refrained from all nourishment, taking into consideration my great age.' When Kālaka reckoned up the days and months and years and centuries he found they came to two aeons, and knew by insight that this must be the Lightning-wielder. [Fig. 51] When the Wise One said accordingly: 'Thou art Indra', the Brāhmaṇa resumed his own form, in fine attire, and wearing dancing ear-rings. Bending low, touching the earth with brow, hands and knees, filled with love, he made obeisance to the lotus feet of the Wise One, saying: 'Honour to thee. Lord of Sages, adorned with every virtue, who even in this degraded Dussamā age knowest the doctrine of the Jinas.' Having thus honoured him, the king of gods returned to heaven. At another time the Wise One, when he knew the end of his days was come, practised the asceticism of abstaining from food, and reached the further shore.

VI. EXPLANATION OF VARIOUS TERMS

I. It should also be observed that every Jina has his own particular complexion, cognizance, and *dīkṣā*-tree. These are as follows in the case of the four chief Jinas whose lives are illustrated in the miniatures:

Jina	*Comple-xion*	*Cogni-zance*	*Dikṣā-tree*
Mahāvīra	Yellow	Lion (*keśari-siṃha*)	Aśoka
Pārśva	Blue	Serpent (*sarpa*)	Dhātakī
Neminātha	Black	Conch (*śaṅkha*)	Veṭasa
Ṛṣabha	Golden	Bull (*vṛṣa*)	Vaṭa (banyan)

II. A more particular account must be given of a *Samavasaraṇa*. [Figs. 27, 28, 54] This is, briefly, a walled enclosure prepared by Indra or the minor gods, intended for the delivery of a religious discourse by a Jina immediately after he becomes a *Kevalin*.

The following description of a *samavasaraṇa* is extracted from the *Samavasaraṇa Sthavana*:[8]

2. Wherever the Jinas exhibit the condition of Kevalin, in which all substances manifest themselves, there the Princes of the Air (Vayu-kumāras) cleanse the earth for one *yojana* all around. 3. The Cloud-princes (Megha-kumāras) rain down fragrant water, the gods of the Seasons spread heaps of flowers and the Vāṇa-Vyantaras make the surface of the earth variegated with ruby, gold and gems. 4. There are three ramparts: the innermost, intermediate and outermost. (The first) is constructed of gems, by the Jyotiṣkas; (and the third) of silver, with the battlements of gold, by the Bhavanapatis. 5. In a round *Samavasaraṇa* the ramparts are 33 *dhanuṣ* and 33 *aṇgulas* wide, 500 *dhanuṣ* high, and 1 *krosa* 600 *dhanuṣ* (counting both sides) distant from each other. Each rampart has four gates made of gems. 9. In the centre is a gem-studded pedestal, with four doors, three steps, and as high as the figure of the

[8] Bhandarkar, 'Jaina Iconography', *Indian Antiquary*, Vol. XL, pp. 125-30 and 153-61

Jina, 200 *dhanuṣ* broad and long, two and a half *krosas* high from the ground level. 10. (In the centre of the dais stands) the Aśoka tree, twelve times as high as the body of the Jina, and exceeding a *yojana* in breadth. Then (underneath) is (a pedestal called) a *devacchaṃda*, (and on it are) four lion-thrones accompanied by (four) foot-stools. (The four lion-thrones are occupied by the Jina himself on the East, and on the other sides by three reflections of the Jina, produced by the Vāṇa-Vyantaras). 12. At every gate the Vāna-Vyantaras put up flags, parasols, *makaras*, ... garlands, pitchers; a triple arch (*toraṇa*), and incense vases. 14. Having entered from the East and from left to right, having sat on a seat facing the East, having placed his feet on a footstool, and having saluted the congregation (*tīrtha*), the Lord discourses on the Law. (The congregation consists of gods, men and animals). 18. ... There are two step-wells in each corner when it is square, and one (at each gateway) when it is a round *samavasaraṇa*.

III. Another term requiring explanation is *Siddha-śilā*. It is merely stated in the *Kalpa Sūtra* that Mahāvīra at death became a Siddha or Mukta, i.e. one perfected or released. A description of this place to which perfected souls pass, leaving their bodies here below, is given in the *Uttarādhyāna Sūtra:*

Twelve *yojanas* above the Sarvātha (heaven) is the place Īṣatpragbhāra, which has the form of an umbrella. It is forty-five hundred thousand *yojanas* long, and as many broad, and it is somewhat more than three times as many in circumference. Its thickness is eight *yojanas*; it is greatest in the middle, and decreases towards the margin till it is thinner than the wing of a fly. This place, by nature pure, consisting of white gold, resembles in form an (inverted) open umbrella, as has been said by the best of Jinas. Above it is a pure blessed place, which is white like a conch. ... There at the top of the world reside the blessed perfected souls, rid of all transmigration, and arrived at the excellent state of perfection.[9]

[Figs. 3, 29, 30] It should be noted that the miniatures, as well as Jaina tradition, appear to identify the place described as Īṣatpragbhāra with the actual *Siddha sīlā*. In the miniatures, the place resembling in form an (inverted) white umbrella, is represented in section as a crescent, very thin at the margins and relatively thick in the centre. This crescent has been pointed out to me by a Jaina priest, in the actual miniatures, as the *Siddha sīlā*; and some of the miniatures, moreover, are thus labelled in a contemporary hand. Hüttemann is certainly mistaken in describing the crescent as that of the moon.[10]

The *Kalpa Sūtra* and the *Acārāṅga Sūtra* do not expressly mention either the Samavasaraṇa or the Siddha Śīlā. But the constant representation of these places in the miniatures shows that the mention of Mahāvīra's preaching (*samosarai*) the Law to gods and men, after attaining the state of a Kevalin was understood to imply also the place of preaching, the *Samavasaraṇa;* and in the same way the statement that he became a *Siddha* implied that he went to the Siddha Śīlā. The Īṣāṭprāgbhāra is inhabited by fifteen varieties of Siddhas, of whom the Tīrthakara-siddhas are first.

IV. The Eight Auspicious Objects (*Aṣṭa-maṇgala*): Representations of the Eight Auspicious Symbols constantly recur in Jaina art. [Figs. 8, 58, 59].

The names of the auspicious objects are given as follows in the *Aupapātika Sūtra*; Sanskrit or English equivalents are added in brackets: 1. *Sotthiya* (svastika); 2. *Sirivaccha* (śrīvatsa); 3. *Nandiyāvatta*; 4. *Vaddhamaṇaga* (powder-box); 5. *Bhaddāsaṇa* (throne of fortune); 6. *Kalasa* (water-jar); 7. *Maccha* (fishes); and 8. *Dappaṇā* (mirror).

In the accompanying black and white reproduction after Hüttemann, from MS.IC.2367 of the Berlin Museum für Völkerkunde, the water-jar forms the central object; leaves and flowers emerge from the neck, which is provided with symbolic eyes. To left and right of the water-jar are represented the powder-box and fishes. The mirror appears in the upper left hand corner, the throne on the right. Below, the *sirivaccha*, *sotthiya* (svastika) and *nandiyāvatta* symbols are represented in order from left to right.

VII. COSMOLOGY

According to Jainas, the universe is eternal. They represent it as having the form of a spindle resting on the point of a cone. Sometimes the same form is likened to a woman with arms akimbo, the junction of spindle with triangle being her waist; in corresponding diagrams, the figure of the woman thus encloses or enfolds the whole cosmos.

[9] Jacobi, *Gaina Sūtras* II, Sacred Books of the East, Vol. XLV, pp. 211-13.

[10] Hüttemann, *Miniaturen zum Jinacarita,* loc. cit., p. 74.

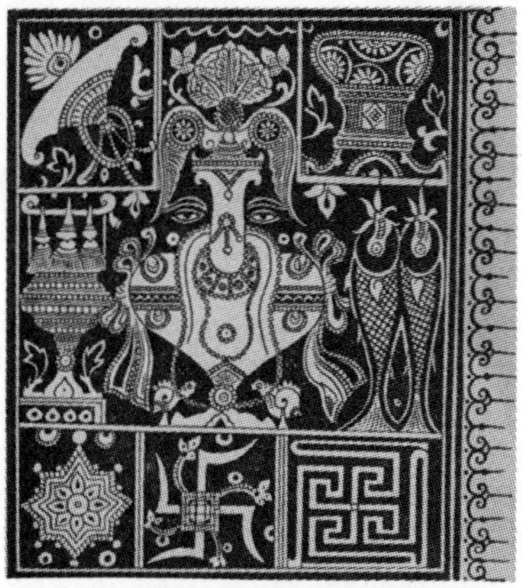

c.

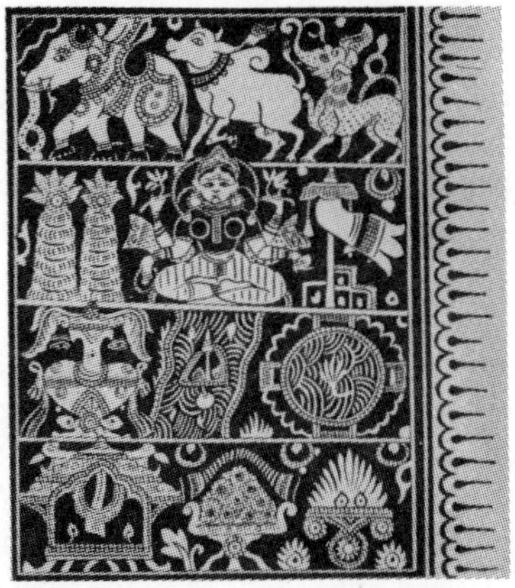

d.

Illustrations from the Berlin MS. IC 2367 of the Museum für Völkerkunde, after Hüttemann, *Miniaturen zum Tinacarita*, Baessler Archiv, 1913.

c. The Aṣṭamaṅgala, or Eight Auspicious Objects.
d. The Fourteen Dreams of the Kśatriyāṇī Triśalā (see p. 83)

The summit of the spindle is formed by the Five Heavens (Vimānas) of the Anuttara gods, that of the Sarvārthasiddhas being central and those of the Vijayas, Vaijayantas, Jayantas and Aparājitas being disposed in a horizontal plane around it. Above these is the Īṣāṭprāgbhāra or paradise of the Perfected; with the exception of this paradise, all belong to the Saṃsāra or sphere of change, mortality and rebirth. Nevertheless, the gods of the higher heavens reside there for periods almost inconceivably long.

Below the five heavens of the Anuttara gods are the nine heavens of the Graiveyakas, arranged one above the other: the Graiveyaka and Anuttara heavens together form the upper half of the spindle.

Below them are the twelve heavens of the Kalpabhavas (sixteen according to the Digambaras), arranged one above the other, completing the lower half of the spindle. All the gods inhabiting the various heavens (vimānas) above the 'waist' are called Vaimānikas.

The 'waist' is formed by Mount Meru, the axis of the universe, and the lands and seas disposed about it horizontally. Here belong the Bhavanādhipati (Asuras, Nāgas, etc.), Vyantara (Rakṣasas, Kiṃnaras, Gandharvas, etc.), and Jyotiṣka (Suns, Moons, Planets, etc.) gods, and finally, also men.

The cone below the 'waist' contains the seven hells or underworlds (Nārakas).

The geography of the worlds about Mount Meru (illustrated in Fig. 56) is as follows: There is a central continent around Meru, called Jambūdvīpa Bharata. Around this is the Salt Sea, separating it from the continent called Dhātukī-dvīpa. Around this again is the Black Sea, separating it from the continent called Puṣkara-dvīpa. The four parts of the two outer continents, and the two parts (Bharata and Airāvata) of Jambūdvīpa, constitute the 'Ten Regions' or 'Worlds'. The inner half of Puṣkara-dvīpa is separated from the outer half by a range of impassable mountains, the Manuṣottara Parvata. Each continent has an elaborate system of rivers and mountains.

The southern segment of Jambūdvīpa, called Bharata-varṣa, is the land of India, where the twenty-four Tīrthakaras of our age (*avasarpini*) have made their appearance. It will be seen that the Bharata-varṣa of the map, with its mountain ranges to the north, its two great rivers, and the sea round it except on the north, corresponds to the actual geography of India, with the Himālayas, Indus and Ganges, and the Indian Ocean.

VIII. AESTHETICS AND RELATIONSHIPS OF JAINA PAINTING

The Jaina MSS., although the illuminated examples are far from common, constitute the chief exception to the general rule that Indian MSS. are not illustrated. It will be seen, however (Fig. 5), that there is no attempt at an organic relationship of text and illustration, such as always appears in Persian MSS. The Jaina miniature is simply a square or oblong picture that looks as if it had been pasted on to the page, rather than designed as a part of it. This may not arise so much from the fact that the painter and writer must have been separate persons, as from the fact that Indian painting was highly developed long before the sacred books were habitually preserved in written form.

We are familiar with the striking continuity of the traditions of Buddhist painting: to give only one example, compare the White Elephant Gift (Vessantara Jātaka) as represented at Degaldoruva in Ceylon (eighteenth century; my *Mediaeval Sinhalese Art*, frontispiece) with the same subject represented at Miran (second century; Stein, *Desert Cathay*, Fig. 147); the latter example, and indeed both, must reflect still older Indian models. Just the same must be true of the illustrations to the Lives of the Jinas: probably nothing in the composition is due to the fifteenth century painter, just as nothing in the text is due to the fifteenth century scribe. This does not mean, of course, that Jaina art has not varied in style, nor that there is no diversity of merit in the mediaeval works; it means that if we had before us Jaina paintings of the fifth century, or even earlier, we should most likely recognize in them compositions almost identical, as such, with many of those in the fifteenth century books, and later.

Probably the illustrations to the Kālakācārya Kathānakam have not so old an ancestry. The story itself is of later origin, and I should suppose the compositions may not go further back than the tenth century. On the whole, they are decidedly less formal and more anecdotal than those accompanying the Lives of the Jinas.

In any case we have before us a purely Indian art derived, like Rājput and Orissa painting and the late Buddhist art of Ceylon, from old traditions; but carrying us further back in actual examples than either of these.

If we seek for definite parallels, other than such obvious resemblances as that of the figure of a seated Jina to a seated Buddha, we are reminded first of the illustrations to the oldest Nepalese palm-leaf MSS. of the Prajñāpāramitā, etc. These illustrations likewise take the form of square frames let into the text, very much as in the Jaina MSS. There are also resemblances in matters of detail: thus, the curious sloping throne (a perspective representation?) seems to be derived from the architectural canopies of the earlier art. There are also striking reminiscences of the Nepalese manner of drawing hands and feet, and general feeling for outline. Also the colouring, where, as in MS. C.A., gold is not employed, or only to an insignificant extent, recalls old Buddhist art.

The pictures are filled with characteristically Indian and ancient motifs: for example, the constant representation of haṃsas, peacocks, lions and elephants, the occasional purely decorative use of the lotus to fill empty spaces (Fig. 1—not here representing a rain of flowers; cf. eighteenth century Sinhalese Buddhist paintings); the fondness for clouds (which have no likeness to Chinese or Persian formulas); the conventions for water; the Hindu costumes (such as the *dhoti*—note the haṃsa and diaper designes of the printed cotton or woven *sāris*, etc.; the lion-thrones (*siṃhāsaṇa*); and the bending of trees (*druma-nātir*) towards the holy man (cf. *Rāmāyaṇa*, exile of Rāma—'the trees incline their heads towards him'). The plain domed arch (Fig. 2, etc.) is of *makara toraṇa* origin; the same is doubtless true of the cusped arches (Fig. 2, r and 1.), which give no proofs of contemporary Persian influences, as they occur also in Nepalese art of the ninth century, and the upper frieze of the Viśvakarma cave temple at Elūrā, still earlier. The distinctively Persian costume of the Shāhis in Kālakācārya pictures cannot be said to prove more than an acquaintance with Persian customs.

The physical type is rather peculiar, the very sharp hooked nose and large eyes being especially striking. The sword-edged nose is also characteristic of mediaeval Nepalese bronzes and Orissan sculpture, and was admired in the most Hindu circles (in Vidyāpati, a beautiful woman's nose is compared to Garuḍa's beak); it was nevertheless a feature no less admirable in the eyes of Persians. The large eyes are of course characteristic of all Indian art; but tney are here drawn in a peculiar manner, not as in Nepalese or Rājput paintings. The further eye is made to project from the outline of the cheek in a most extraordinary way. The prolongation of the outer corner of the eye, almost to meet the ear, is also remarkable; it corresponds to characteristic passages in Hindu literature.[11] Nevertheless, this elongation of the eye by a single fine line stretching to the ear (Figs. 13, 15) is not quite like anything that is

[11] Cf. *Rājatarangini*, I, 210 : 'The corners of their eyes were captivating, and illuminated by a very thin line of antimony, which appeared to play the part of the stem to the ruby-lotuses of their ear-ornaments' (Stein). This description is absolutely realized in Figs. 13 and 15.

familiar in other schools of Indian painting, while it very strongly recalls the drawings on twelfth and thirteenth century Rhages pottery, and seems to me to constitute the most definite suggestion of relationship to Persian art that these Jaina miniatures afford. The use of gold leaf possibly points in the same direction.

The parallels with Rājput painting are naturally closer. Thus, in the Dīkṣā scene of Fig. 1, Mahāvīra is represented with a lion-waist and hugely developed chest; and there are many figures where it would be difficult at first sight to distinguish the representations as those of men or women. This recalls the mannerism of the large Kṛṣṇa cartoons from Jaipur ('Ostasiatische Zeitschrift', I, 2, Fig. 1: *Indian Drawings*, II, Pls. 2 and 3). We have already remarked that the representation of clouds, which appear in twelve out of the fifty-three miniatures reproduced, is anything but Persian or Chinese in manner; on the other hand, it is by no means unlike the manner of the earlier Pahārī and Rājasthānī paintings (seventeenth century Jammu district and Rājputāna—not eighteenth century Kāngrā), where a narrow band of dark blue storm-cloud is constantly introduced above the high horizon. It will not be forgotten that the monsoon clouds in India are as much liked and desired as blue sky in northern Europe. Another resemblance to Rājput art (Jammu) appears in the strong red backgrounds (also in old Nepalese and late Sinhalese, etc.).

The architecture (Figs. 2, 5, 41, 57, etc.) resembles that of Gujarāt, where most of the miniatures must have been painted.

Indian Mughal art did not yet exist when the fifteenth century Jaina miniatures were being painted.

On the whole, the archaeological interest of Jaina painting exceeds its aesthetic significance. In most of the manuscripts the drawing is indeed very highly accomplished, but rather of a workshop character than deeply felt. Many of the miniatures are overcrowded with detail, the statement of fact rather than the expression of emotion. But in some cases the aesthetic values are much higher. The *dīkṣā* scene (Tonsure of Mahāvīra) of Fig. 1, though it conforms to the usual type in most details of composition, attains to far greater dignity, and is comparable in passion with the noble passage of the *Kalpa Sūtra* which begins: 'Reverence to the Saints and Blessed Ones' ... (*supra*, 82). That emotion is really expressed in the picture, which led the chief of the gods to descend from heaven and kneel with an offering before the Wise One. As elsewhere in Indian literature and art (the Great Renunciation of Buddha; Arjuna's Penance, etc.), we are made to feel that the Going-forth of the hero-saint is an event of cosmic and more than temporal significance. Like Blake, the poet thought that 'there were listeners in other worlds than this'.[12] Such examples go far to prove that there must once have existed an Indian school of Jaina painting comparable with the classic Buddhist art of Ajaṇṭā.

Within more secular limits, some of the Kālakācarya pictures have excellent qualities. The Shāhi upon his throne in Figs. 4 and 5 is admirably designed; the vertically striped robe, as well as the pose in Fig. 4, give an impression of great repose and dignity. Other pictures, such as the slaying of the magic ass (Fig. 47) are distinctly amusing, though the humour may be quite unconscious.

The diagrams are chiefly of interest as such; but there are some very well-drawn animals in the outer margins of Fig. 56, especially the running tiger in the upper left hand corner.

The specimens of book-furniture afford examples of excellent craftsmanship. The embroidery of the book-covers is vigorously designed and admirably and patiently executed. The book-strings are still better; nothing could be more successful than the patterns, both geometrical and floral, while two of the examples are of special interest as having interwoven text and dates.

IX. THE ILLUSTRATED MANUSCRIPTS

The reproductions here given in Figs. 1 to 53 are taken from the pages of five Jaina MSS., to which abbreviated reference is made in the descriptions facing the Plates, under the following heads:

I.O. This is the manuscript of the *Kalpa Sūtra* (Lives of the Jinas) of Bhadrabāhu and of the *Kālakācārya Kathānakam* used by Jacobi in his editions of the texts ('Abh. für die Kunde des Morgenländes', VII, I, 1879, and 'Zeit. der Deutsch. Morgenländischen Gesellschaft', XXXIV, 1880) and in his translation of the *Kalpa Sūtra* in the Sacred Books of the East, Vol. XXII. The MS. is dated Vikrama Saṃvat 1484, equivalent to AD 1427, and it is at once the oldest known illuminated Indian MS. on

[12] W.B. Yeats, *Poems of William Blake,* Introduction.

paper, and the oldest known Indian painting on paper of any kind.

The MS. contains 46 miniatures, of which 31 belong to the *Kalpa Sūtra* and 15 to the *Kalakācārya Kathānakam*. Of these miniatures, those on ff. 3, 12, 115, 121, 129 and 144 are here reproduced in figures 9, 12, 45, 50, 5, 51. The MS. is not merely illustrated, but also rather elaborately decorated, as may be seen from the reproduction of a whole folio in colours (Pl. 1). It is written with silver on 113 leaves, of which the ground is coloured black or red alternately. A few pages are written in gold, either on red, or on a plain ground. The borders of the pages are frequently decorated, generally with animal processions (elephants or haṃsas), floral branches or formal lotus-palmette frames, and occasionally with affronted haṃsas, antelopes, or with human figures. These borders have either a blue, vermilion, crimson or red ground. In the Library of the India Office, I am indebted to Dr. F.W. Thomas for facilities kindly granted for reproductions from this manuscript.

The following MSS., C.A. to C.F., belong to the present writer.

C.A. Manuscript of the *Kalpa Sūtra* (98 folios) and the *Kālakācārya Kathānakam* (8 folios), measuring 9.5 x 28 cm, six lines to a page. Prākṛt, with frequent glosses: with 15 miniatures illustrating the Lives of the Jinas, and 2 miniatures illustrating the story of Kālakācārya. Not dated, but probably fifteenth century. The text is written in black ink, and is decorated with plain red borders, and the central circles, etc., are rubricated. The miniatures are painted with yellow (in lieu of gold), crimson, black, green, two shades of blue, and occasional touches of bronzy gold, against a scarlet background (see Figs. 1 and 2). Occasionally a pearly-white pigment is also used. The title of each picture is written in the margin of the MS. or on the picture itself. A rough diagram of each illustration also appears in the margin, as a note to remind the painter of the required subject; possibly the painter was unable to read, and made these spirited marginal notes, according to the instructions of the writer of the MS., or of a reader who went over it with him.

The miniatures in this MS. are remarkable for the accomplishment of the fine brushwork (see Figs. 1, 2, 6, 7, etc.). The *dīkṣā* scene of Fig. 1 is especially noteworthy for its simplicity and dignity.

C.B. Manuscript of the *Kalpa Sūtra* (72 folios) and *Kālakasūri Kathānakam* (5 folios), measuring 11 x 30 cm, nine lines to a page. Prākṛt, with 28 miniatures illustrating the Lives of the Jinas and 6 miniatures illustrating the story of Kālakācārya. Dated Saṃvat 1554 (AD 1497). Text in black ink with red borders and rubricated central circles, etc.; first page with a blue pattern border. Painted with crimson, black, blue, white and scarlet (forming the background of the finished work) on a gold ground (left uncoloured to form the figures, etc.). The miniatures are not labelled. The marginal diagrams are extremely faint.

C.C. Manuscript of the *Kalpa Sūtra* (107 folios), measuring 10.5 x 25.5 cm, seven lines to a page, with 24 miniatures illustrating the Lives of the Jinas. Prākṛt. No date, but probably seventeenth century. Concludes with the colophon '*Iti Gherāvali sūtram*' erased. The colouring is similar to that of C.B., except that the background is bright blue in place of scarlet. The illustrations have marginal legends, but no marginal diagrams. Inferior paper. The execution is generally inferior to that of C.A. and C.B., but a number of subjects which appear in C.C. are not given elsewhere.

C.D. Manuscript of the *Kālakācārya Kathā,* 9 folios, measuring 11 x 26 cm, nine lines to a page, with six miniatures illustrating the story of Kālakācārya. Prākṛt. No date, but of fine quality and probably early fifteenth century. Miniatures coloured as in C.B. Text bordered with red and central circles rubricated.

The two following are mentioned for comparison, but no miniatures are reproduced:

C.E. Manuscript of the *Ratan Sār* (Life of Pārśvanātha, etc.) 21 folios, measuring 10.5 x 26 cm, thirteen lines to a page, text in black ink with red and yellow borders, and rubricated central circles. Dated Saṃvat 1633 (AD 1566). Prākṛt. Illustrated with four crude miniatures, of which one occupies a full page, viz., a woman, with the legend 'Srī Pārśvanātha bhāryā prabhāvatī mūrtti jāṇavī'.

C.F.A. manuscript of 12 folios, measuring 16 x 32 cm, sixteen lines to a page, with a picture of a Jina on each side of each folio. The drawing is quite perfunctory. No date, but probably eighteenth century.

The following MSS. are in the British Museum:

M.S. Or. 5,149. Manuscript of the *Kalpa Sūtra,* 80 folios, nine lines to a page. Has 25 miniatures illustrating the Lives of the Jinas. Text in black ink, with plain borders, central circles, etc., in red. Prākṛt, dated Saṃvat 1521 (AD 1464).

M.S. Or. 5,257. Manuscript of the *Uttarādhyāyana,* sixteenth-seventeenth century, with one miniature.

M.S. Or. Add. 26,374. Manuscript of the *Kṣetra-samas laghu-prakaraṇam,* a system of geography according to the Jainas. Prākṛt, with Gujarātī commentary. With numerous pictures and diagrams. Dated Saṃvat 1826 (AD 1769).

The whole of folio 16 (obverse) is here reproduced in Fig. 55.

The following MSS. are mentioned by Hüttemann:

I.C. 2,367. The *Kalpa Sūtra.* An MS. in the Berlin Museum für Völkerkunde. Studied by Dr. Hüttemann (*Miniaturen zum Jinacarita,* loc. cit.). The MS. has 24 miniatures illustrating the Lives of the Jinas, of which Dr. Hüttemann reproduces 14 (two in colours); four in his figures are here copied in the text figures *a* to *d.*

MS. Or. 799. The *Kalpa Sūtra;* 'mit zahlreichen, sehr schönen ... miniaturen', in the Royal Library, Berlin, mentioned by Dr. Hüttemann, loc. cit.

X. DESCRIPTION OF THE PLATES

Plate I

(The reproductions on this Plate are not in the sequential order of the history, but are chosen as typical examples of colour. Figs. 1-4 size of original; Fig. 5 slightly reduced.)

Fig. 1. Tonsure of Mahāvīra (his initiation as monk). On the left, Indra seated, four-armed, two hands holding a divine garment, one holding a goad (attribute of Indra), the other receiving from Mahāvīra his cast-off royal robes; below, the elephant Airāvata, the *vāhan* of Indra. On the right Mahāvīra, wearing a waist cloth only, seated beneath an Aśoka tree which is slightly inclined towards him, is plucking out his long locks. The foreground represents a hilly park, with Aśoka trees. The horizon is very high; the sky is filled with heavy monsoon clouds. A conventional lotus occupies a space between the figures and the horizon. Cf. figure 26; Hüttemann, Fig. 9 (here text b); B.M. MS. Or. 5,149, folio 37, labelled '*Mahāvīra dīkṣā*'; MS. I.O., folio 50; and MS. C.C., folio 30, labelled '*Dīkṣā*'.

MS. C.A., folio 49, labelled '*Mahāvīraloca*'.

Fig. 2. Pārśvanātha. The Jina enthroned; his crown is surmounted by five snake hoods. The throne is supported by two elephants and two lions, and contained in a mandir, cells of which are occupied by worshippers. The upper arch contains elephants; the upper corners two haṃsas. The upper central part of the throne, just below the Jina's feet, shows the *nāga*, which is the cognizance of Pārśvanātha. Cf. Figs. 32, 57.

MS. C.A., folio 59.

Fig. 3. Mahāvīra as the Perfected One, enthroned above the heavens, in Īṣātprāgbhāra. The inverted crescent represents the Siddha śilā, or Rock of the Perfected. Aśoka trees on either hand lean towards the Jina. His lion-cognizance appears on the front of the throne, which is surmounted by an umbrella. The landscape shows mountains below and a cloudy sky. Cf. Fig. 29; Hüttemann, Fig. 9; B.M. MS. Or. 5,149, folio 37; and MS. C.B., folio 38, labelled '*Mukti śilā*'.

Fig. 4. Kālakācārya conversing with the Śaka Shāhi. The latter sits on a lion throne, holding a flower in his left hand, while the monk faces him with folded palms. The Shāhi seems to be speaking and the monk listening.

MS. C.D., folio 2.

Fig. 5. Folio 129 of the MS. I.O.; with decorated text, and miniature representing Kālakācārya instructing the Śaka Shāhi. As in Fig. 4, but the monk is speaking and the Shāhi listening.

Plate 2

(All the figures of the size of the original)

Fig. 6. The Jina (Mahāvīra) enthroned: he wears royal ornaments and holds a begging bowl.

MS. C.A., folio 1; labelled '*Mahāvīra*'.

Fig. 7. The Jina (Mahāvīra) as Guru (preaching), wearing a monk's robes; the right hand raised in *vitarka mudrā*, and holding a rosary. The Jina is seated in a shrine of simple construction; above it are two parrots. The sky is filled with heavy clouds. Cf. Fig. 8.

MS. C.A., folio 2; labelled '*Guru*'.

Fig. 8. The Jina (Mahāvīra) as Guru (preaching), wearing monk's robes; the right hand raised in *vitarka mudrā*, and holding a rosary. On either side of the shrine are worshippers in niches surmounted by affronted birds. In four compartments above and four below, are represented the Aṣṭamangala, or eight auspicious objects, viz., (in order from left to right, above): *sirivaccha*, *vaddhamaṇaga* (powder-box), *bhaddāsaṇa* (throne), *dappaṇa* (mirror), (and below) the *nandiyāvatta, sotthiya* (swastika), *kalasa* (water-jar), and *maccha* (fishes). In this miniature two subjects, the Guru and the Aṣṭamangala are combined; more often these form the subject of two separate illustrations. Cf. Hüttemann, Fig. 1; MS. I.O., folio 2; and B.M. MS. Or. 5,149, folio 2.

MS. C.B., folio 2; labelled '*Aṣṭamangalāka*'.

Fig. 9. Devānandā's Dreams. Below, Devānandā reclining on a couch. Above, twelve dreams (out of fourteen) in the following order: garlands, Padmāvatī, lion, bull, elephant, palanquin, river, lotus pond, water-jar, banner, and the sun and moon. Cf. Hüttemann, Fig. A; MS. C.B.; and MS. C.C., folio 4.

MS. I.O. folio 3.

Fig. 10. The Court of Indra. Left, Indra enthroned, four-handed, holding goad and trident, some other object on one left hand, and with the right hand raised. Before him are three courtiers, devas resembling himself. Cf. MS. C.C., folio 8, labelled '*Indraya sabhā*'.

MS. C.B., folio 5; labelled 'Indra'.

Fig. 11. Indra, descended from his throne, bows to Mahāvīra. He holds the goad in one left hand, an offering in another, and two other hands are joined in reverence. The curious throne, apparently of the type of a *mandir* built askew, is well seen. Observe the haṃsa and check patterns of the dhotis worn in this and the last picture. Cf. B.M. MS. Or. 5,149, folio 6, labelled '*Indra namokṣaṇam bhaṇai*'.

MS. C.B., folio 6, labelled '*Indra namokṣaṇam*'.

Plate 3

(All the figures of the size of the original)

Fig. 12. Hariṇegameṣī receiving the commands of Indra. Indra is enthroned; Hariṇegameṣī stands with raised joined hands in an attitude of respect and attention. Indra is four-handed, and holds the goad and trident. Hariṇegameṣī has the head of an antelope joined to the body of a man.

MS. I.O., folio 12.

Fig. 13. Hariṇegamesi removing the embryo from the womb of the Brāhmaṇi Devānandā. Devānandā reclines on a cushioned couch, below which are seen a ewer and a dish *of pān supāri*. The embryo is represented as a ball. Above the roof are heavy clouds. Cf. B.M. MS. Or. 5,149, folio 10; and MS. C.B., folio 10, labelled '*Garbhāpahār Hariṇegameṣī*'. MS. C.C. shows this subject and the next in one miniature, labelled '*Garbhāpahār garbha sacaraṇa*'.

MS. C.A., folio 15; labelled '... *Hariṇegameṣī*'.

Fig. 14. Hariṇegameṣī bringing the embryo to the Kṣatriyāṇī Triśalā. Generally similar to the last, but the embryo is more realistically represented, as in Hüttemann's Fig. 3. Cf. also B.M. MS. Or. 4,149, folio 11, labelled '*Garbha sacaraṇa*'.

MS. C.B. folio 11; labelled '*Hariṇegameṣī garbha-prakṣepa.*'

Fig. 15. The Kṣatriyānī Triśalā attended by a maid-servant. The lady reclines on a couch, while the maid plies a fly-whisk (*cāmara*).

MS. C.B., folio 12; labelled '*Raṇī Triśalā*'.

Fig. 16. The Fourteen Dreams of the Kṣatriyāṇī Triśalā, viz.: First row: elephant, bull, lion. Secong row: Padmāvatī, garlands, sun and moon banner. Third row: water-jar, lotus tank, river. Fourth row: palanquin, heap of Jewels, fire. It is noteworthy that the 'lion' *(siha)* of the texts is here, as in Hüttemann's figure 2, represented by a *gaja-siṁha* or mythical elephant-lion. [A true lion is represented in the next figure (17) from the MS. C.A., folio 34.] The water-jar is provided with symbolic eyes. The tank is walled, with four gates or *ghāts*, and a lotus in the middle. A sailing vessel and fishes are seen in the river, and flowers are growing along its margin. Water is represented by intersecting straight lines which are really parts of concentric curves, according to the usual formula. Cf. Hüttemann, Fig. 2; B.M. MS. Or. 5,149, folio 13, labelled '*Svapna 14 lahar*'; and MS. C.C., folio 21, labelled '*Triśalā svapan 14*'.

MS. C.B., folio 13; labelled '*Caūda satraṇā*'.

Fig. 17. The Fourteen Dreams of the Kṣatriyāṇī Triśalā, as above, but with differences of detail. The lion is a true lion. The tank is not walled. There is no ship on the river. The water is represented by intersecting segments of concentric circles, according to the most frequent Indian convention (cf. Figs. 30 and 31). Cf. B.M. MS. Or. 5,149, folio 13; MS. I.O., folio 21; and Hüttemann, figure 2.

MS. C.A., folio 34; labelled '*14 satraṇām*'.

Plate 4
(All the figures are slightly reduced)

Fig. 18. Toilet of Siddhārtha. A maid-servant is dressing his hair, after the bath. Cf. MS. C.C., folio 35.
MS. C.B., folio 21.

Fig. 19. Darbar of Siddhārtha. He is enthroned, to the left. On the right, three kneeling soldiers.
MS. C.B., folio 22; labelled *'Rāja-sabhā'*.

Fig. 20. The Kṣatriyāṇī Triśalā reclining. She is probably listening to the interpretation of the dreams.
MS. C.A., folio 36; labelled *'Rājā-rūpa'* (probably for *'Rāṇī-rūpa'*).

Fig. 21. The interpretation of the dreams. On the left, Siddhārtha seated enthroned, beneath a royal umbrealla; on the left, a Brāhmaṇa reading from a book. Cf. Hüttemann, Fig. 5; MS. C.B., ff. 23, 24; and B.M. MS. Or. 5, 149, folio 24, labelled *'Rājā rāṇī sapna pāṭhaka'*.
MS. C.A. 36; labelled *'Svapna-lakṣaṇa-pāthakāh.'*

Fig. 22. Birth of Mahāvīra. Triśalā, reclining, holds the child in her arm, and is fanned by a maid-servant, using a fly-whisk *(cāmara)*. Cf. Hüttemann, Fig. 6; B.M. MS. Or. 5,149, folio 29, labelled *'Mahāvīra janma'*; MS. C.C., folio 48, labelled *'Vīra janma'*; and MS. I.O., folio 40.
MS. C.B., folio 28; labelled *'Janma'*.

Fig. 23. The Birthday Festival, or 'Apotheosis'. Mahāvīra seated on his mother's (?) lap, while deities on either side offer water of lustration in golden ewers. Two bulls with waving tails descend from heaven towards Triśalā. The figures are all floating in mid-air above the mountains, but the bulls are descending a sort of golden staircase. Cf. Hüttemann, Fig. 7; B.M. MS. Or., folio 30; and MS. I.O., folio 42.
MS. C.B, folio 29; labelled *'Janmābhiṣekha'*.

Plate 5
(All the figures of the size of the original)

Fig. 24. Mahāvīra distributes his wealth. He is seated on a throne before a table covered with gems, which he is presenting to three Brāhmaṇas. Cf. B.M. MS. Or. 5,149, folio 35, labelled *'Mahāvīra dāna'*; and MS. C.C., folio 56, labelled *'Vīra dāna'*.
MS. C.B., folio 32; labelled *'Samvatsarī dāna'*.

Fig. 25. The Indifference of Mahāvīra. He stands, attended by two deities and two antelopes, and is unmoved, though a serpent, a scorpion a lion and a dog are attacking him. Cf. Hüttemann, Fig. 10, where there are two serpents, and the dog is replaced by a woman cooking (representing pleasure). This subject is not given in MSS. C.A. and C.B., nor I.O.
MS. C.C., folio 60; labelled *'Vīra upasargra'*.

Fig. 26. Tonsure of Mahāvīra. On left, Mahāvīra seated beneath an Aśoka tree, plucks out his hair. The tree bends over him (called *drumā-natir,* a mark of gods and arhats), acknowledging his greatness. On the right, Indra, kneeling beneath a royal umbrella, offers a divine robe; one hand holds the trident. The clouds above, usually blue, are here green. Cf. Hüttemann, Fig. 9 (here text fig. *b*); B.M. MS. Or. 5,149, folio 37; MS. I.O., folio 50; MS. C.C., Folio 30; and Fig. 1.
MS. C.B., folio 34; labelled *'Dīkṣā'*.

Fig. 27. *Samavasaraṇa* of Mahāvīra. A triple walled enclosure with four gates, as described in text, *supra*. Mahāvīra seated in centre. A step-well and animals are represented in each corner. Cf. Fig. 28; B.M. MS. Or. 5,149, folio 38, labelled *'Mahāvīra jñāna'*; MS. I.O., folio 53; and MS. C.C., folio 64, labelled *'Jñāna'*.
MS. C.B., folio 37; labelled *'Jñāna samosaraṇa'*.

Fig. 28. *Samavasaraṇa* of Mahāvīra. As Fig. 27.
MS. C.A., folio 53; labelled *'Mahāvīra samosaraṇa'*.

Fig. 29. Mahāvīra as the Perfected One, enthroned above the heavens in Īṣātprāgbhāra. The inverted crescent represents the Siddha Śilā, or Rock of the Perfect, as described in the text, *supra*. Heavy monsoon clouds above, and mountains below. The body of the Jina is bright yellow; he is supported by *haṃsas* and *siddhas* on either side. Cf. Fig. 3; Hüttemann, Fig. 9; B.M. MS. Or. 5, 149, folio 39, labelled *'M. nivaṇī'*; MS. I.O., folio 55; and MS. C.C., folio 66, labelled *'Vīra mukti'*.
MS. C.A., folio 55; labelled *'Siddhi'*.

Plate 6
(All the figures of the size of the original)

Fig. 30. Above, Pārśvanātha in Īṣatprāgbhāra, enthroned above the Siddha Śilā; his head is surmounted by five cobra hoods. Two *dhātaki* trees rise from the peaks below, bending toward the Jina. Cf. MS. I.O., folio 66. Below, Pārśvanātha protected by the *nāga* Dharanendra. The Jina stands in a sea or lake, and is worshipped by a *yakṣa* and *yakṣiṇī*. Cf. figure 31 and B.M. MS. Or. 5,149, folio 46.

MS. C.B., folio 44.

Fig. 31. Pārśvanātha sheltered by the *nāga* Dharanendra. The Jina stands in a sea or lake, supported by a *yakṣa* and sheltered by the *nāga*, whose hoods rise above his head, and tail lies in the water. Cf. B.M. MS. Or. 5,149, folio 46, labelled '*Pā. upasarga*'.

MS. C.C., folio 75; labelled '*Pārśva upasargra*'.

Fig. 32. Pārśvanātha enthroned. The throne is supported by elephants and lions. The Jina's head is surmounted by five cobra hoods and an umbrella. Three worshippers on either side. Cf. Hüttemann, Fig. 11.

MS. C.C., folio 77; labelled '*Pārśva pratimā*'.

Fig. 33. Above, a king worshipping the Śaṅkha, a symbol of Neminātha. Below, a subject not identified; possibly the Jina snatching a sceptre from Indra.

MS. C.C., folio 79; labelled '*Śaṅkha pūriu hari-hāro liu*'.

Fig. 34. Neminātha enthroned. The throne, etc., as in Fig. 2. The figure of the Jina dark blue; below him, in front of the throne, the *śaṇkha* cognizance; observe the *śaṇkha* also indicated beneath the sketch figure in margin. The Jina holds a begging bowl. Cf. MS. C.C. 78, labelled '*Nemi pratimā*'.

MS. C.A., folio 66; labelled '*Neminātha*'.

Fig. 35. Ādinātha enthroned. The throne, etc., as in Figs. 2, 34. The figure of the Jina yellow; below him, in front of the throne, the bull cognizance, and the same in the marginal sketch. Cf. MS. C.C., folio 88, labelled '*Adinātha pratimā*' [*sic*].

MS. C.A., folio 72; labelled '*Śrī Adinātha*'. [*sic*]

Plate 7
(All the figures of the size of the original)

Fig. 36. Episodes in the life of Neminātha.

MS. C.C., folio 80; labelled '*Nemi pasuvāḍa*'.

Fig. 37. prince (?) riding on an elephant, beneath a large royal umbrella.

MS. C.C., folio 89; labelled '*Hasti-mūrtikā umbha*'.

Fig. 38. The twenty Tīrthakaras between Ṛṣabha and Neminātha.

MS. C.C., ff. 63 and 64, show the twenty Tīrthakaras in two groups of ten, each labelled '*Tīrthaṅkara 10*'.

MS. C.B., folio 48.

Fig. 39. The eleven *gaṇadharas* of Mahāvīra; in the centre of the third row, the centre space is occupied by an Oṃkāra figure with a lotus. Cf. MS. C.C., folio 95, labelled '*Gaṇadhara* 11', where the Oṃkāra figure is replaced by the Hrīṃkāra.

MS. C.B., folio 54; labelled '*Gaṇadhara 11*'.

Fig. 40. Four episodes in the life of Ṛṣabha; viz., *Janma, mukti-śilā, dīkṣā* and *samavasaraṇa*.

MS. C.B., folio 47; no label.

Fig. 41. Ṛṣabha enthroned in a *mandir,* with worshippers. His bull cognizance appears on the front of the throne. A parrot and a monkey are seen on the śikhara, which is crowned by a banner.

MS. C.B., folio 72, the last page of the *Kalpa Sūtra* proper, with colophon; the reverse of the same leaf begins the *Kālakācārya Kathānakam,* with a picture similar to that of Fig. 45. No label.

Plate 8
(All the figures of the size of the original)

Fig. 42. Balamittra (nephew of Kālakācārya) preaching to a lion; other monks below. I cannot explain this further; it is, no doubt, a legend connected with the third section of the story of Kālakācārya, but no lion is referred to in the text translated by Jacobi.

MS. C.D., folio 6; labelled '*Balamittra bhāṇae*'.

Fig. 43. Darbar of King Gardabhilla. The king is seated on a throne, beneath a royal umbrella; before him are his general and army, and cavalry. Cf. MS. C.B., folio 84.

MS. C.A., folio 100; labelled '*Gardabhilla*'.

Fig. 44. Kālakācārya instructing the Śaka prince. The latter sits on a lion throne, surmounted by two umbrellas; before him are his bow and arrows hung on a tripod, and two courtiers kneel above. Note the Persian costumes, contrasting with the purely Hindu dress of Gardabhilla in Fig. 43. On the right, Kālakācārya is seated on a cushion, reading from a book. Heavy clouds above. Cf. Fig. 49 (MS. I.O., folio 121).

MS. C.A., folio 100; labelled '*Śākarāya*'.

Fig. 45. Above, Kālakācārya instructing the Shāhi (here an outdoor scene, with hills, trees and clouds). Below, the Shāhi setting out with the army for Hindustān. On the left, a floral border.

MS. I.O., folio 115.

Fig. 46. Above, Kālakācārya instructing the Shāhi, as in Fig. 44. Below, Kālakācārya changing the potter's stuff to gold: he is shaking a powder over the burning kiln, the Shāhi on horseback looking on.

MS. C.B., folio 74.

Fig. 47. Kālakācārya's archers slaying the magic ass. Gardabhilla, within the walls of a fortified city, seated before a fire, performing magical rites, creating the magic ass which stands in the gateway. Above, also within the city, Sarasvatī, within the royal zenāna. Below, horses in the royal stables. Outside the city walls, archers of the Shāhi's army, with Kālakācārya himself on horseback, firing arrows into the ass's mouth. A triangle of cloud in the upper right hand corner.

MS. C.B., folio 75.

Plate 9

(The reproductions are of the size of the originals)

Fig. 48. Above, Gardabhilla is brought a prisoner before Kālakācārya; below, Kālakācārya goes to the zenāna to bring away his sister.

MS. C.B., folio 76.

Fig. 49. Kālakācārya instructing the Shāhi, as in Figs. 44 and 46, *q.v.*

MS. I.O., folio 49.

Fig. 50. Kālakācārya enthroned, holding a book in his right hand, of which also the thumb and first finger are joined in *vitarka mudrā,* with his left hand touches the head of a kneeling monk or nun (probably Sarasvatī, on the occasion of re-admission to the sisterhood), who touches his feet. On the right, above the kneeling figure, appears a sort of table, on which rests a book covered with flowers. A similar table appears in Figs. 48, 51, 53, also Fig. 32. Its construction resembles that of the modern camp-stool. [It is of considerable interest to see such tables represented in use, as they correspond closely with the Sinhalese *daṇḍāsana,* of which an illustration appears in my *Mediaeval Sinhalese Art,* Pl. X, Fig. 1. I had never seen one of these in use, though I knew them as of monastic origin, and was informed that they were used as book-tables.]

MS. I.O., folio 144.

Fig. 51. Above, Indra disguised as an aged Brāhmaṇa, visits Kālakācārya; below, Indra assumes his proper from, and takes leave of Kālakācārya. [See the story related above, Section IV.]

MS. C.D., folio 9.

Fig. 52. A king and queen dancing, possibly an erotic subject. The king is shooting an arrow at a parrot (the *vāhana* of Kāmadeva) on a tree beneath which the queen is dancing.

MS. C.C., folio 100; labelled '*Nṛtya. ...*'

Fig. 53. The Education of Baḍrasvāmi (? Bhadrabāhu, author of the *Kalpa Sūtra*). Above, apparently dedication of the child to the order; below, the child in a swing.

MS. C.C., folio 98; labelled '*Baḍrasvāmi pālanu*'.

The last two figures, the subjects of which I cannot properly explain, occur only in my MS. C.C.

Plate 10

Fig. 54. Diagram of a *Samavasaraṇa*, drawn in black, yellow and red on buff paper. [See description above, Section V.] The diagram is inscribed with details of dimensions, and indicates the positions occupied by the various deities, men and animals. Two step-wells are represented in each corner, although the *samavasaraṇa* is round. The diagram is dated in the top right hand corner, Saṃvat 1680, equivalent to AD 1623. Size of original diagram, 33 by 27 cm. Collection of the author.

Plate 11
(Both figures are reduced)

Fig. 55. Page of a Jaina MS., with miniature apparently representing the Paṇḍaga and Somaṇasa forest. The latter forms a girdle round Mount Meru at its base, and differs from the Paṇḍaga-vaṇa in not being mountainous; it occupies the curved wooded area at the lowest part of the picture. The rocky Paṇḍaga-vaṇa is represented by the six tree-clad arms of the mountains. The temple above is the shrine of a Tīrthakara on the summit of Meru. (I am indebted to the kindness of Dr. L.D. Barnett, of the British Museum, for the above reading.)

B.M. MS. Or. Add. 26,374, folio 16.

Figure 56. Cosmic diagram showing the lands and seas around Mount Meru. [See above, Section VII.] Bharata-varṣa (India) forms the lower segment of the central circle.

From a large diagram painted on cotton cloth. Collection of the author.

Plate 12
(Both figures are reduced)

Fig. 57. Śrī Pārśvanātha. The central panel shows the Jina enthroned in a *mandir*, of which the śikhara, adorned with a flag and approached by a Siddha, occupies the square immediately above. Right and left of Pārśvanātha are narrow panels occupied by the *nāga* Dharanendra and the yakṣiṇī Padmāvatī. On the extreme left, Indra; on the extreme right, Padmāvatī. Above, on the left, the *Samavasaraṇa* of Pārśvanātha [note the Jina with three reflections of himself, occupying the centre, as described in the text, Section V]; on the right the 'Pañca-Pad' [above, five Oṃkāra ideographs, then five seated Siddhas (?) above the crescent of the Siddha-śilā (?). Below, on the left, Suddharma Svāmi (?); on the right, Gotama Svami. The lower central panel I cannot explain.[13]

From a painting on cotton cloth, probably sixteenth century. Size of original, 30 cm. square. Colours: vermilion (background), crimson, pink, blue, green, black, white and gold (chiefly the square of gold leaf over which the central figure of the Jina is drawn). The cloth has been primed before painting. Spots of sandal paste upon the chief figures show that the picture has been used as an object of worship. Collection of the author.

Fig. 58. MS.-cover, embroidered with the Fourteen Dreams of the Mother of Mahāvīra. The subjects are as follows: To right of centre, large panel, Padmāvatī: next column above, the bull; centre, two garlands; below, the sun: extreme right, above, the elephant; centre, the lion; below, moon and stars: left of Padmāvatī, above, the flag: below, the ocean (river) of milk: next column, above, the golden vase: below, the heavenly mansion. The remaining four subjects are not recognizable.

The embroidery is executed in silk on cotton. The colours are crimson, orange, blue, green, cream and black. The narrow border is cross-stitch, as in Fig. 63. The remainder of the work is couched, except the inconspicuous cream outlining in chain-stitch. Size of original, 30 × 13 cm. Probably sixteenth century. Collection of the author.

Plate 13
(The figures are reduced)

Fig. 59. MS.-cover, embroidered with the Fourteen Dreams of the Mother of Mahāvīra, and the Eight Auspicious Objects (*Aṣṭa-maṅgalāka*). The cover consists of two parts hinged together, and is designed to keep together the loose leaves of any MS. resting on the inside of the larger part. The dreams are represented on this larger flap: Padmāvātī occupies the central squares of the two lower rows. The gold vase is on her proper left. The first four squares of the upper row contain respectively the elephant, bull, lion and two garlands; the two squares on Padmāvatī's proper right contain the flag and throne. The remaining subjects are no longer recognizable.

The narrow portion of the cover contains the *Aṣṭamaṅgalāka*, which are upside down in the reproduction. The subjects are, from left to right: *nandiyāvartta,* fishes, golden vase, throne, mirror, *sirivaccha,* powder-box, and *sotthiya* (swastika).

The needlework is of silver thread on red wool; a very little green and purple silk is also used. The silver thread is partly chain-stitch, partly couched.

Size of original, 27.5 × 20 cm. Probably

[13] These are the *navagraha* or 'nine planets'.

sixteenth century. Collection of the author.

Fig. 60. Portion of an embroidered MS.-cover. Silk on cotton canvas, chevron design. Colours: crimson, yellow, orange (two shades), blue, green and white. x 6/7

Fig. 61. Portion of an embroidered handkerchief, for wrapping MSS. Silk on cotton canvas, in striped lozenges; colours as the last. Nearly 1/1.

Fig. 62. Portion of an embroidered MS.-cover, silk on brown cotton canvas, in lozenges; crimson, orange, green, yellow and white in dark blue framework. Nearly 1/1.

Fig. 63. Portion of an embroidered MS.-cover, silk cross-stitch on brownish cotton canvas. Colours: blue, orange, green, yellow, cream and black. x 4/5.

The originals of Figs. 60-3 are all most likely sixteenth century. Collection of the author.

Plate 14

Fig. 64. Book-braid (*kora*), for tying up MSS. Cotton braid, blue and white, bordered with brownish red. The text reads as follows:

Maiṇ samujhyo niradhāra yah jaga kāvokāva-se
Ekai-rūpa apāra pratibimbata kakhiyata jagata

Sambata rasa-rasa-muni-mahi usiyārapura subha kheta
Kora karī Bhagatū Jatī Pūjya Nārāyaṇa heta

I clearly understood, after examination of this world,
God has but one transcendent form, the world is manifest as (His) reflection.

In saṃvat 1766, in the holy land of Usiyārpur
Bhagat Yati made this *kora* in honour of the Reverend Nārāyaṇa.

The first two lines are in the metre 6, 4, 1 : 6, 4, 3; the next two lines 6, 4, 3: 6, 4, 1. In the third line, the metre (6, 4, 3 : 6, 4, 1) requires omission of the syllable 'ār' in Usiyārapura.

Saṃvat 1766 = AD 1709. Width of the braid, 2.1. cm. Collection of the author.

Plate 15

Fig. 65. Book-braid (*kora*), for tying up MSS. Cotton braid, blue and white, bordered with brownish red. The text reads as follows:

Pāpa-pantha pariharahi dharahi subha pantha paga
Para-upagāra nimitta bakhāṇahi mokhi-maga

Sada avaṃcchata-citta ju tāraṇa-taraṇa-jaga
Aise gura-koṅ seva-ta bhāgahi karma ṭhaga 1766

(A guru) who forsakes the path of sin, and sets his foot on the holy path,
who tells the way of salvation for other's good,

Whose mind is ever (*avaṃcchata* ?), who is a saviour from the world,
Such a guru serving, the thief of merit runs away.

These lines are in the metre 6, 4, 2 : (3, 2), 2. 1766 = AD 1709

[I am greatly indebted to the kindness of Dr. Sir G.A. Grierson, who sent me the reading and translation of the texts reproduced in Figs. 64 and 65.]

Fig. 66. Book-braid (*kora*), for tying up MSS. Cotton braid, blue and white, bordered with brownish red. No text. Probably eighteenth century.

The three braids (Figs. 64-6) are in the collection of the author.

PLATE 1

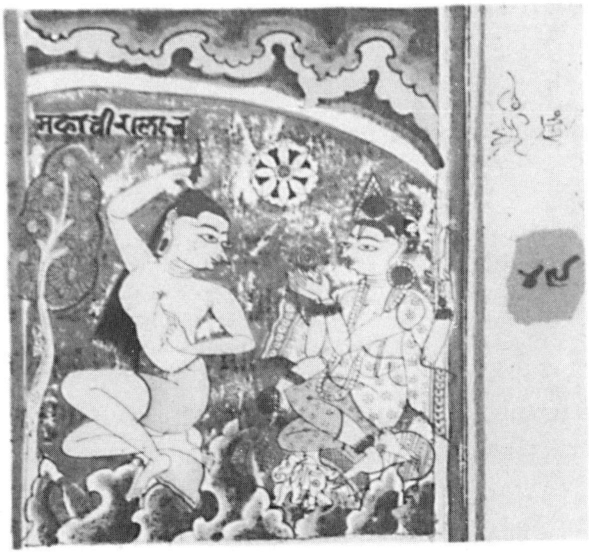

Fig. 1

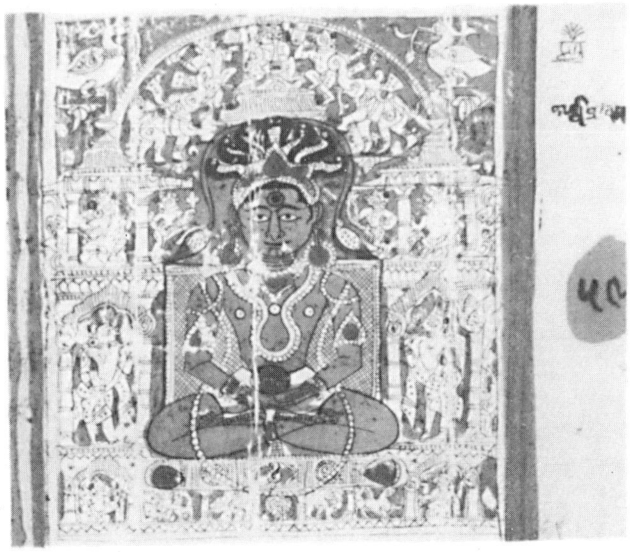

Fig. 2

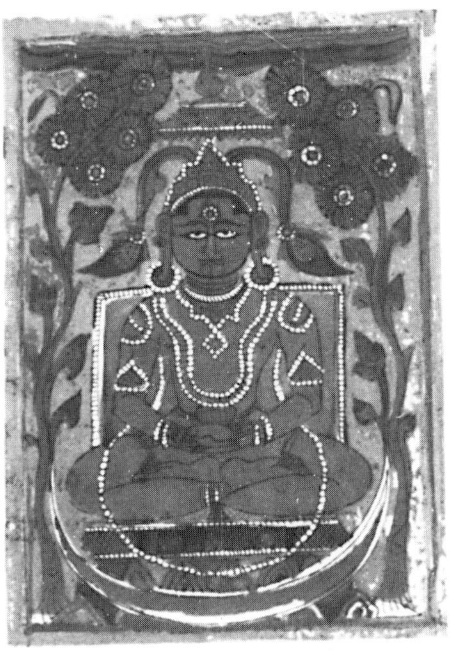

Fig. 3

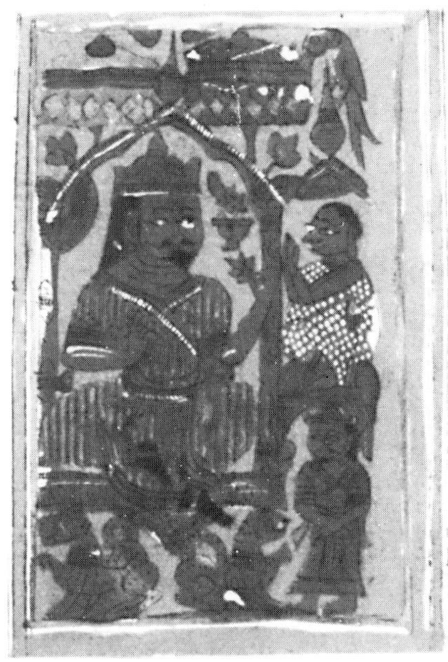

Fig. 4

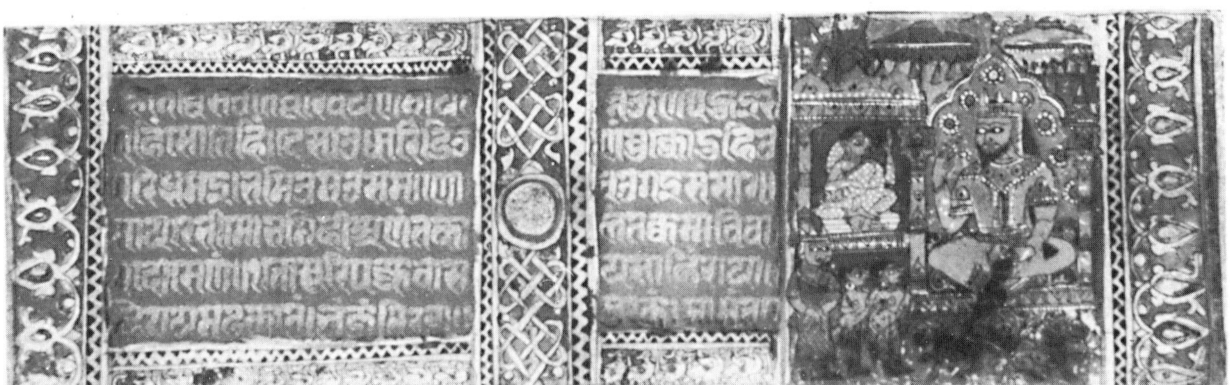

Fig. 5

PLATE 2

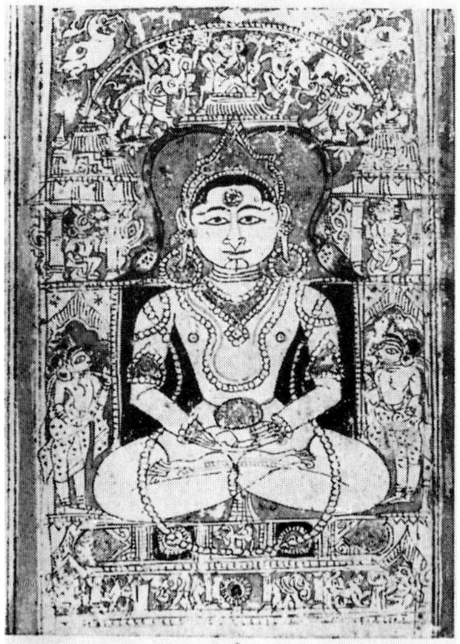

Fig. 6

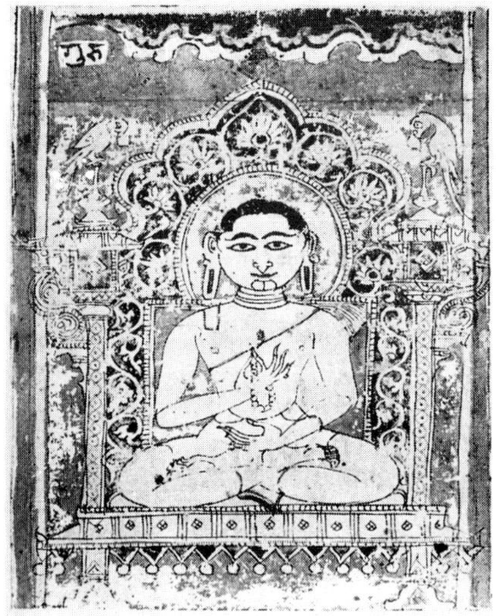

Fig. 7

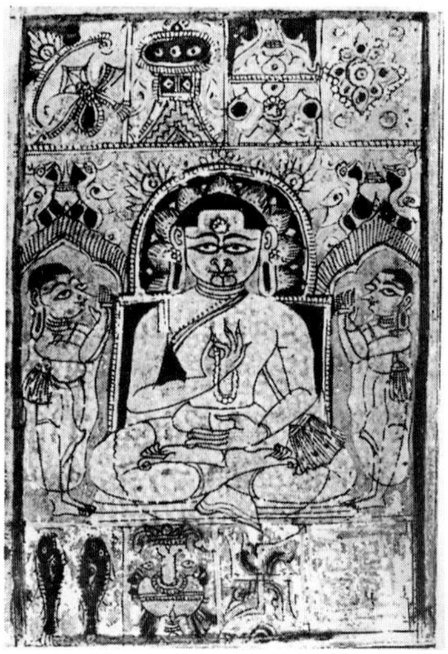

Fig. 8

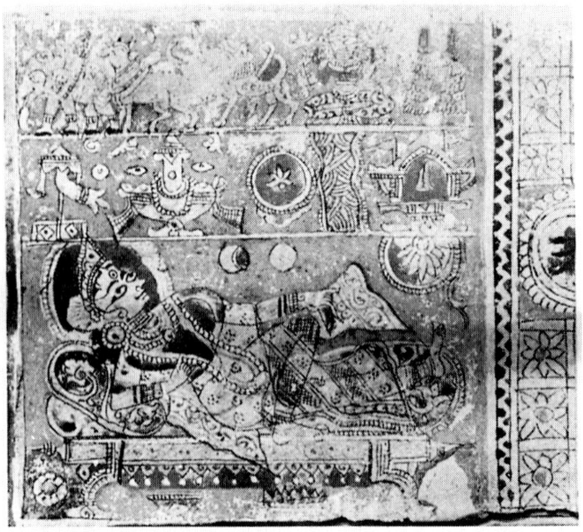

Fig. 9

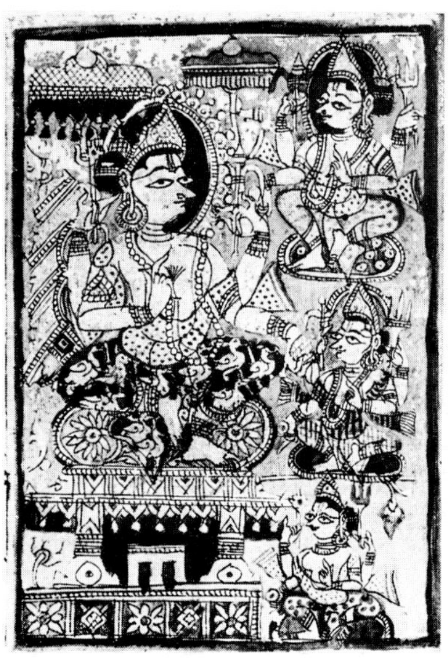

Fig.10

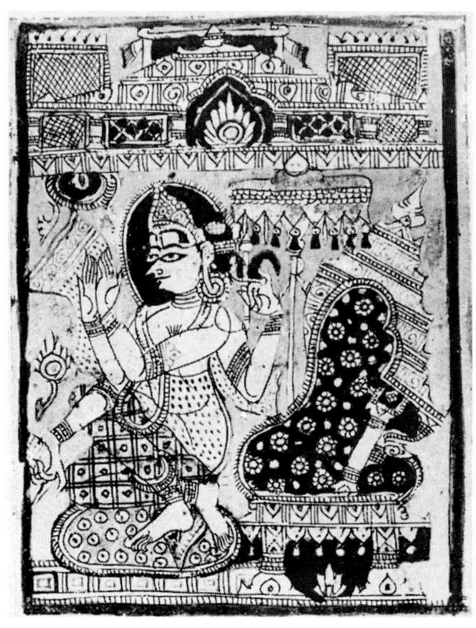

Fig.11

PLATE 3

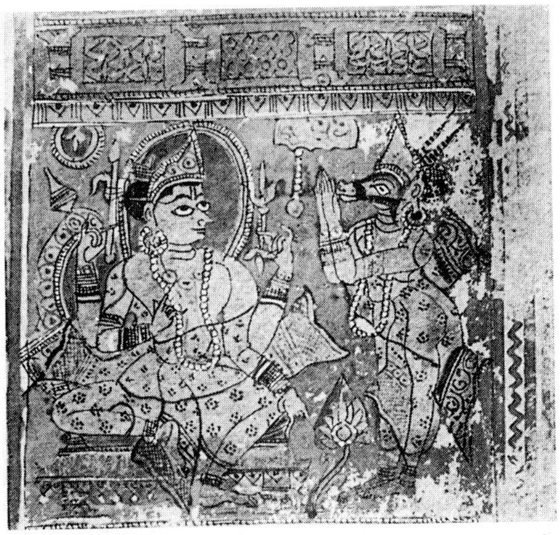

Fig. 12

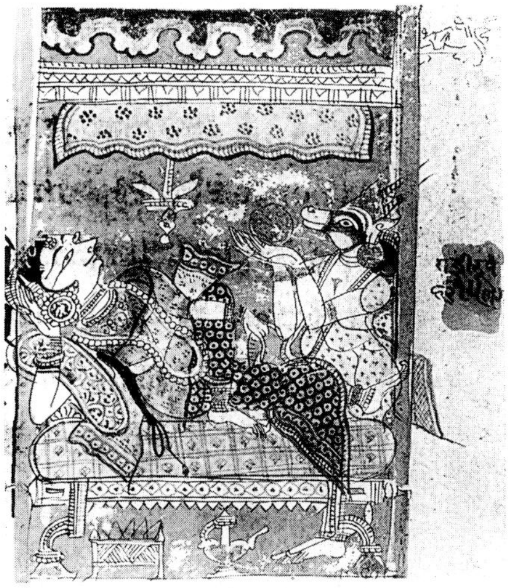

Fig. 13

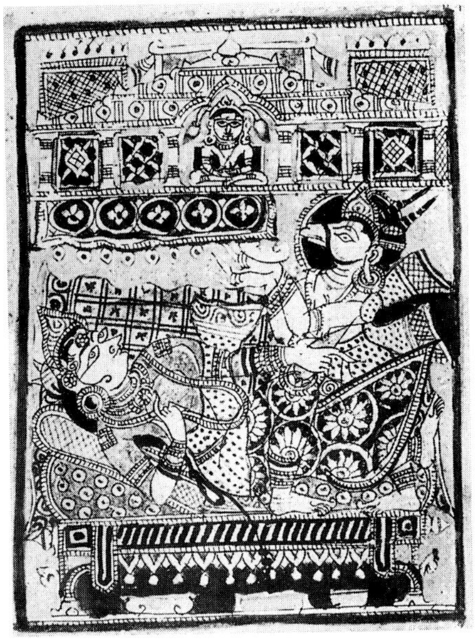

Fig. 14

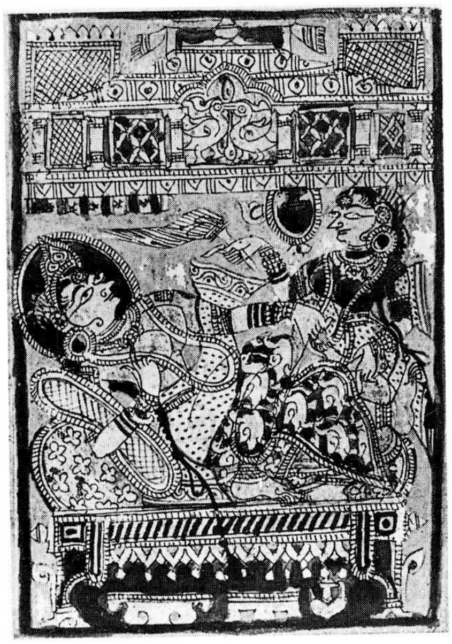

Fig. 15

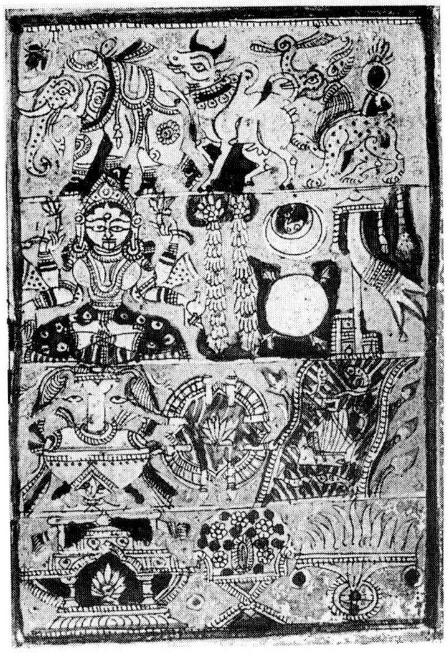

Fig. 16

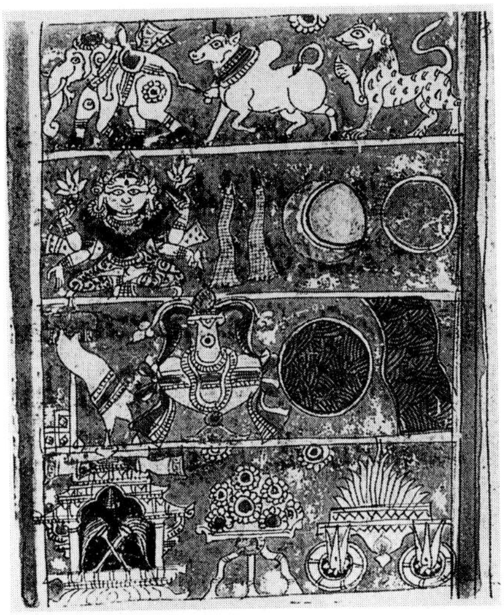

Fig. 17

PLATE 4

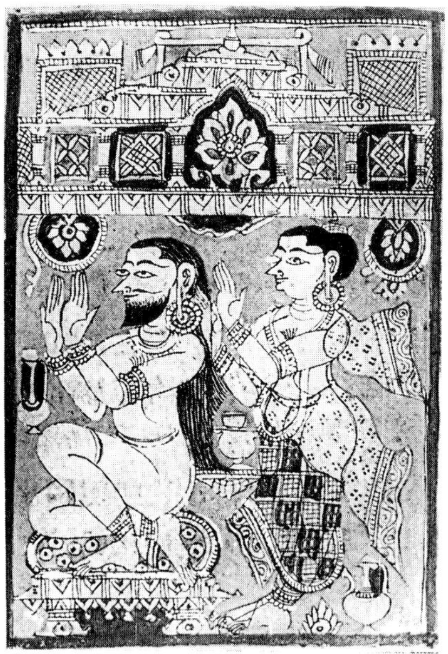

Fig. 18

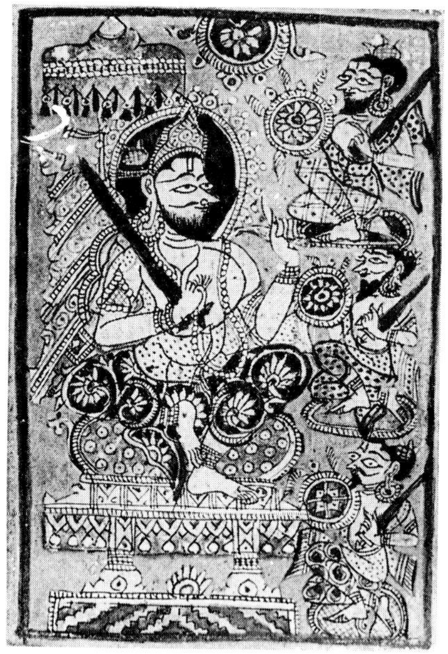

Fig. 19

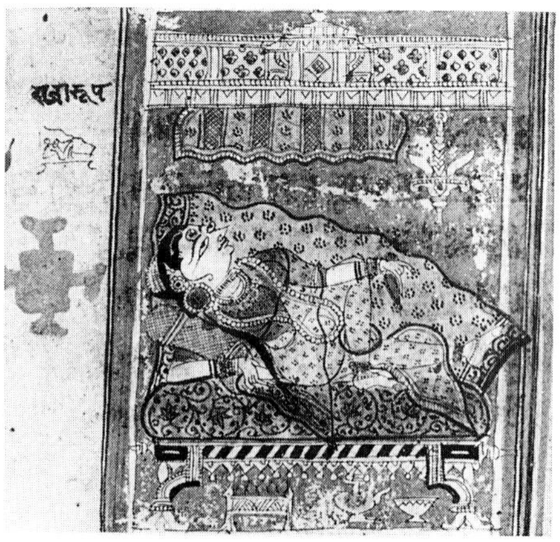

Fig. 20

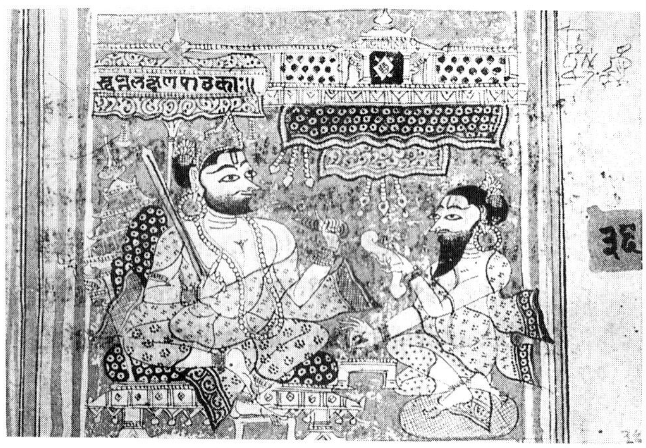

Fig. 21

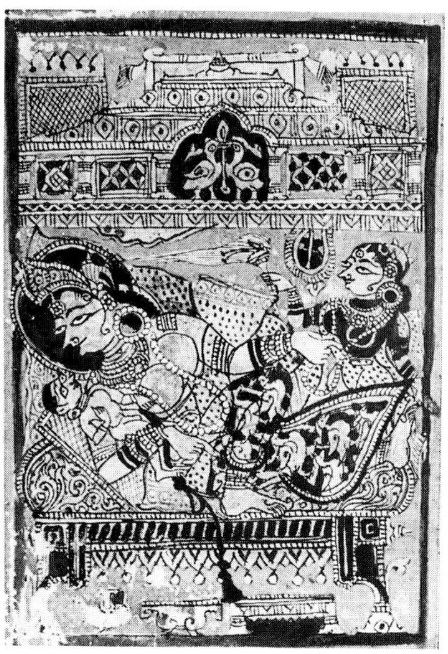

Fig. 22

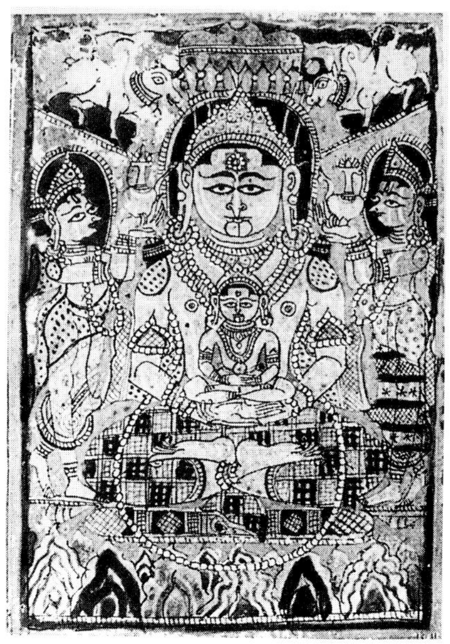

Fig. 23

PLATE 5

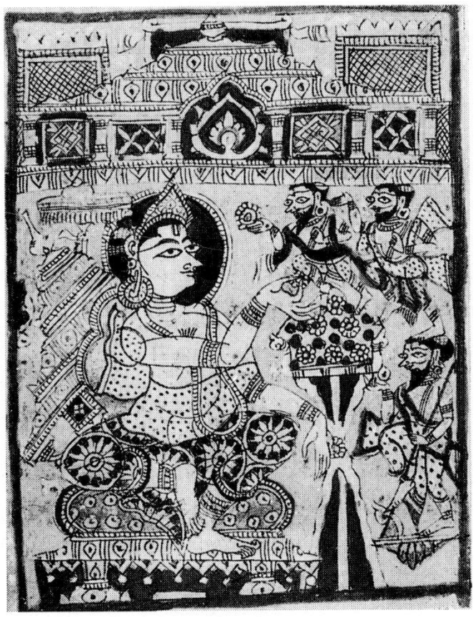

Fig. 24

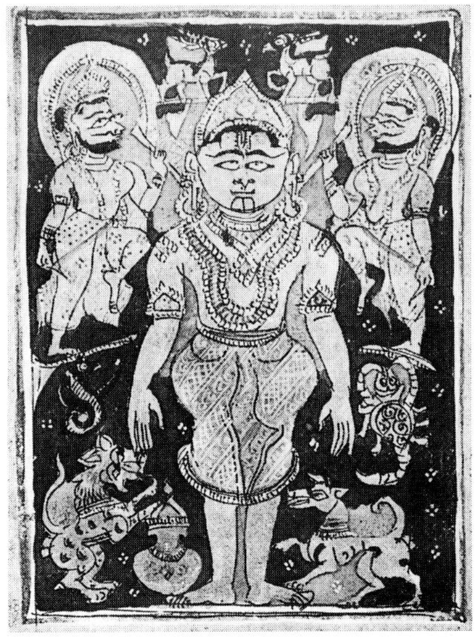

Fig. 25

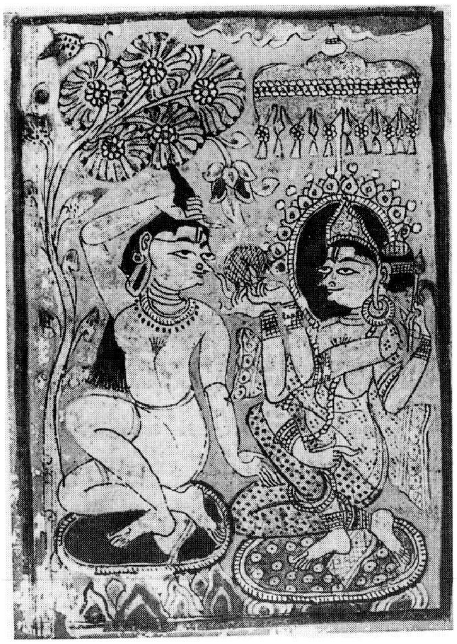

Fig. 26

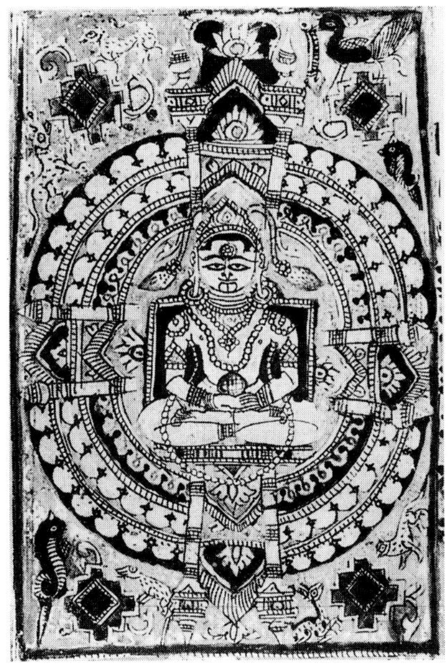

Fig. 27

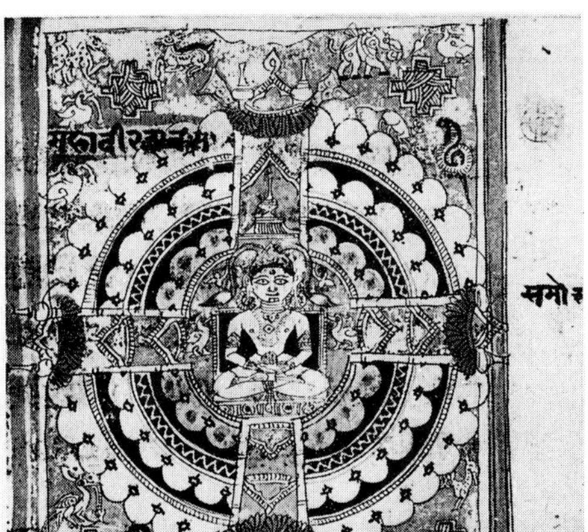

Fig. 28

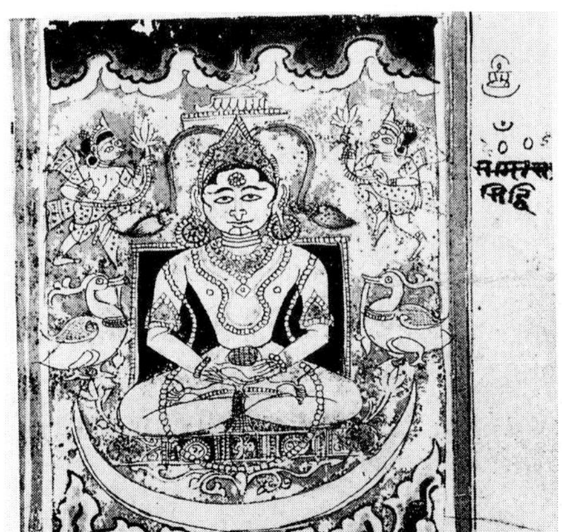

Fig. 29

PLATE 6

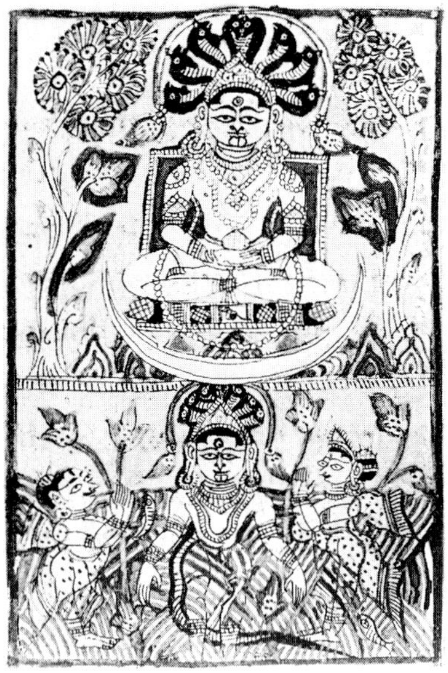

Fig. 30

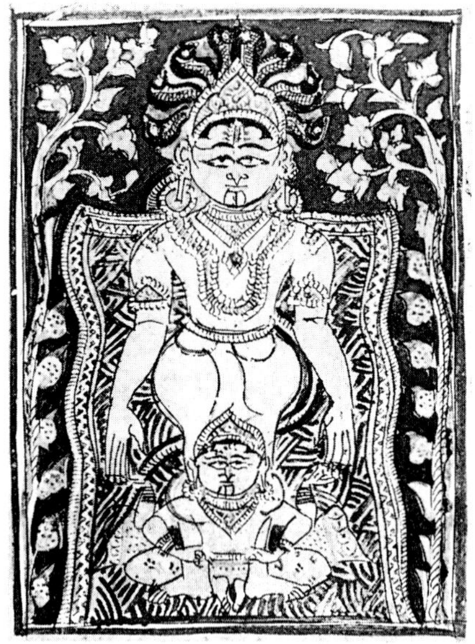

Fig. 31

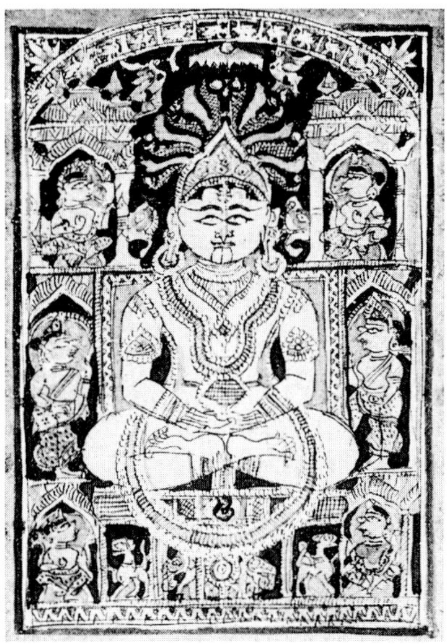

Fig. 32

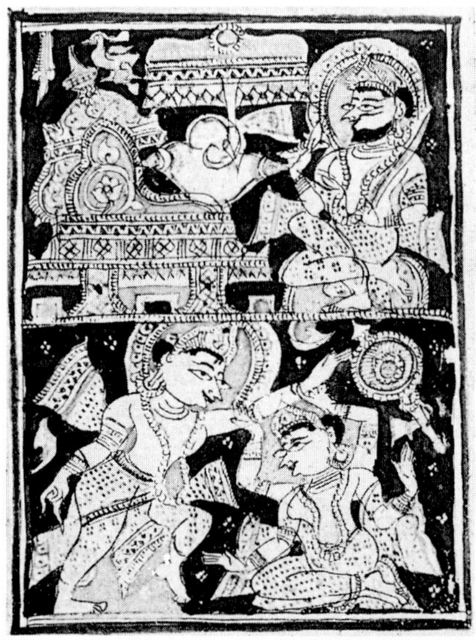

Fig. 33

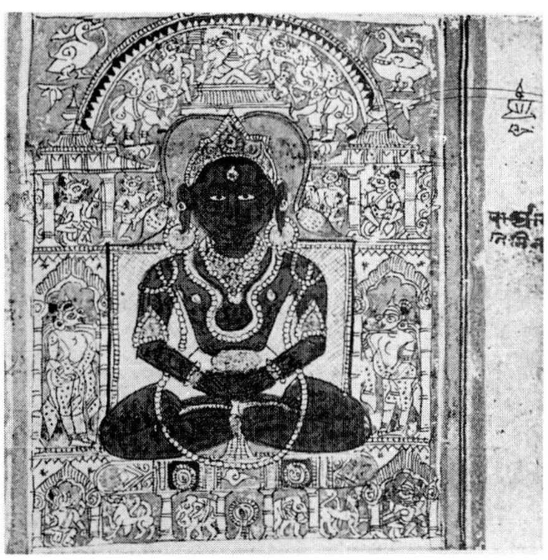

Fig. 34

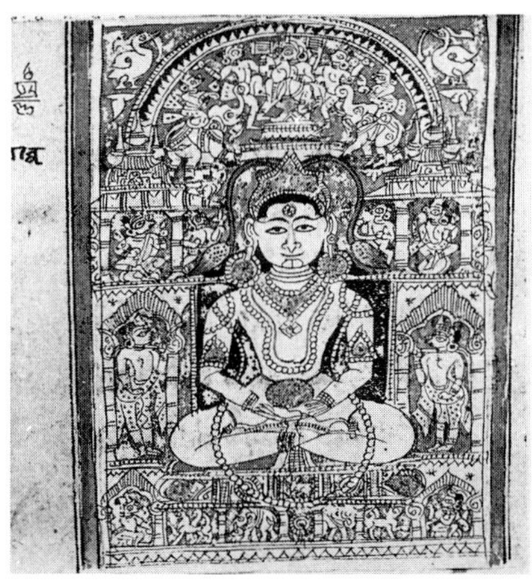

Fig. 35

PLATE 7

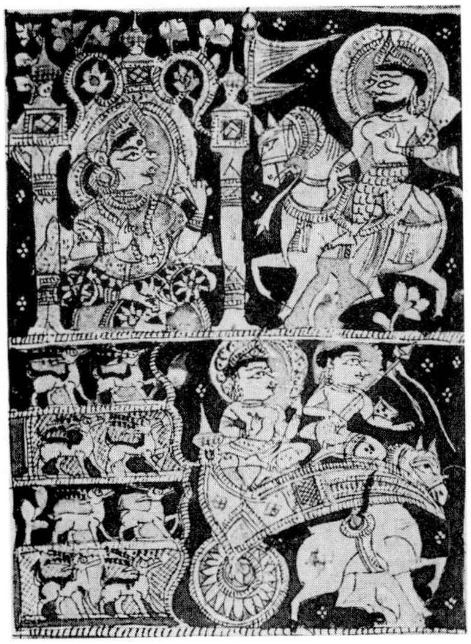

Fig. 36

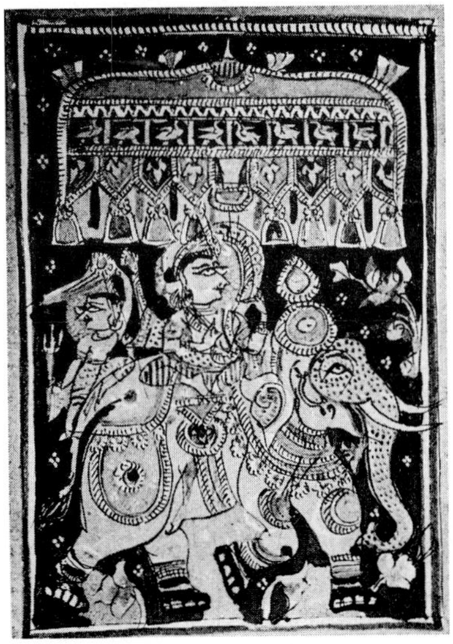

Fig. 37

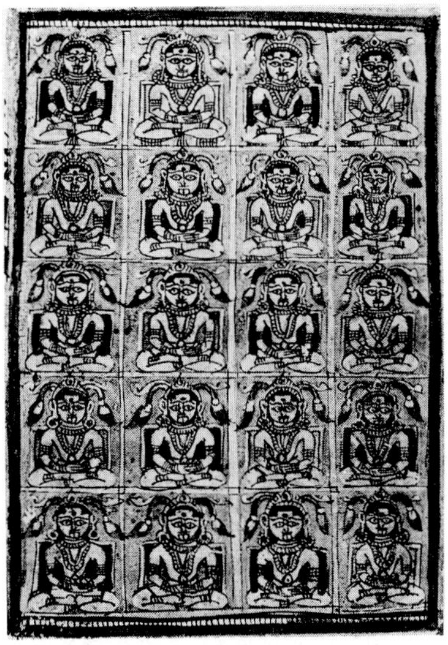

Fig. 38

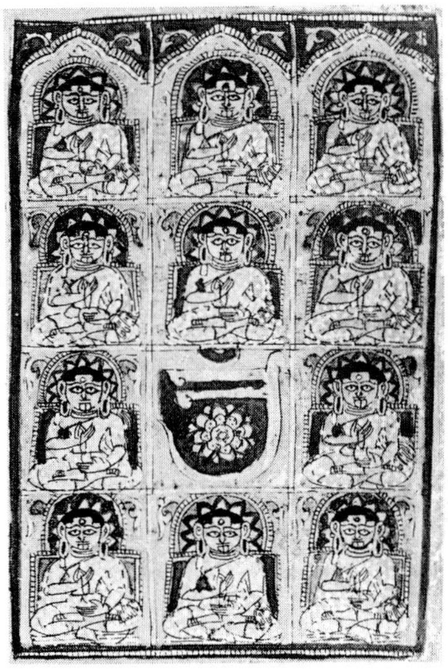

Fig. 39

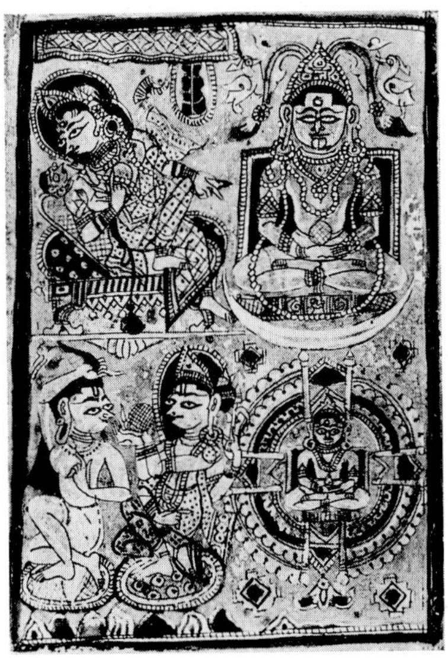

Fig. 40

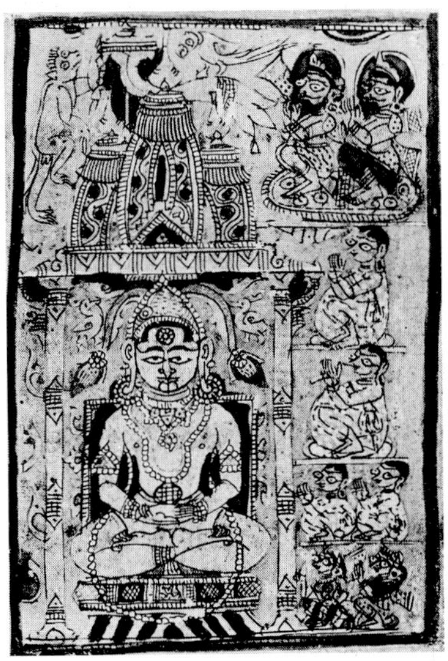

Fig. 41

PLATE 8

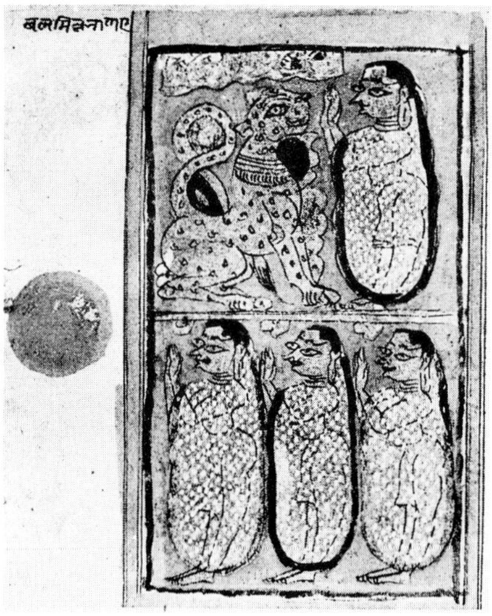

Fig. 42

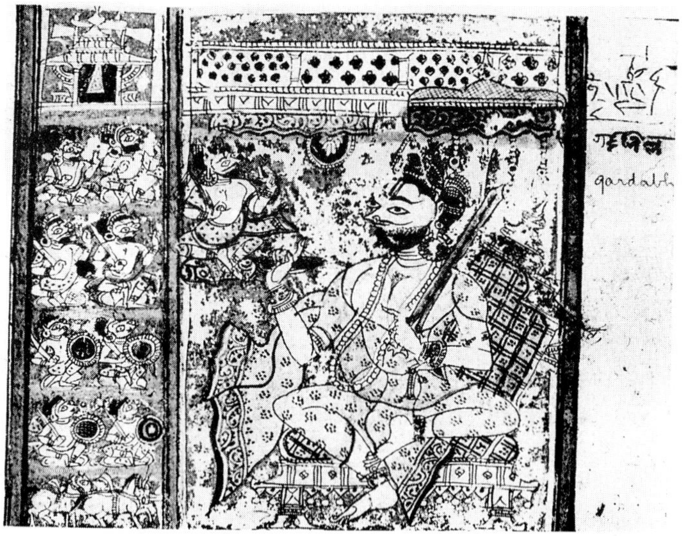

Fig. 43

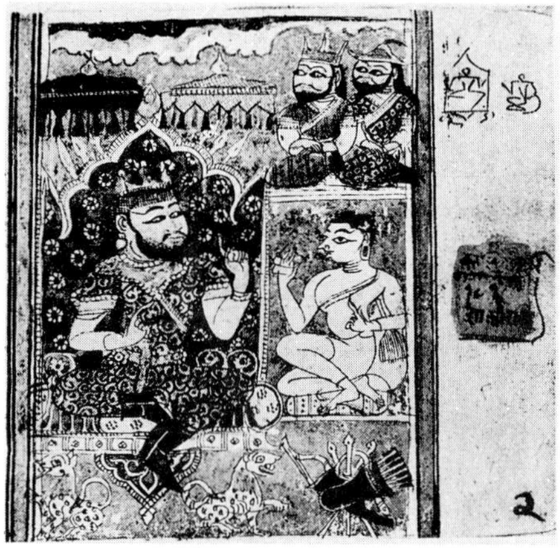

Fig. 44

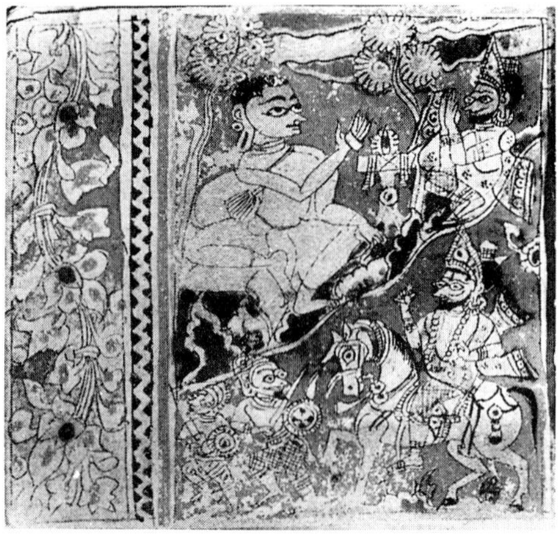

Fig. 45

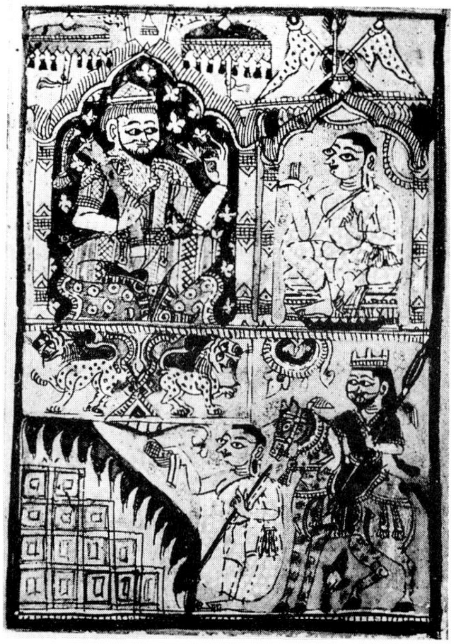

Fig. 46

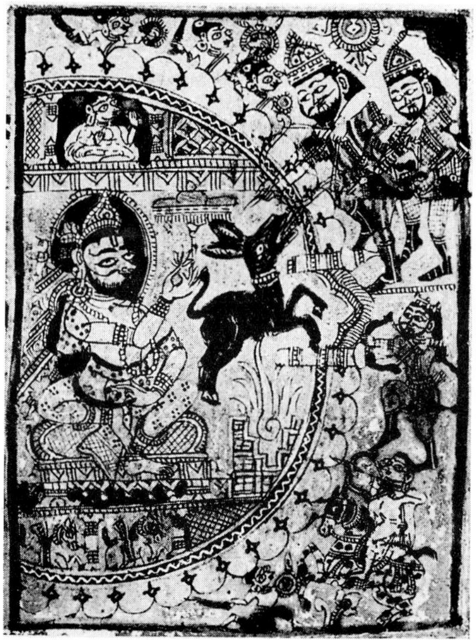

Fig. 47

PLATE 9

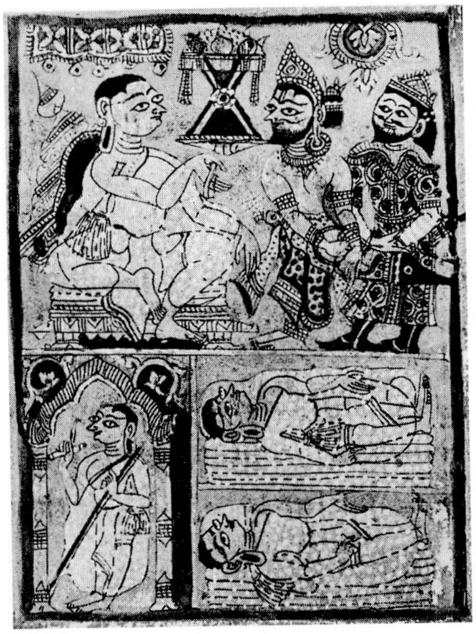

Fig. 48

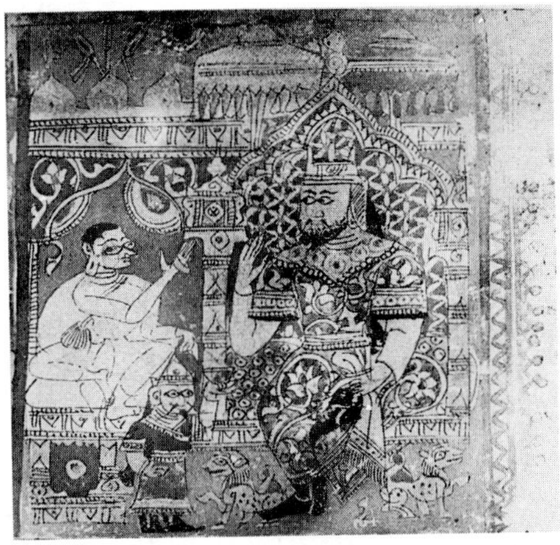

Fig. 49

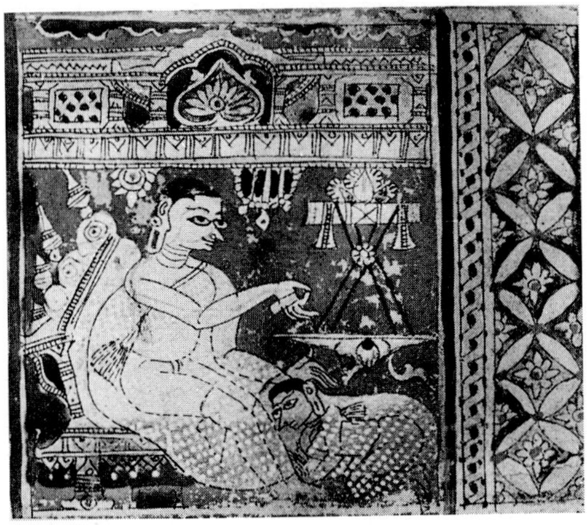

Fig. 50

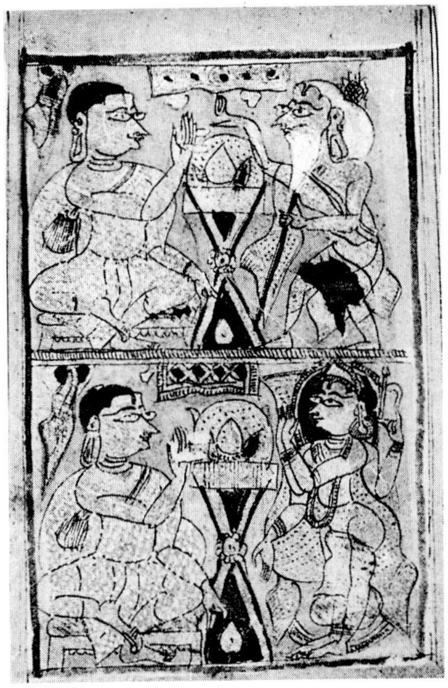

Fig. 51

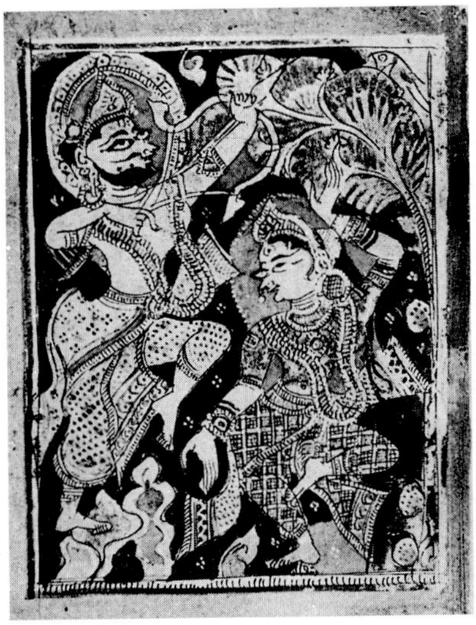

Fig. 52

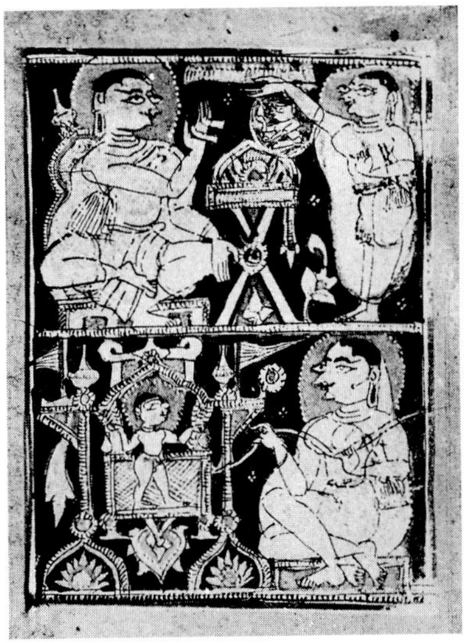

Fig. 53

PLATE 10

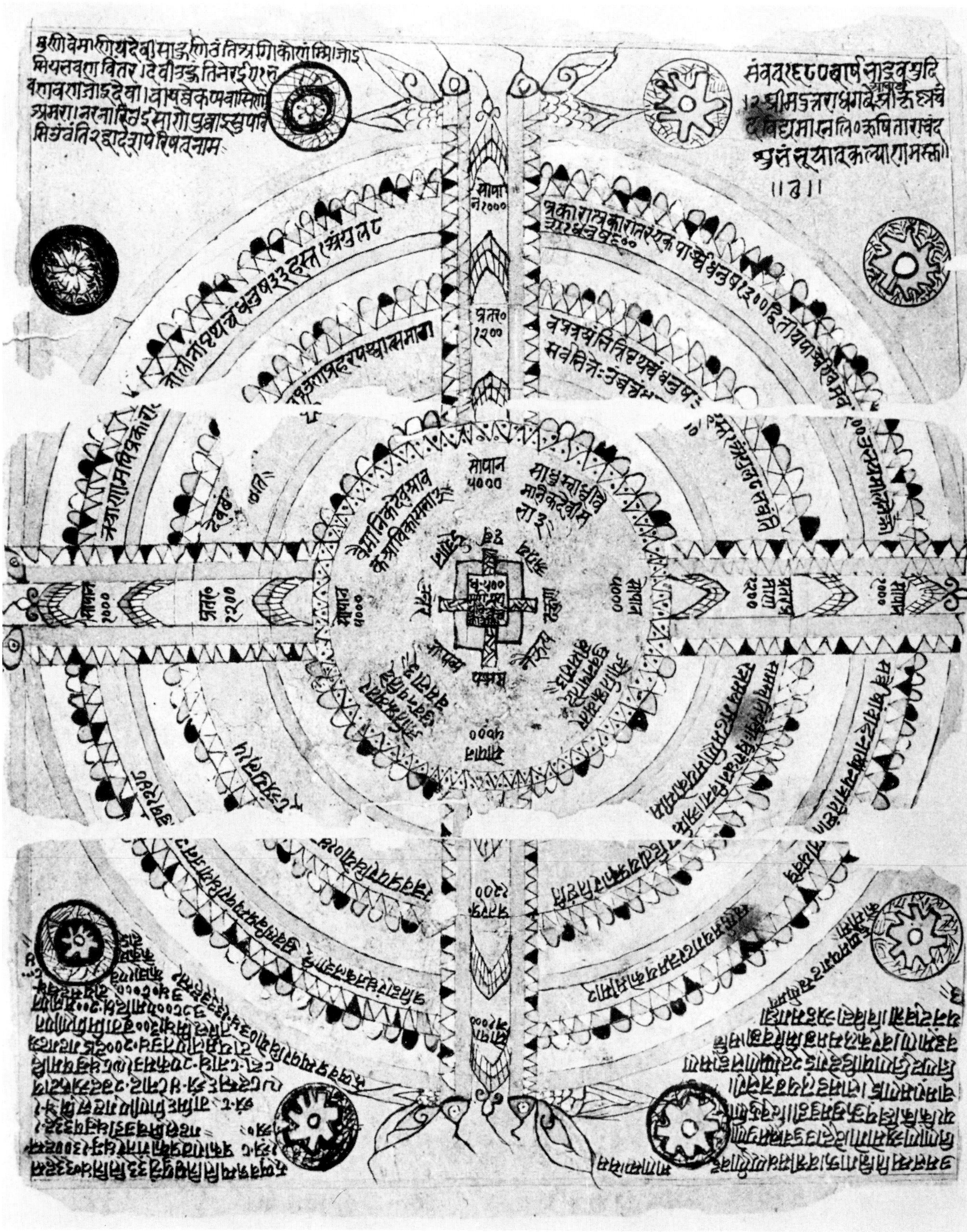

Fig. 54. Samavasaraṇa diagram, dated Saṃvat 1680 (AD 1623).

PLATE 11

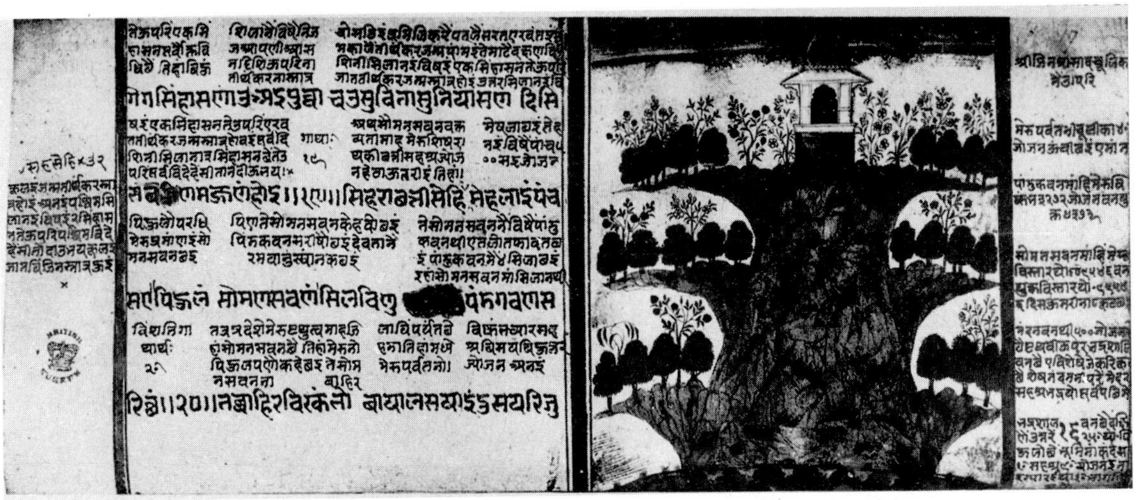

Fig. 55

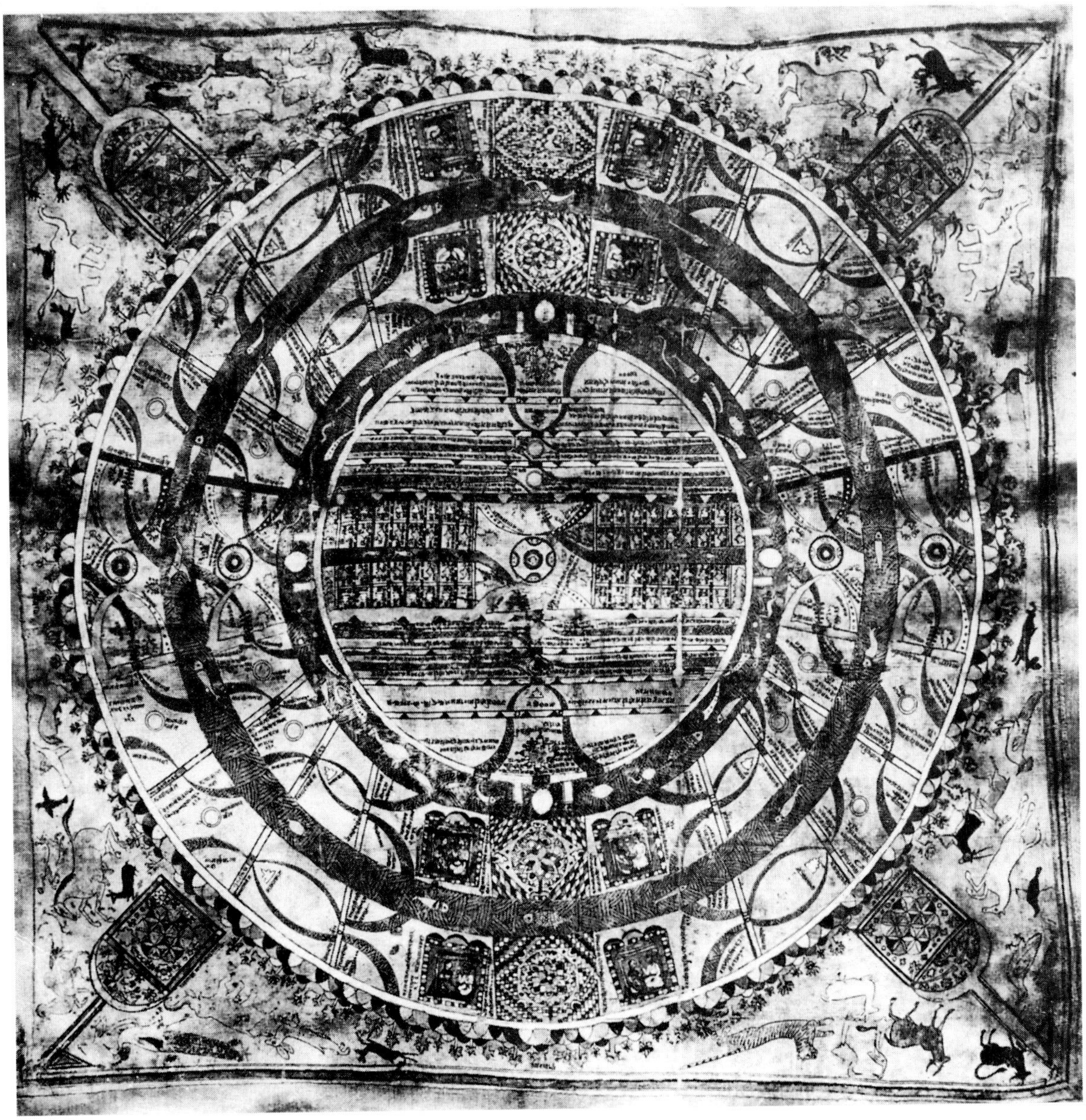

Fig. 56

PLATE 12

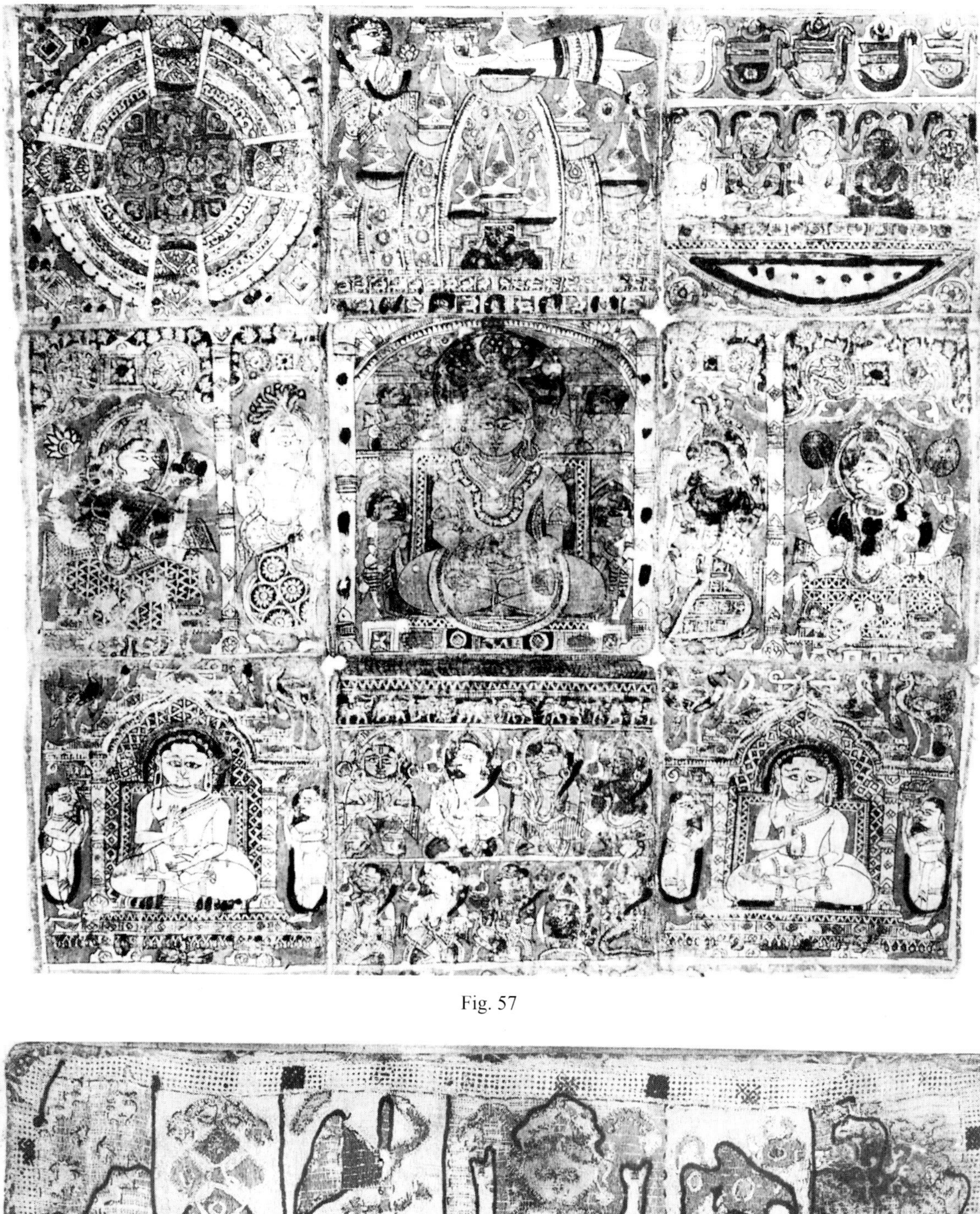

Fig. 57

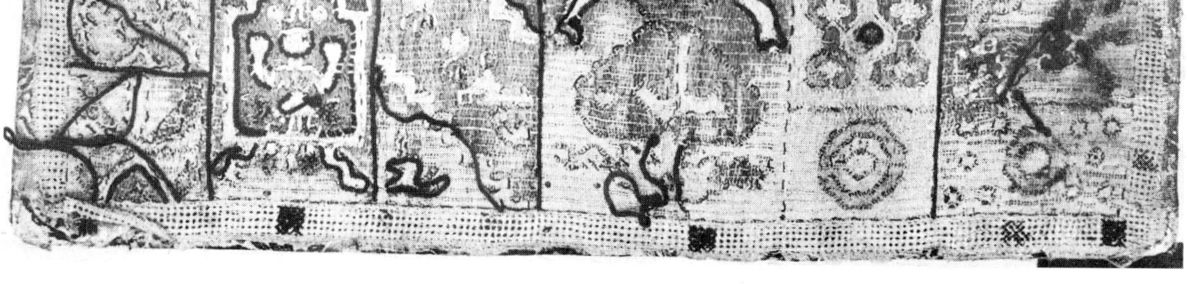

Fig. 58

PLATE 13

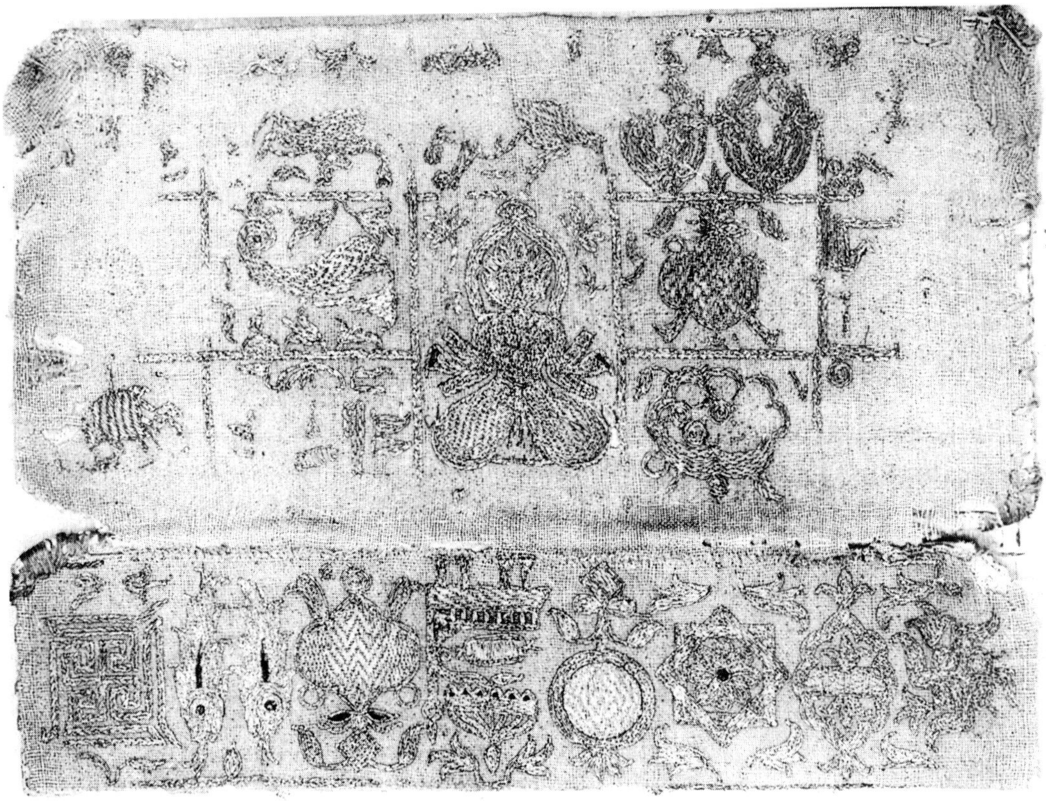

Fig. 59

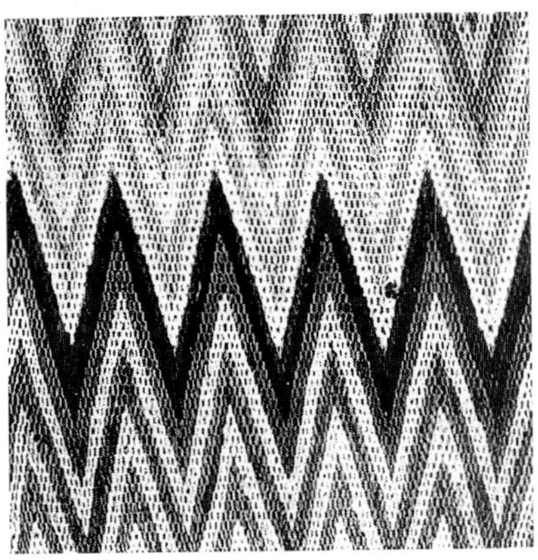

Fig. 60

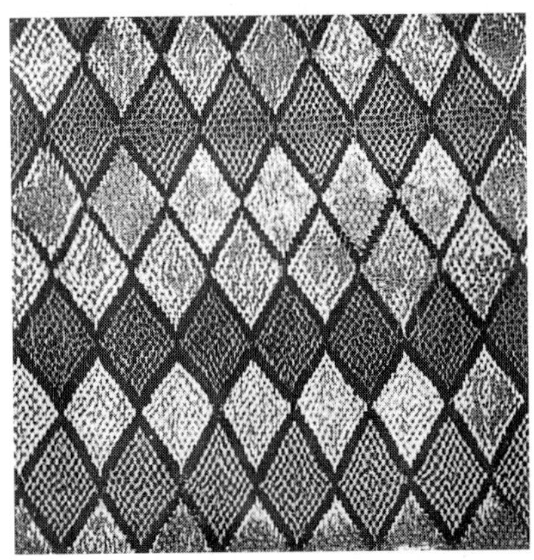

Fig. 62

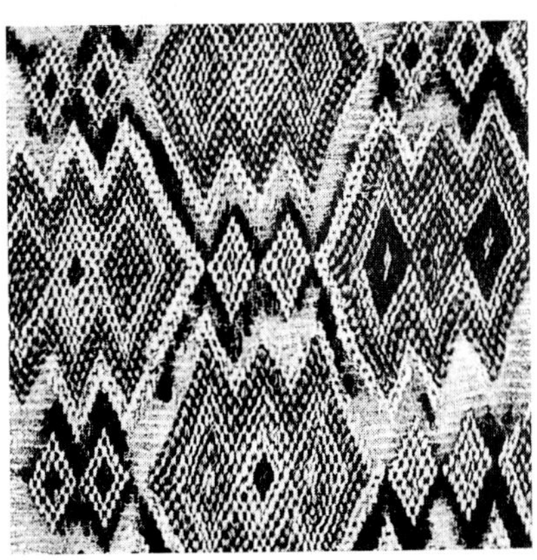

Fig. 61

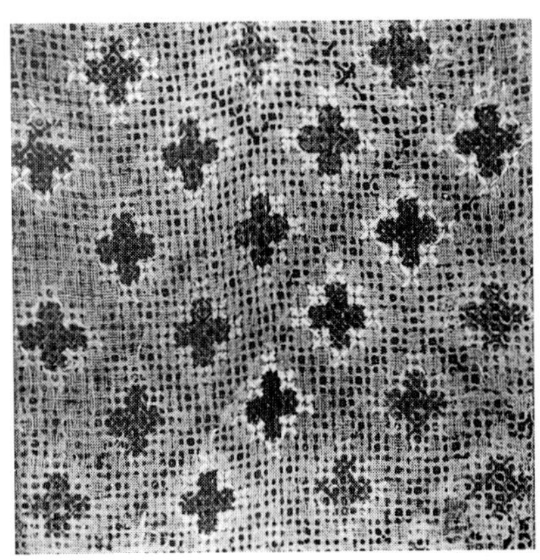

Fig. 63

PLATE 14

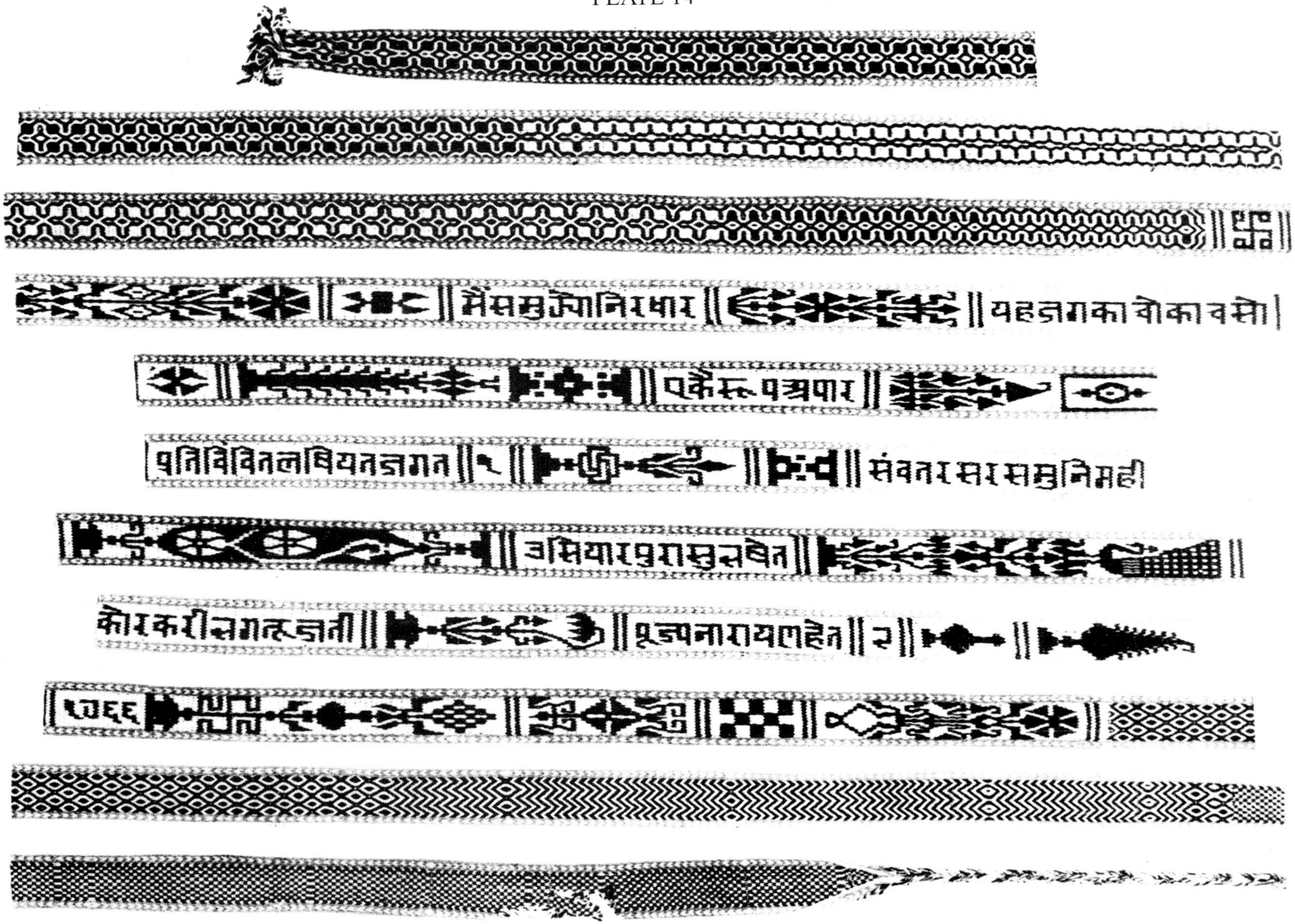

Fig. 64

PLATE 15

Fig. 65

Fig. 66

Illustrated Jaina Manuscripts

The illustrated Jaina manuscripts which the Museum has lately acquired from the writer's collection through the generosity of Dr. Denman W. Ross possess a double interest. In the first place they represent the direct and authentic continuation of the comparatively little known tradition of the Jaina religion, of contemporary origin with Buddhism (sixth century BC), and markedly similar in many details and dogmas, but differing in the fact that it has not, like Buddhism, set its mark on all the culture of the Far East, while on the other hand it alone survives as a distinct cult in the land of its origin. There can be very little doubt, too, that the development of Jain art has closely paralleled that of the art of Buddhism: what was originally a psychology became a cult. The founder, Mahavira, called Jina, 'The Conqueror', and Tirthakara, 'Finder of the Ford', gradually became the object of personal devotion—in effect, a supreme divinity to whom prayers might be addressed and who might be represented by images and worshipped in temples. Tradition has added to the name of the founder twenty-three predecessors. Jaina images, of which the Museum has acquired at the same time a dated example of the thirteenth century, in brass, are only distinguishable from Buddha figures by special characteristics. The paintings now described, together with these figures, go far to prove by internal evidence that there must once have existed an Indian school of Jaina painting comparable with the classic Buddhist art of Ajanta.

Illustrated manuscripts are almost unknown to purely Indian art. Even in Jaina libraries they are very rare. The two books which have been most often decorated in this way are the *Kalpa Sūtra* and the *Kalakacarya Katha*. The first of these relates the lives of the Jinas, and of Mahavira in particular—his miraculous conception, birth (Fig. 2), renunciation of the world at the age of thirty, obtaining *diksa* (Fig. 1), (adopting the rule, garb, and tonsure of a wandering friar), twelve years of ascetic life, attainment of the perfect wisdom of a Kevalin ('one who is single'), first sermon, thirty years' ministry, and final release from this life and from all rebirth.

The story of Kalakacarya is a curious and edifying semi-historical romance. The wicked king Gardabhilla abducted the monk's sister; he betook himself to the court of the Saka king (probably in Persia) (Fig. 3), and, obtaining his help, laid siege to Gardabhilla's capital, Ujjayini, the chief city of Malwa. The greatest difficulty to be overcome was the magic ass: whoever heard her bray fell dead outright. But Kalakacarya's archers stopped her mouth with arrows (Fig. 4), and the city fell. The pious monk re-established his sister in the pure practice of religion; Gardabhilla repented, but wanders still in the ocean of rebirth.

So much for the stories. But the manuscripts are of even greater interest technically, historically, and aesthetically. The majority of Indian manuscripts on paper retain the form of the original strips of palm leaf (or birch bark in the northwest) which were exclusively in use before the introduction of the new material, perhaps in the eleventh century. The language is here Prakrit, the script a mediaeval form of Nagari, differing little from the character still in use. One of the manuscripts bears a date corresponding to AD 1497, and probably two others belong to the early part of the fifteenth century. With the possible exception of a similar manuscript in the British Museum, dated AD 1427, these are the oldest known Indian paintings on paper.

There is here no attempt at an organic relationship of text and illustration, such as always appears in Persian manuscripts, where calligraphy is a first consideration: the miniature is simple a square or oblong picture, more or less in fresco style, that looks as though it had been pasted on the page. This reminds us of the illustrations on certain Nepalese Buddhist palm leaves. The art is purely Indian, with many archaic peculiarities: the Persian costume of certain figures merely accords with the facts of the story. The physical types are indeed remarkable: one could well say of the women's eyes, with the *Rajatarangini* (history of the kings of Kashmir) that their corners 'appeared to play the part of the stem to the ruby lotuses of their ear-ornaments'. In some cases the painting is done direct on the paper, in others upon a gound of gold leaf: in the reproduction of a full page (Fig. 1) it is interesting to note the artist's mnemonic sketch of the subject on the right hand margin. The drawing is exceedingly accomplished: the composition is rigidly canonical, and is repeated with little variation in different manuscripts. The *diksa* scene has real grandeur, and is comparable in passion with a noble passage of the *Kalpa Sūtra*, with which this note may be appropriately concluded: 'Reverence to the Saints and the Blest, the Masters, the Path-makers, highest of men, the lotus-flowers of humanity, givers of safety, light and knowledge, givers and preachers of law, the conquerors and saviours, who have achieved the stainless undying bliss whence there is no return.' We are made to feel that the Going-forth of the Hero-saint is an event of cosmic and not merely temporal significance: the emotion is really expressed in the picture which led the chief of the gods to descend from heaven and kneel with an offering before the Wise One: for, like Blake, the poet-artist thought there were listeners in other worlds than this.

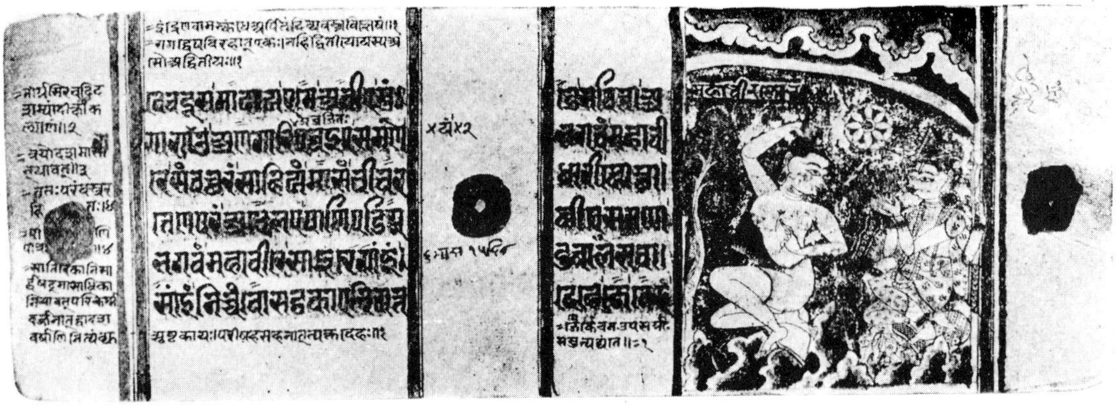

Fig. 1. Dīkṣa or tonsure of Mahavira, attended by the god Sakra. Page of a fifteenth century Jaina manuscript.

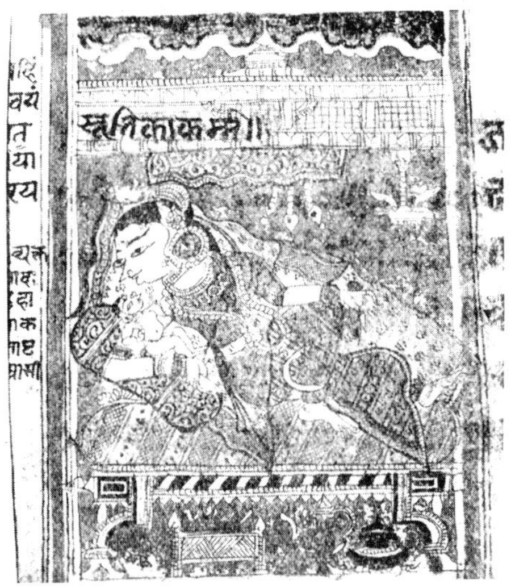

Fig. 2. Nativity of Mahavira: the child with his mother, Trisala, reclining. From the same manuscript as Fig. 1.

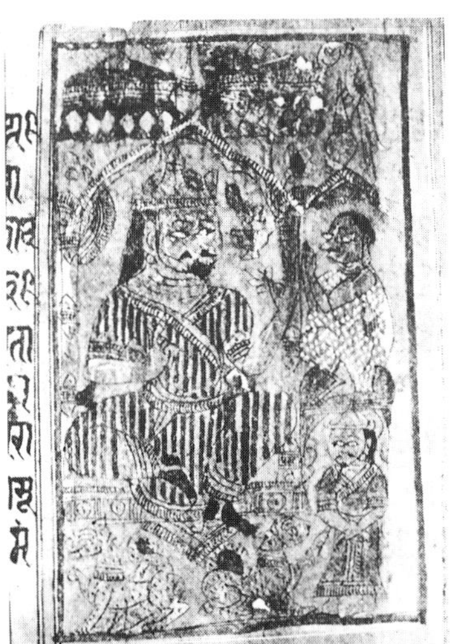

Fig. 3. Ḳalakacarya conversing with the Saka king. From a fifteenth century Jaina manuscript.

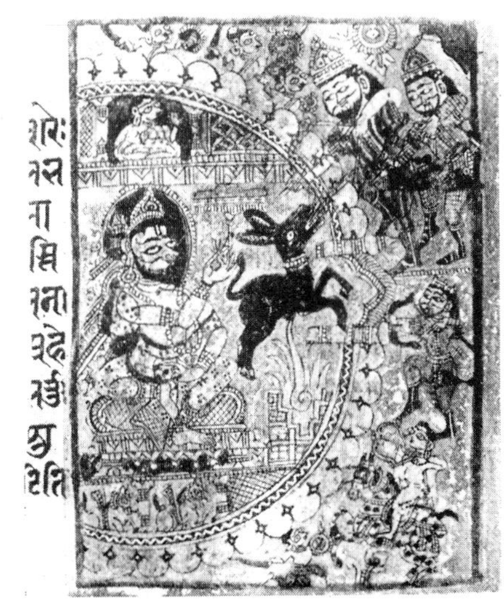

Fig. 4. Siege of Gardabhilla's capital, Ujjayani: Kalakacarya's archers slaying the magic ass. From a Jaina manuscript dated Samvat, 1554 (AD 1497).

Jaina Sculpture

Mahavira, the historical founder of Jainism and contemporary of Buddha, is represented in Jaina art from the Kushan period onwards, as a deified saint to whom prayers may be addressed; though strictly speaking, as a Siddha or liberated soul in the Isatpragbhara, he has no longer any relation with the world. The large sculpture in cream-colored sandstone recently presented to the Museum by Dr. Denman W. Ross consists of the upper half of an image of Mahavira. The head and torso of the Jina are preserved intact; the figure as far as visible is nude. The hair is dressed high in ascetic fashion, with some locks falling on the shoulders. On the breast is the characteristic Jaina sign of the *srivatsa*, a lozenge-shaped mark. Above the head is a triple *chhatra*, surmounted by a crouching figure, and branches of an Aśoka tree, the characteristic enlightenment tree of Mahavira; to right and left in the clouds appear a pair of Vidyadharas, moving toward the centre, with offerings. Behind the torso is represented a throne-back, with rampant lion brackets, the upper horizontal bar ending in *makara* heads. The sculpture is probably from Bundelkhand, North Central India, and may be assigned to the ninth century. It is very like a figure amongst the ruins south of the Adinatha temple, Vaibhargiri, Rajgir, a sacred site of the Śvetāmbara Jains (M.F.A. photo. No. 55511). The height of the part preserved is about 2 feet and 3 inches.

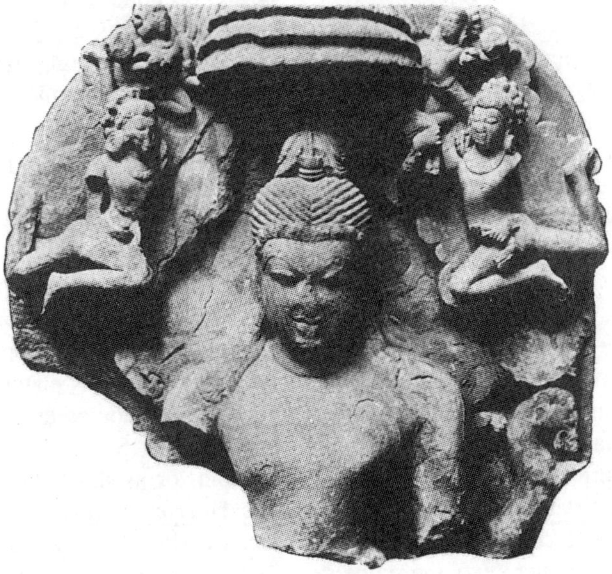

Mahavira. North Central India, 10th century.

An Early Illustrated Jaina Manuscript

Illustrated Jaina or other Gujarati manuscripts antedating the fifteenth century are of extreme rarity. One on palm leaf dated equivalent to AD 1237 has long been known.[1] Professor Norman Brown has recently made a thorough search for other examples in the *bhaṇḍārs* of Western India, and has been able to study and publish three others dated respectively equivalent to AD 1127, 1141, and 1147, the first two of these being on palm leaf, the third on paper.[2] The Museum already possessed a very valuable series of the later manuscripts on paper,[3] and now by gift from Dr. Denman W. Ross has acquired an earlier document of the first importance, and probably the only illustrated Jaina manuscript of so early a date existing outside India. This is a manuscript of the *Sāvaga-paḍikkamaṇa-sutta-cunnī,* a gloss on the *Śrāvaka-pratikramaṇa-sūtra.* This book is written on palm leaves measuring .41 x .055 m. and originally two hundred and eighty-five in number, though fifty-six leaves are missing. Fourtunately, the first and last leaves are preserved, and the value of the manuscript is very greatly enhanced by the exact data recorded in the colophon on the last leaf. From this colophon we learn that the manuscript was written by Kamalacandra, the disciple of Paṇḍit Rāmacandra, at Āghāṭa in the saṃvat year 1317 (i.e. AD 1260) in the reign of a King Teja-siṁha (whose rule at this time is corroborated by other known records). Āghāṭa is the modern Ahar near Udaipur in Mewar, Rajputana. We have thus an exactly dated and localized western Indian illustrated plam leaf manuscript—a document which is of importance in the history of Indian painting and which considerably enriches the already valuable representation of the schools of Indian painting in the Museum collections.

In this manuscript, six illustrations are preserved on the first, second, and last leaves. Some other illustrations may have existed on the lost leaves, but it is quite possible that those preserved are all that the manuscript originally contained. The illustrations are executed on square panel spaces left between the lines of writing and exhibit the characteristically capable and summary draughtsmanship of mediaeval western Indian painting, and the peculiarity of the protruding eye on the side of the face remote from the spectator. Professor Brown has recently suggested that this last peculiarity should be connected with the fact that the eyes of Śvetāmbara Jaina images are actually covered with additional glass eyes extending out in front of the face, so that 'seen three-quarters they protrude beyond the line of the cheek into space'. It should be borne in mind however that there exist also secular and Vaiṣṇava western Indian mediaeval manuscripts exhibiting the same peculiarity, and that it can be recognized in a less exaggerated form in the ceiling frescoes of the Kailāsanātha porch at Elūrā, datable perhaps in the tenth or eleventh century.

The six miniatures of our manuscript represent (1) the Jina Pārśvanātha, (3) a seated Jaina monk instructing a disciple, and (2), (4), (5), and (6) a series of four-armed seated goddess, amongst whom I am at present able to identify only No. 4, who is playing on a *vīṇā* and holds a book and some other unrecognizable attribute, and must be Sarasvatī, goddess of speech and wisdom, or as she should perhaps be styled, in this Jaina environment, Cakreśvarī (cf. Brown, loc. cit., Fig. 2). Another goddess, No. 2, with a child, is perhaps Ambikā. The details of the costumes and textile designs are of interest: the goddesses are dressed in *colī* and *dhotī* as usual, but the former (the bodice) is always shown as open in front, a feature that has not been observed elsewhere. The draughtsmanship, as might be expected, is somewhat superior to that of the illustrations in the later manuscripts but, as in the case of the contemporary Buddhist manuscripts of Bengal and Nepal, the style and

[1] Nahar and Ghose, *Epitome of Jainism,* 1914.

[2] W. Norman Brown, *Early Svetambara Jaina Miniatures*, Indian Art and Letters, N.S. III, 1929, pp. 16ff. The authenticity of the date of the paper manuscript dated 1147 is rather doubtful.

[3] [See] *Catalogue of the Indian Collections, Pt. IV, Jaina Paintings and Manuscripts* [included here].

composition seem to be already stereotyped and a lengthy antecedent development must be assumed.

A more fully illustrated description of the manuscript will appear in Eastern Art, Vol. II, for 1929.

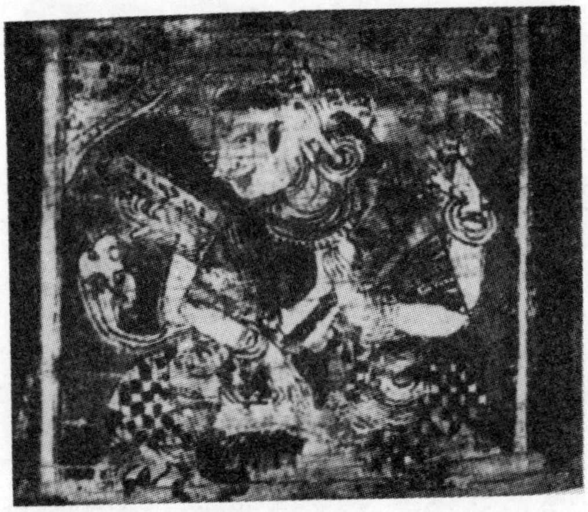

Fig. 1. Jaina Ms. Painting. Sarasvati. Ross Collection.

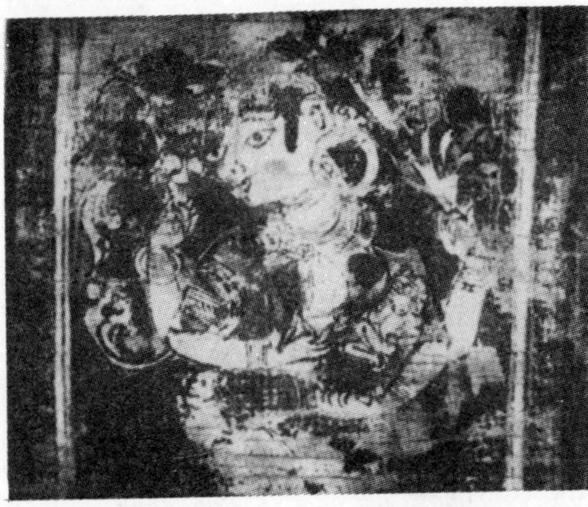

Fig. 2. Jaina Ms. Painting. Ambika. Ross Collection.

An Illustrated Śvetāmbara Jaina Manuscript of AD 1260

The palm leaf manuscript here briefly described and illustrated was recently given by Dr. Denman Ross to the Museum of Fine Arts, Boston and was purchased from Mr. N.M. Heeramaneck of New York. It is an imperfect copy of the *Sāvaga-paḍikkamana-sutta-cuṇṇi* (in Sanskrit *Śrāvaka-pratikramaṇa-sūtra-cūrṇi*), a gloss on the *Śrāvaka-pratikramaṇa-sūtra*. In verse 2, the alternative title *Samaṇovāsaga-paḍikamaṇa-sutta-cuṇṇi* is given. Fortunately, the first and last leaves are preserved. The total number of leaves was 285, of which 56 are now missing; whether or not any of the missing leaves were illustrated cannot be determined. Illustrations are now preserved on leaves 1, 2, and the last leaf, No. 285, reproduced on Plate I. The language is Prakrit, with a Sanskrit colophon on the last leaf; the script is the usual Jaina Nāgarī, with rubricated string holes and numerals; the leaves measure .415 x .052 m. The illustrations, as usual, occupy square intertextual spaces; they are all done on a brick red ground enclosed in a square frame. The following colors are employed: dark blue, green, crimson, and black and white, without gold. As is very often the case in illustrated Jaina sketches, marginal sketches indicate the subject for each picture, and it is to be presumed that the pictures were added by a painter in the empty *ālekhya-sthānas* left by the scribe for this purpose. In style, the pictures are hardly to be distinguished from those of other well-known Jaina manuscripts; there are the same nervous wiry brush outlines, long pointed noses, and projecting eyes,[1] which are elsewhere characteristic of Jaina of Gujarātī painting, however we choose to designate it. But nearly all the known illustrated Jaina manuscripts are of later date and executed on paper, examples on palm leaf and of earlier than fifteenth century date being extremely rare[2] (the earliest known is dated equivalent to AD 1127); the few that are known, of which the present instance is not the least interesting, provide us with almost the only information we have as to the character of Western Indian painting in the twelfth and thirteenth centuries, and as we may fairly assume during some considerable time previous to this date. With the Western Indian Jaina manuscripts, the illustrated Buddhist texts of the Pāla period from Nepal,[3] the frescoes of Poḷonnāruva in Ceylon,[4] and those Pagān in Burma[5] (closely related in style to the Baṅgālī and Naipālī manuscript illustrations), we actually possess material sufficient to indicate the general character of Indian painting in the medieval period, and even this record, fragmentary as it is, represents more than could have been hoped for twenty years ago.[6]

The present manuscript is of considerable interest also from purely historical points of view. The colophon, for a transcript and trans-

[1] The 'projecting eye' is not peculiar to Gujarātī or Jaina painting, but is equally recognizable in the frescoes of Elūrā and those of Pagān in Burma. Cf. Stchoukine, *La peinture indienne*, p. 110, note 5.

[2] See A.K. Coomaraswamy, *Catalogue of the Indian Collections in the Museum of Fine Arts, Boston, Pt. IV, Jaina Painting,* and W. Norman Brown, *Early Śvetāmbara Jaina Miniatures*, in Indian Art and Letters, N.S. III, 1929, and the literature there cited. The other illustrated palm-leaf Jaina MSS. are dated equivalent to AD 1141, and 1237.

[3] See A. Ghose, 'Miniatures of a newly discovered Buddhist palm-leaf manuscript from Bengal', in *Rūpam*, 38-9, 1929, and literature there cited. The Nepalese temple banners found at Tun Huang should also be mentioned. See M.A. Stein, *Serindia,* pp. 1428, 1429, and Pl. LXXXVII.

[4] Arch. Surv. Ceylon, Ann. Rep., 1905, also 1896, pp. 10 and 1897, p. 14.

[5] Duroiselle, *The Ari of Burma and Tāntric Buddhism*, Arch. Surv. India, Ann. Rep., 1915-16; Th. H. Thoman, *Pagan, ein Jahrtausend buddhistischer Tempelkunst*, Heilbronn, .1925.

[6] For the general problem see also H. Goetz, *Die Malschulen des Mittelalters und die Anfange der Moghul-Maleriei in Indien*, N. Ostasiatische Zeitschrift F. 3, 1927.

lation of which I am indebted to the kindness and scholarship of Dr. L.D. Barnet, may be quoted in full:

> *Saṃvat 1317 varse māha sudi 14 ādityadine srīmad-āghāṭadurgge mahārājādhirāja-parameśvara-paramabhaṭṭāraka-umāpativara-labdha-prauḍha-pratāpa-samalaṃkṛta-śrī-tejasiṁha-devakalyāṇa-vijaya-rājye tatpāda-padmopajīvini mahāmātya-śrī-samuddhare mudrā-vyāpāran paripaṃthayati śrīmad-āghāṭa-vāstavya-paṁ(ḍita) rāmacaṃdra-siṣyeṇa kamalacaṃdreṇa pustikā vyaleṣi.* The translation is: 'In the year 1317, on the 14th of the bright fortnight of Māhga, a Sunday, in the fortunate castle of Āghāṭa, during the auspicious victorious reign of His Majesty the fortunate Tejasiṁha, who is adorned by [the titles of] Emperor, Supreme Lord, Supreme Master, receiving boons from Umā's Lord [Śiva], mighty in glory, while the High Minister the fortunate Samuddhara who lives upon His lotus feet was controlling the business of the Seal, the book was written by Kamalacandra disciple of Pandit Rāmacandra, a resident in the fortunate Āghāṭa.'

The king Tejasiṁha referred to is the Guhila king of that time, who was ruling in Mewāṛ at this time. Another record of the same king found at Chitor is dated in saṃvat 1324, or AD 1267.[7] Āghāṭa is now Ahar, near Udaipur.

LIST OF ILLUSTRATIONS

Plate I. ff. 1, 2 and 285 of the manuscript.

Above, f. 1b, on which page the text begins with an invocation of Mahāvīra:

1. Pārśvanātha seated in *siddhāsana,* blue in color, and with the usual serpent hoods above his head; he wears a *dhotī* and jewelry, and has two *caurī*-waving attendants.

2. Goddess, perhaps Ambikā, seated in *vīrāsana*, four-armed, wearing *coḷī* and *dhotī*, and with a child at her breast. The upper left hand holds three fruits or flowers, the upper right a bunch of rose lotuses. Cf. Norman Brown, loc. cit., Fig. 4. Centre, f. 2a.

[7] See *Journ. As. Soc. Bengal.*, Vol. LV, Pt. 1, 1887, p. 17.

3. A Jaina monk seated, apparently on low chair with a back rest, holding a mouthcloth (*mukh-vastrikā, -vastra, -pātrā,* or *-pattikā*) in his left hand, and in his right a broom *(rajoharaṇa),* instructing a disciple seated before him on a cushion and holding a book in both hands. The two monks are very possibly the Rāmacandra and Kamalacandra mentioned in the colophon. Behind these two figures is a table (*hatthapīṭha*) on which is a bundle, probably containing, as Professor Brown informs me, the symbolic representative of an absent guru. Note the sketches of these compositions in both margins.

4. The goddess Sarasvatī,[8] four-armed, seated in *vīrāsana,* wearing a *coḷī* and checkered *dhotī*, the normal hands holding a *vīṇā,* the upper right a book, the upper left a lotus. Note that the *coḷi* is shown open, exposing the breasts not only in Fig. 2, but in all cases.

Below, f. 285b, with the, end of the text, and the colophon:

5. Goddess, possibly Dharaṇendrī, seated in *vīrāsana*, four-armed, normal right-hand on thigh, normal left in the charity gesture (*varada mudrā*), upper right with single-hooded cobra, upper left with three-headed cobra. The outline of the profile of the face is doubled in a curious way, but it is scarcely possible to think that a two-headed figure is intended.

6. Goddess seated in *vīrāsana*, four-armed, normal right hand in the charity gesture (*varada mudrā*), normal left on thigh, upper right with noose (*pāśa*), upper left with elephant goad (*aṇkuśa*).

Plate II. Details of the items 2-5 as numbered above.

P.S. With respect to the open bodice (*coḷi* or *kañcuka* or *kañcukī,* cf. Bāṇa, *Caṇḍīśataka,* 71, *trutyantaḥ pīnabhāge stanavalanabharāt saṁdhayaḥ kañcukasya* 'the seams of her bodice are burst open at the part where it bulges on account of the pressure of her swelling breasts', and ib., 72 *prāntasphuṭatkañcuka* 'the bodice (of Caṇḍī) gapping open at the edges'.

[8] Or possibly Cakreśvarī, of cf. Brown, *Early Śvetāmbara Jaina Miniatures,* in Indian Art and Letters, III, Fig. 2 (a goddess with a book, and accompanied by a *haṁsa:* identified as Cakreśvarī by a Jaina monk of Cambay). Cakreśvarī is one of the most popular of the Jaina Vidyādevīs, but whether she can really be identified with Sarasvatī is doubtful; one would expect Cakreśvarī to carry a *cakra* as attribute.

Additional references to *kañcuka*, *kañcukī*, not given in *Catalogue of the Indian Collections*, *V, Rajput Painting*, Boston, pp. 32, 33, are: *Karpūramanjarī*, I, 13 (women do not wear a *kūrpāsaka* in summer); *kañcukasaṃdhi*, 'fastening of a bodice', stanza attributed to Mayūra, in Quackenbos, *Sanskrit poems of Mayūra*, p. 239; *Padumāwatī* of Malik Muḥammad Jaisī, 38.

CORRIGENDA ILLUSTRATED ŚVETĀMBARA JAINA MANUSCRIPT OF AD 1260[9]

For Plate I read Plate CXXXV; for Plate II read Plate CXXXIV.

[9] *Eastern Art* (Philadelphia), 1931, III, p. 217.

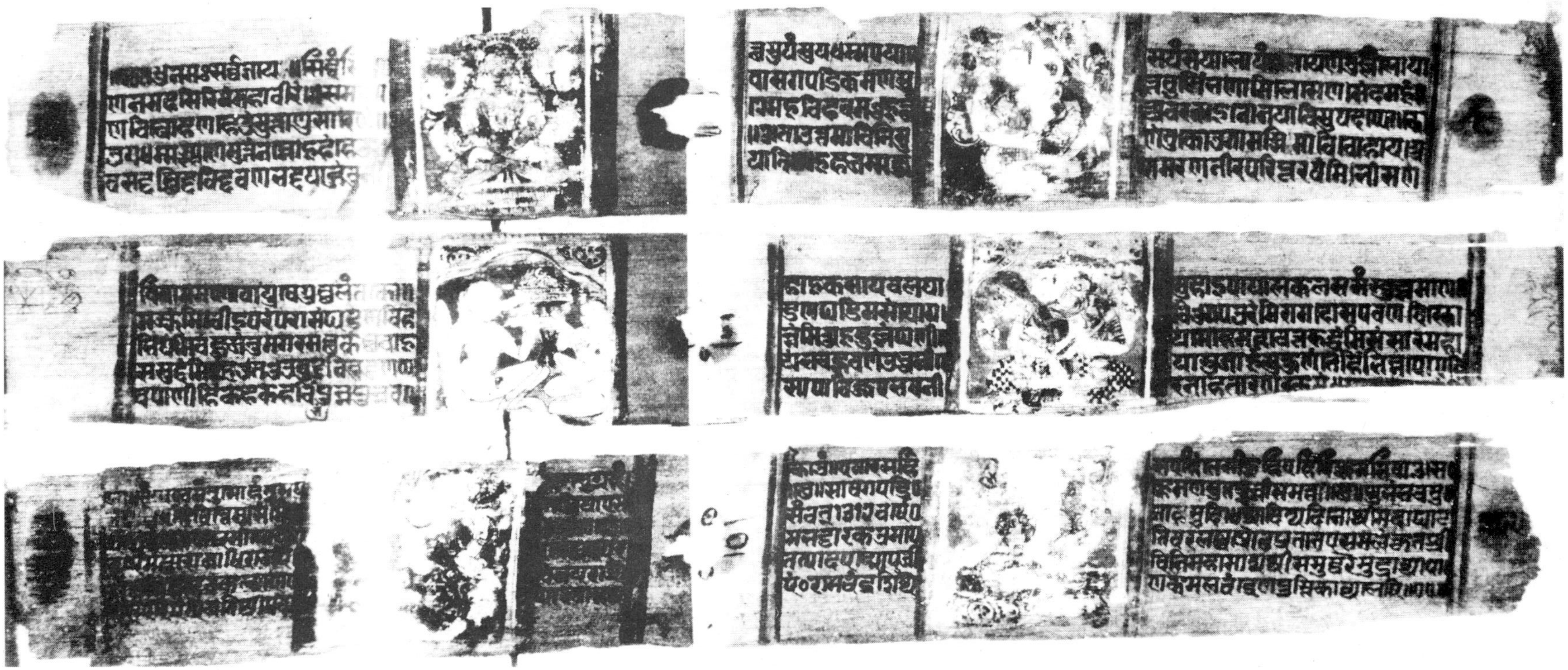

First, second, and last pages of Jāina manuscript, AD 1260.

PLATE CXXXV. Coomaraswamy: An Illustrated Jāina Manuscript.

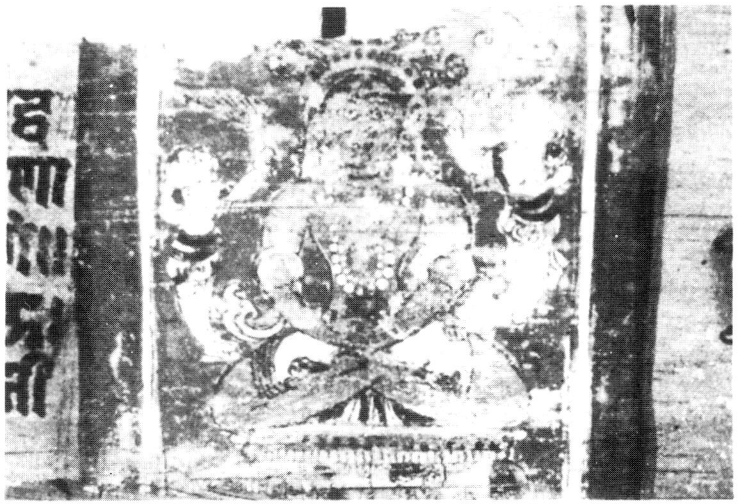

Fig. 1B. Right: Ambikā?

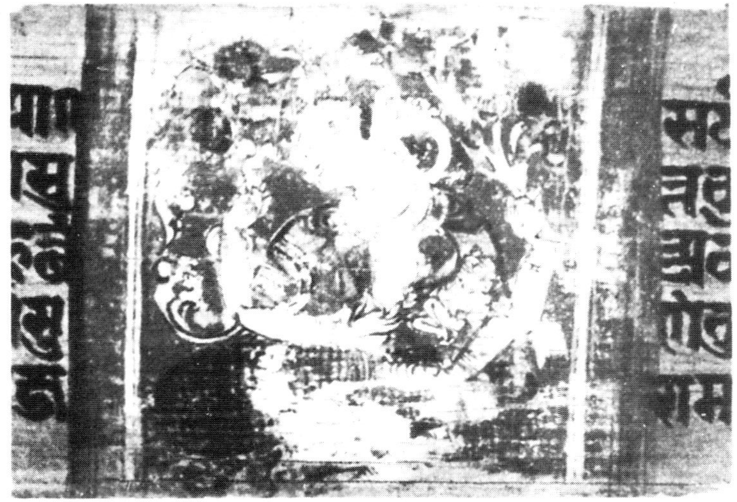

Fig. 1B. Left: Pārsvanātha.

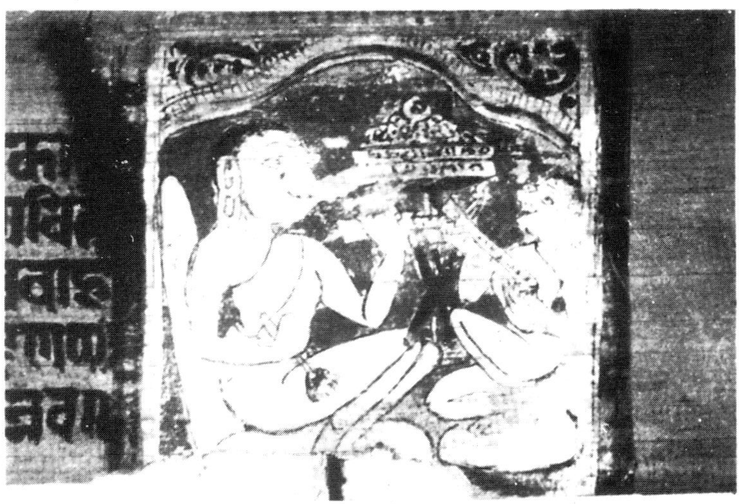

Fig. 2A. Left: Jāina monk and disciple.

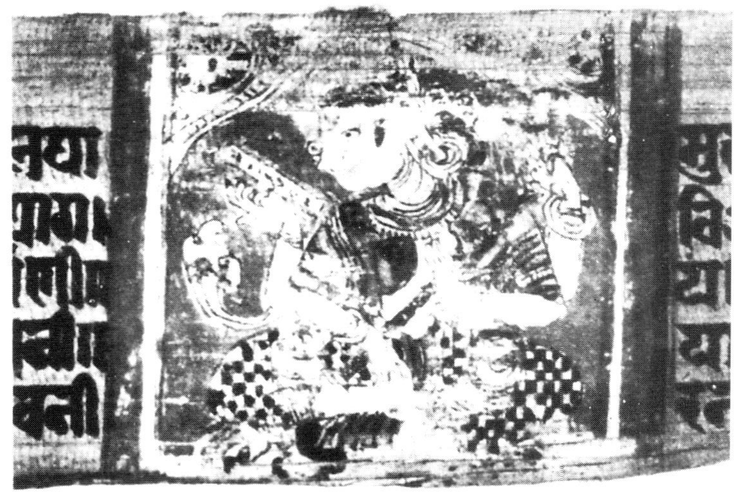

Fig. 2A. Right: Sarasvatī.

Jāina manuscript, AD 1260: four of the miniatures enlarged.

PLATE CXXXIV. Coomaraswamy: An Illustrated Jāina Manuscript.

Two Western Indian Manuscripts

The Museum of Fine Arts has recently acquired by gift from Dr. Denman W. Ross a document of Western Indian[1] painting which Professor Norman Brown, who has published it in full in *Eastern Art*, Vol. II, 1930, justly describes as 'of prime importance in the history of Indian painting'. This acquistion is an illustrated Sanskrit manuscript on paper and the text consists of deveotional Vaishnava poetry; the illustrations are for the most part closely related to the text and represent scenes from the youthful life of Krishna. The manuscript thus adds to the one already known[2] a second example of a Western Indian non-Jaina illustrated text, while the manuscript described below, though in a more Rajput manner, may by regarded as a third.

The present incomplete manuscript consists of thirty-eight leaves, measuring .234 x .102 m., the written area being .19 m. in width. On f. 21-a there is a colophon forming stanza 109 of the text and identifying all or part of it as the *Bāla-gopāla stuti* (Praise of youthful Krishna') of Bilvamaṇgala, distinguished south Indian poet who flourished about AD 1300. Every page is illustrated, two pages on both sides, making forty miniatures in all. Text appears on both sides of the pages but being restricted to such stanzas as correspond to the illustrations, does not fill all the available space; from which it would appear that the book was regarded more as a picture book than as a text, which is the reverse of the usual condition. The manuscript and illustrations may be confidently dated about the middle of the fifteenth century.

In all its main conventions the art is, broadly speaking, typically Indian, and more specifically in its peculiarities similar to that of the Jaina paintings of the same school. It is extremely interesting to see these special mannerisms applied to Vaishnava themes; and this application makes more evident than heretofore the actually close relationship of early Rajput with earlier Western Indian painting. As remarked by Professor Brown, 'The quality of the paintings as works of art is very very high. The drawing has the same careless surety that marks the Śvetāmbara (Jaina) examples, and the same vigorous movement. The composition is almost invariably excellent, the main features of the scene being never crowded by the accessory elements, yet being correctly complemented by them. The color effects are excellent.'

The compositions may be roughly classified as (1) interiors, (2) land-scapes. In both, of course, the vertical projection (perspective a *cheval*) which is characteristic of Indian and other Oriental art, brings the horizon very near to the top of the page, so that in the landscapes only a very narrow strip of sky is seen, and generally what is behind in fact is represented as above on the page. The general background color is a strong red; the bodies, with the exception of Krishna, who is always blue, are yellow, representing the 'golden' complexion of the Indian ideal; this use of yellow is rather rare in the Jaina paper manuscripts, where gold is more usually found, though with less pleasing effect. Clouds are often represented by horizontal color bands, rivers as usual by crossing lines with or without fishes, trees usually as medallion-like masses of foliage. The costumes are purely Indian, in the case of males consisting of *dhotī*, *dupaṭṭa*, and a crown or tiara, but personages of the ascetic type have their long hair bound up and knotted in a Brahmanical fashion not seen in the contemporary Jaina pictures. The female costume consists of the usual rather full *dhotī* and a *colī*, extending rather far down over the stomach. As in the Jaina pictures, numerous varieties of textile design are indicated. The interior representations are of interest architecturally.

Of the four pictures here illustrated, Fig. 1 (f.8) represents the superiority of Vishnu (Krishna)

[1] 'Western Indian' is probably the best term by which to designate the type of painting (twelfth to early seventeenth century) otherwise known as (Śvetāmbara) Jaina (though Vaishnava and secular paintings also occur) and Gujarati (though at least one manuscript is known to be of Mewari origin).

[2] The other being the *Vasanta Vilasa* manuscript dated AD 1451 (Mehta, *Studies in Indian Painting*, and in *Rupam*, 22/3, 1921; O.C. Gangoly, in O.Z., N.F., 2, 1925).

to Brahmā; the latter, as usual, four-headed, is seated enthroned to the left, while Vishnu, four-armed, with the usual attributes, stands to the right of the centre, with two worshipping male figures before him and a female caurī-waver behind him, all in a characteristic landscape environment. Fig. 2 (f. 9), an interior scene, shows on the extreme right the infant Krishna dancing, and in the centre two *gopīs* gazing at his form reflected on the polished surface of a crystal pillar. Fig. 3 (f. 12), another interior scene, a palace, shows two *gopīs* churning butter, the infant Krishna standing by the churn and holding on to the churning stick. Fig. 4 (f. 45) is a typical Brindābana (Brindā-forest) scene showing Krishna as the Divine Herdsman, playing on his flute and followed by the cattle. By a peculiar convention, which survives also in some Rajput paintings, the flute is represented as though held behind the head instead of in front of it; one of the three trees is a plantain (banana).

A second manuscript, likewise, the gift of Dr. Denman W. Ross, is an incomplete text of the *Kumārasambhava* of Kālidāsa and is unique as containing almost the only known and in any case the earliest examples of the illustration of any work by Kālidāsa.[3] The poem is one of the well known works of the most famous of Indian poets and dramatists; it consists of seventeen cantos, and tells, as its title implies, the story of the 'Birth of the War God'. The theme of the poem is as follows: The gods are harassed by the conduct of the demon Tāraka, who has received from Brahmā the boon of immunity to the assault of any existing deity; led by Indra they repair to Brahmā for counsel; he says that only a son born of Umā and Śiva will be able to lead the gods to victory. Now Umā, otherwise called Pārvatī, 'the daughter of the mountain', i.e. of Himālaya, has already set her heart on Śiva, whose wife she had been in her previous incarnation as Satī, daughter of Dakṣa; but Śiva, since the loss of Satī has been immersed in meditation and indifferent to love. The only hope then lies in the God of Love (Kāmadeva), with his arrows. He is despatched to the abode of Śiva, and choosing the moment when Umā approaches with an offering, he lets fly his arrow. But Śiva is roused only to wrath; his third eye opens and blazes, reducing the God of Love to ashes, whence the latter's epithet Anaṅga, or 'Bodiless'. Then Umā resorts to long and arduous penances to win the Great God's attention. When this is at last achieved, Śiva sends the Seven Ṛṣis to ask Himālaya for his daughter; all is now well, the marriage is consummated, Kāmadeva is restored to life, and ultimately Kumāra, or Skanda, the War God, is born and leads the gods to victory over Tāraka.The poem abounds in beautiful descriptions of human feeling and of the sylvan and mountain environment of the events of the legend.

The manuscript consists of twenty-three leaves, consecutive except for the absence of f. 15, written in black Jaina Nāgarī characters, eleven lines to a page, rubricated with ruled margins, each page measuring .25 x .11 m., the written area being .15 m. in width. On f. 1-b the dedication is to Pārśvanātha, proving a Jaina scribe and source; the first four verses of the text following correspond to those of the printed editions, after which some slight variation appears. On f. 5-b the first *sarga* (canto) ends with verse 61, like verse 60 of the printed editions, and the colophon follows: *Iti Kumārasaṃbhave mahākāvye prathamaḥ sargāḥ*. Canto 2 begins as in the printed texts, and ends on f. 9-a with verse 64, corresponding to but not quite verbally identical with verse 64 of the printed editions; the colophon *Iti Kumārasaṃbhave mahākāvye Kālidāsa viracite Kāmonāma dvitīyaḥ sargāḥ*, is a little fuller, naming the author and designating the second canto by the name of Kāma (the God of Love). The third *sarga* begins regularly, ending with verse 46 (f. 18-a), the colophon designating this canto as *Rati pratāpa varṇana*, 'The Tale of Rati's Lamentation'. The fifth canto begins regularly, but the manuscript ends on f. 23-b with the first words of verse 73. The rest of the fifth canto and the whole of the remaining text are missing.

Illustrations are found on ff. 2, 6, 15, 18. On f. 2-a (Fig. 5) the author is represented standing and making a salaam (not the usual *namaskāra* before a four-armed enthroned goddess who holds a lotus and a book in the additional hands, and must be Sarasvatī, though her animal attribute or vehicle looks like a lamb and is

[3] I have seen at Mandi a set of Illustrations to the same text, in the late eighteenth century Kangra style; there are five excellent miniatures of the same period and illustrating the same theme, in the Schneider-Kainer Collection in Berlin (H. Goetz, *Indian Miniatures in German Museums and Private Collections, Eastern Art*, II, 1930, Fig. 13 and p. 165); also one probably from the same series, reproduced in my *Rajput Painting*, Pl. 63.

certainly not a *haṃsa*. Kālidāsa himself is represented as wearing a long *jāma'* reaching the ankles, a sash with long ends, and a turban somewhat of the Jodhpur sort; the goddess wears a *dhotī*, small *coḷī*, and a five-pointed crown (three points being visible in profile). On folio 6-a (Fig. 6) the miniature illustrates the text, II, I.f.: 'Then the dwellers in heaven, harassed by Tāraka, went with Indra at their head to the abode of the self-existent Brahmā, who appeared before them; they propitiated him with pertinent words.' The four-faced four-handed Brahmā, enthroned and holding the Vedas and lotus flowers, is easily recognizable on the left in the upper register; the two deities to the right may be Indra and Varuṇa; the second on the lower register, holding a mace, may be Kubera; the third, 'scratching the ground with his rod,[4] from which all glory has faded (II, 23)', must be Yama; the one uncrowned figure to the left, apparently looking away, but perhaps addressing Brahmā (II, 30), may be Vācaspati (i.e. Brhaspati, the officiating priest of the gods). There is nothing to suggest the presence of Vishnu. Here the costumes are mixed: Brahmā and a deity to the right on the upper register alone wear the strictly orthodox Hindu *dhotī*; the others present wear a *jāma'* extending below the knees, and a long sash, the *jāma'* in one case having the four-pointed skirt which was in fashion at the close of the sixteenth and in the early part of the seventeenth century; all the devas wear the five-pointed Hindu crown.

On 18-b (Fig. 7) two young women, one crowned, are represented in a mountain landscape, with trees and gamboling fawns, and a reservoir in the foreground. These are doubtless Umā (Pārvatī) and one of her companions. Both wear *dhotī* and *colī* Cf. III, 31, and 52-4, 'The fawns, blinded by the pollen of the piyāle blossoms and bewildered by passion, ran wildly against the wind on the forest glade, filled with the murmur of drifting leaves ... Now was seen the daughter of Himālaya, wearing a garment of the hue of the morning sun, swaying like a moving vine, weighted down by its clusters of flowers.' On an unidentified leaf[5] (Fig. 8) is a full page picture representing the marriage of Śiva and Pārvatī: they are enthroned on separate seats beneath a marriage canopy, with a tree (plantain) and a stack of auspicious vessels (*maṅgala kalaśa*) on either side. On the right hand beside Pārvatī are seated female musicians; on the left a standing male, either Himālaya himself or some attendant deity. Śiva's blue color at first suggests Vishnu, but is really that of one of his own darker forms.

All the pictures are unfinished, but they lack only the final outline in black and the details in gold. The usual ground color is a strong red, but a dull blue occurs in the first example, and in the second the background of the upper register is green. Other colors used are an orange red, a pale maroon, and a darker green. The landscape (Fig. 7) shows the usual high horizon and narrow strip of dark sky above the red ground of the middle distance; the two hills in the foreground are very pale maroon. All the faces are shown in profile, though many of the bodies are in three-quarter view. On the whole the stylistic resemblance to the earliest Rājasthānī paintings is much more conspicuous than is the relation to Jaina or Gujarātī painting as typically developed in Western Indian manuscripts such as the one described above; and one is made aware that Mughal painting is already in existence. These facts, together with the character of the costume, especially the association of *dhotī*, long *jāma'*, and *jāma'* with four-pointed skirt, and the representation of the salaam, determine a date about 1600 or quite early in the seventeenth century.

[4] A gesture of perplexity or sorrow; cf. the defeated Mara 'writing on the ground' *(Nidanakatha, Jataka* 1, 78); Amaru, *Sataka,* a verse cited by Keith, *Sanskrit Literature*, p. 185. 'The beloved of thy life standeth without, his head bowed down, drawing figures on the ground'; and in John, 8, 6, 'Jesus stooped down and with his finger wrote on the ground.'

[5] Possibly f. 43; the reverse side was apparently blank, but has preserved the reversed impression of writing from another page.

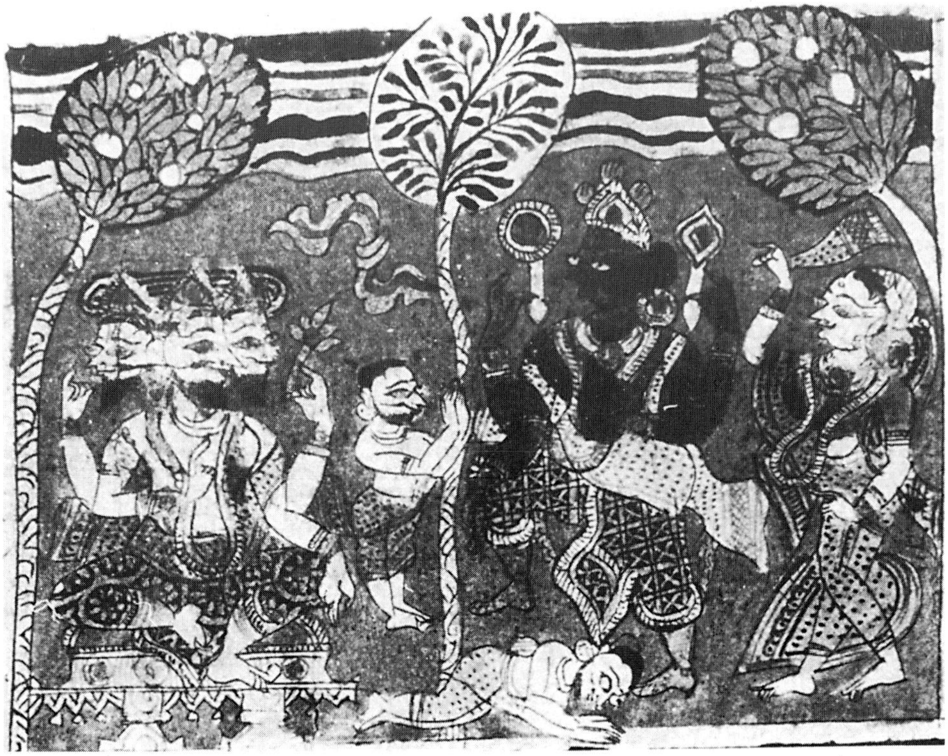

Fig. 1. The Superiority of Vishnu (Krishna). Western India, fifteenth century. Ross Collection.

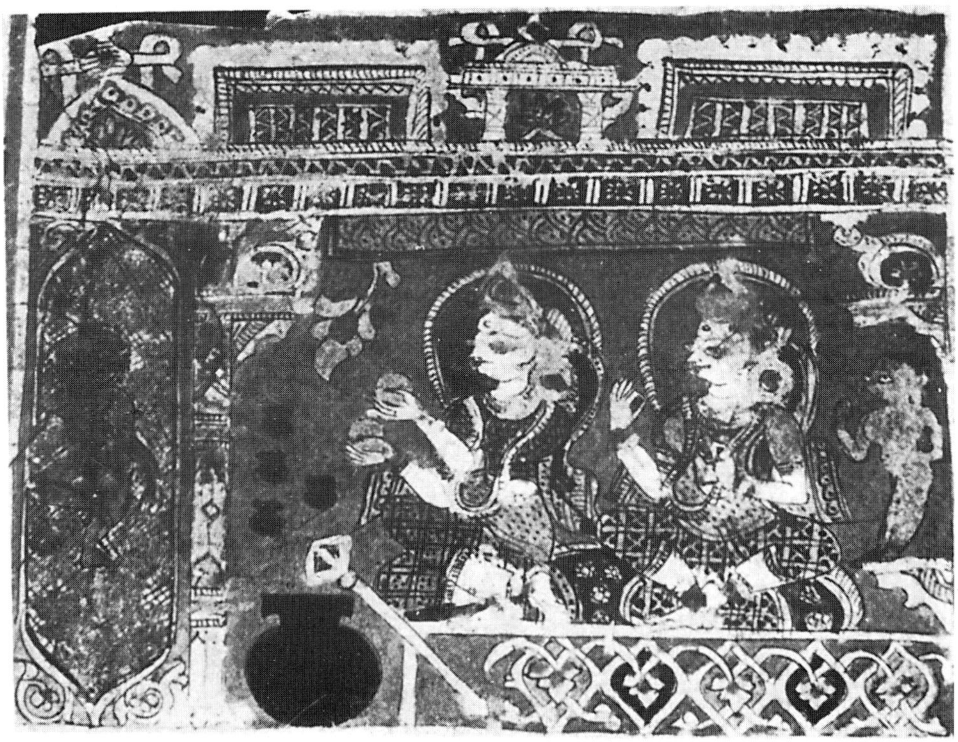

Fig. 2. Krishna Dancing. Reflected in a Crystal Pillar. Western India, fifteenth century. Ross Collection.

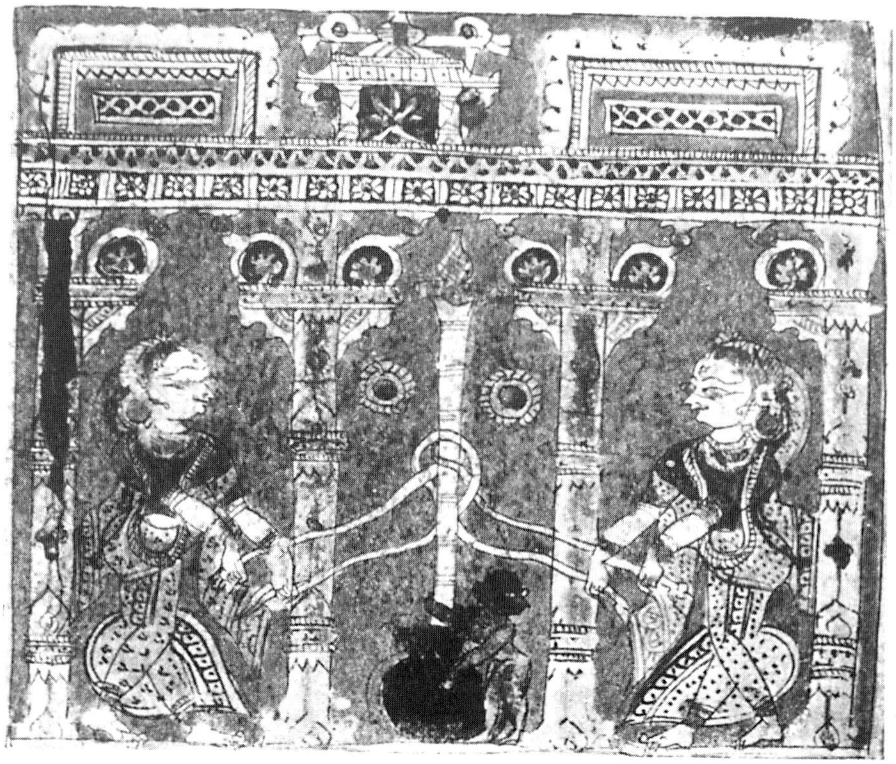

Fig. 3. Gopis Churning; Krishna in the Centre. Western India, fifteenth century. Ross Collection.

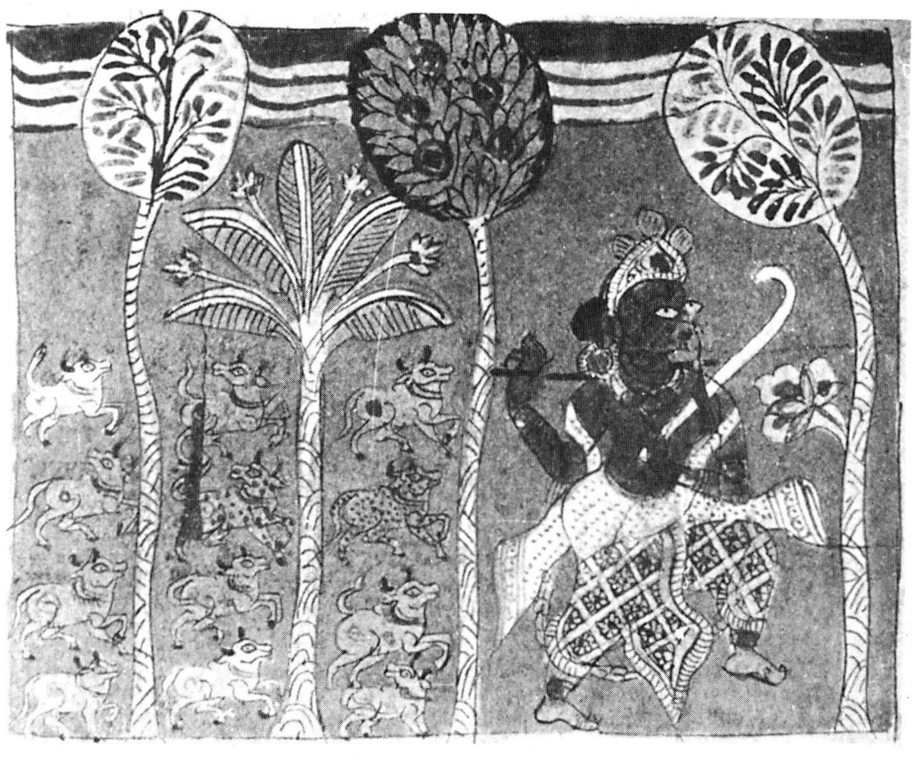

Fig. 4. Krishna with the Flute, as Herdsman. Western India, fifteenth century. Ross Collection.

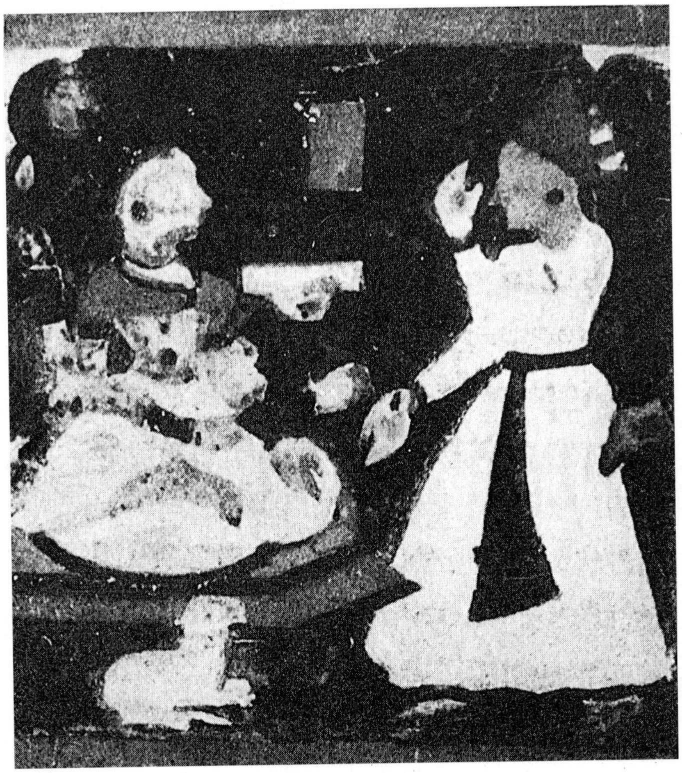

Fig. 5. Kalidasa before Sarasvati. Western India, *ca.* AD 1600. Ross Collection.

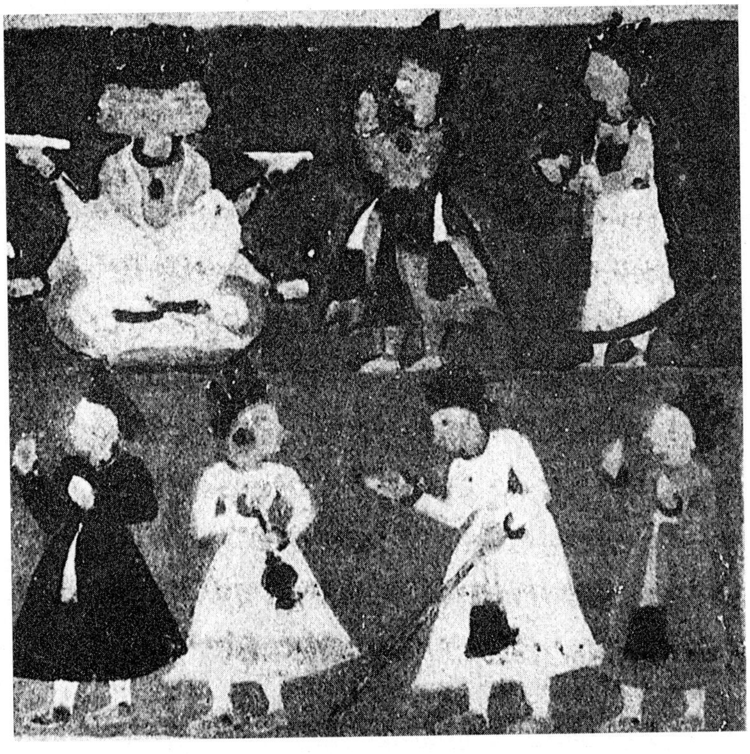

Fig. 6. The Gods Seek the Help of Brahma. Western India, *ca.* AD 1600. Ross Collection.

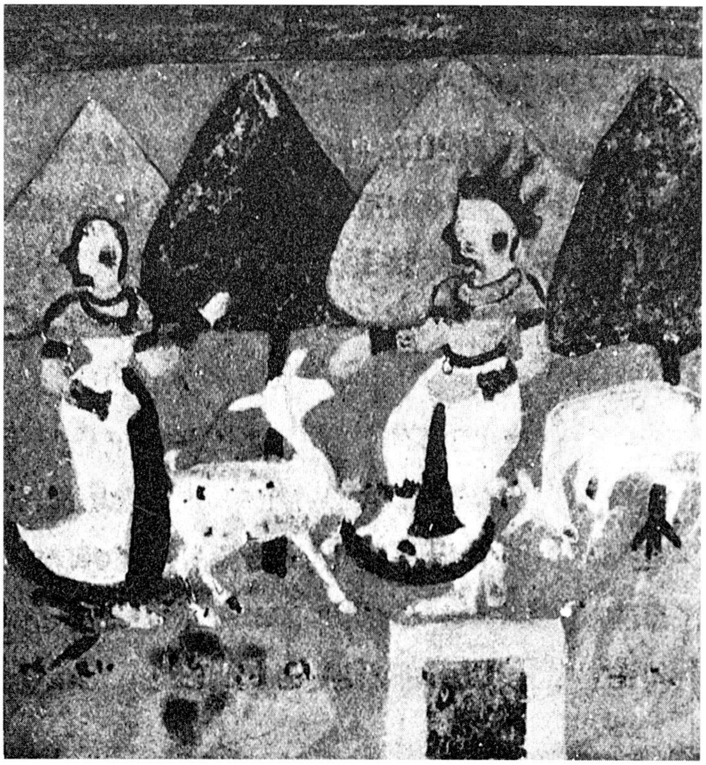

Fig. 7. Uma in the Himalayas. Western India,
ca. AD 1600. Ross Collection.

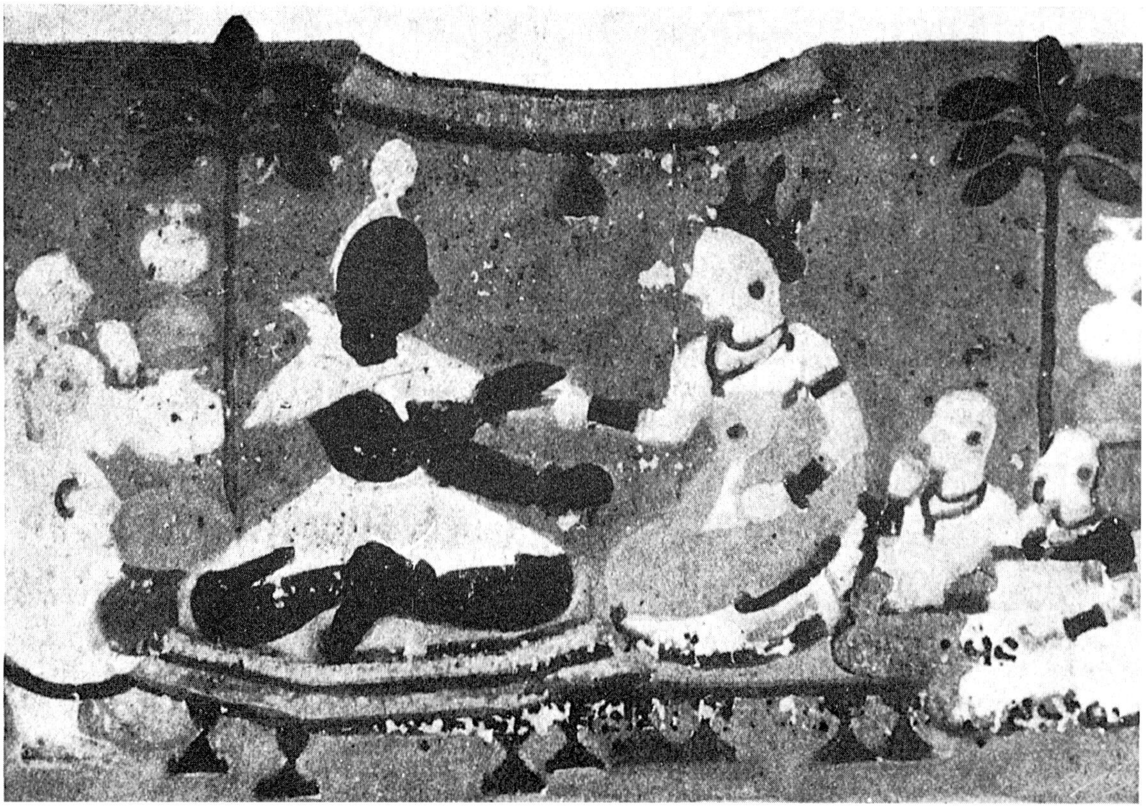

Fig. 8. Marriage of Siva and Uma (Parvati). Western India,
ca. AD 1600. Ross Collection.

An Illustrated Jaina Manuscript

The Museum has long possessed what is probably the finest collection in the world of manuscripts illustrated in the Jaina, Gujarātī, or as it is now preferably called the Early Western Indian Style.[1] An additional paper example has now been acquired,[2] viz., the MS Ha., which has been described by Professor W.N. Brown as follows: 'MS of the Kalpasūtra and Kālakācāryakathā. 162 folios (nos. 52 and 53 missing, with their nos. written on no. 51; 2 folios bearing no. 28), with 87 miniatures (79 of the Kalpasūtra; 8 of the Kālakācāryakathā), Not dated, probably sixteenth century.' Forty-two of the miniatures are reproduced in Professor Brown's *Miniature Paintings of the Jaina Kalpasūtra*, from which the foregoing description is cited.

The prevailing background of the finished pictures is blue, painted over gold leaf, which remains as the flesh color and that of the costumes and architecture, with superadded detail in white, scarlet, crimson, pink, green, and black. The technique and mannerisms are those generally characteristic of the school. The miniatures of the present manuscript are rather more than usually animated, and include a number of compositions which are either unique or which vary in some way from the stereotyped formulae. By far the most important of the unique compositions is the 'Glorious Sunrise' (Śrī Sūryodaya) of Fig. 1, which has been called the only known example of an Indian landscape painting without figures,[3] but is in fact only a 'landscape' in the same sense that the Byzantine mosaics of the 'Days of the Creation' can be called 'landscapes'. As described by Brown, 'The bright golden ball of the sun, with first a blue and then a white rim against a red background, is just above a variegated mountain peak. Trees flank the scene.' The sunrise is that of the morning of the conception of Mahāvīra, following the night in which Queen Triśalā has reported her Fourteen Dreams to King Siddhārtha. As described in the *Kalpasūtra*, 59, 'He, the thousand-eyed maker of day, shining in his radiance, awakened the groups of lotuses. When in due time the god of day had risen and by the blows of his hands (or rays) the darkness was driven away, while the inhabited world was, as it were, dipped in saffron, the Kshattriya Siddhārtha rose from his bed, descended from the footstool, went to the hall for gymnastic exercises, and entered it.'[4] This is virtually a description of the First Sunrise, in the beginning of days (*agre ahuān*) so often celebrated in the *Ṛg Veda*. This will be more apparent if we recall that the Nativity of Mahāvīra (like that of the Buddha, but in certain respects even more literally) repeats the pattern of the Nativity of Agni, Indra, and the Sun as formulated in the *Ṛg Veda*. The most peculiar feature of the

[1] Coomaraswamy, 'Notes on Jaina Art', *Journal of Indian Art*, No. 127, 1914; *Catalogue of the Indian Collections, Part IV, Jaina Paintings and Manuscripts,* Boston, 1924 (bibliography, p. 38); 'An Early illustrated Jaina Manuscript', *MFA. Bulletin*, Feb. 1930; 'An Illustrated Svetambara Jaina Manuscript of AD 1260', *Eastern Art*, II, 1930; 'Two Western Indian Manuscripts', *MFA. Bulletin*, Feb. 1931; Brown, 'Early Vaishnava Paintings from Western India', *Eastern Art,* II, 1930; *The Story of Kalaka*, Washington, 1933 (bibliography, p. 13; History of the Style, pp. 13-24); *Miniature Paintings of the Jaina Kalpasūtra,* Washington, 1934 (bibliography, p. 3).

[2] Reg. No. 35.58; dimensions of the leaves, .266 x .113 m.; stiff board covers, of silk brocade, and brocade pocket of later date.

[3] 'The first pure landscape I have seen in Early Western Indian miniature painting', Brown, *Miniature Paintings of the Jaina Kalpasūtra*, p. 24. Cf. Kramrisch, 'Landscape without human figures is rare indeed in Indian painting, and it would be difficult to quote more than one pure precedent', in *Journal of the Indian Society of Oriental Art*, II, 1934, p. 122 (the late Bengali examples although very different in style are nevertheless comparable in intention, inasmuch as they derive in the last analysis from the Tree of Life motif).

[4] The world is illumined by the conception, and even before the birth of the child; as also in the Vedic, Buddhist, and Christian traditions. What is said of Siddhārtha, as rising from his bed, etc., may be expressed in other words by saying that with the conception of the Son, the Father proceeds from interior to exterior operation.

Nativity of Mahāvīra is the miraculous transference of the embryo from the womb of the Brahman lady Devānandā to that of the Kṣatriya lady Triśalā, which implies the passing over of dominion from the spiritual to the temporal power; this transference, which is described at length in the *Kalpasūtra* and is circumstantially represented in all the illustrated manuscripts, corresponds exactly to *ṚV.*, I, 113, 1-3, where Night 'when she hath conceived for Savitr's (the Sun's) quickening, yields, the womb (*yonim*) to Dawn,' I, 124, 8 where 'sister to mightier sister yields the womb', and III, 2, 2, where Agni (often referred to elsewhere as *dvimāta*, 'having two mothers') 'becomes the son of both mothers'. It may be added that Indra himself, who as Light defeats the powers of Darkness, is at least once referred to by the essential name of Mahāvīra, 'The Great Champion' (*ṚV.*, I, 32, 6) and that he speaks of the womb from which he is born as *mahāvīryā*, 'that of the Great Champion' (*Śatapatha Brāhmaṇa*, III, 2, 1, 27). The mountain is evidently Mt. Meru, the Vedic *parvata*. coincident with the Axis of the Universe and trunk of the Tree of Life, as also in Fig. 2.[5]

The foregoing analysis of the content of the miniature has been requisite to explain its composition, which is evidently no less traditional than is the phrasing of the corresponding text. The same may be said of another miniature. Fig. 2 (not in the Museum of Fine Arts but reproduced here as another example of 'pure landscape'), illustrating the last of Triśalā's Fourteen Dreams, prefiguring the birth of Mahāvīra. 'She saw a fire in vehement motion, fed with much-shining and honey-colored butter, smokeless, crackling, and extremely beautiful with its burning flames. The mass of its flames, which rose one above the other, seemed to interpenetrate each other, and the blaze of its flames seemed here and there to burn the very sky' (*Kalpasūtra*, 14): and this is essentially, alike in the miniature and the text, a picture of the first kindling of Agni, the first Fire lit by the proceeding powers on the occasion of the First Sacrifice, when the Light is brought forth out of Darkness.

The episode illustrated in Fig. 3 is related only in Hemacandra's *Triṣaṣṭiśalākāpuruṣacaritra* (*parva* 10, summarized by Brown, loc. cit., p. 32), and belongs to the *enfances*. One of the deities, unnamed, is jealous of Mahāvīra's champion powers (*vīrya*), and upon an occasion when Mahāvīra was at play with his companions 'assumed the form of a serpent and appeared at the foot of a tree'. All but Mahāvīra run away. Then the serpent takes the form of one of the boys, and all set about to climb the tree. Mahāvīra naturally reaches the top first, where he 'shines like the Sun above Mt. Meru', while his companions hang below like birds.[6] It had been arranged that the winner in the climbing contest should have the privilege of riding on the others' backs. The picture in fact illustrates two parts of the story; on the right, Mahāvīra is shown about to engage in a struggle with the serpent, as such; on the left, he is seen riding upon the shoulders of the jealous deity, who had assumed the form of one of Mahāvīra's companions in order to take part in the climbing contest. The serpent and dragon forms assumed by the jealous deity, and all the details of Mahāvīra's conflict with him in various guises from the moment when Mahāvīra's companions deserted him down to that of the final victory when the defeated deity assumes his own form, does reverence to the Lord, and returns to his

[5] Cf. the theme of Fig. 3, in connection with which, Mahāvīra having climbed to the top of the tree is compared to the Sun shining on Mt. Meru (Hemacandra, *Triṣaṣṭiśalakāpuruṣacaritra*, parva 10, used by Brown, p. 32). The description of the Sri Suryodaya is moreover almost the same as that of Trisala's seventh dream, prefiguring the birth of Mahavira, where the Sun is referred to as 'always circling around Mt. Meru' (*Kalpasūtra*, III, 7).

[6] The world employed, literally translated, is 'branch-creature'; Brown suggests constellations or monkeys, but the traditional imagery suggests that 'birds' are really intended. The tree is evidently the Tree of Life, in which the Sun, like an eagle, nests above, the companion powers on the lower branches, according to the simile of the nest (*nida*, *kulaya*) so often employed in the *Ṛg Veda* and Upanisads, and met with also in Dante's 'power that is form unto the nests' (*Paradiso*, XVIII, 10). All of Mahāvīra's companions are of course his like, that is to say Devas, among whom he is pre-eminent. The whole episode is related to *Pancavimsa Brahmana*, XIV, 1, 13, where the question is put, 'Those who ascent to the top of the great tree, how do they fare thereafter?', and answered 'Those who have wings fly away, those who are wingless fall down.' Cf. *Ṛg Veda*, VIII, 21, 25 'perched like birds, we sing aloud to thee', and I, 164, 21, 'where the eagles celebrate in concert their share of aeviternity'.

own place, show that the whole episode is a version of the conflict with Death (Mṛtyu) in which the proceeding Powers of Light are always involved;[7] in other words, and like the Buddhist Mārayuddha, the present episode is the Jaina version of the Vedic battle of Indra with Ahi-Vṛtra. It is always in this way that the metaphysical formulations of the older tradition, where it is well understood that the 'events' related are not historical but eternal and symbolic, are preserved in the pseudo-historical and partially euhemerized lives of the Messiahs in the form of miraculous 'episode'.[8] All this has an important bearing upon the interpretation of the art, as such; for evidently, just as the narrative is not intended to be historical, so the illustration is not intended to be representative. 'Art in its manner of operation imitates Nature', i.e. 'naturanaturans, creatrix, Deus'; it is not an imitation of the results of Nature's operation. The 'truth' of the picture, then, like that of the narrative, cannot be proved or disproved by observation; the vocabulary of the art, whether verbal or visual, is algebraic rather than arithmetical (as Emil Male observed in connection with Christian art, the symbolism is a 'calculus'); the locus of the equations that are displayed in the picture or narrative has no material existence. Even the method of 'continuous narration' employed in the picture under discussion reflects the timelessness of the acts of being that are referred to. In the same way the spatiality or traditional art is not dimensional, but logical. When these principles are forgotten, and in failing to make the distinction of symbol from sign, we often commit the solecism of seeing in 'primitive' art merely an unsuccessful attempt at representation. That the composition, especially as regards the tree and the serpent, recalls the formulae of Christian art in its representations of the Fall is neither accidental nor derivative; for although the moment is distinct, the situation is identical, viz., 'in the beginning' (*in principio*, Skt. *agre*), and the association of the serpent (Death) with the tree inevitable.

The remaining miniatures chosen for illustration may be described more briefly. In Fig. 4 the parents of the Jina Pārśvanātha, the predecessor of Mahāvīra, are shown in Benares, as explained by the caption in the left margin; King Aśvasena is seen in a palace chamber overlooking the Ganges, and Queen Vāmā his wife stands before him, no doubt informing him of the dreams, which are the same as Triśalā's, for 'Every mother of a Finder of the Ford (Tīrthaṃkara) sees these Fourteen Dreams in that night in which the renowned Perfection (*arhat*) enters her womb.'[9]

Fig. 5 is an example of the rare cases in which the entire page of a manuscript is devoted to the illustration of a single theme. Indra (Śakra) is seated in state, surrounded by his court. Indra is four-armed, and bears his characteristic attributes, the *vajra* or 'thunderbolt', and the *aṅkuśa*, or elephant goad. On the right, in the lower register, are seated four ministers, probably the Regents of the Four Quarters; and in the upper register are two male musicians and a female dancer. The arrangement in two tiers according to what is known as vertical projection or *perspective à cheval* does not of course imply that the musicians are seated in a gallery, but merely that they are behind the courtiers, who are seated close to the throne.[10]

[7] Cf. Scheftelowitz, *Die Zeit als Schicksalsgottheit in der indischen Religion*, 1929, p. 34 and *passim*.

[8] *Ṛg Veda*, 1, 170, 1, 'There is in fact no now and no tomorrow'; X, 54, 2, 'All that they call thy battles, Indra, was thy magic.' In later times the historicity of the Messianic 'events' as recorded in epic or gospel is, from the popular point of view, taken for granted; and the scientific approach, according to which the 'events' are regarded as *fictitious* history, is equally native. Even in the gospels, however, the situation is often perfectly clear, cf. *Bhagavata Purana*, X, 46, 39 'No action can be attributed to Him' (Krishna); and in connection with the story at this point, the commentator (Nilakantha) remarks, 'The narrative is not the real point.'

[9] The miniature is discussed by Brown, loc. cit., p. 41. The situation is implicit in *Kalpasūtra*, 150. 'Finder', or more literally 'Maker of a Ford', has reference to the crossing of the river of life, from the dark into the light world, as in the *Ṛg Veda*, *passim*, and in Exodus; the designation Tirthankara corresponding to such expressions as *krtam tirtham*, 'Make ye a ford'; X, 140, 7, 'Who will declare to us the ford?' *Arhat* is 'qualified'; in the *Ṛg Veda* the supreme powers are so-called, and it is in fact 'by *arhana*' that they have become what they are (X, 63, 4; I, 127, 6); and the conception is retained in Jainism and Buddhism.

[10] The miniature is discussed by Brown, loc. cit., p. 14. The situation is described at length in the *Kalpasūtra*, 14 f. It was when thus enthroned that Indra, being aware of his omniscient vision of the whole world (a motif derived from the Vedic concept of the all-seeing Sun) perceives that Mahāvīra has

In the interesting composition, Fig. 6, Krishna and his wives are urging Ariṣṭanemi to marry, pointing out that all of the Tīrthaṃkaras have married and had a family before adopting the religious life. The picture shows a bathing ghat or step-well, with Krishna and Nemi standing on the steps, the former holding up an object that looks like a horn, the latter in an attitude of expostulation. The two women standing above on either side are Krishna's wives, who add their persuasions to Krishna's.[11]

In Fig. 7 a monk is standing before another and evidently superior monk, who is seated on a spired throne of the usual type. That the standing figure is not that of a nun is clearly shown by the fact that the robe does not extend above the neck and behind the head, as is normal in the representation of nuns. The disciple stands with raised and joined hands in an attitude of respectful attention, and the seated monk, who has in his hands the usual monastic mouth-cloth, is addressing him. Both monks are provided with the small whisk broom used for brushing away insects from the path, so that they may not be trodden upon. The miniature would be difficult to identify if taken by itself, but as it occurs in the Kālakācārya section of the manuscript, on f. 161 (1), that is after the defeat of Gardabhilla and in connection with the latter part of the Kālaka story, but preceding the episode in which Indra appears disguised as an old Brahman, there can be no doubt that it is Kālaka himself who is seated on the throne and that he is admonishing the stubborn disciples, who are typified by the single standing figure.

Figure 8 illustrates one of a pair of Jaina manuscript covers acquired two years ago from the Harriet Otis Cruft Fund.[12] Both covers are imperfect, but they are of exceptional quality and unusual technique. The covers are of paper board, painted and lacquered. The outer side of each is divided into three compartments. The central compartment in each case is occupied by a large 'Full Vase' or 'Vase of Plenty' (*pūrṇa kalaśa* or *pūrṇa ghaṭa*) symbol, provided with the eyes that are peculiar to the Jaina representations, though the symbol is otherwise of universal application in Indian art. Brown, loc. cit., p. 12, discusses the symbol briefly, with references, suggesting that it represents the Sun, or the sky full of rain; I incline to an only slightly different interpretation, viz., that the Vase itself represents the Year (*saṃvatsara*), which is one of the most familiar equivalents of Agni-Prajāpati as supreme deity in the Brāhmaṇas (the same idea is implicit in the *Ṛg Veda*, where Agni is called the 'Lord of the Season'), the eyes representing the Sun and Moon respectively. The side panels in the illustrated cover are occupied by large equestrian figures facing the central panel. The drawing is very vigorous and may be regarded as the prototype of the equestrian figures later found in Rajput art; similar figures occur in the manuscript illustrations, when required by the narrative. In the other cover, not illustrated, the lateral compartments are similarly occupied by riders on elephants.

---

entered the womb of the Brahman Lady Devananda, and sends his angel to transfer the embryo to that of the Kśatriya lady Triśalā.

[11] The miniature is discussed by Brown, loc. cit., p. 46. The incident is implied in *Kalpasūtra*, 172 and explicit in Devendra's commentary on the *Uttaradhayana*.

[12] Reg. No. 33.678. The imperfect cover illustrated measures .087 x .172 m. A date not later than the fifteenth century may be assumed.

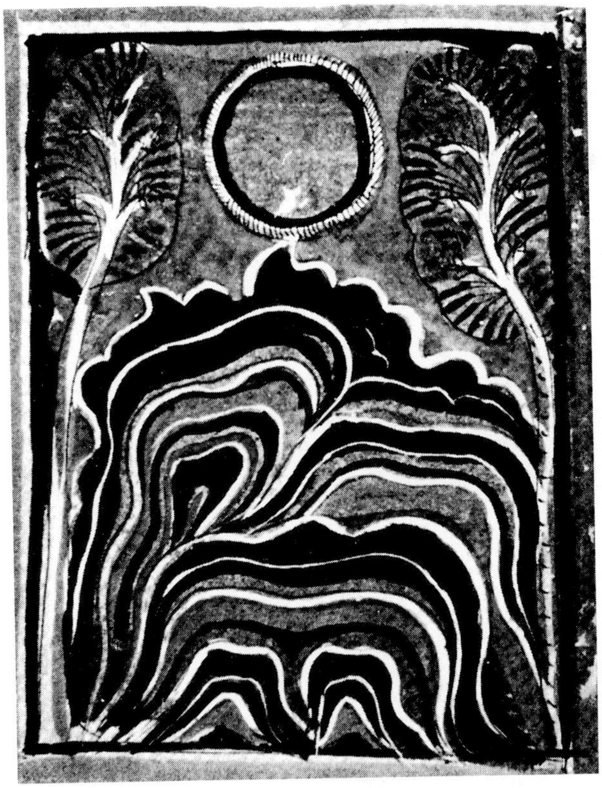

Fig. 1. 'Glorious Sunrise'.
Harriet Otis Cruft Fund.

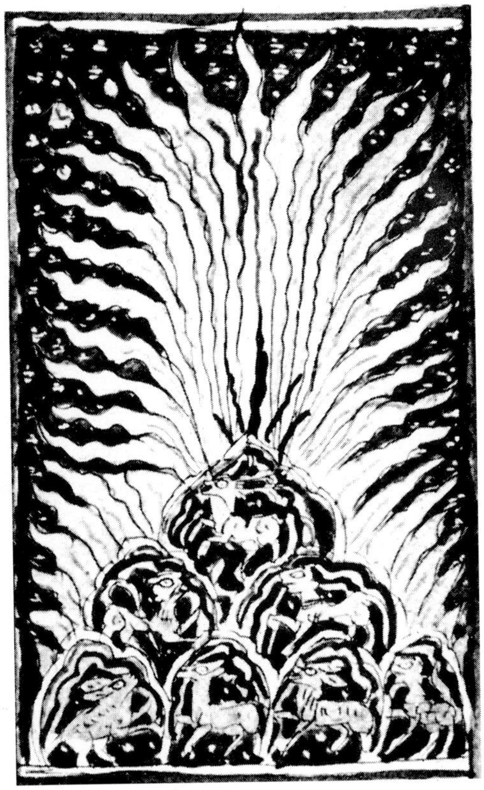

Fig. 2. Cosmic Fire.
N.M. Heeramaneck Collection.

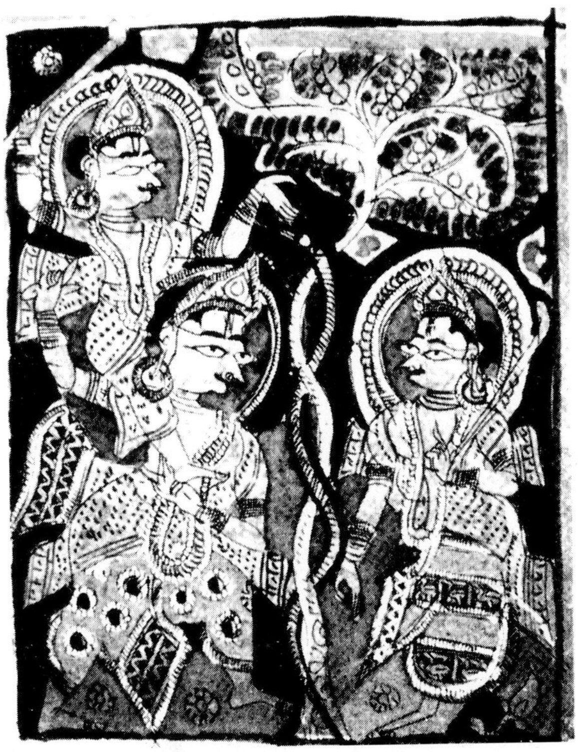

Fig. 3. Mahāvīra's Defeat of Death.
Harriet Otis Cruft Fund.

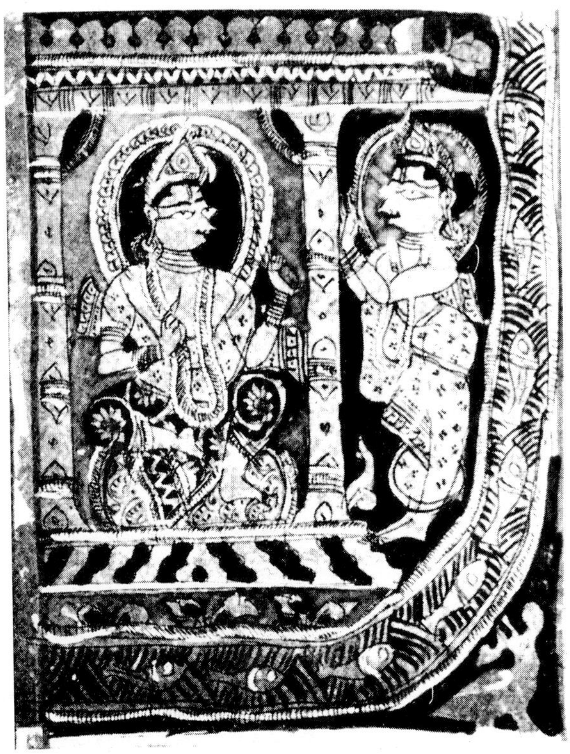

Fig. 4. Pārśva's Parents in Benares.
Harriet Otis Cruft Fund.

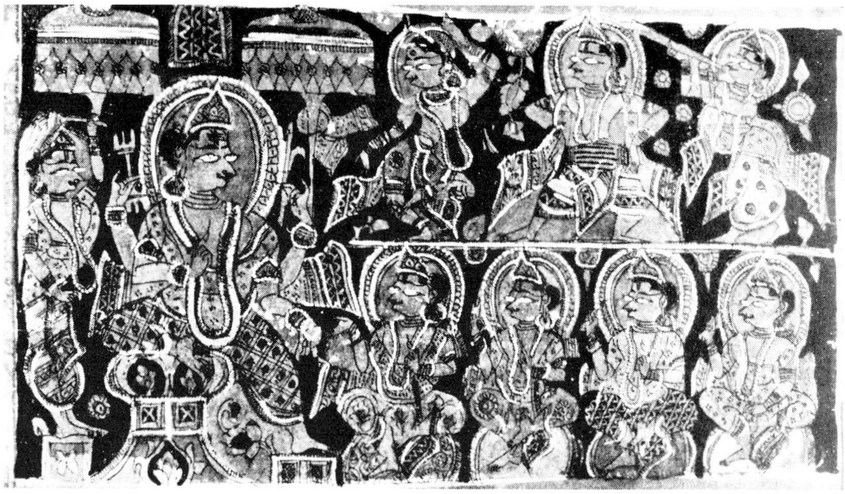

Fig. 5. 'Entertainment in Indra's Court'. Harriet Otis Cruft Fund.

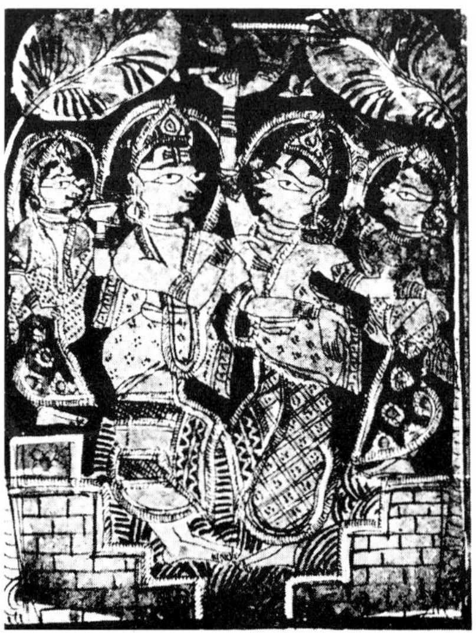

Fig. 6. Nemi urged to Marry.
Harriet Otis Cruft Fund.

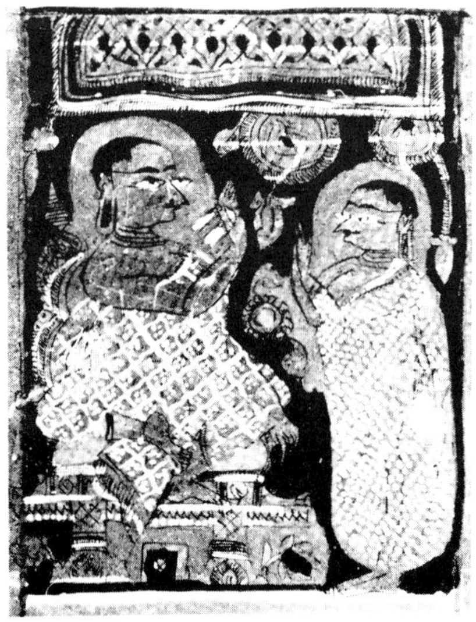

Fig. 7. Two Jaina Monks.
Harriet Otis Cruft Fund.

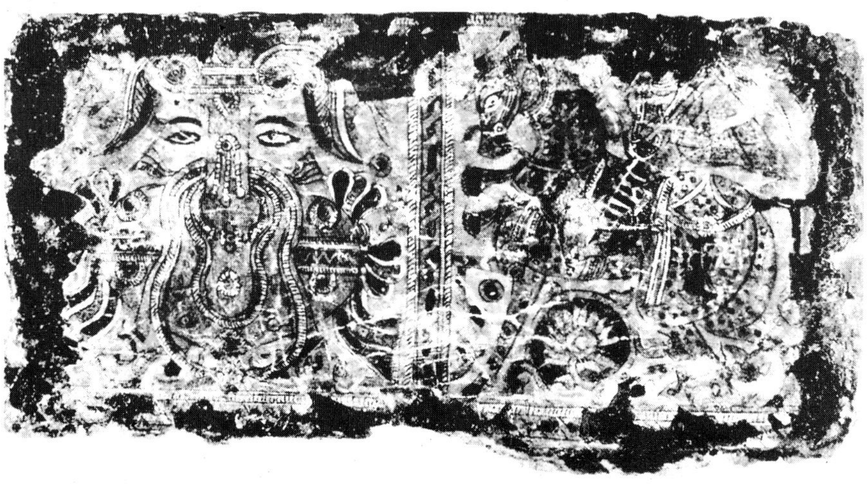

Fig. 8. Cover of a Jaina Manuscript. Harriet Otis Cruft Fund.

Review of *The Story of Kālaka* by W. Norman Brown

This most admirable monograph combines two connected lines of study, offering on the one hand critical editions and translations of various versions of the Kālakācārya legend, and on the other summarizing and coordinating all that is known of the history of Jaina, Gujarātī, or as the author prefers to say, Western Indian, miniature painting. The reviewer cannot contribute to the criticism of the Prakrit texts, and as regards misprints has noted only *patola* (*for paṭola*) p. 19. The additions to our knowledge of Western Indian painting are very welcome, for though 'the importance of the school is such that no account of painting in India can nowadays afford to ignore it', it has been and still is unduly neglected, even M. Buhot finding nothing better to say than that 'quelques enluminures jaïnes et krishnaïtes surprennent par leur barbarie et n'ont guère qu'une saveur décorative' (*L'Art, des origines à nos jours*, 1933, p. 365); according to Professor Brown, however, 'The great merit of the art is the vigor of its drawing, the nervous force of its line, its high decorative quality.'

Examples of the school range from AD 1127 to the end of the sixteenth century, those of early date occurring in palm-leaf, those of the fifteenth and sixteenth centuries in paper Mss. Some changes in style and coloring take place, and there is a great change in the range of subject matter. The interesting point is brought out that in illustrating the Kālaka Mss. the artist may represent subjects not referred to in the actual text, and was thus illustrating the legend as a whole, rather than the particular text in hand. While the Jaina compositions are constantly repeated with merely minor variations, the Vaiṣṇava and secular illuminations present a much greater variety of subject matter and composition, and are more definitely related to the earlier productions of the Rajput school. Professor Brown discusses the peculiar treatment of the eyes at some length. Without rejecting any possible connection of the projecting eye in the paintings and the actual treatment of the eye in Śvetāmbara images, I will only say that this seems to me an inadequate explanation of the distortion: in European art, we should not explain the elongation of the figure in Ms. paintings as due to a copying of images, but rather think of the elongation in both as having a common psychological source. The projecting eye can hardly be isolated from the exaggeration of other features, and the angularity of the style as a whole. These exaggerations, moreover, correspond to those of the poetical literature, in which the eyes are said to reach the ears, and the nose is compared to a parrot's. A similar angularity and distortion may be remarked in the Javanese *wayang* figures, cf. Verneuil, 'Interpretation de la figure humaine dans l'art javanais', *Rev. As.*, IV, 1927, pp. 67-76. As a more direct contribution to the history of the mannerism of Western Indian painting, reference may be made to an engraving, to all intents and purposes a drawing, representing Garuḍa, and occurring on a copper plate of Vākpatirāja of Dhāra, AD 974, see Burgess, *ASWI*, Vol. III, Pl. LXIII: here, even discounting the elongation of the nose as proper to the subject, the Western Indian style is already clearly recognizable, and even the projecting eye is unmistakably thought not conspicuously developed.

As regards the symbolic representation of the Guru (Figs. 5, 18, 34, 35), I have received some further information from Mr. N.C. Mehta, who quotes Pandit Sukhlāl of Ahmadabad. A symbol of this sort is used only in Śvetāmbara circles; the symbol is employed alike by cleric (*sādhu*) and layman (*śrāvaka*). Commonly spoken of as *sthāpanācārya*, and more technically as *kasiṇa*, the symbol consists of a tripod, supporting a white cotton, wool, or silk cloth in which is wrapped a conch, cowrie, piece of sandal-wood, or similar object, the nature of the object varying with the Gaccha. In case the proper object is not available, a book, pen, or staff may be employed, and the *sthāpanācārya* is then spoken of as *asthāī*, 'temporary'. No one should pass between the worshipper and the symbol, which is accorded a respect similar to that which would be due to the Guru in person.

I may add that Professor Brown informs me

that he has recently, and since the publication of the present monograph, received from India reproductions of five miniature paintings from a plam-leaf Ms. of the *Kalpasūtra* of which the last page, reproduced in full, bears the date Saṃvat 927, equivalent to AD 870, that is, 257 years earlier than any similar Ms. hitherto published.

The monograph is illustrated by 15 plates, of which 5 are in color. The author, the Guggenheim Foundation, and the Freer Gallery are to be heartily congratulated on the appearance and value of this first volume in the series of 'Oriental Studies' projected by the latter Institution.

Review of Manuscript Illustrations of the *Uttarādhyāyanasūtra* by W. Norman Brown

So far as a piece of research can be considered 'complete' this excellent volume completes Professor Brown's series of studies on the Western Indian style of miniature painting which flourished from the early twelfth to the end of the sixteenth century, and which was chiefly preserved in the Jain Mss. of Gujarat. Of the three texts most frequently illustrated, the *Kalpasūtra* and *Kālakācāryakathā* have been described previously. The *Uttarādhyāyanasūtra* can be dated somewhere about the fourth century AD, while the illustrations reproduced are from Mss. of the fifteenth and sixteenth centuries; one of these exhibits the style of the transition towards the early Rajput paintings of about 1600. The text contains discourse supposedly addressed to monks by the Jain founder Mahāvīra, and the many stories and parables embodied in these discourses readily lend themselves to illustration, which illustrations fall into set types that recur in many Mss., but there are many types not found in the two other texts; Fig. 100 may be cited as an excellent piece at once of story-telling and decorative composition; Fig. 74 as an example of what is already a Rajput style.

Review of Ancient Vijñaptipatras by Hirananda Śastri

Vijñaptipatras are a sort of report or letter, sent by members of a Śvetāmbara Jaina community to the ācārya of another community, inviting a pastoral visitation. These reports were written on long rolls of paper, and always richly illustrated; all known specimens come from Gujarat or Kathiawad, and the present publication makes an addition to our knowledge of Western Indian painting. Of greatest historical interest is an example dated Vik. 1667 (AD 1610) containing portraits of Jahangir and Prince Khurram, and of several courtiers, and an allusion to a *farmān* (prohibiting animal slaughter during the Paryushaṇā week) that had been granted by Akbar and later confirmed by Jahangir. The pictures in illustration of these events are in a Mughal style and by the painter Śālivāhana, and are of considerable interest although notof very high quality. In addition to the actual Vijñaptipatras, which range from the seventeenth to the nineteenth century, Dr. Śastri reproduces an illustrated Ms. of the Saṅgrahaṇī Sūtra, which he calls the oldest dated example known of painting on cloth from Gujarat (AD 1397); this Ms. begins with a fine painting of the characteristic Jaina Maṅgala-kalaśa with eyes, a form of which the author's discussion is rather inadequate. The vase, with its arborescent outgrowths, and flanking birds represents the Fountain and the Tree of Life, and may be compared to many almost identical Byzantine forms. The eyes are in all probability representations of the Sun and Moon: they are strangely impressive. It is significant that similarly eyed vessels are met with in Greece and Egypt, and that *kalaśa* = kulix = chalice, each of these vessels being ritually the container of an *eau de vie* that represents the blood of a sacrifice. On the 'Eyes of Soma' cf. *JISOA* 3 (1935), 136, 137.